Eskimo

Eskimo

Kutchin

North Athabaskan

North-west Coast

Aleuts

Nootka

North Algonkians

Ojibwa

BEOTHUK

Micmac

Penobscot

West Shoshone

Maidu

KARANKAWA

Seri

LOWER CALIFORNIA INDIANS

PUELCHE

TEHUELCHE

CHONO

Alakaluf

Yaghan

ONA

The Hunting Peoples

Books by Carleton S. Coon

The Story of Man
The Seven Caves
The Origin of Races
The Living Races of Man (with E. E. Hunt)

The Hunting Peoples

Carleton S. Coon

Maps and Drawings by Aldren A. Watson

BOOK CLUB ASSOCIATES
LONDON

FIRST PUBLISHED IN GREAT BRITAIN 1972
COPYRIGHT © 1971 BY CARLETON S. COON

THIS EDITION PUBLISHED 1974 BY
BOOK CLUB ASSOCIATES
BY ARRANGEMENT WITH JONATHAN CAPE LTD

PRINTED IN GREAT BRITAIN BY
LOWE AND BRYDONE (PRINTERS) LTD
THETFORD, NORFOLK

To: John Batchelor, Martin Gusinde,
Bill Harney, E. H. Man,
Neil G. Munro, Patrick T. L. Putnam, George Augustus Robinson,
Frank G. Speck, R. P. Trilles, and W. Lloyd Warner

Prime Observers of the Early Hunting Scene,
In Memoriam

Contents

Tools come first. Making stone tools. Choppers, ancient and modern. Flake tools. Stone blades. The kinds of stone used for toolmaking. Shell tools. Hafting tools. Tools made of native metal. Ground stone tools. Axes and adzes. Uses of fire as a tool. Peoples ignorant of fire making. Two ways to make fire. How hunters get water in deserts and on frozen ground. Environmental protection: shelter and body covering. Camping in the open: caves, rock shelters, and hollow trees. The domed hut: man's most basic house type. The lean-to. The pit house. Conical tents. Thatched houses. The plank houses of the Northwest Coast Indians. Nootka house-building. The domed snow igloo of the Central Eskimo. How hunters keep warm out of doors. The human body: a walking billboard. Hair as symbol and protection. Painting the body with pigments. Three basic kinds of clothing. Covering the loins. The robe. Tailored garments. Waterproof garments. Head covering. Mittens and footgear. Curing skins. How Yaghan and Eskimo women cut and sew skins. Thongs and lines. Making cordage of vegetable materials and of human hair. Andamanese rope making. Conclusion.

Walking and climbing. Aids to walking on sand, snow, and ice. Carrying things. Dragging things. Dog sleds and sled dogs. Water transport. Balsas, or reed rafts. Bark boats. Birchbark canoes and moosehide boats. Kayaks and umiaks. The three-plank skiffs of the Alakalufs. The cedar-wood dugouts of the Nootka. Outrigger canoes. Conclusion.

The food quest: a cooperative effort. Geographical differences in the food supply. The primacy of hunting as a day-to-day activity. Weapons: the club. The simple spear. Spear-throwers. Bows and arrows. The S-shaped bow of the Andamanese. Arrowmaking among the Ona. Poisoned arrows. Hunting by stalking: Australia. Tracking: North America. Hunting with lures. Hunting with disguises. Killing many animals at once. Driving animals into fences and pounds. Hunting by sea: the harpoon. Slings and bolas. Hunting with nets: water, air, and land. A Mbuti net hunt. A Birhor monkey hunt. The interband annual deer hunt of the Birhors. The supposed antagonism between hunting and sex. Trapping. Kinds of traps. Conclusion.

5. Big-Game Hunting

Elephant hunting: the Akoa Pygmies. The Mbuti Pygmies. Whale hunting: a rare and complicated enterprise. A Nootka whale hunt. A Nootka chief calls a whale ashore.

6. Fishing

Methods of fishing: driving and hooking. Raking and spearing. Shooting fish with arrows. Stunning fish with poison. Fishing with nets. Fishing with weirs, dams, and traps. Nootka fish traps. The Ainu fishing calendar. Ainu fishing rites.

7. Gathering

A truce with tigers: the nonhunting Kadar. The Chenchus: hunters forced into yam digging. Wild yams and honey bees in the Old World tropics. Honey ants and honey bees. Collecting honey from trees. Collecting honey from cliffs in India and Ceylon. Collecting insects for food. Windfalls of wild fruits. Collecting wild grass seeds. Collecting molluscs for food. Shells used as ornaments and as currency.

8. Food and Drugs

How food is shared. How people with graded ranks divide the meat. Trading food. Eating food raw and cooking it. Roasting food as practiced by the Tasmanians. Australian cooking techniques. Broiling, boiling, and pottery. Boiling without pottery. Preserving food. The unimportance of drugs among hunters.

9. The Social Organization of Hunters: Territories, Bands, and Kinship

Introduction. Space, territories, and bands. Relations within bands. Symbolic ties to the land. The Yaghans, a decimated and disrupted people. The Alakaluf, the Western Shoshone, and the nonhunting Kadar. Composite bands in Canada, India, and Australia. Boundaries. The troublesome subject of kinship terms. The three primary incest tabus.

10. Marriage

The ideal choice of spouses. The so-called "joking" relationship. Marriage among the Kadar. The !Kung Bushmen and their same-name tabu.

List of Illustrations

List of Maps

Introduction

For nearly half a century I have been reading about the peoples of the world who managed to survive into modern times as hunters and gatherers. It has also been my good fortune to visit some of them, albeit briefly. Today a scant quarter of a million hunters are left, no more than .003 percent of mankind. Ten thousand years ago they numbered about ten million, one hundred percent of the earth's population.

Ten thousand years ago all men were hunters, including the ancestors of everyone reading this book. The span of ten millennia encompasses about four hundred generations, too few to allow for any notable genetic changes. Insofar as human behavior, like the behavior of other animal species, depends ultimately on inherited capacities (including the capacity to learn), our natural tendencies cannot have changed very much. We and our ancestors are the same people.

If we can find out how hunters live, it might help us to discover what we would be able to do if we could make a fresh start as of ten thousand years ago.

This is neither science-fiction nor idle speculation. It is a sober, professional conclusion. I need not belabor here the well-known and frightening facts about the cumulative effects of radiation upon living organisms, the irreversible thinning of the earth's atmosphere through the wasting of its oxygen, or other aspects of the global crisis that we began to wrinkle our brows about yesterday, or was it the day before? Others can describe these perils with greater authority. I write about something equally important, the key to the whole chain of destruction, the nature of man himself.

We may define living hunters and gatherers as peoples who survived into the nineteenth century without agriculture and without domestic animals other than dogs. There are some quasi exceptions. The Tlingit Indians of the Northwest Coast of North America grew tobacco, which is not a food but a drug. Some of the

Ainu living on the island of Hokkaido in Japan had begun to raise a little millet, mostly for brewing beer.

Our definition excludes from the list of hunters all of the circumpolar reindeer breeders of Eurasia, from Lapland to the Chukchi Peninsula. They are just as much food-producers as the camel and sheep-breeding Bedawin of Arabia. It also rules out the historic Plains Indians who shot buffalo from horseback, and the mounted Indians of Patagonia. In both cases, the horses came from Spain.

In screening my list of hunting peoples I wondered, for a long time, what to do about the presence or absence of dogs, because they were first domesticated only about ten thousand years ago, the point in human history that we are trying to re-create. When first discovered, by Europeans, some hunters had no dogs. They were the Tasmanians, the Andamanese, and probably the Fuegian Indians. The Australian aborigines had dingoes. These are feral dogs introduced on the continent about 6000 B.C. They breed in the wild, are captured as puppies, and are little used in hunting because they are hard to control. Various other hunters living in Africa, Asia, and the Americas kept half-starved mutts, more for barking at night than for hunting.

Only two breeds of native dogs owned by hunters are really useful enough to matter. One is the Ainu deerhound, the other the husky or sled dog known to us mostly through the Eskimo. Both were concerned with snow, the Ainu hounds in winter hunting, the Eskimo dogs for winter transport on land. Both were native breeds, parts of the cultural equipment of the peoples concerned. Neither the Ainu nor the Eskimo will be blackballed from the hunter's club because of their dogs.

When I started this work, I described the culture of one food-gathering people after another, moving eastward from Africa around the world, but before I reached the Chukchi Peninsula I realized that it was still a long way to Cape Horn, that I was repeating myself here and there, taking more time than expected, and running the book into two thick volumes. Then I decided to shift to a cross-cultural method, from ethnography to ethnology, organizing my material by subjects rather than by peoples. This approach allowed me, among other advantages, to pick and choose between lucid and lively sources and duller and more pedantic ones.

Despite its apparent carefree manner, this book is not just

Ainu *Eskimo* *Dingo*

1. *An Ainu hunting dog, an Eskimo sled dog, and an Australian dingo*

descriptive nor meant simply for entertainment. I am not making fun of hunters. I respect and admire them. Before being overrun by the snowball of modern civilization they led full and satisfactory lives, and it will do us no harm to reflect on the advantages of some of their age-old ways of dealing with nature and with each other.

If any fellow anthropologists read it, they may notice that I have followed no particular or single school, be it historical, evolutionary, functional, culture-areal, *Kulturkreislich,* or even

Lévi-Straussian, because no one of them, in my opinion, to the exclusion of the others, gives us exactly what we need.

My greatest problem has been how to explain the subjects of kinship, incest tabus, and marriage in Chapters 9 and 10, so as to make them comprehensible to the general reader, for whom the book is intended, and at the same time to satisfy the specialists in these subjects. I cannot expect to succeed on both counts, and the first one has priority.

In my opinion some of the soundest work yet done on the cultures of hunters, and of some other peoples on a "primitive" economic level, is being done by workers following new approaches. Among them, Irven DeVore takes his cues from animal behavior; Richard B. Lee studies "cultural ecology"; Richard A. Gould entered the field through "living archaeology"; and Robert G. Gardner uses film as a means of collecting pertinent information. From these relatively young men and others like them we have much to expect, as long as there are any unspoiled peoples left for them to study.

In the following accounts of the activities of hunters I have alternated between the present and past tenses of verbs: The present tense indicates customary or habitual actions in *the ethnographic present,* a term coined by Eliot D. Chapple and myself thirty years ago* to designate the time span during which a culture being referred to was still functioning unimpaired by outside influences. The past tense designates specific, single events, all of which actually took place in the past. As in the "imperfect" form of an Arabic verb, the present also represents incompleted, continuous, repetitive, or habitual action. Our past tense is thus comparable to the Arabic "perfect" form, which denotes completed action, whenever it may occur or have occurred.

My thanks go out to both Desmond Morris of the London Zoo and Charles Mack of the Museum of Comparative Zoology at Harvard for having identified the mysterious "raccoon" of Hokkaido as a species of wild dog; to Dr. Ruth Turner of the same museum for help on clams; to Professor Edward Osborn Wilson of Harvard for information on wild bees and honey; to Professor Norman J. Wilimovsky of the University of British Columbia for

*E. D. Chapple and C. S. Coon, *Principles of Anthropology* (New York: Holt, 1940).

having identified the taimen, a large, migratory fish of both Hokkaido and the Northwest Coast; to Mrs. Albert H. Matano of Queen's Village, New York, for photographs of her Ainu dog; and to Paul Willis, curator of Natural History at the Peabody Museum of Salem, Massachusetts, for information on the anatomy of the bowhead whale. Two veteran librarians, Miss Margaret Currier of the Peabody Museum Library at Harvard and Miss Cynthia Griffin of the University Museum of the University of Pennsylvania have again given me their invaluable help. Finally, I would like to express my warmest gratitude to my two editors, Peter Davison of the Atlantic Monthly Press and Graham C. Greene of Jonathan Cape, Ltd., in the hope that what follows may not disappoint them.

Carleton S. Coon
Gloucester, Massachusetts

B

1.

Living Hunters of the World, a Synopsis

Long ago by our reckoning, but only a tick or two ago on a cosmic clock, our ancestors roamed forests and grasslands in the most favored parts of the earth. There they picked wild fruits, dug up juicy tubers, robbed wild bees of their honey, stalked swift-footed animals with spears and bows, gathered basketfuls of shellfish from the shores at low tide, and cooked and ate tasty meals.

Our ancestors built weathertight houses with their own hands, went naked when it was warm enough, and wore skin garments when they needed to. They lived in small communities in which everyone knew everyone else so intimately that there was no need for pomp and pretense and nothing to be gained by one trying to cheat another.

They lived as many of us try to do on hunting and fishing trips and while camping during vacations in national parks. Few of us can survive in the wild very long without matches, axes, and other manufactured equipment, but how did our ancestors manage it? How can we relive in our own minds those happy days that few of us have ever experienced? There is no problem. It is easy.

Right up to the present century, time crept at an almost imperceptible pace. Tucked away in the corners of the earth, there could still be found isolated peoples of all races,* to whom time is the change of seasons when different fruits ripen, when animals breed and migrate, and when men are born, grow up, reproduce, grow old, and die. Once dead they join their ancestors and continue to live in a timeless world, to reappear to their descendants in dreams.

Compared to most of us, these are peoples unhaunted by doubts and guilt, and in a sense, happy—or they were until we ourselves turned their clocks jarringly ahead and disturbed them, just as we are now disturbing ourselves in a period of climax when time is approaching zero and the power we have unleashed approaches infinity.

*In what follows I have no good examples of Negro hunting cultures, which are very scarce in Africa as nearly all Negroes are agricultural, pastoral, or both. Remnants of a few Negro hunting tribes in Angola remain to be fully described. (See Antonio de Almeida, *Bushmen and Other Non-Bantu Peoples of Angola.* [Johannesburg, Witwatersrand University Press, 1965]) Another group, the Bergdama of Southwest Africa, are Negroes and probably pre-Bushmen. (See H. Vedder, *Die Bergdama* [2 vols.] (Hamburg, 1923) Bergdama culture is almost indistinguishable from that of the Bushmen.

2

As the maps on the end papers show, the living hunters covered here are the Pygmies of the African rain forest, the Bushmen of the Kalahari Desert, some of the hill tribes of southern India and Ceylon, the Andaman Islanders in the Bay of Bengal, the Australian and Tasmanian aborigines, the Ainu of northern Japan, the well-known Eskimo, and many tribes of Indians in northern and western America and a few in the southernmost part of South America. None of them were growing crops or breeding food animals when Europeans arrived.

At this point one may ask, why weren't they? It was not because they lacked the intellectual capacity to do so. We know this because some of the techniques the living hunters employ in obtaining foodstuffs from their environment were every bit as complex and ingenious as those employed by some of the peoples who grow crops and raise food animals today. In some departments of life the hunter's social organization is just as complex as the crop grower's, or more so.

Three simple reasons come quickly to mind. The first is geographical isolation or sheer distance. Because of their remoteness from the centers where food production began—no more than ten thousand years ago in the Old and New Worlds—the techniques of husbandry had not yet reached them. The second is that some of the hunters still lived in climatic regions beyond the range of profitable agriculture, where the growing season was too short for available crops or where the rainy season came at the wrong time.

The third reason is that they did not want to change. The hunter's life gave them all the food they needed and an eminently satisfactory way of living together in small, intimate groups. The hunter is free from tedious routine, and his daily activities are more exciting. He hunts when he needs food. In most environments he can relax when he and his family have had enough to eat. Why raise crops, by back-breaking work, when his women can dig yams in abundance, or when the whole family can camp under a tree that bears tasty and nutritious nuts? Agriculture brings with it a whole new system of human relationships that offer no easily understood advantages, and disturbs an age-old balance between man and nature and among the people who live together.

Whatever the reason or combination of reasons, it is our good fortune that some of the hunters live in steaming forests, some on deserts, some in cool forests like those our ancestors took away from the Indians in northern New England, and others in the frozen polar regions. In fact, within the last century such peoples have inhabited all of the kinds of climate and terrain still existing in the world.

But despite the differences in climate and in the kinds of food hunted or gathered, these groups have much in common: they live out of doors, get plenty of exercise, know every rock, stream, and stand of trees, and the habits of every kind of animal that shares their bit of the earth's surface, as intimately as they know each other.

They are part of nature and they feel it. They are not bent on the destruction of the earth, through a lack of humility and a heedless ignorance of the rules that govern the birth and death of planets in the boundless universe.

They have not yet, as we have, fully opened Pandora's famous box, though they long ago began to tamper with its lid and to peek inside.

While they peeked, three of the disruptive forces locked in the box managed to creep out, in what order we are not sure. One was language. When some people first learned to speak they were few in number, and by the time that all could speak, their bands were widely separated. Whatever language they had spoken in the first place, each group developed its own idiom, and when such groups met later they could not understand each other.

This peculiarity, confined to man, at once separated human groups in the same way that animals of different species are separated by their inbuilt, private means of communication — through movements of the body, special positions of tail and ears, cries, and nuptial dances. When bands unable to communicate with each other chanced to meet on the borders of their territories, it was easy for each to consider the other as something less than human and to fight, for they both sought the same food. Fighting within one's own species is something unique to man, at least on an intergroup scale; and misunderstanding, either linguistic or otherwise, lies at its root. It has been proposed that warfare, also uniquely human, required a matching of wits not needed in hunting less intelligent animals, and is partly responsible for the growth of the human brain to its present size, and for our much-vaunted and suicidal intelligence which is endangering the continuation of all life on earth.

A second force to creep out was not death itself, because death has always been a part of life in both the plant and animal kingdoms, but the knowledge of the inevitability of death. This is a somber realization. Other animals do not know that each of them has to die.* Fear

*Several times when I have mentioned this statement I have been told, "You are

4

is a momentary thing. Death is a quick surprise. But all of us know that we must someday die, and the knowledge haunts us, albeit subconsciously much of the time, until death comes.

Sleep is the death of a day's activities, and while we sleep we often dream. When a dog dreams, we can tell so by its twitchings. What the dog dreams about is its own concern, not ours, except that we may notice by the movements of its legs that it seems to be running in the open while its body is actually lying on the floor. When a person dreams, he too is moving about in his mind's eye, going to different places, seeing other people, and talking with them. But when he wakes up, if he remembers his dream, he may, if he has not had a modern education, accept the following explanation:

In his body are housed two vital principles, two spirits, two souls. One remains inside him as long as he lives and disappears when he dies. The other is the one that leaves his body temporarily while he dreams, for a longer period when he is in a coma, and permanently when he dies. What happens to it after death? It has been in the habit of leaving his body from time to time during life, and during death it must also have gone away. But where has it gone? If the deceased was a troublemaker in life, he becomes an antisocial spirit, and that spirit is likely to linger around its former haunts to molest and disturb his kith and kin.

But if the deceased was an agreeable, well-tempered person who behaved well in life, his spirit will not linger very long to disturb the living, thus changing its pattern of behavior, but it will join the spirits of its ancestors in some special place, like a great rock or an impressive tree, or it will be wafted up to the sky, and may even become a star. From time to time a man's spirit may return to his descendants in dreams, giving them warnings and useful advice, such as where to hunt.

It is easy to see why dreams recalled after awakening are taken much more literally by people who have not studied psychology than they are by us, who are told that most dreams are only automatic ways of relieving tension during sleep. No dreams came out of

wrong. Elephants know that they have to die." On pages 16–20 of *The Social Contract* Robert Ardrey (who does not take sides in this discussion) cites several eyewitness accounts of the behavior of both African and Indian elephants, members of different genera, when one of a troop has been shot. A large female walks up to the recumbent pachyderm, strips some branches off nearby trees, and lays them over the victim's head and forequarters, then the troop disappears. Branches and leaves are what elephants eat. It seems to me that this act is done to provide the apparently sick or wounded animal with food to give it strength to stand up and follow the other members of its troop. People do the same thing, as we shall see later on. The Tasmanians used to leave food with a sick person left behind.

Pandora's box, but the stuff of dreams—the power of speech and the knowledge that all men must die—did.

And so did the third force, the knowledge of how to use fire, the only force which we can hope to date. From archaeological evidence we know that man has used fire for at least four hundred thousand years. Despite the antiquity of man's discovery of fire, hunters are still impressed with it, for they have myths that tell of a time when people lacked fire. Then, in most of these myths, a man stole it. He may have snatched it from an errant spirit or an animal, but in most cases the women had it first and hid it from the men, and one bold man stole it from them.

This explanation symbolizes either or both of two constants in human life: the rivalry for importance between the sexes in their different but compensatory roles in getting vegetable versus animal foods; and the shift in authority between them in bringing up their male child. While he is a baby a boy's mother feeds him, comforts him, and controls his actions, but as he grows older he gradually joins the company of men, initially under the guidance of his father, a maternal uncle, or both.

But fire is both a useful and a destructive force. It must be kept burning or it will be lost, and it is a woman's job to see that it doesn't go out. Fire cooks food. Fire keeps people warm. At night fire gives light to dance by, and in some parts of the world where it is useful, hunters set fires to burn over the brush, making it easier for them to see and to hunt game. But an untended baby can roll into a fire and be burned, and uncontrolled brush or grass fires can burn down people's camps or spread widely and scorch a whole landscape. By such uncontrolled game-fires the patterns of vegetation of some parts of the earth's surface may well have been altered tens, if not hundreds, of thousands of years ago.*

The knowledge of using fire thus gave our ancestors their first chance to alter the face of the earth, a power that has been progressively used at a rate at first imperceptible, and eventually accelerating at an ever-quickening pace to the crisis in cosmic history which we have now reached, a heritage from our over-inventive ancestors who knew not what a mess they were leaving us in.

Some of the culturally simplest peoples intuitively understand this dilemma, and express it in their own terms. Well over a century ago two native Tasmanian women were sitting on a granite ledge over-

*See Omer C. Stewart, "The Forgotten Side of Ethnogeography," in Robert F. Spencer, ed., *Method and Perspective in Anthropology* (Minneapolis, University of Minnesota Press, 1954), pp. 221–248.

looking a stream. One of them had placed lines of burning coals on the surface of the ledge, to crack the outer layer of the granite and make the heated stone flake off in sections that she could shape into discs on which to grind seeds. While the fires were still burning she had already begun to pound one of the pieces already removed, and the other woman said: "Don't make so much noise. The river will hear you and it will rise and drown the land."

That statement could have been made many thousands of years ago.

Water quenches fire, and fire dries wet things. A Tasmanian chief may jab a burning torch into a driving rain to make it stop. A dead tree struck by lightning may burst into sudden flames and the ensuing rain may put them out. In an instance recorded in the western desert of Australia, some natives had lost their fire, a tree was struck, and a man ran to it and retrieved a brand before the rain fell.

Water may thus become personified, or be identified with a snake that wriggles in the water, and the snake may become a rainbow, a path to the sky. Thus people came to personify other forces of nature besides the lightning, rain, snake, rainbow, and seasonal storms; notably the sun, moon, and stars.

The sun lights the day, the moon the night. They are thus polar opposites, like fire and water. But the moon waxes and wanes, and its variations in shape and brilliance may need explanation. The sun may be an insatiable woman periodically draining the moon of his sexual powers, or the full moon may be a woman who sends out her dangerous emissaries, evil spirits, to harm people. On a more factual level, a full moon is a time to beware of nocturnal predators, like leopards, or for a night raid. The stars may be animals pursued by hunters into the sky and immobilized there forever. Or they may be ancestors of the living people, or the children of the moon. An eclipse is an animal eating the sun or the moon and it must be driven away by making noise.

Explanations of natural phenomena are as many as the human mind can invent, among people living in small groups in the open and getting their food by hunting and gathering. Being intelligent human beings endowed with lively imaginations, most of these people need to find ways to explain everything that they observe in order to satisfy their curiosity. But the matter does not end there. When changes in natural events that upset their routine of life occur, they will try to influence them, as in the case of the Tasmanian poking his torch into the wind-driven rain, or others making a great variety of noises to stop an eclipse.

The same is true of their sources of food. Animals move about. Some of them migrate with the seasons, particularly in lands distant from the equator, where the animals' own food varies with the time of year. Animals too are intelligent, but not as intelligent as people. Hunters must know their habits intimately in order to outwit them. But this is easier than outwitting other people because animals of a species tend to behave more or less the same, given differences of sex and age.

In order to ensure the success of the hunt, some peoples refrain from sexual intercourse beforehand. Although this prohibition may be subrational among the people concerned, several reasons for it may be and have been suggested. One is the polarity between men's work and women's work; another is that animals are most easily caught when copulating. Copulation is a "strong" act, one of maximum intensity. So is killing. In other words, you can take your choice between copulating and killing, the rationalization being that if you copulate too soon before the hunt you will alert the animals. And if your wife copulates with another man while you are hunting you will come home empty-handed.

Not all hunters make this association, but many of them do, and they also take it for granted that animals can understand human speech, even at a distance. This is why, when preparing for a hunt as well as when on it, the hunters are wont to refer to the animals by circumlocution, never pronouncing their real names.

Animals too are believed to talk among themselves, and they can converse with people, usually in dreams. In many tales told around the fire at night, some animals try to deceive each other and come to a bad end. These are essentially moral tales, meant to impress on young people the punitive rewards of antisocial behavior among men.

Useful trees and edible plants may also be endowed with personality. Among the Indians of central California the oak bearing sweet acorns will bleed if felled, for it is sacred, and in southern India a magic tree is believed to give milk from its branches to abandoned babies, at least in tales. Yams may belong to a storm god who becomes angry if he sees women digging them. So the women who dig them cut off their tops and replace them in the ground, to fool the god. From such a practice, one kind of agriculture may have begun.

In view of the close contacts between hunters and animals it is only natural that individual men identify themselves with particular animal species, to accentuate their own differences. Among the Ainu of northern Japan, people who use the bear as their totem may say that a bear once transformed himself into a man, entered a lone woman's house, and begat on her a son. The identification of this boy with bears was handed down from father to son from then on. Or, as among certain Northwest Coast Indians, a raven once helped the ancestor of the Raven lineage in some way, and hence the bond. In most cases people do not eat the flesh of their totem animals, for it would be like eating their own kin, and few hunting peoples are cannibals.

The number of persons living together varies according to the food supply, and it may vary seasonally as the abundance of food varies. Like members of other small, isolated communities (as with European royalty), people recognize their relationships to each other both by descent and through marriage, and designate these ties by terms denoting kinship, close and distant. But kinship terms serve more than one purpose. They indicate through well-known rules of behavior not only who may marry whom, but also who shares food with whom, and which individuals must avoid close contact with one another.

The automatic observance of these rules, impressed on youthful minds, programs them, so to speak, in the optimum procedures of human relations. These procedures keep the persons who live together at various times in the state of relative harmony and cooperation needed to ensure the survival of the group as a whole, however formed.

As a human being is born, suckled, learns to walk and to talk, joins a play group of his or her peers, comes to puberty, marries, lives an adult life, ages, and dies, he passes through a number of biological and social changes, including sickness, that would disturb the lives of the others with whom he [or she] lives if steps were not taken to soften each blow. These steps are rites. Each step symbolizes a transition, often a simulated death and rebirth. The rites of different peoples vary in detail, but the purpose served is the same, because all people are human, biological organisms. The constant factor is life itself, the variations cultural.

By these means and subject to the usual exceptions, a generalization may be made. Hunting and gathering peoples whose lives have not yet been distorted or shattered by too much pressure from uninvited contacts with technologically more advanced outsiders are, in many cases, less subject to continuous anxiety than most of the outsiders, including ourselves, of course, among the outsiders.

These outside contacts vary in degree. In some cases the hunters still lead lives of their own, but their cultures are truncated. Most frequently they are spared the need to make their own tools because they obtain iron ones in trade for foreign products. As the volume of trade increases, growing to include cloth, bananas, rice, tobacco, and alcohol, the hunters may visit their trading partners' villages and markets, and come to partake more and more of village life. As their own cultures deteriorate they may end up as outcast hangers-on at the edges of villages, where they make baskets, become potters, perform public dances, and gradually merge into the lower echelons of the social structures of the outsiders without whom they now cannot live.

Contacts with modern European invaders are usually more disastrous, and take less time. They bring epidemics against which the hunters have no built-in immunities, and they effect a general dependence which disrupts the hunters' social systems and leads to lassitude and, in some cases, to extinction as a full-blooded people.

Nearly all of the peoples to whom we shall refer in the following pages have suffered from one or the other of these outside contacts, and to different degrees. Luckily in many cases enough details of the whole culture have been recorded during the last century to serve our purpose. It is our intention to reconstruct, albeit briefly, the principal aspects of the cultures of the survivors from the time when all men were hunters and led full, well-rounded, and meaningful lives. It is not our intention to follow the tradition of Jean Jacques Rousseau and draw a glowing picture of the noble savage. Who is nobler or more savage than whom is beside the point. We are interested in more practical matters — those concerned with our own survival, as well as with theirs.

As we stated on page 2, hunting and gathering peoples have survived into modern times in all of the climatic regions of the world. From our point of view this is good news because it allows us to cover most aspects of preagricultural human behavior on a global basis.

But all parts of the globe have not been inhabited for equal lengths of time. North and South America had no human fauna before the latter part of the Ice Age, let us say since between twenty–five thousand and eighteen thousand years ago; we cannot be sure because we do not know. Australia was first invaded by human beings during the same time-span, and those parts of northern Europe and Siberia that were pressed miles below the surface of the ice cap could not have been inhabited until it melted, only about ten thousand years ago.

From our present point of view, this excursion into time and space will help us to explain some of the more obvious cultural differences between the hunters and gatherers living in the tropics and the subtropical parts of the southern hemisphere and those who are able to endure the bitter cold of winter in the far north of Asia and North America. Human beings evolved in the warm parts of the Old World, and as long as they remained in their original climatic zones they had little need to invent warm clothing or warm shelters, or to store and preserve food. They could live from day to day, and some of them still do. The powers of invention that are part of our common human heritage could thus be employed more in the field of human relations than in that of physical survival. At opposite extremes in this respect are the cultures of some of the Australian aborigines and those of some of the Eskimo.

But how, then, can we explain why some of the Indians living on the western and southern coasts of South America, in latitudes between forty-five and fifty-five degrees south, wear little if any clothing if their ancestors had to cross the Bering Strait land bridge during the peak of the last glaciation? Either their ancestors who came out of Asia then had warm clothing and abandoned it once they reached the tropics where they didn't need it, and failed to reinvent it, or they made the crossing without it. We do not know the answer, but there is evidence to support both theories.

When the land bridge existed, it was not glaciated. The Japanese current warmed the southern shore of the bridge and those people on either side. They could conceivably have gotten from the coast of Asia to that of Alaska without warm garments, and proceeded down the narrow coastal strip of North America, still under the influence of the Japanese current, to California. Also, the western shores of the Magellanic channels and of Tierra del Fuego have a maritime climate like that of the Northwest Coast, and close to the water's edge the temperature seldom falls below freezing. The Indians could and did survive there without warm clothing, into the present century. As physiological tests have shown, these Indians have a high cold tolerance.

Although this discussion is inconclusive, it brings up another point. Why do most of the hunters and gatherers still living in the

Old World survive mostly in the tropics and south temperate regions, while those in the New World are found mostly toward the poles? The answer is simple. Most of the Old World agriculture began in the North Temperate Zone. In the New World it began in the tropics. In each of these major regions agriculture spread most rapidly and most easily within the climates where its principal food plants would grow. We can thank the ingenuity of human beings in inventing agriculture in more than one part of the world for the geographical limits of the spread of food production by this means, and thus for the survival of our nonagricultural subjects in all of the unglaciated climatic zones of the world.

2.

The Basic Equipment
of Hunters

Tools come first

Hunters have survived in the very diversified climatic regions in which they now live because, aside from knowing how to get their food and to cook it, they are also able to build adequate houses or other shelters from local materials, and to clothe their bodies as much as local conditions require, from the equator to beyond the Arctic Circle. As well as weapons, they also need cords, thongs, and threads for binding, tying, and sewing things together, and containers to carry and keep them in.

It would be impractical to try to build the simplest rainproof and windproof shelter, to make a skin robe, or to strip the sinews off an animal's carcass without being able to cut things. We cut with tools. Modern tools are made of metal by specialists and we buy them in hardware stores. With a few exceptions, hunters' tools are homemade, and of stone.

Making stone tools

Some of the simplest kinds of stone tools may be made quickly by almost anyone. Others require considerable skill, and in a few cases they are made by part-time specialists and traded. The latter is particularly true of stone axes, which need to be pecked and ground, and sometimes polished. Suitable stone is not to be found everywhere, and it may take a man a good two weeks to finish one. While he is pecking and grinding away on a single axe head, someone else may have to feed him. Thus an incipient division of labor may arise out of toolmaking, even among hunters. The clearest examples of this may be seen in Australia, where the fabrication of stone tools has persisted the longest.

Choppers, ancient and modern

Nearly every kind of stone tool unearthed by archaeologists has been made in modern times by someone or other. The oldest tools yet discovered are the pebble tools and choppers excavated by Richard Leakey in a site east of Lake Rudolf in Kenya, and dated at about 2,600,000 years. As they were made and used by manlike creatures that had not yet attained a human status in terms of brain size, it may be said that toolmaking is older than man himself.

Some of these ancient implements are simply water-rounded pebbles taken from stream beds and struck with other stones so as to produce, in each case, a single, sharp, cutting edge. Others are lumps of stone that the toolmaker picks up and hammers until he has produced a comparable cutting edge. Either would be good enough for felling a sapling and shaping it into a digging stick or club.

In modern times such choppers are still used by women in Australia for cutting down small trees, or for removing a piece of bark from a convex bend in a treetrunk. (This piece of bark serves her as a container). During the last century, the Shoshone Indian women of our own American plateau country were making such choppers for their own use while their men were pressure-flaking sophisticated stone arrowheads. The Alakaluf Indians of southern Chile used choppers almost until the arrival of Europeans in the sixteenth century.

In Europe, Africa, western Asia, and India, choppers were gradually replaced by two kinds of tools: bifacially flaked, almond-shaped hand axes, and flake tools, which are quicker to make than hand axes and lighter in weight. The hand axes, made for over three hundred thousand years, yielded at last to flakes, and no people now living have ever been known to make hand axes. From India eastward, flakes simply replaced choppers, and flake tools are still made in Australia and were made until recently in the Americas.

A man fabricating flake tools must have a definite image in his mind of what he plans to produce. Sometimes the flake is good enough to use without further alteration, but more often it needs trimming, either by tapping it with another stone, which removes rather coarse spalls, by striking it with a stick, which, being softer, removes finer ones, or by pressing the edge with a piece of bone or horn, which may produce a virtually unindented cutting edge.

Flakes can be made into many kinds of simple tools, such as

steep scrapers for notching and planing wood, chisels, perforators, and burins for engraving grooves in wood, bone, and antler, as well as a variety of knives and projectile points. In Australia a special knife is used for circumcising boys; it has a convex cutting edge and the other edge is blunted so that it may be held in the curve of the operator's index finger.

Stone blades: their invention and distribution

About 35,000 B.C. a new kind of stone tool began to appear in western Asia and Europe, and as far as we can tell now it was invented by people hunting in the Syrian Desert.* It was a technique of striking long, thin blades from a carefully prepared conelike piece of flint. Such a matrix takes much skill to prepare, but the blades may be struck off it by placing a punch of some elastic material like bone or antler along the flat top of the matrix and delivering a single, accurate blow. The blades can then be retouched into a large variety of special forms for special uses. Blademaking spread to Africa, and the Bushmen were still making them in historic times. It did not get to Asia or the New World until quite late; up until about the fifteenth century A.D. the Ainu of northern Japan were still making their knives of flakes. Most of the American Indians were still using flakes at the time of European discovery. In Australia, blades seem to have been invented independently, but they were not used over the entire continent and never reached Tasmania.

The kinds of stone used for toolmaking

So far we have not specified the tool materials except for flint, which, along with obsidian, is the most easily worked and can be made into relatively elaborate forms. But all parts of the world do not have these glassy stones. Quartzite can be worked, but not as easily, and basalt is even harder to shape by flaking. Quartz is the most intractable of those commonly used, and it takes the eye of

*The only site in which a clear transition can be shown is Jerf Ajla near Palmyra, which I excavated in 1955 and which was reexcavated by Bruce Schroeder a decade later.

Alaskan Eskimo arrowpoints

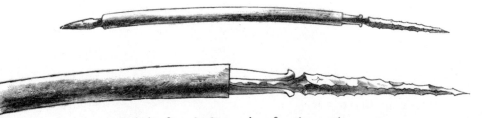

set in foreshaft made of walrus rib

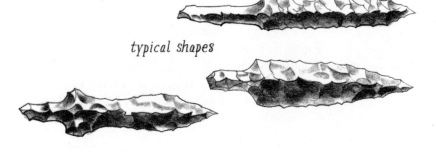

typical shapes

2. An Eskimo arrow (archaeological): bone foreshaft and stone point, showing method of hafting. (After John Witthoft, **Expedition,** Vol. 10, No. 2, 1968)

a professional to tell whether a piece of it was really a tool. The Ovatchumba people of Southwest Africa use quartz today, and into the nineteenth century the Andaman Islanders were shaving each other's heads with crude quartz flakes, discarded after use.

Shell tools

The same Andaman Islanders also used bivalve shells for working wood, and the Alakaluf of southern Chile did the same. The Pygmies of Gabon use the shell of a large land snail for cutting the hearts out of small animals they sacrifice and for circumcising babies. The same Pygmies trim the staves of their bows with the rasplike leaves of an epiphytic creeper that acts like sandpaper. Some of the Australian aborigines use kangaroo incisor teeth as chisels.

Hafting tools

The simplest stone tools made by flaking and chipping are held directly in the hand, as in Tasmania, but others are hafted. The Australians collect gum from eucalyptus trees, and, in the treeless desert, they reduce gum from spinifex grass by heating it. The toolmaker then heats the gum and joins his tool to a wooden handle. When the gum hardens it is as strong as epoxy glue. The Andaman Islanders do the same with a combination of a vegetable gum and beeswax.

Because such adhesives are not available in the colder climates, the hafting is usually done by lashing the head on with sinews. The Eskimo are particularly adept at setting stone blades in handles of bone or walrus ivory, and some of these handles are perfectly shaped to fit the hand.

Tools made of native metal

Alone of living hunters, the Greenland Eskimo made tools of local iron, and not just from spikes and nails from shipwrecks as the Andamanese did. The sources of Eskimo iron were four meteorites in Thule and telluric iron found in basalt deposits at Disko Bay, both in Greenland. Their technique was to saw the metal with strips of sandstone, grind each piece into shape with other stones, and then pound the edges.

The Central Eskimo of Coronation Gulf worked native copper, from the Coppermine River, in the same way, and so did the Tlingit Indians of the Northwest Coast, who got their copper from an unknown source. In Alaska some Athabascan Indians took copper from the Copper River, and others, in the Northern Territories of Canada, obtained it from the same source as the Central Eskimo. The Tlingit

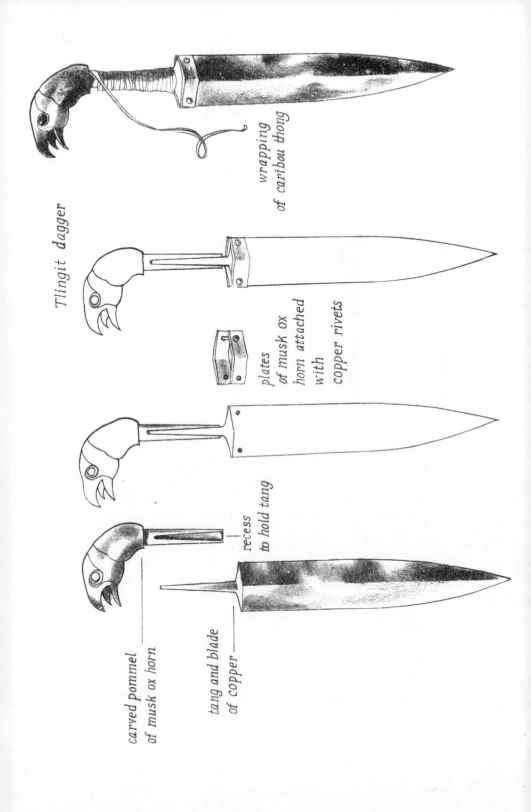

Tlingit dagger

wrapping
of caribou thong

plates
of musk ox
horn attached
with
copper rivets

recess
to hold tang

carved pommel
of musk ox horn

tang and blade
of copper

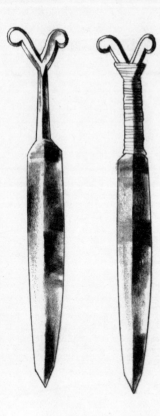

Dagger of native forged copper

3. Two copper daggers; one cold hammered by the Tlingit, the other forged by Canadian Indians of the Northern Territories. (After John Witthoft, Expedition, *Vol. 11, No. 3, 1969*)

worked their copper cold, as the Eskimo did. But the Copper River Indians, uniquely in North America, forged it hot with stone hammers.* Most of the copper implements made by these Eskimos and Indians were daggers meant for fighting, but the Copper River Indians also forged copper arrowheads.

Ground stone tools

Except for this diversion into the subject of metalworking, so far we have been discussing only stone tools and only those that are flaked and chipped. When the materials are siliceous stones, like flint and obsidian, they are as sharp as glass, sharper than iron and most steel. Experiments have shown that a well-made flint arrowhead penetrates more deeply into an animal's body than an

*John Witthoft and Frances Eyman, "Metallurgy of the Tlingit, Dene, and Eskimo" (*Expedition*, Vol. 11, No. 3, 1969) pp. 12–23.

iron one. Their only disadvantage is that they break easily and have to be replaced.

For felling trees and working hard wood, ground stone tools are more durable and efficient than flaked ones. Here the best materials are tough stones like basalt. Ground stone axe and adze heads go back only to about 8000 B.C. in western Asia and Europe. From these centers they diffused in many directions. They were, really, initially invented for the purpose of clearing land when agriculture began, but they spread beyond the reaches of agriculture, particularly to the north. They formed part of the tool kit of hunting peoples in Siberia and North America, and seem to have been separately invented in Australia almost as early as in Western Asia and Europe, if not earlier.

Although a relatively soft stone, slate is easily split and ground into tools that do not need to have very hard edges. A well-known example is the crescent-shaped woman's knife of the Eskimo, used especially in cutting skins to make garments.

Axes and adzes

Once a stone axe has been made it has to be hafted. The North American hunters and the Australian aborigines did this by splitting a stick at one end, inserting the stone head, and binding it fast. The Indians did this with rawhide, which would shrink when it dried. Some of their axe heads were grooved at the hafting point to keep the head from being driven out when used, but the Australians, who used vegetable fibers and did not groove their axe heads,* were constantly having to rehaft their axes.

With an adze, hafting is easier and more efficient. An adze head is different from an axe head in that one face is relatively flat and the other curved, and it is set in a right-angle plane to the handle. Thus it can be hafted on an L-shaped shaft made from a curved piece of wood, and lashed directly to the handle, which does not need to be split. It is not as good for felling a tree as an axe, but much better for working the wood once it has been felled. The Northwest Coast Indians were particularly expert at using such adzes, and they had soft, straight-grained cedar to work with.

*With the exception of two partially grooved pieces that have been found archaeologically.

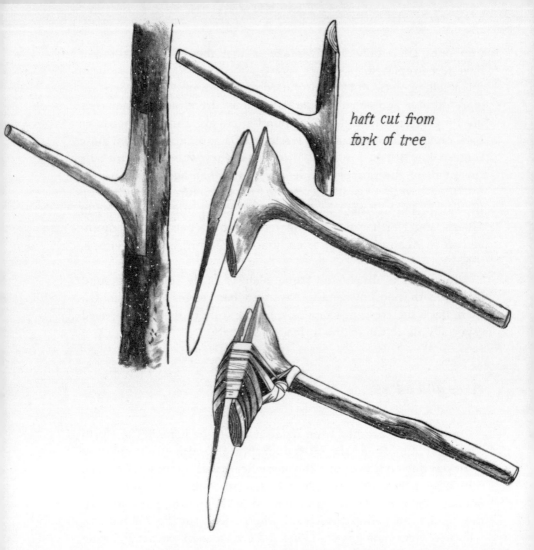

*haft cut from
fork of tree*

4. *An Andamanese adze; blade ground originally out of Pinna
shell, later of iron from shipwrecks*

Apparently uniquely among nonagricultural peoples, the Andaman
Islanders used to grind adze heads out of sections of large mollusc
shells. Instead of the giant Tridacna, used in Micronesia, they chose
the Pinna, a smaller, wedge-shaped bivalve with a thick shell
equipped with a sharp, toothless forward edge, hard enough for
cutting some kinds of wood. With these adzes they used to hew out
the pith-centered trunks of soft-wooded trees into canoe hulls, before
they began making their adzes out of scrap iron, ground in the same
fashion.

Uses of fire as a tool:
Tasmanians and Yümbri

Fire is also used, as in Tasmania, in hardening spear points. The tip of the spear is exposed to fire enough to dry out the wood but not enough to let it char. Dry wood will penetrate an animal's body better than green wood.

Fire can also be used in felling large trees. Over a century ago in Southwest Africa, Sir Francis Galton noted that Bushmen felled trees with fire in order to make posts for game fences and pounds. Recently in West Africa Thurstan Shaw saw some men fell a tree 130 feet high in the following manner. First they stripped off all the bark at the base of the trunk, to bare the wood. Then they heaped burning logs around it. The logs ignited the trunk at that level, and the fire charred it through until it fell. The whole operation, excluding the bark stripping, took sixty hours.*

In Laos, near the big bend of the Mekong River, lives a hunting-gathering people named the Yümbri, or Ghosts of the Yellow Leaves. Their densely wooded country is rich in stands of bamboo. The Yümbri not only cut down the bamboo trunks with fire, but they also use fire to shape pieces of the bamboo into knives. As bamboo has a siliceous crust, these wooden tools can be used to cut skin and flesh. In other words, people with fire and bamboo can survive without stone tools.

Peoples ignorant of fire making

Although all peoples of the world have used fire for tens or hundreds of thousands of years, some hunters still survived into the nineteenth century without knowing how to make fire. Three are outstanding, the Tasmanians, the Andaman Islanders, and the Pygmies of the Ituri Forest in the Congo. All three live in wet country where it is not easy to keep fire going or to carry it about when moving camp, as all three do. They must keep on hand a supply of punky, dry wood, wrapped in bark or leaves. Many tribes of the Australian aborigines carry fire too, because, even if they know how to make it, suitable kinds of wood are not available everywhere.

*Thurstan Shaw, "Tree Felling by Fire" (*Antiquity*, Vol. 43, 1969) p. 52 and plate VI (a).

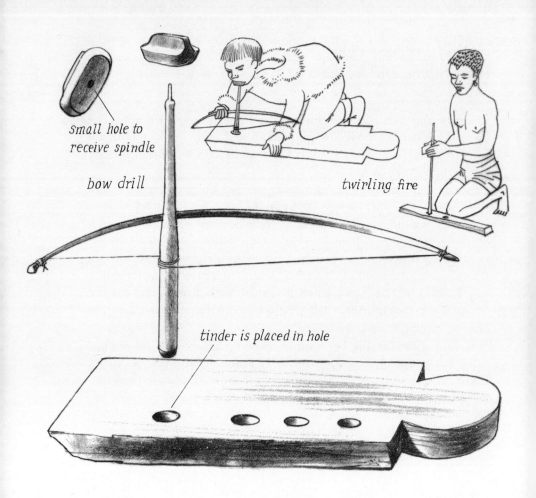

small hole to
receive spindle

bow drill

twirling fire

tinder is placed in hole

5. Fire drills

Two Ways to Make Fire

The commonest technique of firemaking is to rotate a shaft of hard wood in a cup-shaped depression in a piece of soft wood held on the ground. The fire maker must rotate the drill back and forth between the palms of his hands, pressing the shaft down as well as turning it. This is hard work, and it is easiest when two men take turns. Once the powder ground out of the hearthboard has begun to glow, it must be caught in tinder and blown on to make it flame. This last step is the critical one because it depends on the type of tinder used.

Recently I had several students try to make fire by this method, and the only one who succeeded used the silk from dried milkweed pods as tinder.

People who use bows in hunting can rotate the shaft with one hand, while holding it from above with a piece of shell, a dimpled pebble, or a wooden socket with a piece of smooth stone inserted in the cavity like a jewel in a watch. This method requires less effort than the first one and less time, but the problem of tinder is equally crucial.*

An alternate method is to strike a lump of iron pyrites on the edge of a piece of flint or quartz; this is the same principle as that of firing a flintlock. Sparks fly into the tinder, which with skill and luck, is blown into a flame, and the fire is burning almost at once. While this is a much easier method than even the bow drill, few peoples use it because surface deposits of the materials needed are not found in combination in many places.

The principal examples reported of fire making by flint and pyrites are from the Greenland Eskimo, the Yaghans of Tierra del Fuego, and some of the Australian aborigines. Because these three peoples are widely separated in space, and cannot have been in contact for thousands of years, if at all, it is more than likely that each of them invented the method independently.

How hunters get water
in deserts and on frozen ground

Other mammals that live in deserts and on frozen ground have special physiological adaptations to living with little or no drinking water. We have none. Our adaptations are cultural. In dry parts of Australia the aborigines know where water lies close under the surface in dry stream beds, and in these places they used to dig shallow wells at points within a day's walk of each other. These lines of wells thus became trade routes. In the north, they tapped water from the

*Some of the aborigines of Northern Australia and the Western Desert use the fire-saw method, probably introduced by Indonesians before the discovery of Australia by Europeans. By drawing a piece of wood rapidly back and forth across a notch in the shaft of a spearthrower, a man can make fire in a few seconds. Also H. Ling Roth (1899 Appendix H) believed two early accounts of the use of the Polynesian fire-plough method by Tasmanians, but this evidence is still, and probably always will be, *sub judice.*

bulbous trunks of "cream of tartar" trees, and in Queensland they sucked it through filter-tipped tubes from under pandanus roots.

In parts of South Africa the Bushmen also cache water in ostrich egg shells for emergency use. From the rumen of a gemsbok and its vegetable contents, they could also squeeze enough water to last several persons a week. The Eskimo melt snow in soapstone bowls over blubber lamps, and in northern forests American Indians melt it in watertight birchbark kettles kept out of direct contact with the flames.

Environmental protection: shelter and body covering

Such ingenious solutions to the water shortage problem helped hunters extend their habitats far beyond those of other species native to tropical and temperate climates, but water was not enough. Particularly in the north, hunters also needed to keep warm, and the chill of night in a desert has to be experienced to be believed. During the night a number of people sleeping together in a small, enclosed space can preserve the core temperatures of their bodies at a comfortable level. These enclosed spaces are dwellings. In the daytime anyone who sallies out of doors needs to keep warm individually. This means clothing — a portable, enclosed space. Let us start with housing in its simplest form, which is really no house at all.

Camping in the open: caves, rock shelters, and hollow trees

Fire keeps people warm and dry, but it keeps them warmer and drier in a confined space than in the open air. Even when walking about with torches, people can receive some warmth from them, but not enough in a really cold climate with subzero temperatures. When some of the aborigines of the Australian desert sleep in temporary camps, they lie down between two rows of smoldering fires that raise the temperature enough to keep them from waking from the cold.

26

But there is little rain in the desert, and when it rains anywhere fires need to be protected. If the people don't know how to relight them, fires need the protection more than people do. Caves and rock shelters offer shelter, and people have lived in them as long as they have had fire. Before that they camped in the open, as archaelogical evidence shows. Caves are damp places. They also offer shelter to predatory animals against which men are helpless at night without fire, particularly if a man's way out may be blocked.

In recent times the Veddas, an aboriginal hunting people of Ceylon, lived in cave mouths and rock shelters during the rainy season but left them in the dry season to camp near permanent water, where the deer they hunted congregated. The Chenchu people of southern India moved seasonally in the same way, from the hills where they hunted during the rains to the banks of the Kistna River during the drought. But in the hills, where there are no caves, they lived in brush shelters, while on the riverbanks they camped under overhanging cliffs in rock shelters.

The Crystal Mountains in West Central Africa have caves, but the local Pygmies do not live in them. They deposit dead bodies in them instead, and fear the ghosts of the dead. But the same Pygmies protect themselves from rain when caught in the forest by crouching between the flying-buttress-like root-flanges of some of the giant trees. Early navigators who visited the southern coast of Tasmania in the nineteenth century found some of the natives sitting inside the hollow base of a tree trunk of great circumference. Its opening had been enlarged by fire.

Nature does not provide enough caves and hollow trees to house everyone. All peoples, hunters included, build some kind of dwelling. Most dwellings are variants of five types: the domed hut, the lean-to, the pit house, the conical tent, and the gabled, rectangular cabin or house. Whichever kind is built, in each camp or village the dwellings are all alike, inside and out, except that some may be larger than others. Everyone knows how to construct them.

The domed hut: man's most basic house type

The most widely distributed of all the five types, the domed hut is small, with a low entrance just large enough to crawl through. In the Ituri Forest of the Congo, the Pygmy women build them, usually working in pairs. First they cut thin, flexible saplings about eight to ten feet long and stick them into the ground in a circle. Then the women stand inside. One of them bends the tips of two opposite poles together and holds them while the other woman lashes them with bark from vines, and so on around the circle until that part of the job has been completed. The next step is to move outside and lash more saplings to the uprights in the form of concentric circles, leaving a space for the doorway. Then all that is left to do is to collect large leaves with stout stems, notch the stems, and fix them to the frame hoops. Such a hut is six to eight feet wide and high enough for a Pygmy to stand up in in the middle. It is watertight enough to protect a man, his wife, and small children from the rain.

Pygmies, South African Bushmen, most of the food-gathering peoples of southern India, some of the Australian aborigines, and some of the Tasmanians made such huts. They are basically similar to North American Indian wigwams, and the Alakaluf Indians of southern Chile still made them as late as the 1950s. While the frame is basically the same throughout, covering varies from leaves to bark, mats, and skins.

The famous architect Buckminster Fuller, who invented the geodesic dome, actually reinvented, in a more modern form, a house

6. *A domed hut of the Kalahari Bushmen*

type that once had a worldwide distribution and may well be over a quarter of a million years old, judging by archaeological evidence from southern France. One might almost say that the domed hut is as specific to man, in a cultural sense, as the oriole's special kind of nest is instinctively specific to orioles. One advantage of the domed hut is that it can be put up in no more than two hours wherever there is suitable wood, and can be abandoned whenever a band of hunters decides to move camp.

The lean-to

A second widely distributed kind of shelter is a simple rectangle of sticks and branches, covered with leaves, that is set up at an angle by means of poles, and facing away from the wind, with a fire in front. This is used by the Kadar of southern India, the Semang of the Malay Peninsula, the Philippine Negritos, and some of the Australian aborigines. In hot weather the latter cover the lean-to with bark and set it up as a flat roof with open sides to protect them from the sun. Like the domed hut, the lean-to is found among the Fuegian Indians, but with a guanaco-skin cover.

The Onas, guanaco hunters of the northern and eastern sides of Tierra del Fuego, used to erect several of these shelters in an arc away from the wind, with their fires built in front. This type of tent, for that is what is was, had one disadvantage. Being used on mostly treeless, grassy plains, it had to be carried from camp to camp, and the skin covers and poles made heavy bundles. The Ona women strapped them on their backs while the men carried only their weapons. The men were not abusing their women. They had to be mobile and alert, on the lookout for game and enemies.

The relatives of the Onas, the Tehuelche of Patagonia, who acquired horses from the Spaniards, were able to transport their shelters on horseback, and consequently they made larger ones which they built in pairs facing each other, in effect, a gabled dwelling.

The pit house

Neither of the previous two dwelling types gives protection from intense cold. In northern regions of Eurasia and North America we find a third and warmer kind. It is the pit house, large enough to hold several families. A hole is dug in the ground and a framework erected of available materials. If wood is abundant, a dome of logs is made by crisscrossing, and a hole is left in the top. During the late Pleistocene in southern Russia, Upper Paleolithic hunters used mammoth bones instead, and the Chukchi and Eskimo of the Bering Strait region used the ribs and jaws of whales. Some of the Eskimo farther east used slabs of shale. In any case, the framework is completed with smaller sticks, bones, or stones, and earth piled on top. In the colder regions the entrance may be through a vaulted tunnel, with a depression in the middle to serve as a valve to reduce heat loss.

In North America such dwellings were used as far south as Central California and into the Plains. The entrance was usually through the hole in the top, plus a notched log for a ladder. The Beothuk Indians of Newfoundland built octagonal pit houses with eight partitions converging on a common hearth, and the entrance was through one side. In Hokkaido, Sakhalin Island, and the Kurils the Ainu formerly lived in pit houses, in some cases multiple ones connected by tunnels.

Wherever used, these pit houses were essentially winter dwellings, and required a more or less sedentary life dependent on an abundance of animal food: either mammoths, as in prehistoric Europe; or whales, walruses, and seals, as in the Bering Strait region; or salmon, deer, and bear, as among the Ainu. The disadvantage of these underground habitations was the problem of sanitation. For that, and because of a need of greater mobility, many of the peoples who wintered in them moved out in warm weather to live in temporary and more mobile dwellings.

Conical tents

Northern peoples who hunted land mammals such as reindeer, caribou, moose, and what Americans call buffalo and elk, could not remain in one place all winter, and they lived in tents, usually conical, the year round. They are used all the way around the arctic and subarctic regions from Lapland to Maine. In forested regions the poles are easy to cut and need not be carried, and the frames are usually covered with birchbark. In open country the covers are usually of skins, and the poles have to be carried. The largest tents of this type are the tipis of the Plains Indians, but they could afford large ones because, like the Tehuelche, they had horses to transport them.

Thatched houses

While permanent, thatched houses are usually made by agricultural peoples, there are some hunters whose food supply is constant and who also have plenty of wood and thatching material. The Önge Negritos of Little Andaman Island live along the shore, where fish, molluscs, sea turtles, and dugongs are abundant. They build large, oval, communal houses of poles and thatch. Inside, each family of the band has its own section and fireplace just inside the walls, leaving an open space in the middle for a dance floor. Food-producing Indians in the Amazon Basin today live in similar one-house villages. The similarity between them and the Önge in house type is due to two things; they live in similar climates where similar building materials are available, and both can obtain enough food locally the year round to permit sedentary life.

As stated earlier, the Ainu of Japan used to winter in pit houses, and in the summer they probably bivouacked in deerskin tents with a three-pole frame. These were still used in the nineteenth century on hunting forays. In modern times, equipped with Japanese steel axes, the Hokkaido Ainu build rectangular, gable-roofed, single-family houses with frameworks of logs and poles and thatched walls and roofs. Although drafty and inflammable, they are lived in the year round. Each house has two outdoor privies, one for each sex.

The plank houses of the Northwest Coast Indians

The ultimate in nonagricultural house-building was probably reached by the Indians of the American Northwest Coast, who had an abundant supply of easily worked cedar. They split and adzed out planks and boards, with which they walled and roofed large, weather-

C

7. *A thatched house of the Önge of Little Andaman Island.
Such a dwelling is inhabited by an entire band*

8. *An Ainu thatched house and storehouse*

proof, and ornate buildings with gabled roofs, as impressive as many European wooden buildings.

The tree is the western red cedar (*Thuja plicata*), from which most of the shingles used in North America are sawn. The nature of its wood made it possible for the Indians to obtain large planks of it with simple stone and bone chisels and wedges. As these trees run from 150 to 200 feet in height and have trunk diameters of from six to ten feet, the Indians would have found it difficult to fell them with stone tools, but by a simple and ingenious method the Nootka, for example, obtained half sections of a trunk while leaving the rest of the tree standing.

The most suitable trees for house-building do not grow along the shore, but deep in the forest where the limbs branch off high up. The trunks are straight and free of knots. A single man, walking in the forest and finding such a tree, would first cut a narrow notch with chisels, halfway across the trunk, just above the level where the root-buttresses begin to flange out. Then he would cast a line over the lowest branch and climb up, some twenty or thirty feet above his notch. Below the lowest branch, he would cut a wider notch, also halfway through the trunk.

The next step was to drive wedges downward into the trunk at the bottom of the upper notch, until the wood began to split. When the split was wide enough, he thrust in a pole, below the wedges, and climbed down. Then he went home. The weight of the pole and the action of the wind rocking the tree gradually extended the split to the lower notch, at which point the half-section of trunk between the notches fell off, and it could be either hewn into a boat or split into planks for house-building. The latter process was best done by two men. First they would drive a row of small wedges into the edge of the slab, and as the split widened, put in larger wedges. Usually it was necessary to drive wedges along both sides to keep the split straight, and one man might hasten the process by using a pole between the piece split off and the rest of the slab as a lever. Still, as the men neared the center of the slab it was impossible to avoid completely the influence of the curvature of the growth rings, and this meant adzing the board afterward to flatten its sides.

The reader is probably already familiar with the external appearance of Northwest Coast houses of the totem pole period, constructed after the introduction of iron carpenters' tools. More pertinent to our present subject is an account of how some of them were made in earlier times, when the Indian carpenter's kit consisted of only stone

9. A Nootka plank house. (After Philip Drucker, 1951)

mauls, chisels, adzes, wedges, simple drills, grindstones of sandstone for smoothing wood surfaces, and sharkskin for polishing them. To these implements may be added a knowledge of two techniques: steaming wood to bend it, and scorching it to produce a dense, smooth, surface finish. Not only in house-building but in making wooden boxes, and canoes, they used ten different units of measurement, all based on a man's fingers, hands, arms, and span, from a finger-breadth to a fathom.

Nootka house-building

The best documented available account of precontact house-building again concerns the Nootka,* who changed their residences twice a year. Their winter villages were located near the heads of inlets, for shelter, and their summer villages were near the shore. In each site they erected house frames, with one house sheltering at least four families, often including that of a chief. But each household owned only one set of planks to serve as walls and roof. Every spring and fall they carried their planks back and forth between their residences by canoe. The number of planks thus transported depended on the size of each house. The houses ranged in length from forty to one hundred feet and were between thirty and forty feet wide, and were built with a long side facing the shore.

The framework of an ordinary house consisted of two solid posts ten to twelve feet high set in front-center a few feet apart, and supporting a crossbar on top. This crossbar in turn held up the front end of the ridgepole. A single post, carved in human form before being set up, bore the rear end of the ridgepole. At each of the four corners of the house stood a post nine to ten feet high, and the pair on each side of the house bore the weight of the plates. In exceptionally long houses, there would be three posts on each side.

The wall planks were held in place between pairs of poles the ends of which were driven into the ground, and if the planks were not long enough to reach the length of the house, their ends were made to overlap between a pair of poles. Rather than have the planks support one another, each plank was hung from the paired posts in

*Philip Drucker, "The Northern and Central Nootkan Tribes" (Washington, D.C., Bureau of American Ethnology, Bull. 144, 1951).

slings of cedar-bark rope, in such a fashion that each plank over-lapped the one below it, as with clapboards.

Whatever its length, the ridgepole was always a single log, adzed down so that its diameter, usually a good three to four feet, was the same from end to end. Between ridgepole and plates were laid rafters, then horizontal poles were lashed to the rafters, and over the poles the roof planks were laid, overlapping each other, and loose. The longest and most perfect planks were used for this purpose. They were left loose so that people inside could shift them about with poles, to let out smoke and keep out the rain. During stormy weather they weighted down the planks with stones and logs to keep them from blowing off. The doorway was located in the front end of the house, between the two center posts and covered with a hang-ing mat. Inside the doorway, a siding of planks on either side kept the wind from blowing on the fires in the nearby corners.

Such a house was inhabited by several families, four in corners and others along the sides. Each had its own raised bed and in-dividual fireplace, but there was also a communal hearth in the center for use on ceremonial occasions. The highest-ranking member, whether or not a chief, occupied the right rear corner, and the other positions followed protocol.

Being of cedar, the house frames lasted for many years and did not have to be set up often. If one post or beam rotted, it was replaced. The portable planks were naturally more vulnerable and needed re-placement more often, and as we have seen, splitting off and adzing a set of planks took considerable time and effort. Actually the most frequent occasion for building a new house frame and making new planks was after enemy raiders had burned a house down.

Both transporting the lumber to the site and erecting the frame required the combined efforts of a considerable number of persons, as in an old-fashioned, American country barn-raising. The way that the house-owner got them together was to send out invitations and make a merry feast out of the occasion. This meant that stores of food had to be laid in to feed the participants, and they had to be en-tertained.

From the place where they were cut the posts and beams were usually floated to the water's edge nearest the house side, but now they had to be moved up the slope. As many as a dozen men would work together, some levering, others blocking, and still others heav-ing on ropes, all to the heave-ho rhythm of a chantey-man. Setting the center and side posts in holes, and raising the crossbeam, side plates, and ridgepole required the use of levers, shears, and temporary cribwork towers. Setting up these towers was a tricky method, because if any of the crosspieces should roll or shift, the whole tower might collapse. The men working on it therefore had to lash the units together and wedge them, and then roll the pole off the tower onto its support.

Without reasonable doubt, the kind of house we have just described was the most elaborate type of habitation constructed by hunting peoples in historic times. The key factors were of course an ample supply of food and the availability in abundance of what is probably the world's best timber. Add to this the consummate craftsmanship of the Indians with a minimum tool kit, and their ability to work in teams on different aspects of a single task, and the reason for their success is clear. This is the only account I have found which reveals so much organization and coordinated teamwork in a hunting society when devoted to a technical operation.

The domed snow igloo of the Central Eskimo

But the Northwest Coast Indians were not the only skilled housebuilders. As this brief survey has shown, hunting and gathering peoples in all climates have shown much ingenuity and inventive capacity in building the kinds of shelters that they need. They use local materials; they need hire no masons, carpenters, or plumbers, nor do they have to worry about strikes, or a sudden doubling in the price of building materials. They do their work with tools of their own making, none of which are of metal. Without geometry, trigonometry, or architectural plans — for they are all illiterate — they have discovered many of the principles of house construction used by modern peoples, even that of the self-supported dome. The latter is the product of the genius of the Eskimo, the snow igloo, a temporary and at best, by its very nature, a seasonal dwelling. All Eskimo did not make it, but some of them did, particularly the Netsilik and the Caribou Eskimo living on the barren lands west of Hudson Bay.

With a bone snow-knife, a man cuts a number of rectangular blocks of closely compacted snow. He then stands in the middle of the area to be covered, and a companion, often his wife, hands him the blocks.

10. An Eskimo snow igloo

First he sets some of them on edge in a circle on the surface of the ground, and then he tapers the upper edge of each block so that this bottom layer takes the form of an incipient spiral. Then he lays on the second tier, one block at a time, so that each block is held in place not only by the block or blocks below it but also by the block next to it, on which it leans. Owing to these two surface contacts he can also taper the walls of his house inward until he has walled in a dome except for a hole in the top, which he covers with a single piece of snow. Thus walled in by his own efforts, he kneels down and cuts a doorway, out of which he emerges.

These are essential steps. He may add a window of isinglass or ice, and, if the snowhouse is to be lived in during most of the winter, he may line the dome with skins. Such a lining will permit an inside temperature up to 60°F., instead of a maximum of 35°F. without it. There is always a little melting, but the melting fuses the dome into a solid shell. Melting was of no concern to the Caribou Eskimo, for they had no heat in their igloos except that of their own bodies.

In order to reduce heat loss, the igloo-maker may also add a vaulted snow tunnel to the doorway, like the tunnels that other Eskimo use as entrances to their pit houses. These tunnels are in the form of arches. Neither domes nor arches were invented elsewhere in the world before the rise of literate, metal-age civilizations, and professional architects.

How hunters keep warm out of doors

With or without the help of fires, human body heat within a confined air space provides enough environmental protection to keep the people who spend the night together in domed huts, tents, igloos, or other dwellings alive and warm and ready to face the rigors of the outside world once the sun is up.

In a surprisingly wide range of temperature, humidity, and water vapor pressure, hunting peoples can go about their daily activities without a stitch of clothing. They can do this because of the remarkable efficiency of our most conspicuous but least understood organ, the more or less hairless human skin. In comparison with the hairy hides of most other mammals, our skins are highly vascular. The flow of blood beneath the surface compensates to a certain degree for a partial or complete failure of the follicles on our trunks and limbs to sprout the hair to which they are genetically entitled.

In cool weather, blood flowing through a network of capillaries gives warmth. In hot weather it supplies the fluids exuded by the sweat glands, and the evaporation of sweat cools the air immediately encasing the skin, particularly if there is any breeze. If there is none, the evaporation creates a highly local, miniature current of air, which does the trick.

People do not really need body covering in many of the tropical parts of the world, or even in some regions where the temperature may fall close to the freezing point. The Tasmanians, Alakaluf, and Yaghan Indians are examples of the latter. Their bodies were, or are, able to tolerate air temperatures in the thirties and forties Fahrenheit, and immersion in icy water. During the night fire and shelter kept them warm.

In 1959 members of a physiological expedition studying the cold tolerance of the Alakaluf on Wellington Island, Chile, used each

c*

night to place two Indians in an unheated tent under thin blankets. Each man had thermocouples attached to his skin in various places, and a rectal thermometer inserted in the appropriate place. Wires led from the men to a room in a building where the scientists read gauges.

One night one Indian panicked. He leapt off his cot and ran up the mountain naked, trailing his wires behind him, until the one attached to his rectal thermometer caught on a bush and pulled the instrument out. It was winter, and the mountain was covered with snow. The refugee from science remained on the mountain for nearly a week, until the expedition departed. No planned experiment could demonstrate the cold tolerance of the Alakaluf more clearly than this event did.

The human body: a walking billboard

Man is a social animal. People see each other every day, and their mutual behavior depends on such matters as age, sex, degree of maturity, kinship, and relative positions of authority. If everyone went about stark naked and unadorned, these distinctions would be blurred, and some would disappear. Society needs structure, structure needs symbols, and the most obvious place to put symbols is on the human body.

One way is to mutilate it, by knocking out a few incisor teeth, lopping off finger joints, stretching earlobes, putting plugs through holes in the lips and cheeks, scarifying black skin, tattooing lighter skin, circumcising, subincising, cutting out clitorises, and the like. These practices are not confined to hunters. Some of our most civilized peoples employ some of them.

A second way to use the human body as a billboard is to paint it. Paint can be removed, so the number of designs a person can wear is limited only by his or her palette and imagination. Most often body paint is put on on ceremonial occasions when people are either very happy or very sad, and wish either to dress up or to show their state of disturbance. We do the same thing with clothing, and some members of our younger generation have unwittingly rediscovered body paint, over and above cosmetics.

Hair as symbol and protection

They have also rediscovered long hair and full beards. As any parent knows who has tried to send a shaggy-locked teen-ager to a barber shop, hair is a prime human symbol in any culture, including those of hunters. For example, the Ainu men used to wear their hair and beards at full length. They believed that they would sicken and die if they cut either. When the Japanese conquered the Ainu they forced the men to cut their hair, and this action created more resistance than any other.

Like skin, hair also has a protective value. For one thing, it enlarges the sensory range of the scalp. While moving about in a cave, a bald-headed man is more likely to smack his head on the roof than is a man with a full crop. Hair also offers some protection against heat and cold, depending on the person's race. A Bushman with tightly coiled hair, distributed on his scalp in patches like peppercorns, can tease them out to their full length, and by smearing them with pomade he can convert his hair into a natural helmet to shield his scalp from the summer sun. The Tasmanians, who also had spiral hair, did the same thing against cold. In neither example was the symbolic aspect of the hairdo lost.

Painting the body with pigments

Most of the hunting peoples of the world, and some nonhunters as well, paint their bodies with three natural earth pigments, red ochre, yellow ochre, and white pipe clay (kaolin). Some of them also use ordinary olive-gray potter's clay. For black, they use charcoal. Natural deposits of the ochres and kaolin are not found everywhere, and the search for these cosmetic materials is one of the chief reasons for primitive trade. Food is traded very little. In other words, social needs have priority over economic ones among hunters too.

If earth pigments and charcoal are rubbed on dry, they do not stick to the skin very long. If they are mixed with a liquid medium they can be painted on with chewed sticks or other impromptu brushes, in more detailed and delicate designs. The two mediums used by hunters, and others, are water and oils, or fat. This brings us back to the real subject of this section, portable environmental protection. To my knowledge, no one has technically studied the thermal properties of red ochre, yellow ochre, pipe clay, or charcoal when applied to the naked human skin with water. They may offer some protection from sunburn, windburn, and insects; and red and black paint may absorb heat, white paint repel it. If they do, these are side effects. The overt purpose is decoration.

The other medium in which pigments may be applied to the skin is oil, usually in the form of animal fats, but sometimes, as in the tropical forests, in the form of vegetable oils. Among the African Pygmies, it may be termite oil, boiled out of the bodies of those insects and having a very pungent odor. Oil, of course, protects the human body from a certain amount of cold, which is why channel swimmers grease their bodies. It also repels insects.

The little-known and now extinct Karankawa Indians of the Texas Coast, who were true food gatherers, smeared their bodies with the fat of sharks and alligators. The New England Indians who greeted our Pilgrim ancestors used to grease themselves in wintertime from the waist up, giving them an aroma often commented on by the settlers. At sunset the Andaman Islanders used to cover their bodies with sea turtle fat, usually mixed with red ochre, against the chill of evening. The Tasmanians, Yaghans, and Alakaluf, all of whom lived in cool climates, used animal fats as their chief means of keeping warm, along with the fires in their boats. But in subfreezing climates, fat is not as efficient as clothing, and fat and clothing do not go well together.

Three basic kinds of clothing

Not counting head, hand, and foot covering for the moment, we may broadly classify clothing into three categories: loin coverings, robes, and tailored garments. Variants of all three are worn, at least out of doors, by those hunters who do not go completely naked.

Covering the loins

In individual cultures it is sometimes hard to say whether the loins are covered out of modesty or to protect the genitalia—or to call attention to them. Some peoples in the tropics wear a bunch of leaves hanging from a waistband. Others gird their loins with a strip of beaten bark. In the Ituri Forest of the Congo, a Pygmy man will climb nearly to the top of a wild fig tree, well over one hundred feet, to strip a piece of bark from a limb. He takes this risk because there the bark is softest. Back in the camp he beats this bark into a sheet six to eight inches wide with a flat-sided hammer, often of ivory, on a fallen log. This sheet is as soft as cloth and will not chafe the skin. If he is to wear it himself, he will pass it between his legs and then around his waist, and tie it in front. Such a piece of bark needs to be a good eight feet long. If he is making if for his wife, he gives her a piece little more than two feet long. She passes it between her legs and under a tight fiber belt in front and behind.

The robe

The robe seems to be the most widely distributed and basic of garments. It is essentially a rectangle of some material worn over the shoulders, or under the armpits, and wrapped around the body. In its simplest form, it is a single skin. It may be held in place by thorns and thongs.

When the Yaghan and Alakaluf Indians went fishing and harpooning in their canoes, they either went naked or wore a single pelt of seal or sea otter, tied over their backs. Additional thongs would enable a woman to carry her baby on her back, inside the robe, with its face peeking over her shoulder. These robes did not impede the motions of their arms or hands. In each canoe a fire, burning on a clay hearth, provided additional warmth. The Yaghans knew how to sew skins together into larger robes, but they used them mostly indoors as bedding.

The climate of Tasmania is not as chilly as that of Tierra del Fuego. It is comparable to the climate of England. Still it is cold enough to require clothing, in addition to fat and ochre. Most of the robes worn by the Tasmanians were single skins, wallaby or kangaroo, but they also knew how to make warm, composite robes by sewing together the skins of a dozen or more "opossums." These marsupials are phalangers, given their local name because of their arboreal habit and resemblance to the American opossum, but they are smaller, about the size of a cat.

Across Bass Strait in southwestern Australia more of these "opossum" skin robes were being worn by aborigines encountered by early nineteenth-century settlers. Some of the robes were large and elegant; those worn by men of rank had decorated borders.

The guanaco-hunting Onas of the plains of Tierra del Fuego made voluminous robes by stitching together several guanaco skins. These robes are very warm, because the guanaco is a wild relative of the llama, alpaca, and vicuña, whose wools are among the lightest and warmest in the world. An Ona who was out hunting kept his arms inside his robe, holding the edges of the garment together. When ready to shoot, he dropped his robe to the ground, even in the snow, and pursued his quarry naked. Lucas Bridges, the son of Thomas Bridges, missionary to the Fuegian Indians, once asked an Ona why he exposed his body to the cold and was told, "For the same reason that you keep your face uncovered."

Even the Northwest Coast Indians, whose technological skills were outstanding, wore the simple robe as their basic garment, but they were not skins. Their robes were highly ornate, woven blankets, made of shredded cedar-bark fibers plus various animal hairs. Their manufacture will be described in Chapter Twelve. In the cool, maritime climate of the Northwest Coast, robes were all that the Indians needed, as long as they stayed on the coast. On trips into the mountains, they dressed more in the style of the Indians of the interior.

Tailored garments

When a person is sitting still, or even walking about with no critical need to use his hands, nothing is warmer than a robe, because it encloses the whole body as a unit. But for people who have to remain out of doors all day at below-freezing temperatures, garments with separate coverings for the arms and legs are needed. These garments were originally limited to northern Eurasia and North America, and apparently go back to the Upper Paleolithic Europeans.

There are two degrees of tailoring, partial and complete. Partial tailoring is limited to the North American Indians, including the

Northern Athabascans and Northern Algonkians of the boreal forests and mountains. Basically this consists of a sleeveless pullover shirt and a breechclout, with separate sleeves and leggins tied on when needed, although some of the most northerly tribes had shirts with sleeves.

Of all the native peoples of North America, only the Eskimo wore fully tailored suits, consisting basically of two pieces, a hooded parka and a pair of trousers. In winter they wore two such suits, one inside with the fur facing in, and the other outside with the fur out. Caribou hide is particularly efficient at retaining body heat because caribou hair, like that of other members of the deer family, is hollow, thus providing maximum insulation with minimum weight. But if caribou skin is worn too close to the nose and mouth, the moisture from exhaled breath freezes on its hairs. For that reason the Eskimo sewed wolf and wolverine fur ruffs around the edges affected, for the breath will not freeze on the fur of these animals.

On the Asiatic side of Bering Strait, both the Eskimo and Chukchi wore essentially the same kind of garments as the American Eskimo, but inland the reindeer-hunting tribes wore hooded coats cut down the middle, overlapped, and held together by belts. The Ainu of Hokkaido wore several layers of sleeved shirts reaching just below the knees, and without hoods. The oldest shirts were on the inside, the newest one outside. Originally they made these shirts of deerskin, but after they got the idea of looms from Japanese contact, most of them were made of woven elm bark.

Waterproof garments

In the Amur River country of Siberia, the Goldi, who were fishermen, made their clothing of salmon skin, and the Aleuts of the stormy islands bearing their name protected their undergarments, which were basically robes, against the rain with waterproof parkas made of sewn strips of seal gut. The Eskimo, whose country has little rain, sewed their seams so finely as to make them impervious to water, and when they removed their clothing to go indoors, they beat their fur parkas and trousers with special implements to remove the snow, which otherwise would melt indoors.

Head covering

Apart from the special treatment of their hair by the Tasmanians and Bushmen, which was previously described, special head coverings were rare in the southern hemisphere. The Onas were an exception; they wore pointed caps of guanaco skin, which served as disguises in hunting as well as providing protection. In the northern hemisphere, the Northern Athabascan and Northern Algonkian Indians wore fur caps, and the Eskimo needed none because of their hoods.

From California up the Northwest Coast to Alaska the Indians wore caps or hats of tightly woven basketry, some of which were decorative and elaborate. The Aleuts made visored hats of thin strips of wood.

Mittens and footgear

Only in the cold regions of the North do hunting peoples cover their hands, to keep their fingers from freezing, and there they wear fur mittens, more efficient than gloves. To keep from losing them when they have to bare their hands, the Eskimo tie their mittens together by a thong which is threaded up their sleeves and over their shoulders.

Of all the hunters of the New World, only the Eskimo make boots, the well-known mukluks. They make their soles of the skin of the bearded seal (*Erignatus barbatus*) which, when properly greased, is water-resistant. The Indians of the North American forests wore moccasins, which are essentially two pieces of skin sewn together, one for the sole, sides, and back, and the other for the upper and tongue. In South America the Onas seem to have reinvented a kind of moccasin for hunting in the snow. It is made of one piece of skin in which the upper and tongue, simply a forward extension of the sole, are doubled back over the toes and sewn to the sides.

These are the principal kinds of footwear worn by hunters, but there are a few others. The Bushmen of the Kalahari wear skin sandals to protect their feet from the hot, sandy ground when hunting in the summer. This gives them an advantage over the game animals, for the latter usually seek shade in the middle of the day.

In summertime the Ainu of Hokkaido wear slipperlike shoes of wide, plaited strips of elm bark, comparable to those that country people used to wear in Russia. In winter they protect their feet with waterproof boots of salmon skin. In all seasons they cover their calves and ankles with elm-bark leggins.

Curing skins

Many hunters who live in warm climates prefer nudity to wearing clothing because dressing skins is lengthy and tedious work. Also, the skin of an animal cooked whole is good to eat. In cool climates a mixture of fat and ochre not only keeps people warm enough for comfort, but it also keeps their bodies dry. Rain water simply runs off it. When untanned skins, however cured, get wet, they stiffen and have to be softened over again, in many cases by chewing. Tanning is a specialized and laborious process confined to modern civilizations.

To illustrate what steps are involved in dressing a skin, let us follow the activities of a Yaghan man and wife team. Having harpooned and beached a sea lion, the husband turns it on its back and makes a long incision with a mussel shell, from its neck to the end of its rump. Then he makes a circular cut around its neck — so deep that he can break the cervical vertebrae with his hands — and removes the head. He peels off the skin on both sides, slashing with his shell to free the skin from its underlying fat. When he gets to the flippers he leaves them on the body by skinning them from the inside.

Once the skin has been detached he cuts off the flipper skin, and his wife sews up the holes with fibers made of tendons. With a bone awl, he punches holes all around the edges of the skin, about a finger-length apart, and stretches it with sticks cut to the proper length. Some run lengthwise, others crosswise, as in a grid. He adjusts them in such a way that the skin is smooth and unwrinkled. He sets the stretched skin against his hut, with a stick propping it to keep it upright. The inside is toward the hut. The circulation of air will dry it on both sides. After two or three weeks it is stiff enough so that he can remove the sticks.

If it is to be used for covering a hut, he leaves the fat that remains on the inside, but if it is to be used for a garment or for thongs, his wife now gets to work scraping the inside with a sharp-edged mussel shell. With short strokes, she removes both the adhering bits of fat and the inner layer of the skin. Otherwise the latter will rot. For some purposes, as for making thongs, the hair too must be removed. There are two methods. One is to place the skin hair-side down on the bare earth on the floor of the hut, with rushes and other covering over it, until the outer layer of skin has begun to ferment; then, after about two more weeks, the wife scrapes the outer side, removing that layer with the hair. By the other method, the wife collects her own urine and rubs it into the outer side, and then the family sleep on it. This method is quicker, and the finished hide is softer, suitable for thongs and straps. If the skin is to be worn, the oil on the wearer's body constantly lubricates it. Sometimes, in addition, the woman rubs it with a mixture of burnt clay and fat.

The South African Bushmen also cure gemsbok hides, to be worn as robes, with human urine, then they scrape the inner sides thin, and from time to time they rub in bone meal, making the hides as soft as chamois. The Micmac of Nova Scotia have another method of curing moose and deer hides, one of which is an approach to tanning. They boil pieces of fir root until the water is red, add ashes, and soak the hide in this mixture for a week. Then they take it out, wring it, hang it over a rope stretched between two trees, and scrape it with a knife. Variants of these three methods may be found among many other hunting peoples.

How Yaghan and Eskimo women cut and sew skins

In making clothing, including caps, mittens, boots, and moccasins, it is usually necessary to cut skins with matching edges and to sew them together. This is women's work, and apparently the women of every hunting people who wear skins for clothing, however simple or complicated, knew or know how to do it.

A Yaghan woman lays her skins on the ground side by side and, with a sharpened shell, trims the edges of each piece to be matched in an approximately straight line. Then she pierces small, matching holes in the two skins with a bone awl and laces them together with a thread of twisted tendon fibers, making a continuous spiral stitch. The sinews most preferred are taken from the tail of the coypu

(*Myocastor coipu*), a large aquatic rodent with webbed feet that lives in underwater burrows. In default of these animals, which are rare in Yaghan country, they use sea otter sinews.

The woman does this stitching by punching one hole at a time, and pushing the end of the thread through the hole after licking it to keep its point from fraying. Only then does she bore the other hole. The result is a quite coarse and uneven joint. When finished, she pounds the two edges with a round stone to flatten them and to tighten the stitches.

At the opposite end of the spectrum is the tailoring skill of an Eskimo woman who, because she lives in a cold climate, needs more skill. She must cut the skins not only in straight lines but also in curves. This she does with an *ulu*, or woman's knife, a thin piece of slate curved like a half moon on the cutting edge, and kept sharp by grinding. Along the straight upper edge is a handle which allows her to exert the needed pressure. By rocking and sliding this implement on the inner side of the fur or skin, she achieves precision.

When ready to join the pieces together, she lays one on top of the other, the bottom one with its inside down and the top one with its inside up, so that the stitches will match exactly. She sews them together with a fine bone needle that has an eye in its head. This is blind stitching; when the joined pieces are viewed from the outside, no stitches can be seen, and the joint is tight. The Eskimo use a variety of stitches, some with overlapping, and some waterproof.*

Thongs and lines

People who wear skins for clothing also use them in making thongs and long, stout lines. A clearly stated account of the latter may again be taken from detailed observations of the Yaghans. They prefer to use the thick skins of the adult male southern fur seal (*Artocephalus australis*), an animal reaching six feet in length and weighing from five hundred to seven hundred pounds. After a woman has removed its hair, her husband spreads the skin smoothly on a flat piece of ground.

He punches a hole in the center of it and, with a sharpened shell, he carefully cuts a finger-wide strip in an unbroken, concentric

*See E. W. Hawkes, *The Labrador Eskimo* (Canadian Geological Survey, Memoir 91, 1916, No. 1637).

spiral until he has used up the skin. He then ties one end of the line to a tree trunk, pulls it tight, and runs it around other trees to stretch. After it has dried it is ready for use.

The Yaghans make shorter and finer cords by plaiting strips of gut. These are very commonly used for sling cords, for every male Yaghan goes about with his sling hanging around his neck and over his chest, ready for instant use. Their fishlines are either seaweed stems or cords of plaited sinews.

Northern hunters use similar methods for making thongs and lines. For long, heavy lines needed in harpooning large sea mammals, the Alaskan Eskimo prefer the skin of the bearded seal, also used for making boot soles as previously mentioned. As a male bearded seal may reach twelve feet in length and weigh up to eight hundred pounds, one skin can make a very long line when it is cut by the spiral method described for the Yaghans.

Making cordage of vegetable materials and of human hair

In warm parts of the world where hunters have little use for skins, they make most of their cordage out of vegetable fiber. As one exception, some of the Australian aborigines make it of hair shorn from women's heads. The men wind up to thirty feet of such strings around their waists, ready for use when needed. The simplest and commonest way to produce cordage out of short fibers, vegetable or human, is for the person to lay them out on his or her thigh and roll them together with the palm of one hand, twisting them by this means, and adding more fiber as needed to get the desired length. By doubling such a cord and then letting the two pieces snap together, it can, if needed, be kept from unwinding.

Andamanese rope making

In order to make long, strong ropes, the Andaman Islanders practiced a more sophisticated technique. A man would select a long, straight, smooth and clear branch of an hibiscus tree and remove its bark at full length. He would then scrape off the outer layer with a Cyrena clam shell, baring the fibers, and dry the strips in the sun. When it was ready he would separate the fibers, select several strands, and tie them to his big toe. Meanwhile he had assembled a second bundle of fibers and laid them on the ground. Holding the first set taut, he would twist the second one around it in a spiral. As the cord grew longer than the original strip of bark, he would blend in new fibers until it reached the desired length, which might be as much as thirty yards. Depending on its intended use, he might coat it with beeswax. If he planned to make it into a turtle net, he would leave it uncoated so that it could absorb salt water, because salt water stiffens this kind of fiber and stiff meshes are advantageous in catching turtles. If he wanted the cord to be limber, as for a harpoon line, he would wax it.

His next step was to make, or to reuse, a wooden reel, created by lashing two sticks of light, hard wood together in the middle, in the form of a cross. Then he would wind no more than half of his cord around the arms of this device. The other half he placed on the ground behind his back, and draped the end of it over his left shoulder. Then he ran a length of cane through the reel and its contents, to form an axle. He sat down again, and then he held the ends of the cane between his toes with the reel in the middle. He proceeded then as before, except that he played the first line off the reel and drew the second one over his shoulder, winding the second one spirally around the first. Now he had a rope. These ropes and lines varied in thickness depending on their intended use. For a people who did not know how to make fire, this was a considerable technological achievement.

Conclusion

In reviewing the information surveyed in this chapter, our first observation is that it is incomplete. It has to be because otherwise it would fill an entire, immensely detailed book. Nevertheless it covers in varying degrees of detail the basic technologies of hunting and gathering peoples living in the world's different climates.

All hunters know how to make and use tools, and how to use fire, if not how to make it. Everyone builds shelters or houses adequate for local needs. Everyone manages to keep the human body warm in one way or another, and to make some kind of cordage. In this sense they all end up equal, but some have to work harder at it than others do, and the hardest workers show the most inventive creativity and engineering skill.

Since life is easiest in the tropics and subtropics, technology is naturally simplest there. In the colder parts of the world technology is more advanced in the northern than in the southern hemisphere, if only for one simple reason. In the south, chilly climates like those of Tasmania and Tierra del Fuego are maritime ones, with little seasonal change, because the land masses are small. In the north the climates are continental, with great seasonal extremes. As we proceed with other aspects of technology such as transportation, hunting, fishing, collecting, and cooking, we shall see these same geographical differences repeated, as might be expected. But when we go on to survey the social organization and ceremonial life of the same peoples we will see some of the tables turned. The peoples who have to work least to get a living have the most time to play, and in inventing ways of getting married and of staging spectaculars, they show as much imagination as the gadgeteering Eskimo.

One of the brightest men that our civilization has given birth to, Charles Darwin, considered the Yaghans to be the most brutish and debased people on the earth. As the examples of their technical skills cited in this chapter show, and as we shall see even more clearly later on, that judgment was probably the most erroneous he ever made; no unpolluted hunters are brutish or debased. Darwin's target lay closer to home.

3.

Travel and Transport on Land and Water

Walking and climbing

Without motor vehicles, horses, or bicycles, most hunters rely principally on their feet for locomotion, and although they move about constantly in their own territories they do not travel nearly as far in a year as an urban commuter does in a month. Lack of advanced transportation limits the number of persons who habitually see each other, and it is one of the chief reasons for differences between the social systems of hunters and our own. In the rest of this chapter we shall ignore ordinary walking and describe some of the technological devices by which hunters improve on nature in moving about on land and sea.

Probably the simplest of them has to do with climbing, because all that it involves is an ordinary rope, the manufacture of which was the last item on the agenda of the preceding chapter. If a tree has low branches, or is draped with convenient creepers, or even has a trunk thin enough to shinny up, no rope is needed. But a majestic, tall, thick-trunked, smooth-barked forest giant of a tree could not be climbed by an ape, let alone by a man, without a rope. He uses the rope as a linesman uses his waist-belt in climbing a telephone pole. If he cannot make the soles of his feet adhere to the bark, he needs a second piece of equipment, something to cut notches with in the bark, and this may be no more than a crude flake of stone. That is the way Tasmanian women used to climb trees after "opossums" and how Pygmies climb for honey. But if the bees have nested on the side of a steep, high cliff, the rope has another use, to suspend the beeman brave enough to dangle from it and risk being stung as well.

Aids to walking on sand, snow, and ice

Simple walking, which we have decided to ignore, is not always easy or even possible in sandy deserts, snowfields, and on ice. Hunting peoples have invented ways to overcome all three of these hazards.

11. *An Australian aborigine making a sandshoe. (After D. F. Thomson,* Illustrated London News, *Dec. 6, 1961, p. 1012)*

In the Great Sandy Desert of western Australia, men of the Bindibu tribe make special sandshoes. They lash together, at both ends, two flexible sticks of wood, then spread them apart in the middle with crosspieces. The forward end of such a sandshoe curves upward as in a ski, and the central, foot-bearing portion is cross-webbed with strips of bark. During the 1960s an explorer photographed a Bindibu man who was making a pair; the chance that the latter was imitating snowshoes is out of the question. His was one of the few tribes that had not had previous contacts with white men, who have no need for snowshoes in Australia anyway.

The snowshoe is the oldest and most widely distributed device for walking in snow. Except among the Eskimo living on the barren lands west of Hudson Bay and in Greenland, and among the horse-borne Plains Indians, they are universal among hunters in the parts of North America where there is deep snow in winter. The Ainu have them, as do the Asiatic Eskimo and Chukchi, and they are widely distributed in Europe among peoples who are no longer, in our sense, hunters.

Snowshoes take many forms, depending on the terrain and the kind of snow. Some are simply two pieces of board lashed together with crosspieces, as at Little Whale River in Labrador. Others are circular frames made of two lengths of wood lashed together at both ends, without crosspieces, and with a few thongs. Good enough for wet snow, these were worn by Indians in northern California and the Columbia River basin. The Ainu snowshoe is similar except that it is lashed tightly across the middle to give it a figure 8 form.

The Chukchi and Asiatic Eskimo use fully evolved snowshoes with crossbars and webbing, except that they are double ended, with frames of two sticks lashed together at both ends. The rest of the North American snowshoes take on familiar forms, varying from the long, narrow, finely webbed ones of the Indians of the boreal forest, to bearpaws better suited for hilly country and dense woods. We Americans got our snowshoes from the Indians, rather than using the cruder types found in Europe.

Skis originated either in northern Europe or Siberia and are associated mainly with reindeer herding, because speed is needed to round up and to drive the reindeer. In eastern Siberia some of the hunting peoples adopted skis from herders, but they never reached the aboriginal New World.

As for walking on ice, some of the Eskimo made creepers with bone prongs, to lash to their boots. These devices were similar to mountain climbers' crampons. In Siberia some of the Tungus, who were not bona fide hunters in our sense of the word, skated on frozen rivers with bone-bladed or iron-bladed skates.

Carrying things

While moving about, hunters carry their weapons, women their digging sticks, both in their hands. Women also carry things by hand in bags or other containers, of which one kind is presumably very ancient because it is widespread. It is what the Australians call a dilly bag, usually made of vegetable fibers by a technique known as spiral braiding, or coil without foundation (See Figure 12). Both the

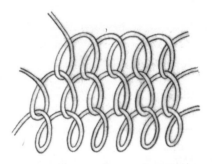

12. Coil without foundation

Tasmanians and the Fuegians used them for carrying shellfish, the Australians for yams, and many other peoples for anything collected by women.

But heavy loads are better carried on the head or back. Australian hunters living in open country carry kangaroos on their heads, with the animals' legs and heads lashed together to make a compact package of the bodies. Their women carry water in wooden troughs in the same way. Head porterage, however, is of little use in forests, or for very heavy loads. The Ona women of Tierra del Fuego carry the poles and skin covers of their windbreaks on their backs by straps under their armpits and over their breasts. This is women's work of necessity, because the men have to be unencumbered in case they sight game or encounter enemies.

Much commoner is the tumpline, a strap over the forehead, holding a load on the back. This is used by the Pygmies of Africa, the

Ainu, and many of the American Indians, none of whom practiced head porterage before the Spaniards introduced it from the Mediterranean region. The tumpline is a very efficient way of distributing the load on the body, but it has its disadvantages. The person using it has to bend over, so that he or she has to follow a beaten trail. It may irritate the forehead, and even produce a depressed groove in the frontal bone. California Indians wore stiff basketry caps to avoid these effects.

Shoulder poles, common among agricultural peoples, are of little use among hunters. One of the few examples to the contrary is found among the South African Bushmen. There two men sometimes bring home an animal too heavy for either to carry alone, suspended from the middle of a pole over one shoulder of each man.

Dragging things

A better way to move heavy burdens, where the terrain permits, is to drag them on some device, of which three are used by hunters: the travois, the toboggan, and the sled. The travois is an A-frame attached to a domestic animal's back with the burden lashed behind its tail and the ends of the two poles trailing on the ground. The Plains Indians had used the travois with dogs before they obtained horses after their introduction by the Spaniards. Then the Indians were able to haul much heavier loads, including large tipi covers.

Toboggans, having flat bottoms and upcurved bows, are ideal for dragging loads over deep, soft snow, particularly by men wearing snowshoes. The Northern Algonkian and Northern Athabascan Indians of the United States and Canada were using them when the white men arrived. Once the French and British had introduced the fur trade, and the Indians had become professional trappers, winter travel and transport increased and so did the weight of the loads. The traders encouraged the Indians to adapt Eskimo sled dogs to pulling toboggans through the forest, in tandem hitch, rather than with the fanwise hitch used by Eastern Eskimo on open ground.

Dog sleds and sled dogs

Archaeologists studying Eskimo prehistory in Alaska and Canada believe that the husky or malemute breed of dogs was of relatively recent pre-Columbian introduction in Alaska, and that dog-sled driving was older in eastern Siberia. In northern Eurasia, reaching as far east as Lapland, dog sleds become gradually replaced by reindeer sleds as one moves westward, and the people who drive reindeer also herd them, and are not, according to our definition, hunters, but pastoralists.

The situation of the Eskimo is thus anomalous. For winter transportation they use animals of a special breed imported from another continent, and this breed probably did not originate with hunters at all. It would be ludicrous to exclude the Eskimo from our roster of hunters on account of these dogs, because no other people on earth relies as much on hunting as they do, nor are there better hunters anywhere. They are just hunters with a special advantage derived indirectly from pastoralists, an advantage particularly suited to their special environment.

The sleds themselves, probably also of early Asiatic inspiration, are superior to toboggans in snow which is not too deep for the runners, and on ice. The runners, of course, offer far less traction surface than flat bottoms and can be driven with less effort on the part of the dogs, and faster. In summer they can be driven over the springy muskeg.

In order to reduce friction to a minimum, some of the Eskimo used to freeze an intermediate coat of muck or blood onto the wooden or bone face of the runner, and then froze water onto the frozen muck or blood. The reason for this double coating is that ice will not stick to the runner directly.

Water transport

So much for land travel. Let us now go down to the shore, to the lakes and rivers, to see how hunters and gatherers take advantage of the water. The roster of peoples who have some means of water transport is greater than that of the peoples who have invented special devices for travel on snow, ice, and sand, because there is navigable water in many parts of the world, and because travel by boat is easier and faster, in many circumstances, than travel by land.

As expected, the watercraft made and used by hunting peoples are made of local materials including reeds, bark, skin, and wood, either for frames or hewn. They can carry anything from one person, like an Eskimo kayak, to well over sixty, as in a Northwest Coast war canoe. Propulsion is usually by poles and paddles. During the history of European and Asian contacts with hunters, some of the latter have changed their boat types rapidly after the acquisition of metal tools; some have learned to row instead of paddling; and some have adopted sails.

Balsas, or reed rafts

In the summer of 1970 Thor Heyerdahl sailed across the Atlantic in a reed raft based on an ancient Egyptian model. For centuries, Indians have been sailing such rafts on Lake Titicaca. Judging by its wide geographical distribution this kind of watercraft seems to be very old, for it is or was also made by such widely separated peoples as the Akoa Pygmies of Gabon, the Seri Indians of Tiberón Island in the Gulf of California, and the Tasmanians.

In its simplest form, a balsa is a collection of three or five spindle- or cigar-shaped bundles of reeds or bark. Each bundle is tied up with a cord, and then all of them are lashed together so as to produce a double-pointed raft. Usually the bow and stern are raised, and the middle part concave. At sea they may be propelled with poles or paddles, and in two places, Gabon and Tasmania, women who are swimming push the balsa ahead of them.

In 1832, a Tasmanian man made one in less than half a day, with the help of two women who brought him paperbark and binding materials. As many as seven men and women used to push out in one of these boats across the stormy waters of the island's southern shore to visit some rocky, uninhabited islands five miles out to sea. They went there to spear seals. Many boatloads were drowned, but the reward in seal meat and skins was considered worth the risk.

Bark boats

Almost any kind of a real boat is faster and easier to handle than a balsa, but it is harder to make. Without efficient axes, it is easier to make a boat out of bark than of wood.

In the Riverina region of South Australia, where there are naviga-

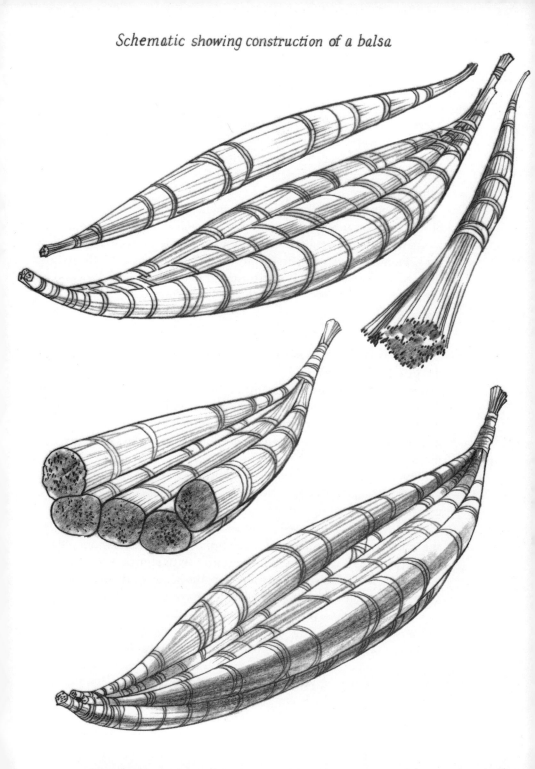

Schematic showing construction of a balsa

13. *How a balsa raft is made of bundles of reeds, as among the Akoa Pygmies and the Seri Indians. The Tasmanians made them of bundles of paperbark*

ble lakes and streams, the aborigines made one-piece bark boats between ten and twenty feet long, by stripping the trunk of a large eucalyptus tree, and shaping the hull with fire. They needed no thwarts or gunwales because the bark is very thick and tough. Such a boat could hold up to ten persons. Along the east coast of the continent, from Cape York to Adelaide, they built flat-bottomed, skifflike boats of three pieces of bark sewn together and calked with gum. With a fire burning on a clay hearth amidships, they used to go line-fishing offshore.

The Yaghans of Tierra del Fuego made similar three-piece boats of the bark of an evergreen beech *(Nothofagus)*, and also kept fires in their boats. It was the sight of a multitude of such waterborne fires, along with signal fires atop the hills to warn of their arrival, that led the early Spanish navigators to name the island Fireland.

Birchbark canoes and moosehide boats

The best-known and marvelously efficient bark boats are of course the birchbark canoes used throughout the boreal forest of the United States and Canada, as well as in the Siberian taiga. Most familiar is the canoe made by the Penobscot Indians of Oldtown, Maine. It is the most complicated piece of equipment made by the Indians, and it takes two men about a week to build one, in warm weather when the bark is soft.*

First they carefully strip off the bark of a large birch tree, large enough to make a canoe between twelve and sixteen feet or sixteen and twenty feet long; they come in two sizes. The men use only three cutting tools—an axe, a crooked-knife, and an awl. They lay the sheet on the ground white-side up; that will be the inner side of the canoe. They weight down the center with stones, lay false gunwales along the edges, then bend up the sides and hold them in place with stakes in the ground which have wooden clamps at the top. While so doing the men slit the bark where needed to allow for the upward curves of the bow and stern. Then they attach the gunwales to each side, carefully measuring the height as they go along, with a notched stick. Next they attach two other pieces of bark at bow and stern to give the canoe raised points, set in a watertight partition between bow and stern and the rest of the boat, and add flaps of bark on each side at both ends to keep water from splashing

*F. G. Speck, *Penobscot Man* (Philadelphia, University of Pennsylvania Press, 1940), pp. 57–68.

in when the boat dips. Inside the bow and stern they fix curved pieces of cedar to form keels for these ends; no keel is needed in the rest of the boat because of the lining.

This consists of a number of thin cedar strips laid lengthwise between the bulwarks, starting from the middle and covering the whole inside of the canoe. They then cover these strips horizontally with about forty-five (more or less, depending on the size of the canoe) ribs of cedar which they have kept bent into a U-shape in bundles, tied with cedar-bark cord. They hammer the ribs in with a special mallet, and spread them with a two-piece wooden lever. Now that the hull is in shape inside and out, the men attach the top rail of the gunwale with pegs. The spruce roots used in sewing have been kept in a vessel of water to keep them soft. Now the final sewing and the pitching of slits and cracks remain, and the canoe is ready for the water. Today such canoes may be seen mostly in museums, for the thread industry has cut down most of the canoe birches for spools. The canoes are still made with other hull materials but in the same basic design, for none could be better.

The Penobscots also made a cruder canoe out of moosehide, for a special purpose. In the spring, when the ice broke up in the rivers, two men who had been hunting as partners in the woods upstream would want to bring home the meat and skins they had accumulated, and their birchbark canoes were back in the village. So they sewed together two moosehides, neck to tail, or three if necessary, to make a piece about twelve feet long, and waterproofed it with grease. They also built a frame with elmwood gunwales and thwarts, and a keel of white birch, and placed the skins over the frame. Next they set in the lining strips and the ribs, spaced farther apart than in a birchbark canoe, and finally they calked the hull with a mixture of pitch and moose tallow. The whole operation took less than two days, and the two men were able to carry about four hundred pounds with them down to their village. There they could take the boat apart and cut up the moose hides to make moccasins and thongs.

Kayaks and umiaks

The skin boats made by the Eskimo and Aleuts were, of course, no temporary constructions, and they differed from the birchbark and the moosehide canoe in one critical respect. The frames were

D

made first and the skin covers could then be put over them and re-moved seasonally, or replaced when needed. The Eskimo kayak and the Aleut bidarka are double-ended, decked boats in which a man sits with a skin skirt reaching from the surface of the deck to his armpits, under which it is lashed by a drawstring. Thus he can tip over and right himself without swamping the hull. Propulsion is by means of a double-bladed paddle. While the Eskimo kayak is a one-man boat, the Aleut bidarka may be two-holed. A man in the rear may steady the boat while the man in front hunts sea otters with a spear-thrower and darts. Under the Russian regime the Aleuts made some three-seater bidarkas, which were used as water taxis.

The large boats, called umiaks by the Eskimo and nixalax by the Aleuts, might run as much as thirty feet long and carry twenty peo-ple, or a corresponding amount of cargo. The frame is of driftwood, the cover of walrus hide, in the case of the umiak. The Eskimo use it for whaling, and it is found only in Alaskan waters and on the coasts of Greenland and Labrador; there are no whales in the shallow waters between Beaufort Sea and Baffin Bay. The Aleuts covered their nixalax frames with sea-lion skins, and used them for general trans-portation. In historic times, Alaskan umiaks were both rowed and sailed, the sails being made of gut.

The Eskimo, Aleuts, and in former times other circumpolar peo-ples as far as Lapland, made boats of skin because of a shortage of wood. Even where wood is available, wooden boats replace bark ones only where special species of timber are at hand and where the boatmakers have suitable tools. There are several types of wooden boats, three of which were made by hunters. One is a three-plank, flat-bottomed skiff, like the Australian and Yaghan three-piece bark boats. Another is a simple dugout made by hewing, with or without fire. A third is a dugout with raised coamings.

The three-plank skiffs of the Alakalufs

The Alakaluf Indians of southern Chile, and their neighbors, the now extinct Chonos, who lived north of them from the Gulf of Peñas to the island of Chiloé, made the first kind of those skiffs, because the forests along the shores of their coast and islands contained two special trees, the cypress and the alerce tree (*Fitzroya patagonica*), also a conifer. Cypress wood is easily split into planks or boards with simple wedges, and trimmed down with fire and clam shells. As cypress wood is flexible, these boards are easily bent to form the sides of the hull, the bottom being made of between three and seven planks, depending on size.

The alerce tree provides the calking material that makes the joints between the planks watertight. The sapwood of this tree, lying just under the innermost layer of bark, is spongy and elastic, especially after being pounded between two stones. The planks are laced together through parallel holes by pairs of whole lianas, and the holes calked. These plank boats vary in size from small, one-man skiffs used in inland creeks to twenty-footers capable of use in the open Pacific where the seal rookeries are located. But the Alakalufs and Chonos avoided open-sea navigation as much as possible by carrying their boats across the isthmuses of peninsulas with stormy headlands. When the sea level was higher than at present, these isthmuses were channels and the peninsulas islands; thus portaging did not involve climbing, although the large boats, being heavy, had to be taken apart and reassembled on the other shore.

After they obtained metal axes, the Alakaluf Indians began to make dugouts, and some were still to be seen in the 1950s. The tree used was the evergreen beech (*Nothofagus*), the same one from which bark was taken to make the three-piece bark canoes of the Yaghans, also made by some of the Alakalufs. Beeches with trunks large enough to be converted to dugouts grow inland several miles from shore. There the Alakalufs search for dead ones, still standing, and mark them.

One man can build a dugout, but the work goes better with two men. They fell it and cut it in two below the lowest limbs, and then start hewing out the inside of the hull. The butt end of the log will be the bow. Except at the two ends, they cut it to a thickness of about an inch and a quarter, following the outside shape of the log. By this time the boat-to-be is light enough to be moved to the shore. The men prepare a path through the forest, and summon eight or ten other Indians, both men and women, who haul it over the mossy floor of the forest, and lift it over fallen trees and rocks. When they reach the shore they tow it to camp, where they set it on the ground, near the owner's hut, on dry land.

The next step is to thin it still more with an adze, either obtained in trade or made of a file; after this has been done they raise it on posts for the most critical part of the process — stretching the sides of the hull to widen the boat. They keep it wet, and rake under it glowing coals of cypress wood. When it is flexible enough they stretch it with thwartlike boards put in obliquely and hammered into a position at right angles to the axis of the boat. Then, with shells, they scrape off the char on the outside caused by the heating, and patch up any cracks or holes in the hull with various substances, including beaten-out tin cans. Finally they raise the sides with boards of cypress or driftwood and put in the rowing seats, rowing tholes, and tholes for a steering oar in the stern.

Both men and women row them, facing forward, with oars staggered as in a racing shell. They make good time and travel great distances. For example, in 1959, in response to a radio call, a crew of Alakaluf men rowed 160 miles from Puerto Eden, Wellington Island, all the way to Rio Baker simply to ferry a lady passenger back and forth off a visiting steamship. When they got there, they found that she had decided to stay aboard the steamship after all.

The cedar-wood dugouts of the Nootka

The Northwest Coast Indians, who built the most elaborate wooden houses of any hunting peoples, also made the largest wooden boats. The best boatmakers on the coast were the Nootka, who went out whaling in their boats. A man who wanted to build a boat would first obtain a half section of a large cedar trunk in the manner described under house-building. With the help of others, he would haul it to his home at the water's edge. Then he and one helper would hew it into the hull of a canoe.

Unlike the Alakalufs, who do not shape the outside of the log except at the ends, the Nootka adzed out the outer side first. Then they drilled holes into the prospective hull to a depth marking the desired thickness, and drove into the holes pegs of fire-blackened, and easily seen, wood. As they hollowed the hull by alternately chiseling and wedging out sections, they stopped when they reached the ends of the pegs, and smoothed the inside surface with adzes. It was not always necessary to spread the sides, but when they did they filled the hull with water and dropped in hot stones to steam the wood, and then spread the sides with thwarts.

The Indians made these boats in all sizes, from a small craft paddled and poled by a single person to chiefs' canoes, war canoes, and craft used for carrying cargoes, reaching a maximum of forty to sixty feet in length. In historic times they sailed some of these larger boats.

Outrigger canoes

One final kind of dugout needs to be mentioned: the outrigger canoe, well known from Polynesia, Micronesia, Melanesia, Indonesia, and the shores of the Indian Ocean. With two known exceptions, outriggers were not made or used by hunting-gathering peoples, and in both cases their presence was due to recent outside influence. Some of the Australian aborigines living near the tip of Cape York Peninsula made them in imitation of New Guinea craft, and the Andaman Islanders constructed single-outrigger, double-ended canoes by hewing out pithy-cored trunks as mentioned on page 22.

In the latter case the outriggers were attached to booms by pegs and lashing. It is most likely that these canoes, of prime use in harpooning turtles and dugong, were made only after A.D. 1500, when the Andamanese came under Malay influence. But once they could see their usefulness the Andamanese did not take long to learn how to build them, and, on Little Andaman Island, where a native population is still to be found, they are still in use.

Conclusion

The same points may be made about land and water transport as for housing and clothing—that peoples on a hunting and gathering level of life show ingenuity in technology comparable to their needs, kinds of tools available, and local materials, and that they quickly take advantage of new tools and new models when they have a chance, provided that they are not decimated, swamped, and confused by the impact of the bearers of the new cultures. Again, peoples living in cold climates need better transport than do those living in warm ones, and have responded accordingly. Superior means of transport have much to do with success in hunting in adverse climates where food is plentiful and mobility essential, as will be shown in the following chapters.

4.

The Food Quest: Hunting and Trapping

The food quest: a cooperative effort

The work that hunters and their wives do to achieve environmental protection and mobility in different climates enables them to pursue their primary objective, obtaining food for themselves and their dependents. The food quest is a total family effort with, in most cases, a division of labor between the men who hunt and the women and children who bring in more easily collected edibles. Usually it is also an effort involving more than one family because it is more efficient for several men to hunt together than for one man to hunt alone.

When women go out collecting they also make out best in groups, partly for companionship, and partly because older women can show the younger ones where to look for food, and teach them when it is likely to be in season. In those societies in which a bride comes to live with her husband's people, it takes her some time to learn the lay of the land from other women who have lived longer in that particular territory.

Collecting includes such diverse activities as digging up roots and tubers, picking fruit, diving for marine molluscs or gathering them at low tide, catching swarming insects, prying grubs out of rotten logs, robbing birds' nests of their eggs and fledglings and bees' nests of their honey. Thus collecting is not limited to procuring vegetable foods, but also covers the techniques for finding edible animal species that cannot run, crawl, fly, or swim away, or at least not very rapidly or very far. These species are known as *slow game*.

Whether food is obtained by hunting, fowling, fishing, or gathering, another distinction may be made—between animals and plants that are widely spaced or solitary, and those encountered in herds, flocks, schools, beds, fields, groves, and the like. The first kinds require individual attention; the second can be slaughtered or harvested en masse. The latter can obviously support denser and more nearly sedentary populations.

Geographical differences in the food supply

In tropical forests, few species of animals are migratory and few feed in herds. One exception is that of the leaf-eating monkeys. On the ground the cover is dense and a hunter may stand within a few feet of an edible animal and not be aware of its presence. Or the roles may be reversed; the edible animal may be the hunter. In African forests leopards are man-killers; in India and Southeast Asia, tigers.

Because in really barren deserts grass and leaves are in short supply, herd animals are also rare, as in parts of South Africa, the Australian deserts, Lower California, and the North American Great Basin. In the boreal forests of North America between the ranges of the caribou and bison, the principal game animals are deer and moose. They too rarely congregate in large groups. In the deserts the hunters move about from the smaller to the larger water holes as the former dry up, following the game. In the northern forests hunting is best in the winter, when the animals move slowly on account of the snow. Summer is the fishing season, when the rivers and lakes are free of ice and survival does not depend so much on animal fats as it does in wintertime.

Herd animals are most commonly encountered on grasslands and thinly forested terrain, where grazing is rich. Examples are the gray kangaroo in Australia and Tasmania, many species of antelope in East and South Africa, and the bison in North America. But in northern regions of Eurasia and North America open tundras and barren lands also support herds of reindeer and caribou, and in Hokkaido the sika deer used to migrate seasonally from the mountain slopes to the riverbanks in numbers great enough to warrant mass slaughter.

Some species of sea mammals, notably seals, sea lions, walruses, and sea elephants, also congregate in large numbers during the breeding season, usually on rocky islets and headlands, where they are then relatively helpless and can easily be killed. Of the birds the aquatic species are the ones most commonly hunted en masse, during migrations or in the breeding season. These include ducks, geese, swans, petrels, auks, and penguins.

Even more critical in the economy of those hunters located where they can harvest them, are marine fish that swim upstream in great numbers to spawn. These include several species of salmon and the less well known and larger taimen (*Hucho perryii*), a relative of

D*

the chars. In modern times the principal regions where these fish are seasonally most abundant are the Columbia River basin and, farther north, the rivers emptying into the Northwest Coast; those of the Japanese island of Hokkaido; and the Amur River in eastern Siberia. The abundance of these fish made a virtually sedentary life possible for the Northwest Coast Indians of North America and for the Ainu and Goldi, all of whom had some way of preserving them.

Marine molluscs, such as mussels, clams, oysters, limpets, whelks, and abalones can also be harvested, in a sense, in certain favored inlets and shores, as, for example, Tasmania, the Andamans, southern Chile, and along the New England coast. In these places, as in others long since occupied by agricultural peoples, huge, deep middens attest the importance of this kind of food to earlier peoples. Some of them, like the natives of the western coast of Tasmania and of the Andamanese shorelines, were also nearly sedentary.

Most of the parts of the world where wild seeds were once harvested have become agricultural lands, but an exception is California, particularly in the Sacramento Valley. Until the white men came, the local Indians had a relatively dense population of villagers who collected not only grass seeds but also acorns. The reason why agriculture had spared them is that New World cultivation depended mostly on maize, grown in the Pueblo country, where the rain falls in summer. Having a Mediterranean climate, California was unsuited to maize cultivation because of its winter rains, which favor the Old World grains of the Mediterranean and Near East: wheat, barley, rye, and oats. Another exception occurs in the Great Lakes region, where the Ojibwa Indians harvested wild rice directly into their canoes. Indians living today in the Minneapolis–St. Paul area are paid quite handsomely to gather into their boats a certain rare rice (used for making beer) that ripens in various fresh-water rivers and lakes each fall.

In central California, as in the lands bordering the Mediterranean Sea in remote antiquity, edible acorns also provide a staple food supply in season. In the Kalahari Desert some of the Bushmen gather the nuts of the mangetti tree *(Ricinodendron rautanenii)* the year round. Mangetti groves are within walking distance of their seasonal camps, which are shifted periodically, a few miles at a time, as the minor water holes dry up and are later replenished. While they eat as much meat as they can, these Bushmen derive the bulk of their food from the vegetable kingdom.

Again speaking very generally, vegetable foods are most important in hunters' diets near the equator and animal foods near the poles, and techniques of hunting and fishing reach their highest degree of complexity where vegetable foods are in least supply owing to the limitations of the climate. Because there is more land north of the tropics than south of them, we may expect to find hunting techniques to be more highly elaborate in the northern than in the southern hemisphere. In the north, hunting techniques go hand in hand with those already described concerning environmental protection and transportation. All three are parts of a single picture.

The primacy of hunting as a day-to-day activity

At this point we are faced with a choice, whether to go on with hunting, or to postpone its discussion until after having described the techniques of fishing and gathering. I have opted for the primacy of hunting. While it does not bring in the most food everywhere, it produces the kind of food that most people like best if they can get it; it is more nearly universal in the preagricultural world than fishing; and it has more impact on social structure than gathering. Hunting is, in short, the hunters' favorite activity. It separates the men from the boys. It is highly stimulating and distinctly human. There are really two kinds of hunting; a day-to-day activity, and big-game hunting. We shall start with the first of these and work up to the latter.

Weapons: the club

In order to kill animals on the run and birds in flight, a hunter needs both weapons and catching and holding devices. These include clubs, spears, bows and arrows, harpoons, slings, bolas, fences, pounds, and traps.

Clubs are the simplest and perhaps oldest weapons, in their crudest form little different from a woman's digging stick, itself the most nearly universal implement used in procuring food. But among most if not all known hunters, the club is a secondary weapon used for despatching wounded or slowly moving animals and for throwing at game at short distances. The Tasmanian club, known as a waddy, was about eighteen inches long, an inch and a half thick, and pointed. It was made of the hard and heavy casuarina wood, fluted with straight or spiral grooves, and its tip fire-hardened. With it Tasmanians killed the smaller species of marsupials, such as bandicoots, mostly on the ground. But when an opossum was in the lower branches of a tree they would throw waddies at it. Once a chief cast one at a nearby kangaroo and missed. He remarked that it was an old waddy; the kangaroo can see an old waddy and dodge it, but he can't see a new one.

On Melville Island, off the coast of northern Australia, the Tiwi use clubs for hunting migratory ducks. A group of grown men and adolescent boys station themselves in a row along a ridge over which the ducks may be expected to fly low. When the flock flies nearest one of the fowlers, he casts his waddy into the midst of the birds overhead, giving his club a spiral motion with a twist of his wrist. His weapon thus achieves a maximum spread, like that of shotgun pellets, for all he needs do to fell a bird is to injure a wing.

On the Australian mainland the boomerang, unknown on the offshore islands and really a specialized throwing club, is expressly designed to have the same effect, both on birds and on kangaroos. The well-known return boomerang is also a native Australian invention of considerable sophistication, but it is less used in hunting than the other kinds.

Weapons: the simple spear

The primary weapon designed to pierce an animal's body is also the oldest one known archaeologically, the simple spear. In England one made of yew has been found in deposits considered to be a quarter of a million years old. In recent times its use as the only piercing weapon was mostly limited to Australia and Tasmania. The Tasmanians made spears with great care. When possible they were made of the slender trunks of the tea tree, a species of *Melaleuca*, related to the myrtle. Its wood is hard, straight, and springy and the trunk is thin enough to need little if any scraping.

The men made their spears at night beside a fire, and each man made his own. First he would shape the point with stone flakes, then peel off the bark, then toast the spear in a fire, then hold it in his teeth with both hands on the shaft to straighten it, and finally he would blacken it all over. All the time they were working, the men sang. They made the spears in two lengths, about ten and about fifteen feet; the shorter ones were for hunting, the longer ones for fighting.

In childhood the boys first learned to cast spears, and throughout life they practiced constantly. A skilled hunter could throw a long spear 250 feet, a short one over 300 feet, and he could hit targets with bull's-eye accuracy at 180 feet. One ex-hunter who found himself in prison was seen to cast a broomstick thirty-five feet across a jailyard through a hole in the opposite wall one half inch wider than the shaft.

In other parts of the world, including much of Australia, spears are tipped with stone, bone, or sting-ray-barb points which give them greater penetration than can a simple wooden tip. In Australia the tips are cemented on with either eucalyptus or spinifex gum, as stated on page 18.

Spear-throwers

Some of the mainland Australians also used a spear-thrower, there called a wommera. (In America we use the Aztec word, atlatl — Aztecs made them too.) Its function is to increase the range of the missile by lengthening the radius of the casting arc of the thrower's arm. The spear-thrower is a piece of wood of variable length, depending on the range sought; it has a handle of some kind at one end, and at the other end either a cup or a prong, to engage the butt of the spear.

The missile cast from such a device is a light spear or dart, usually shorter and lighter than a spear cast by hand, and because of the increase in leverage, it has a greater velocity. In Australia such spears were sometimes made with a reed or cane shaft and a hardwood fore-shaft. At the other end of the Pacific Ocean, the Aleuts carried a number of stone- or bone-headed darts of pinewood, painted red, and lashed to the decks of their bidarkas or skin-boats. Presumably the red paint made it easy to see the darts in the water and thus to recover them. They threw them with notched "boards," and the early Russian accounts state that the Aleuts cast them with deadly accuracy and killed men, animals, and birds as efficiently as the Russians could with firearms.

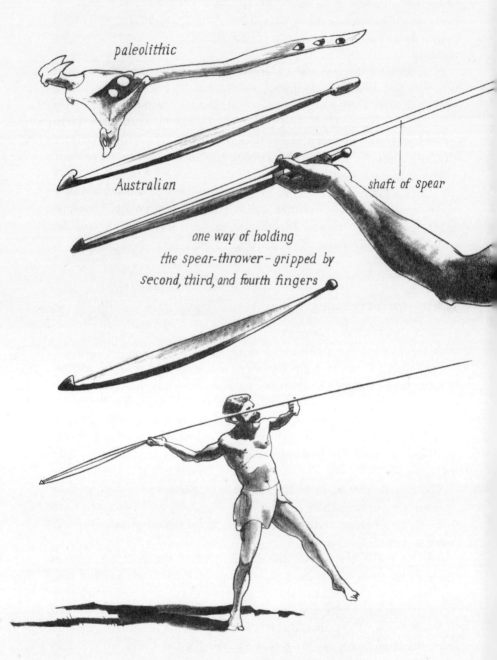

Spear-throwers

paleolithic

Australian

shaft of spear

one way of holding
the spear-thrower - gripped by
second, third, and fourth fingers

14. Spear-throwers in action

Weapons: bows and arrows

In Europe, spear-throwers go back to the Upper Paleolithic period, at least to 15,000 years ago. Bows and arrows succeeded them only near the end of the Ice Age, about ten thousand years ago. We do not know when, where, or by whom bows and arrows were invented, or even if they were invented more than once. Mechanically they are more advanced than the spear because they depend on the spring rather than on the use of human muscle alone.* At any rate, during prehistoric times their use had spread over most of the world, with the notable exception of Australia and its largest island, Tasmania.

Bows are made of local wood where suitable trees are available, but in other regions, as in the Far North, they may be made of driftwood or unsuitable timber and made elastic by the addition of sinew, horn, or baleen either glued or tied on. The Caribou Eskimo, who didn't even have driftwood, made them of musk-ox horns.

The S-shaped bow of the Andamanese

One of the most unusual is the S-shaped bow of the southern Great Andamanese, Andaman Islands. It takes a man about four days to make one. First he selects a tree of a certain species of hardwood, possibly a nutmeg (*Myristica fragrans*) — we are not sure. Sometimes his choice may be a trunk itself, or more likely a branch, about four inches in diameter, with a bend in it of 160°. The bend is the critical feature. He cuts out a piece of this wood about four and a half feet long, with the bend located at about two-thirds of the way down from what is to be the upper end of the bow.

After he has roughed out the stave with a shell or scrap-iron adze, he trims it with finer strokes of the same tool, incises it with a Cyrena shell, and then planes it to its final form with a boar's tusk sharpened with a whetstone. When this is done he rubs it with white clay and ochre, and equips it with a bowstring of waxed Anadendron fiber. The stave of the bow is round in section at the grip, but it widens out above and below, like an hourglass, narrowing again at each end. The broad upper and lower parts of the stave

*One pulls it back slowly, then it snaps forward quickly — time-energy factor.

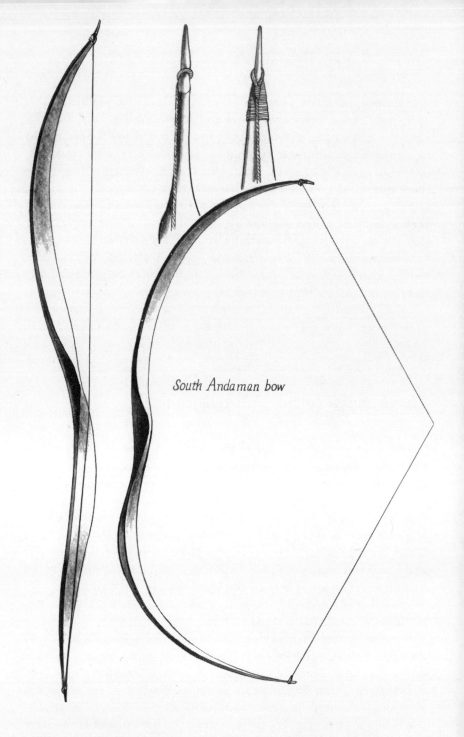

South Andaman bow

15. *A South Andamanese S-shaped bow. On left: bow after arrow has just been shot*

are planed quite thin, and the lower part thinner than the upper.

When the bow is strung, the lower third of the stave points downward and forward, as it did in the first place, but when the archer draws the string, the stave becomes a single arc, as in an ordinary bow. When the arrow is released the string slaps against the shaft with a sharp noise. While this is a disadvantage in warfare, it makes little difference when shooting fish or, for that matter, in the forest, for pigs, the only game animal, move about singly, and in the dense undergrowth one miss is enough to make a pig disappear at once, with or without the noise. Owing to its shape, the bow has one special merit. It does not have to be kept unstrung when not in use, because the bowstring can be slipped past the lower arm and the tension on the stave relieved. Thus the bow is always ready at a moment's notice.

Arrowmaking among the Ona

There is just as much variation in arrows as there is in bows, in terms of material, length, whether of one piece or composite, what kind of head is used, whether or not fletched and if so with what, and whether notched or unnotched, depending on the kind of bowstring. We leave these details to the experts, and shall describe their manufacture by a single people, the guanaco-hunting Ona of Tierra del Fuego.

They made the arrow shafts from a species of bush or shrub,* the trunk of which grows twisted. The arrowmaker split a section of suitable length into four quarter-pieces, which he then heated and straightened with hands and teeth, just as the Tasmanian straightened his spear. Each shaft was then trimmed down, smoothed in a grooved stone made specially for this purpose, and then polished with a fox-skin and dust. It was fletched with the two sections of a split feather and fastened with a fine sinew threaded between the barbs. White clay was applied to the feathered part of the shaft to make the sinew stick. Then the arrow was notched at both ends, and the point was set in the front notch and lashed. Originally the points were made of finely retouched stone, but when observed by anthropologists, the Ona were making them of glass. A little pitch

*Probably either *Berberis ilicifolia*, a wild barberry, or *Maytenus magellenica*. In the latter case, the branches rather than the trunk would be used.

from a wreck, placed above the nock, gave a better finger grip.

The significant point about the manufacture of these arrows is that to make them the Ona used six different materials from widely distant parts of their country, seven out of the nine kinds of tools they had, and fourteen different processes. The arrow was their highest technical achievement, and well it should have been, because, propelled by an equally efficient bow of beechwood, it could be shot 250 yards, and could bring down a guanaco, with great penetration, at over 100 yards. There being little wild vegetable food in Ona country, they were almost wholly dependent on these weapons for their food.

Poisoned arrows

For one reason or another, and in totally different environments, some hunters poison their arrows. Four groups are best known for this practice, the South African Bushmen, the Maidu of Central California, the Ainu of Hokkaido, and the Pygmies of the African rain forest.

The Bushmen's use of arrow poison allows them to shoot relatively large and swift animals at short range with small, weak bows, and reduces the distance the hunter has to walk in following the animal until it drops. While some other Bushmen use vegetable poison, the !Kung of the Kalahari Desert (the exclamation point represents a palato-alveolar click) make theirs of the pupae of the beetle (*Diamphidia simplex*). These grubs are dug from under the roots of a certain species of tree. Some grubs are yellow, others orange. According to the Bushmen, the yellow ones are males, and carry their poison only in a special sac, while the orange ones are said to be females, and their whole bodies are full of the poison. The Bushmen crush these grubs and smear the paste on the foreshafts of their arrows, rather than on the small points, which are made of gemsbok shoulder-blades, other bones being too soft for good penetration. The tips are left unpoisoned in order to avoid accidents in handling.

The Maidu poison their deer-arrows with rattlesnake venom. This poison is made only by village chiefs, in the following manner. The chief obtains a deer liver and holds it up for rattlesnakes to bite, and when it is full of venom he dries it. Before setting out to stalk deer, hunters are allowed to pass their arrowheads through it. The Ainu arrow poison, used for hunting bear and the sika deer, is aconite from the dried, tuberous root of the monkshood plant. The African Pygmy poison is a blend of vegetable and animal substances of which strychnine is the principal ingredient.

Poison, as used by the Ainu, facilitates the mass slaughter of deer in season in an orderly manner. The Pygmies' use of poison makes it possible to retrieve the small animals that they normally shoot which otherwise might get lost in the brush before dying, and to relax the muscles of monkeys shot in trees so that the animals' hands will be unable to grasp the limbs in a death grip, and their bodies will fall to the ground.

Toward the end of the last century a French missionary priest, Father Trilles, was invited to accompany a chief of the Akoa Pygmies of Gabon into the deep forest to watch the latter make arrow poison, an operation normally veiled in secrecy. On the evening before they first set out, the chief pronounced some ritual spells. Then he decapitated a stolen chicken, and holding it by the feet, sprinkled its blood in the direction of the four cardinal points, and finally toward the sky, for the benefit of the moon, "Chief of the Night." Then he danced, imitating the actions made by the various animals commonly hunted as each was hit by a poisoned arrow, staggered, and dropped dead.

The next morning the chief and the priest collected the ingredients —ten kinds of plant specimens, samples of which Father Trilles sent back to Paris for botanical identification; the larvae of a small beetle; and the venom of a horned viper, which the chief extracted by pinning the snake's head to the ground with a forked stick and irritating him. The ten plants included two species of *Strychnos*, one of *Strophanthus,* one of *Erythrophloeum,* a species of amaryllis close to belladonna, a wild pepper, and the juice of a wild yam and latex of a wild fig. The last two were not poisonous, but included to give the mixture body.

The chief did not really need all twelve ingredients because some duplicated the effects of others, stopping the heart directly, working on the nervous system, and paralyzing the muscles. But by combining some of each category he could be sure to halt the animal as quickly as possible, paralyze it, and kill it, before it could disappear and die in hiding. It is clear that the chief understood the properties of the different ingredients, because once when he was making spear-poison for an elephant hunt, he changed the formula to make the effect last longer.

After he had collected all his ingredients, the chief hid them in the crotch of a tree, for he would not bring them into camp.

On their third trip to the forest, Father Trilles watched the chief make the poison. The latter worked with extreme concentration because he had to take care not to get any of the dangerous material on his hands or in his eyes. First he trimmed the bulbs, bits of bark, and other vegetable substances to remove fibrous appendages that might affect him, and he buried the trimmings. Then he crushed the vegetable ingredients in a bowl with a stone, mixing in a little water from time to time and spitting in it. Each time he spat he muttered a spell against the animals he hoped to kill with the poison. He stirred it with a spoon until it had become reddish brown and then added bits of a fire-dried white marsh toad whose skin is dangerous to touch.

Next he boiled his concoction until the mixture had been reduced by evaporation to a thick paste. When it had cooled he added the crushed beetle grubs, but if these were not available he could use instead a kind of black ant whose sting paralyzes at once. He then wrapped the completed poison in a sheet of soft, pliant bark, and put it inside the body of a monkey that he had shot for the purpose, and buried the body in the black earth of a marsh.

Several days later he dug up the monkey, now putrefied, and removed his package, touching it only with leaves covering his fingers. Taking it back into the forest he opened it and added the sap of a euphorbia tree to make it adhere to the tips of his arrows. Having placed a suitable amount of his paste on a leaf, he laid out his arrows in a row, and picked one up, rotating its tip slowly in the paste. Then he held the shaft between both palms and twirled it rapidly. Once he had poisoned all the arrows brought with him he packed them carefully in a bark quiver, and was ready for the chase.

A tourist driving along a forest-lined road, seeing an elderly, diminutive black man clad in a bark-cloth breechclout, would have no reason to suspect that this child of nature knew the properties of many medicinal plants, some still undescribed in Western science, and how to combine them for their greatest effect. With the forest and marsh his pharmacy, his laboratory a secret nook in the shade of tall trees, and a minimum of equipment, the Pygmy poison-maker performs a delicate, dangerous, and highly skilled sequence of operations as exacting as some modern professions.

The possession of poison bears with it a sobering responsibility. Its use requires both great caution and firm self-discipline. A poisoned arrow must not be discharged until the bowman knows where his companions are. He must handle the arrows with great care, even in the excitement of sighting an animal. If a campmate has been seducing his wife, he must avoid the temptation to scratch his sleeping rival with an arrow. Yet the literature on Pygmies, Bushmen, Maidu Indians of Central California, and Ainu that I have read contains no instance of a deliberate clandestine use of arrow poison against fellow hunters. But, as we shall see on page 238, the !Kung Bushmen used to shoot poisoned arrows at each other in open, public fights, and the Akoa Pygmies shot them from trees at Fang Negroes raiding their camps.

Hunting by stalking: Australia

The primary weapons, clubs and spears and arrows, with and without poison, are used in stalking, the most widespread hunting method through the parts of the world with which we are concerned. This means that one or more hunters leave camp to locate, to follow if necessary, and to kill individual animals or small groups of them. Success in stalking depends not only on skill in handling weapons but also on an intimate knowledge of animal habits, which are species-specific; in other words, all animals of a species, given variations in sex and age, and whether or not they are in rut, may usually be counted on to behave in the same general way.

The Australian aborigines are justly famed for their skill in tracking. In postcontact times the police have used native hunters for tracking criminals. The hunter can identify a man by his tracks just as we can by his handwriting. He can tell that a person unknown to him is knock-kneed, or limps, whether or not he is fatigued, how tall he is (by his stride), and how much he weighs. They have acquired this detailed ability from tracking animals.

In the open desert of western Australia, the hunter comes upon a set of kangaroo tracks, leans over, and smells them. Whether or not the aborigines possess an unusually keen sense of smell is a moot point that can only be settled by experiments. In either case it is well trained. With it a hunter can tell how fresh the tracks are. When he finds kangaroo droppings or places where the animal has urinated, he has a still better test of the passage of time.

Once he has found a reasonably fresh set of tracks, with or without spoor, his next step is simply to follow it, sleeping on the tracks at night, until he has brought the animal within sight. The principle involved is that, unless it knows it is being chased, the animal is in no hurry. It will stop now and then to nibble at a succulent bush and rest in shade in the heat of the day. The man keeps up a steady pace from dawn to dusk, and before long he will come within sighting distance of his quarry.

Having viewed it from afar, he approaches the kangaroo from downwind, exercising great caution by creeping from bush to bush or rock to rock, moving only when the animal is looking in another direction. When he has arrived within distant range he may cast a spear over the animal's head to make it react as if it were being attacked from the opposite direction. Then it may run toward the hunter, who will cast a second spear more accurately within close range.

Tracking: North America

Tracking is easier in snow. As the accompanying diagram shows, a Kutchin Indian of the Upper Yukon country on either side of the Alaskan-Canadian border will hunt a moose in a special way. He knows that the animal follows a certain vegetation zone, feeding in early morning and late afternoon, and resting during the middle of the day. Before stopping to feed or to lie down, the moose will double back on its trail on the downwind side, so that it can smell any person or other animal following it. When he comes upon a moose's trail, instead of following it, the Indian hunter walks in a series of loops downwind of it, until he comes to where he has overshot it. Then he walks back in smaller loops, still downwind, being careful to make no noise, until he comes within bowshot.

These two examples apply not only to Australian and North American Indian hunters but also, with many local variations, depending on the species hunted and the terrain, to spearmen and

Kutchin moose stalking

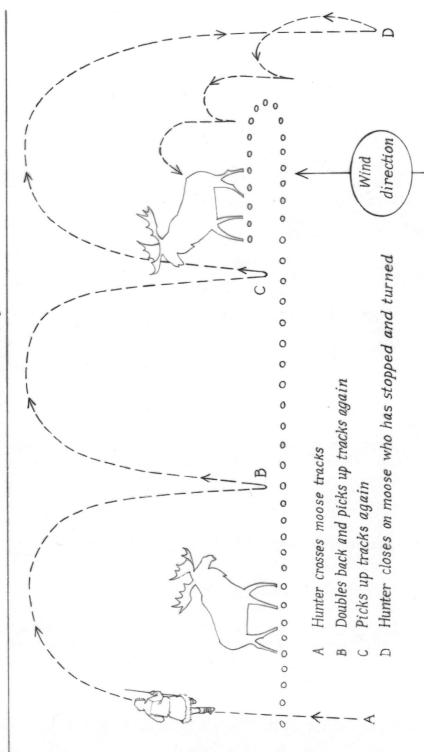

Wind direction

A   Hunter crosses moose tracks
B   Doubles back and picks up tracks again
C   Picks up tracks again
D   Hunter closes on moose who has stopped and turned

16. How a Kutchin hunter stalks a moose. (After Cornelius Osgood, 1936)

Ainu deer decoy, actual size

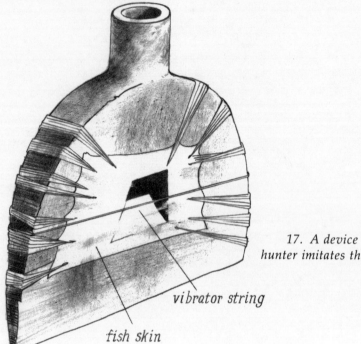

17. *A device with which an Ainu hunter imitates the cry of a lost fawn*

vibrator string

fish skin

bowmen in many other parts of the world, as for example to the South African Bushmen and the now extinct hunters of Lower California.

Hunting with lures

Many hunting peoples who stalk animals also use lures. The Penobscot Indians of Maine attract male moose during the mating season by imitating the amorous call of the cow moose through a cone of birchbark. At closer distance, if near a pond or stream, the hunter fills the cone with water and lets it splash out into the body of water below in such a way that it sounds like a cow moose urinating. This last gesture is calculated to arouse the bull moose's libido to a high pitch.

The Ainu make a more complicated deer call out of a piece of wood about four inches long and two inches wide. It is wedge-shaped in section and curved on the upper, or thick, edge. Through the middle of the curved edge they bore a hole which comes out in the middle of one side, and stretch a very thin piece of fish skin over that surface, lashing it on with twisted lengths of fish gut string, and one of these strings is stretched tightly over the lower hole to act as a vibrator. When a hunter, in hiding, wishes to decoy a deer, he first wets the string that runs over the bottom hole, and then blows through the upper one, meanwhile drawing his thumbs over the fish skin. The sound that comes out closely resembles the cry of a fawn, attracting a doe to within range of his bow.

Hunting with disguises

Some hunters disguise themselves as animals in order to mingle among them and to kill them at short range, and silently. The guiding principle behind these disguises is selection, as in any other form of art. Animals of a species recognize each other by parts of the body rather than by the body as a whole, and by characteristic postures and gaits. Hunters know this and thus imitate the animals selectively.

One of the clearest examples known comes from the Maidu Indians of Central California. During the rutting season, one or two hunters used to walk into a herd of deer, wearing deerskins and antlers which had been hollowed by grooves to reduce their weight.

The hunters' chests were painted white, and each man carried a pair of sticks to represent forelegs. Now and then they would rub the sticks together to imitate the sound of bucks scraping each others' antlers as part of the mating procedure. At suitable moments, the hunters would shoot one deer after another with arrows poisoned with rattlesnake venom, the manufacture of which has been previously described.

In the cave of Trois Frères, Arriège, France, is a famous engraved and painted figure of a man wearing just such a disguise. It is called "The Sorcerer." Had the French archaeologist who discovered it known about the Maidu practice, he might rather have named it "The Deer Stalker." The figure comes from the period known as Magdalenian IV, roughly fourteen thousand years ago.

Killing many animals at once

Hunters who stalk game kill the animals one by one. But, as previously mentioned, there are ways of slaughtering them in large numbers and getting much meat at once. The simplest of these is the communal hunt, or surround. For example, the Efe Pygmies of the Ituri Forest in the Congolese Republic are bowmen. During most of the year they hunt by stalking individual animals in teams of two to four men, such a team being often one-half the total manpower of a band.

But once a year all the families of a band unite for a communal surround. Men, women, and children spread out in a large circle, the men armed with bows, and the women and children with sticks. At a signal, they begin beating the brush and screaming, making as much noise as possible, and frightening the game. This is the opposite of the procedure employed in stalking, when women and children are left behind and silence is essential. As the circumference of the circle is reduced by the beaters converging toward its center, there is less and less chance for the animals to escape between the beaters, and the game finally mills about in the middle of the ring. Then the bowmen go in to despatch the animals, taking care not to shoot each other.

Naturally this hunt depletes the local game, and it takes about two months for the animal population of that part of the forest to restore itself by moving in from outside, but this temporary scarcity of flesh-food does not bring hunger to the Pygmies. The communal hunt is held just before the honey season, the time of year when not only honey but also many kinds of vegetable foods are abundant. During these two months the hunting bands, limited to about four to eight families each, now split up into even smaller units to feast off the honey, ripe fruits, tubers, and mushrooms.

In such a communal hunt the energy of the entire band is expended at once. But there are ways of using natural forces such as fire and water to replace some of the beaters, or to make their work easier. Before they acquired horses, some of the American Plains Indians used to set fire to dry grass, downwind of a herd of bison, when the latter were grazing near bluffs over a river. As the wind carried the fire toward the bluff, the bison stampeded, fell over, and were despatched by hunters waiting on the riverbank.

The Klamath Indians of South Central Oregon employed a variant of this technique to drive deer in the fall. At that time the deer had congregated in herds, browsing on the slopes behind Pelican Bay of Lake Klamath. The men of a village situated near the shore got behind the deer and drove them down into the lake, where women were waiting in canoes to kill them with clubs.

Driving animals into fences and pounds

A third method is to drive animals between fences into a narrow gap where they may be despatched, or into a pound. It takes only a few men to set up the fences, but they can do this work at any convenient time of year, and the structures may be used over and over again, with a few repairs. In some cases the fence is only a row of piles of brush, with spaces in between. Men stationed between the piles will pop up when animals try to escape through the sides, and will drive them back in. This technique has been reported from as far afield as Tasmania and California.

This method of hunting is made more efficient when combined with devices that operate automatically, such as snares. An example is the caribou drive of the Kutchin Indians of the Upper Yukon country, whose territory straddles the Alaskan-Canadian boundary. These Indians made permanent or semipermanent circular pounds, some of which were a mile and a half in diameter. Construction and repairs took place in summer, in preparation for the autumn and winter hunts.

Except for the entrance, such a pound was bounded by a ring of posts about four feet high. Poles and brush closed the interstices between the posts except for narrow gaps, wide enough to let one caribou through at a time, and each gap was equipped with a noose. As these gaps were only about eight feet apart, their nooses could hold a large number of animals.

The entrance to the pound was flanked by two rows of other posts, about six feet high, converging like a funnel. Each post was decked out with moss hanging in such a way as to represent a man and thus dissuade the caribou from escaping between them. At the far ends of the rows, the posts were quite far apart; as they approached the entrance, they were set closer and closer together.

To operate such a pound efficiently required more Indians than

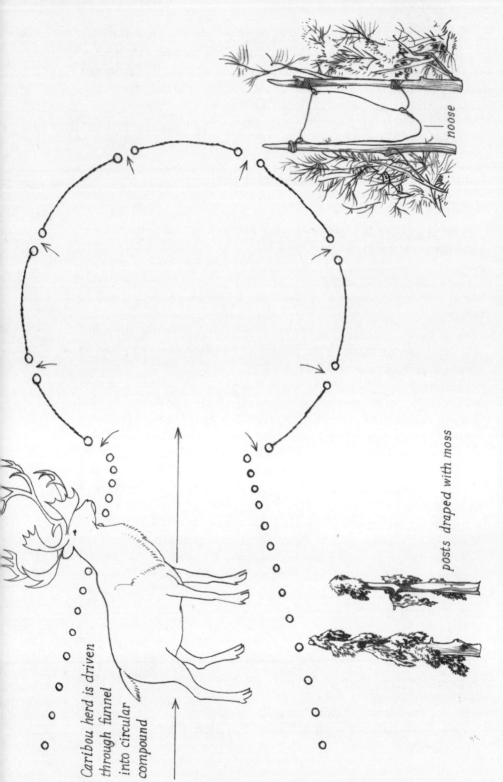

noose

posts draped with moss

Caribou herd is driven through funnel into circular compound

18. A Kutchin caribou pound. Some of them are a mile and a half in diameter

the population of one camp or village; several bands united for this purpose. Having located a herd of caribou grazing, the hunters surrounded them and drove them toward the pound by howling like wolves. Once the herd was inside the pound, the hunters stood in the entranceway. Some of the men shot the deer that tried to escape and frightened the others so that they would dash for the exits and get snared. No one entered the pound until the hunt was over.

An even fancier variant was that of the Ainu, who built straight fences parallel to a stream bed rather than pounds, and also used lassos and set bows. Every year in mid-October herds of sika deer migrated down from the forested slopes of the mountain ranges into the valley bottoms, along paths that they followed every year. Their habit was to browse on the flatlands bordering the streams before the snow began to fall. The Ainu settlements were also located near the riverbanks, because of the salmon fishing, and also because (except in winter when the streams were frozen) the Ainus' chief means of travel was by dugout canoe. Two or three miles away from their houses the Ainu set up deer fences of poles, mostly in groves but sometimes on open land too. These fences varied from a few hundred yards to a mile in length. At intervals in the fences they left gaps. These gaps were armed with set bows and poisoned arrows. Cords across the gaps pulled triggers when the deer came through, and released the arrows.

Before the hunt men and women repaired the old fences and built new ones when needed, and finally the men set the bows, under the direction of the village headman, whose duty it also was to dismantle them after the hunt was over. When the deer had assembled on the upper slopes, young men, women, and dogs drove the deer to the fences and along them, lassoing and clubbing some of the deer, while others were shot by the set bows.

In the middle of March, they also hunted deer, but from camps higher up the slopes, too far from their settlements along the river for commuting. Because they went there each year, the hunters had cabins to sleep in. They also took along a few women as cooks. The cabins were set within easy walking distance of groves of fir, under which the deer congregated to browse on bamboo grass and other vegetation which they could reach because the snow ur.der the trees was thin. Outside in the open the snow had partly melted and again frozen, thus producing a crust hard enough to keep the deer from running when their hoofs broke through, but not strong enough for them to walk on. Outside the shelter of the groves, the deer were nearly helpless.

First the hunters would drive the deer out of the grove into the deeper snow and shoot them with poisoned arrows. While this was going on some of the hunters would enter the grove and attach set bows to the trunks, and when the deer that had not been killed outside returned to the sanctuary of the trees, some of them too would be shot.

Another account of an elaborate preparation for driving game into fences comes from the pen of no less an observer than Sir Francis Galton, who visited Southwest Africa in 1850–52. At that time game was very abundant in the well-watered hills of the country still occupied by the Cape Bushmen, large numbers of whom used to join forces to drive herds of game down from the heights into the valleys. Some of the latter were wholly enclosed with fences, except for openings through which the animals fell into deep pits.

According to Galton: "We passed a magnificent set of pitfalls which the Bushmen who live about these hills had made. The whole breadth of the valley was staked and bushed across. At intervals the fence was broken, and there deep pitfalls were made. The strength and size of timber that was used gave me a great idea of Bushman industry, for every tree had to be burned down and carried away from the hills, and yet the scale of the undertaking would have excited astonishment in far more civilized nations. When a herd of animals was seen among the hills, the Bushmen drove them through this valley up to the fence; this was too high for them to jump, so that they were obliged to make for the gaps, and there they tumbled into the pitfalls."*

An enterprise of such magnitude, involving felling trees with fire, carrying the trunks several miles, and digging postholes and pits must have required considerable organization, and the same must have been true of year-to-year maintenance, the management of the hunt itself, and the division of tons of meat. The surviving Bushmen, confined to deserts, have no opportunity to hunt in this fashion, and we may never know the details.

*Francis Galton, *Narrative of an Explorer in Tropical South Africa* (London, 1853), p. 160.

Hunting by sea: the harpoon

Except for the incidental and minor use of the lasso by the Ainu, and the major use of the snare by the Kutchin, so far we have been describing the use of piercing weapons — throwing clubs, boomerangs, spears, darts, and arrows held in the hand or set, that leave the hunter's control once they have been thrown, shot, or discharged. On land, his chances of retrieving his quarry's body are usually good if the wound has been crippling or fatal.

In hunting by sea, the situation is different. A wounded seal can sound, and remain on the bottom without a chance of being recovered. The same goes for any other sea mammal except the right whales, which float, and for sea turtles or large fish. The answer is, of course, the invention of the harpoon. The harpoon has a detachable head attached to a long line, and the casting or thrusting shaft comes loose and can be recovered in the water or retained in the harpooner's hand. Being barbed, the head is supposed to remain imbedded in the victim's flesh, and the harpooner can eventually haul in his prey with the line, which is usually attached to a float. We use harpoons in catching swordfish, and a few generations ago some of our ancestors used them in whaling.

I was once told that there was a native Andaman Islander living on Nantucket, having been brought there by Yankee whalers, whom he served as a harpooner, but I was unable to confirm or refute this. It is not surprising that the whaling captains should have employed such a man, because in their home islands the Andamanese are harpooners too, their principal prey being both green and hawk-billed sea turtles, weighing respectively up to one hundred and four hundred pounds. In addition to delicious meat in large quantities, these chelonians supplied the Andamanese with turtle fat, their favorite body ointment.

Before they possessed harpoons the Andamanese say that they caught turtles only in nets, along with large fish. When European and oriental ships began to be wrecked in considerable numbers on their stormy shores, the Andamanese obtained a supply of nails, spikes, and other hardware from the timbers, and only with nails and spikes could they pierce the tough shells of the sea turtles and hold them with lines.

But even iron heads could not be depended on to penetrate a turtle's carapace if the harpoon were merely cast. The metal had to

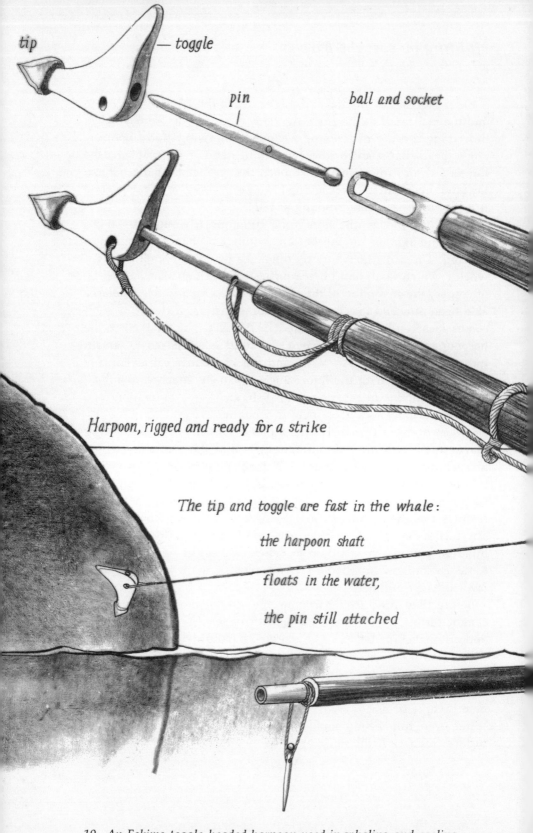

tip — toggle

pin

ball and socket

Harpoon, rigged and ready for a strike

The tip and toggle are fast in the whale:

the harpoon shaft

floats in the water,

the pin still attached

19. An Eskimo toggle-headed harpoon used in whaling and sealing

be jabbed through it by hand. With this problem in mind, the Andamanese built their canoes with long, projecting platforms at the bow, and made particularly long harpoon shafts. Having drawn as close to the turtle as possible, the harpooner, holding his weapon, runs onto the platform, leaps off, and thrusts the head into his victim. Now the shaft, which he has released, floats loose, and the paddler left in the canoe casts out two floats of buoyant wood attached to the line. After this, hauling in the turtle and lashing it to the hull is only a matter of time.

Whether they caught them in nets or with harpoons, the Andamanese never molested the turtles when they waddled ashore to lay their eggs in the sand, nor on their way back to the water. When asked why they performed this act of conservation, the men looked embarrassed and gave no reply.

At the mouth of the McArthur River in the Northern Territory of Australia, some of the local aborigines harpoon dugongs in the same way. The chances are very good that in both cases these are techniques that the people using them learned from outsiders coming by sea, but from our point of view that interpretation is not of vital importance. What really matters is that both the Andamanese and the northern Australians were alert. When they saw a new technique of getting food in large quantities, and the technique was within their capacity to imitate, they jumped at it.

Most of the bona fide hunters who are also harpooners use these weapons in killing sea mammals in chilly salt water. These animals provide them with skins and fat as well as meat. In this respect we think at once of the Eskimo, Chukchi, Northwest Coast Indians, and the Yaghans and Alakaluf of the Fuegian country. Although the harpoons of all of these peoples have detachable heads, they vary in technical details and in degree of mechanical complexity.

The Yaghans and Alakaluf make relatively simple ones, with a barbed head cut from a piece of whale's rib and set in a slot in the end of a cypress-wood shaft, where it is held by the elasticity of skin wrappings until the animal is struck. In the case of a small harpoon, a thong tied to the lower end of the head is twisted around the upper portion of the shaft and made fast to its midsection. When the head penetrates the animal's body it is either jarred loose or becomes disengaged when the animal thrashes, dragging the shaft behind it, while the hunter retains the line. In the case of a larger harpoon, a skin cord, as much as sixty feet long, passes from the head down the shaft through three skin loops, and the harpooner recovers

E

the shaft when he is in the process of pulling in his prey.

As might be expected, the Eskimo make more ingenious harpoons, combining the ball-and-socket principle with that of the toggle. They mount the harpoon head on a bone or ivory foreshaft loosely tied to the end of the wooden shaft by a thong. The line goes to a hole in the middle of the head. When the animal is struck, the foreshaft comes loose from the head at one end and is left hanging from the shaft by its thong. In this way the shaft is not likely to break from the animal's movements, and this is important because wood suitable for making into harpoon shafts is scarce. As the head penetrates the animal's flesh a pull on the cord turns it sidewise so that the end of the head and its barb act like a toggle and the head cannot be pulled out. (See Figure 19.)

Slings and bolas

In addition to the primary projectile weapons — the club, spear, and bow and arrow — some land hunters also throw stones. A rough stone, picked up on the spur of the moment, is better for street-fighting than for hunting, because it meets considerable air resistance and is hard to aim. A smooth, round stone is better in both respects and people who carry them about as premeditated missiles either select water-rounded pebbles or peck rough stones into a globular shape.

Such a stone gains velocity and distance if it is first whirled around the hunter's head in the pocket of a sling or tied to the end of a thong. The mechanical principle is essentially the same as that of the spear-thrower, to serve as an elongation of the thrower's arm. While the sling is common enough among shepherds as an aid to controlling their flocks, it is used by relatively few hunters. The chief exceptions are those of the Yaghans and Ona of Tierra del Fuego, who hunt birds with it.

The Tehuelche of Patagonia, mainland relatives of the Ona, used to throw a baseball-sized stone attached to a single thong. When released after twirling, the thong trailed the stone through the air like a comet's tail. Its impact could stun a guanaco or a rhea, the South American equivalent of an ostrich. Some of these stones, which antedate Spanish contact, had grooves around them for attachment, a sign that they were important enough weapons to warrant careful preparation.

But all of them were not thrown singly. More often the Tehuelche tied two stones together, one at each end of the thong. Holding one stone in his hand, the hunter swung the other, and after their release the two turned in the air by centrifugal force until one of them, or the thong, struck a guanaco. Then the impact caused the stones to entangle the animal with the thong. As a variant, the Tehuelche sometimes used three stones, two large ones and a smaller one to hold in the hand while swinging the other two before release. After the introduction of Spanish horses and cattle, the Indians and the gauchos who succeeded them used these bolas as a cowboy does a lariat, replacing the stones with imported brass balls.

The Eskimo also make bolas of their own design for catching birds in flight. They tie as many as five to eight pieces of bone together with a knot in the center, and in its flight this device has a spread comparable to that of bird shot. Once entangled, the bird drops to the ground.

Hunting with nets: water, air, and land

If we continue to pursue this survey of hunting weapons more or less systematically, bolas lead us into the subject of catching and holding, rather than killing, devices. At the end of this line of weaponry come traps, which operate in the hunter's absence. Somewhere between bolas and traps fall nets, relatively complex devices that, unlike traps, still require the hunter's presence.

Technologically, nets also bridge part of the gap between simple, open basketry made with pliant cordage, like women's carrying bags, and textiles. Nets of any considerable size require a good supply of cordage, and if they are to be well made, the use of the netting needle, which spaces the meshes evenly, and a knowledge of the netting knot. Under these circumstances it is not surprising that few hunters made them, even for fishing, for which nets are particularly suited.

Before obtaining scrap-iron from wrecks to convert into harpoon heads, as we have seen, the Andamanese caught sea turtles with hibiscus-fiber nets, and they made them as expertly as they did the cords themselves. Even with harpoons in the weaponry, the Alakaluf too used nets, as an occasional, alternate means of catching sea lions. The nets were not large and were made of thongs. When the Alakaluf spotted from their boats a rookery of these animals basking on the rocks of a small island, they would come ashore out of sight and creep up to hide in caves or behind rocks, a short distance away. Thence they would dash out, nets in hand, and throw the nets over large, adult animals to entangle them and to hold them back from the sea until the hunters could club them to death.

The Eskimo of Labrador, Smith Sound, and Bering Strait use small nets on the ends of poles to scoop low-flying birds out of the air in places where the birds are flying through gaps in the hills. In the Murray River country of southeastern Australia, where there are many permanent streams, teams of aborigines used to stretch a net shaped like a tennis net across streams where ducks were feeding, downstream from the ducks, and just above the surface of the water. Then most of the men would go upstream and drive the ducks down, slowly at first, so as not to make them rise. Then, when near enough the net, the men would frighten the ducks and make them rise. The ducks would start to fly downstream. One man, left behind in hiding, would imitate the whistle of the duck hawk and throw a piece of bark into the air, to flutter like the hawk's wings. The ducks then dived, flying low, skimming the water and smacking into the net, where their neck feathers got caught in the meshes, holding them until the other men had arrived.

Most of the peoples who drive land animals into nets are forest cultivators who like to have an extra supply of meat now and then to balance their predominantly starch diets. They also know how to make nets. Net hunting for land animals is so rare among hunters that I have found only three cases in the available literature. One comes from a heavily forested part of Queensland where the aborigines were reported, nearly a century ago, to be catching wallabies in nets. We have neither details nor verification.

The other two are richly documented. One group includes bands of the Sua and Aka branches of the Mbuti Pygmies of the Ituri Forest, living west of the Efe branch of the same people, who hunt with bows and arrows. The other one is a people known as the Birhors, who live in the Chota Nagpur Hills of India, near Ranchi in the state of Bihar. Both are symbiotic. The Pygmies get some of their nets from their Negro neighbors, who themselves are part-time net hunters. The Birhors make their own, because they specialize in rope making, and trade their ropes to their rice-growing neighbors. In return for meat the Pygmies receive bananas from their trading partners, and the Birhors get rice. These cultivated vegetable foods free the women of both peoples from part of their daily work in collecting wild plants, and allow them to take part in routine hunts. We shall review the hunting routines of each of the peoples because the details are available, they are our best examples of how symbiotic hunters get their meat supply, and they give us a chance to introduce the important subject of hunting magic.

A Mbuti net hunt

Net hunting takes almost as many people as a surround does, while stalking requires small teams of a few men each. Consequently the Mbuti net-hunting bands are larger than those of the bow-hunting Aka. The net hunters deplete the local game more rapidly than the stalkers do, and have to move camp to other parts of the forest more often.

Let us visualize ourselves in a net-hunting camp. Except for old people and babies, most of the men, women, and larger children have been hunting together, and they have returned and eaten their late afternoon meal. The men converse, and finally decide whether or not they will go out the next day. Their decision will depend partly on their predictions of the weather and partly on how much food they have left. If the answer is yes, they further decide where they will hunt, and this depends on the location of game.

Before they retire for the night they will also dance, imitating the actions of the animals they hope to kill. In the morning before they set out, some of the younger men light a fire near the beginning of the trail to be followed, and make it smoke by throwing on green leaves. They do this to call the attention of the forest to their hunt. On the way out and back, the women may pause to dig a few roots or pick mushrooms to put in their bags along with the game they hope to bring back.

Each active hunter who is a married man owns a net, and so do a few bachelors who have proved themselves equally competent. The nets are about four feet wide and vary from one hundred to three hundred feet in length. Between seven and thirty such nets are set up in a semicircle, tied to bushes and creepers, and each man conceals himself behind his net. As a rule the older men are stationed in the center and the younger men on the flanks, and brothers like to be next to each other. A man will not cross the ground in front of the net unless some other hunter needs his help.

The women take up their positions in another semicircle facing that of the nets, and at a signal they begin beating the brush with sticks and shouting. The frightened game then rushes into the nets, and the hunters do not kill it until it seems to be ready to escape. Then they shoot it with arrows poisoned with stropanthus, and with spears. If too few animals are killed in the first drive, it may be repeated at a new location until the hunters either have enough game or give up. The women bring the smaller animals back to camp in their bags, while the younger men carry the larger ones in on their shoulders. Whether or not they hunt again the next day depends on how long the supply of meat will last, on the weather, on a decision to shift camp, or one to carry some meat into the village for a change of pace.

A Birhor monkey hunt

While the Mbuti are welcome in the villages of their agricultural neighbors, the Birhors have no such convenient accommodations. Although their women rather anonymously trade rope for rice, cloth, cutlery, pots, and other goods in the markets, the men stay in the forest for a good reason. They kill and eat monkeys, and monkeys are sacred to the Hindus, being identified with the Vedic monkey-god Hanuman, a benevolent deity. In the Congo villages the Pygmies partake, in a rather tongue-in-cheek way, in the rituals of their hosts, and have no need of elaborate hunting rites in the forest. The Birhors, on the other hand, are ritually on their own, and to them success at the hunt depends on the proper performance of ritual acts and the keeping of ritual tabus.

While the Birhors also catch macaques, the most abundant monkeys in the forest are the leaf-eating langurs, which have black coats and long tails. These monkeys feed in bands of considerable size. Each man in the camp owns a net, of about the same dimensions as the Pygmy net, and the Birhors make them themselves. When tied together they will stretch out several hundred yards. On the hunt the men take their iron axes with them, but no bows; in fact, few men own bows.

When the chief has decided to lead his followers out on a monkey hunt, he washes, dons a clean breechclout, and makes sacrifices to each spirit concerned with the hunt, calling them by name and scattering a few grains of rice on the ground for each one as he names him. He takes along most of the active women who are not out trading, or menstruating. The women that go are to serve as beaters. On the way out of camp the men make sure that the women left behind are not looking at them, and that they themselves don't see an empty pot, or someone defecating. Otherwise the hunt might fail.

As they approach the hunting ground one of the men, who serves the chief as a herald, assembles the nets in a heap, and hands the chief a special wand to touch them with. The chief prays as he does so. Now that the nets have been consecrated, the further preparations for the hunt can begin. The chief sends out scouts to locate the monkeys, and when they have been located men tie their nets together and stretch them between bamboo poles in the rear of a piece of open ground.

Now the men divide up into teams, with a special flanker and his beaters stationed on either side. They drive the monkeys out of the trees and onto the ground on the open space, and then across the ground into the nets. Once they are entangled, other men, armed with clubs, emerge from hiding places in the bushes, and club them. It may be observed that this is more delicate work than the Sua Pygmy net hunt because monkeys are intelligent animals. It is not easy to drive them while they are overhead in the trees or to make them come down to the ground. The anxiety expressed by the rites and restrictions is based on a chance of failure if anything goes wrong with the procedure.

Once the monkeys have been killed one of the hunters kindles a fire by twirling a bamboo shaft on a hearth board. The hunters then singe the bodies, cut them up, and remove the hearts, brains, and other organs to be cooked and eaten on the spot, but not at once. First the chief roasts a little of this meat, and offers it to the spirits. After the men have eaten their snacks, the chief divides the rest of the meat according to fixed protocol, and the hunters and beaters carry their shares home.

The interband annual deer hunt of the Birhors

In the latter part of April and early in May, members of several neighboring bands of Birhors join forces to hold an annual deer hunt. The deer is either the sambur *(Cervus unicolor)*, or the axis deer *(Cervus axis)*, both of which form large enough herds at that season to warrant the effort. In this hunt only men participate. The women are left behind in camp where they have to observe strict sexual tabus.

Before the members of the different bands have assembled, their heralds have carried messages back and forth between their chiefs, to determine the time and place. Once together, the chiefs meet in council to agree on the rules.

Each man takes along his net and two bamboo poles, his axe, and a club. A few men also carry bows to shoot birds on the way. Having arrived at the netting place, one of the chiefs takes charge, as agreed on beforehand. Now everyone sits down with his net in front of him, and a herald, also specially chosen, touches each net with a wand. He hands the wand to the presiding chief, who prays to the sky-god, facing the direction from which they have come, and twirling the wand in his hand. The prayer ended, he lays the wand across the path they had followed, as a spirit-barrier. Now he prays, again, but silently, for everyone left in camp, to counteract possible evil influences.

He next appoints two flankers, each of whom has about a dozen beaters under his command, and the nets are tied together and spread in a long line. The hunt proceeds; the beaters and flankers drive the deer into the nets and club them, as with monkeys. Whenever a deer is killed the headman of the killer's band (not just the head of the hunt) smears some of its blood on a leaf of a special tree and offers it to the different hills and streams, saying: "Today we take away your goat (the Hindu animal of sacrifice), so we offer you this in sacrifice."

If the first drive fails, a shaman who has been serving as hunter or simply accompanying the others, strikes the ground with a wand of his own and looks into a handful of leaves to see what spirit or spirits are hindering the hunt. These are usually identified as the spirits of ancestors who died hunting. Once the shaman has called out the names of these spirits the presiding chief offers them each a pinch of tobacco. If after this a second drive fails, then the chiefs are sure that at least one of the women left in camp must have been sexually incontinent, offending one of the gods watching the hunt, who in reprisal has held back the game.

The supposed antagonism between hunting and sex, as tested by the examples of the Mbuti and Birhor net hunters

In Chapter 1 we mentioned the common but not universal feeling among hunters that sexual intercourse and success at the chase are mutually antagonistic. This attitude may be partly related to their common observation that while animals are copulating they are most easily killed, because their precautionary guards are lowered. But that cannot be the whole story. The examples of the Mbuti and Birhor net hunters may serve as test cases of this generalization.

Now the Pygmies, who hunt nearly every day, have sexual intercourse whenever they please, whether or not they plan to hunt the next morning, and some of them even slip off into the bushes on the way back to camp. To them, sex has nothing special to do with hunting. Taking their women with them, the Pygmies cannot be any more adulterous in the forest then they are in camp, and when they visit Negro villages, all the members of the camp go along. If a Negro takes a Pygmy woman as a plural wife, she leaves her band and stays in the village. The Negroes worry about the ritual contamination of women, but this idea has found little acceptance among the Pygmies, who live their own lives in the forest.

When the Birhors hunt monkeys, as they do frequently, they take along some of the women as beaters, and no sexual tabus are observed except that they leave menstruating women behind, in seclusion, and that all women, menstruating or not, who do not go out should avoid glancing at the departing men. During an interband annual deer hunt, all women are left behind, and the hunters may not copulate with any women during the preceding night. The waiting women, who may belong to more than one band, must remain continent until the men have returned, in the belief that their sexual activities would spoil the hunt.

E*

When men and women who have known each other before come together once a year as members of different bands, the temptation to overstep marital ties must be great. No sex for anyone is preferable to quarreling over women at a critical time. There is method in the Birhors' magic, and comparable situations do not arise among the Mbuti net hunters.

Trapping

Net hunting is a step in the direction of trapping, for trapping is a way of catching animals with devices that operate in the hunter's absence. But there are no hunters on record who rely heavily on traps for meat and skins, except when those devices are combined with fences and pounds, as with the Kutchin, Ainu, and Bushmen, who are certainly on hand when they are used.

The hunters that need unattended traps the most are those that live in the cold north and need furs for clothing. They are the Indians of Canada and Alaska, the North American Eskimo, the Asiatic Eskimo, Chukchi, and other East Asian hunters that wear fur clothing. All of them are able to construct rather complicated traps because they have the tools and the skill to build boats, sleds, and toboggans.

Trapping was not a full-time occupation for any of these peoples before the Hudson Bay Company and other traders had arrived on the scene. For example, the whale-hunting Eskimo of Tigara, the Tikerarmiut, used to go out by families in the summer to catch wolves, wolverines, foxes, and marmots in snares and deadfalls. They made the wolf and wolverine furs into face ruffs for their parkas, and the fox and marmot skins into soft, warm undergarments.

On these expeditions no hunter was supposed to trap more than four animals of any of the species named in a single day. If he did, he ran the risk of turning into such an animal. Many generations ago, according to a local tale, a greedy hunter broke this tabu, and soon he began to grow claws. His hair turned into fur, and his nose became a snout. Once the white fur traders had begun coming to Tigara in the summer, the magic spell was broken. The Tikerarmiut trapped as much fur as they could, and no one turned into an animal, although the animals themselves became scarcer, harder to find.

Kinds of traps

Although traps may be classified in various ways, the most functional system seems to be based on a consideration of the forces used in catching the animal, as follows: the weight or momentum of the animal itself; the torsion of a spring; and the weight of a suspended object. In the last two, some triggering device is needed to release the spring or weight.

No method could be simpler than the use of so-called bird lime, which consists of smearing a sticky substance on the limbs of trees so that perching birds will get their feet caught in it and be unable to fly away. This is done mostly in warm countries where suitable gums are available, as in Australia. In southeastern Australia and western Tasmania, where the aborigines were relatively sedentary, a favorite trick was to imbed in the ground sharp, pointed stakes. They placed these along paths habitually followed by kangaroos and wallabies, so that the animals would impale their feet when hopping.

In addition to the open pits into which they drove game through holes in fences, the Bushmen used also to dig unattended animal pits, with concealed surfaces. These were true traps in which the animal's own weight was the critical force. There were two kinds, used respectively in the north and south of the Bushman country. The northern Bushmen dug them in the dry season, either on paths to water holes or on the banks of streams. Such a pit, excavated with ordinary digging sticks, would be about twelve feet long and of equal depth, but narrow — a little less than a yard wide. Inside it consisted of two chambers separated by a wall of earth left standing in the middle, but not quite as high as the ground level. The pit was oriented lengthwise to the direction the game was likely to take, and covered with brush. The earth removed in excavation was scattered elsewhere.

A long-legged animal (as most of them are there) that fell into the first chamber would try to scramble over the dividing wall, and be strung up on its belly with its feet dangling fore and aft. Even a giraffe could be immobilized in such a trap.

The southern Bushmen, the ones that drove game as previously stated, also dug unattended pits. These were single chambered, had sharp, pointed stakes set in the middle, and caught animals as large as rhinoceroses, which had to be killed with spears.

The Chukchi of the Siberian side of Bering Strait made a smaller, and mechanically more sophisticated, kind of a pit trap, one with bait and a lid, for catching foxes. Going to a frozen river, a man would chop a chamber out of the ice, one as much as five or six feet square, and of equal depth. He covered it with a slab of ice with a hole in it just large enough for a fox to get through. Below the hole he set a square piece of ice or wood, balanced on two stakes imbedded in opposite sides of the chamber, and baited. A fox jumps through the hole after the bait, lands on a swinging platform, falls into the lower part of the chamber, and the platform swings back. He cannot get out. Other foxes may follow him, until the chamber is full.

We have already mentioned the use of nooses in the caribou pounds of the Kutchin Indians. Single nooses, set along game trails, are widely used to catch single animals, and by their own force. The Penobscot Indians used to catch hares in nooses hung from crossbars between pairs of notched poles. Led into the noose by convergent piles of brush on either side, a hare would put its head through the noose which would tighten, and as it leaped forward the crossbar would fall down and be dragged in the bushes, stopping the hare. Being made of rawhide, the nooses were stiff enough to stay open until activated.

Few devices invented by the Eskimo show greater ingenuity combined with simplicity than a wolf trap using the force of a spring and the animal's own body heat as a trigger. An Eskimo coils a strip of baleen, pointed at both ends, so that it looks like a watch spring. He ties it to keep it from unwinding, sets it out of doors in water, and when it is frozen he cuts the binding. Then he inserts it into a piece of meat, which he also freezes, and leaves it in a place where wolves have been seen. A passing wolf gulps it down, it thaws in the wolf's stomach, the spring uncoils and pierces the wolf's vitals, leaving him to a painful end.

A widely used device depending on the flexibility of wood is the spring pole. Some of us remember the childhood pleasure of climbing a small birch tree and having it bend over with our weight, depositing us gently on the ground, and then springing back again. If instead of letting it spring back we attach a noose to the end of it and then find some means of keeping the noose just over or on the ground until released by an animal who gets caught in the noose and pulled up into the air, we have a spring-pole trap.

The critical element is the trigger, which is attached not to the noose, which hangs free or may be propped up on sticks, but to a cord tied to the end of the pole and strong enough to withstand the force of the spring. In an American Indian marmot trap, the cord passes in back of the noose, and the noose is dangling in an opening through which the marmot tries to pass. Once he has his neck in the noose he still has to get by the cord, and to do so he gnaws it, and hangs himself. For animals that do not gnaw cords but will take bait, the end of the cord may be lopped over a notched stake driven into the ground; or better, a truncated sapling or bush held in the ground by its own roots. When bait is tied to the cord, the animal tries to take the bait away, pulls the loop out of the notch, and up he goes.

Hunters who trap with spring poles in summer may find them too brittle in winter when the sap is gone. Instead they may build a kind of a well-sweep with a noose instead of a bucket on the business end. It will be a log balanced in the crotch of a tree, with the thick end heavy enough to lift up any animal likely to trip the noose. The principle at play here is the use of the force of a suspended object; which leads us to deadfalls that crush the animal instead of hanging it.

There are many variations on this theme. The Bushmen not only dig pits but also make deadfalls out of propped-up slabs of stone, to catch small animals. But the greatest proliferation of deadfalls is found in the northern regions previously designated, where people need furs for clothing; and as dead-falls are more efficient than simpler traps, they are the ones most used. Some of them crush the animal between two logs, and sometimes the logs have spikes to prevent escape.

A caribou trap, made by some of the Athabascan Indians of Alaska, is a combination deadfall and noose. The noose hangs from the limb of a tree, and the noose cord passes through a hole in the upper end of a log propped diagonally against the foot of the tree. A trigger holds the log up, and when tripped, it lets the log drop, strangling the caribou with the noose.

Traps that depend on the weight or momentum of the animal being caught do not need tripping or triggering devices. Bird lime, stakes, pits, and nooses do not need them. Neither does a very clever but simple mink trap used by the Penobscot Indians. They merely cut a hole in the side of a tree, about six feet up, and insert two sharp wooden stakes, pointing upward, at the mouth of the hole. The mink climbs to the hole and sticks his head in to take the bait. When he tries to back out, he impales his neck on the stakes.

Spring poles and deadfalls need triggering devices, and the kind to be used depends on a combination of the trap maker's ingenuity and the amount of force the animal is likely to exert in tripping it. A trap that needs too much force to trip it may let an animal get away with the bait. A heavy deadfall that must be released with a light tug poses a problem of leverage. If the prop holding the weight up comes in two pieces, one resting on the other, a light pull sidewise will collapse it; this is the principle of the Eskimo whaling harpoon. Or if a wooden toggle is poised between the two arms of a forked branch of wood, and the tug slides the toggle along the fork to a point where it is shorter than the gap it fills, it can be released with a minimum of pulling force.

These sophisticated mechanical devices are only part of a highly evolved technological complex limited to the northerly regions of the world and, as far as hunters are concerned, to northeastern Asia, including Hokkaido; and to northern North America, including the Aleutians and the American Northwest Coast as well as Eskimo country and the forested interior.

Conclusion

Trapping is a specialized and secondary way of hunting, and also a lonely one. It can supplement the meat supply, and it can provide furs needed for survival in the Far North. As it does not require the cooperation of many people and is not emotion inspiring, it has no contribution to make to social structure. It is not the kind of action of which myths are made. It does not make a man feel important, or even exalted, for that kind of hunting comes with the killing of big game face to face.

5.

Big-Game Hunting

M ost of the hunting methods that we have surveyed, except for fur trapping, are primarily ways of getting animal food. The hunter does not have to pit his wits against the animals he kills because he is more intelligent than they are, and he runs little risk of being killed. Most of them are no larger than he is. A predatory animal does not ordinarily tackle an adversary much larger than himself, and this is true even of lions, tigers, and bears.

But owing to the combination of his intelligence and his weapons, a man can tackle as large an animal as an elephant or a whale, both of which are intelligent and can fight back. In this sense big-game hunting bears some of the dangers, and the rewards in prestige, of fighting. Not every man is qualified by temperament, boldness, and skill to hunt big game, and those who do are outstanding individuals, both for the amount of meat they supply to their fellows, and for the respect that they receive, if they survive.

When we see the engravings and paintings of mammoths on European cave walls, we realize that big-game hunting goes back thousands of years among our European ancestors. But they were not the only ones. American Indians killed mammoths too.

A few years ago, only a few miles from where these words are being written, a site was found in Ipswich, Massachusetts, that contained a number of beautifully fashioned, fluted flint spearheads. They were made of a kind of flint that does not occur nearby, and were dated at about eight thousand years ago, at a time when the continental ice sheet that scoured our granite outcrops bare had just retreated, and forest trees had grown up on what are now our salt marshes. Even more recently a local inhabitant brought me a disc-shaped bone that he had found between the peat and blue clay. It was a mammoth's astragalus, or ankle bone. Later on an ulna, or front lower leg bone, of the same or a similar animal turned up in the same place.

The ancient Indians that had brought or traded these flint spearheads from some unknown place, and had killed the mammoth, were great hunters, for a mammoth was a wily as well as a huge and powerful beast, able at a few seconds' notice to pick a man up in his trunk and dash his victim on the ground, to trample and crush his body underfoot. Not every man had then, or has now, the stamina and skill that it took to kill mammoths with a spear, and those that possessed these qualities must have acquired personal satisfaction and great prestige.

Elephant hunting: the Akoa Pygmies

A mammoth was the cold-weather cousin of the living elephants, themselves equally formidable adversaries to contemporary hunters. On the face of a cliff deep in the Libyan Desert stands an ancient rock engraving depicting a duel between a long-legged elephant and a man, in which the elephant seems to be winning, for it is holding a small man, who could have been a Pygmy, high off the ground in the curl of his trunk.

The part of the southern Sahara where that combat was depicted is now almost as barren as the face of the moon. The forest has retreated southward, and with it the elephants and their hunters, the living Pygmies. They still hunt elephants, and we know the details of some of their hunts, because Father Trilles, who watched an Akoa Pygmy chief make arrow poison as narrated on pages 81–83, also went hunting with them several times and recorded in detail what they did, said, and sang.

These Pygmies live in year-round camps hidden in forests and marshes, in elephant country. They used to hunt elephants several times a year, and would kill as many as three or four at a time, or they might come home empty handed. They believe in the existence of a giant white elephant (white is the color of death and of ghosts) that appears to them in dreams, giving them advice. But if the chief, who is identified with elephants in a spiritual way, dreams of the white elephant, this is a warning and a bad omen, and the camp must be moved to another site without delay. While out on hunts they also notice that certain elephants behave in special ways resembling the walks and gestures of other hunters who have been killed by elephants, and they believe that the spirits of these men have somehow or other been incorporated into those of these living animals. When a Pygmy hunter has been crushed under an elephant's feet, there is no mourning, for he has died nobly and joined the elephants in a sense, but still the camp has lost a man.

When a troop of elephants has been reported nearby, the Pygmies are eager to go out, for there is nothing that they enjoy more than an elephant hunt, with its excitement, danger, and promise of more meat than they can eat. But before the decision is made to embark on such an expedition the chief must carefully weigh the risks. His first consideration, therefore, is whether or not any men may be expected to be killed, and if so, how many.

Once when such a report had been made, the chief, named Nkita, invoked certain spirits regarding the prospects of a successful hunt. In a dream the spirits told him that several men would be killed. He recounted this warning to his followers, but the men said: "We are still hungry." Not wishing to take the responsibility for the outcome Nkita sent a message to the chief of a neighboring camp, whose name was Akhor, inviting the latter to come with his men and to share the hunt. Akhor arrived with all his people — men, women, and children. Nkita considered this a good sign.

Now Akhor took over the auguries. First he held a geode (a hollow nodule of stone with a crystal lining) on the ground. The smallest girl in the camp, stark naked and without ornaments, brought fresh water and poured it into the open mouth of the geode, which Akhor then covered with the palms of his hands, invoking water spirits. The geode began to sway. Akhor let it be seen as he moved his hands, and the water appeared to be bubbling, as if boiling. An assistant brought some fresh flowers which Akhor put in the water, then splashed it about and spilled it on the ground. When it had dried somewhat the wet patches on the ground where the water had fallen and flowed were interpreted. A long, straight, broken line in the middle meant a long, difficult trail, but one leading to eventual success. A circle symbolized a dead man, and triangles dead elephants. There were five triangles — a good hunt.

But one forecast was not enough. Akhor spread a piece of bark on the ground and deposited on it eight lots of divination, comparable to the Urim and Thummin of the Ark of the Covenant. They consisted of two ram's astragali, two water chevrotain's astragali, and four pieces of tortoise shell, all differently marked. The ram's astragali were not easy to come by. A ram had to be stolen from a Negro village, where the rams were kept for stud and closely guarded. The water chevrotain had to be caught alive, its hoofs and horns cut off, and the rest of its body burned to ashes.

First Akhor smeared the eight lots with a mixture of termite oil and red wood powder, red being the color associated with marriage

The Elephant's Revenge

From a rock engraving at In Habeter, Fezzan, Libya

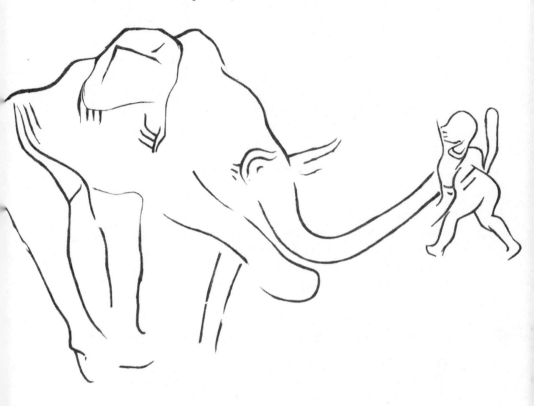

20. *Rock engraving of an elephant about to crush a small man,
found in a country now devoid of vegetation. (After Leo
Frobenius,* Ekade Ektab, *1937, Plate 63, Leipzig, Verlag Otto
Harrassowitz)*

and childbirth. By casting these lots a number of times to see which way up each would fall, he could get over a hundred combinations, for each astragalus alone could fall in four different positions, on its top, bottom, outer edge, or inner edge. At the end of his casting Akhor predicted that not five, but eight elephants would be killed — five of them males — and one hunter. Father Trilles, who went with them on the hunt, reported that the prediction was completely accurate, if only because he had shot one of the elephants himself.

Before setting out for the hunt the members of the combined camps sang a song, with a solo by the chief and a chorus, to the twanging of a musical bow. Father Trilles rendered the lyric in scanning French, which may be anglicized as follows. With a double translation plus multiple editing of the priest's manuscript, the exact words may not be fully accurate, but the spirit is probably correct.

THE ELEPHANT SONG

In the weeping forest, under the evening wind,
The night, all black, lies down to sleep, happy.
In the sky the stars escape trembling,
Fireflies flash and go out,
Up high, the moon is dark, its white light is out.
The spirits are wandering,
 Elephant hunter, take up your bow!
   Chorus: Elephant hunter, take up your bow!

In the timid forest the tree sleeps, the leaves are dead,
The monkeys have closed their eyes, hanging high from the branches,
The antelopes glide by with silent steps,
They nibble the cool grass, cocking their ears, alert,
They raise their heads and listen, a little frightened,
The cicada falls silent, cutting off his grating sound,
 Elephant hunter, take up your bow!
   Chorus: Elephant hunter, take up your bow!

In the forest that the great rain lashes,
Father elephant walks heavily, baou, baou,
Carefree and fearless, sure of his strength,
Father elephant whom nothing can vanquish,
Among the tall forest trees that he breaks, he stops and moves on,
He eats, trumpets, and searches for his mate,

Father elephant, we hear you from afar,
  Elephant hunter, take up your bow!
          Chorus: Elephant hunter, take up your bow!

In the forest where nothing moves through but you,
Hunter, lift up your heart, glide, run, leap, and walk,
The meat is in front of you, the huge piece of meat,
The meat that walks like a hill,
The meat that rejoices the heart,
The meat that will roast at your hearth,
The meat your teeth sink into,
The beautiful red meat and the blood that we drink steaming,
  Yoyo, Elephant hunter, take up your bow!
          Chorus: Yoyo, Elephant hunter, take up your bow!

The hunters then left the camp, followed by their women and children. When the scouts found elephant tracks, some of the men laid their tongues on the compressed earth to taste how fresh the tracks were, and by close observation of the tracks themselves, they could tell its maker's sex and estimate its age and stature.

Having located their first elephant, they then glided in close to shower it with poisoned arrows, aiming at particularly penetrable places, but if the elephant showed no immediate effect of this barrage some particularly brave and impatient man risked his life. He dashed between the elephant's legs and thrust a poisoned spear as deeply as he could into its belly, and with good aim and luck he might pierce the stomach and push the poison into blood vessels higher up.

The punctured elephant's first reaction was revenge. He tried to seize the hunter with his trunk, but if the hunter jumped out of the way soon enough and escaped, the elephant tried to pull the spear out of his belly with his trunk and then to cover the wound with mud.

Once the elephant had fallen and was dead, the women and children surrounded its body, crying shrilly: "Nkukuru! Nkukuru!" a Pygmy ululation. Standing with their bodies bending backward and their heads held by their arms, the men said: "Master Elephant, Master Elephant."

At this point the chief in charge of the hunt walked up to the elephant's body and placed a garland of flowering creepers around its neck, while singing an appropriate song. Then he placed another garland about its tusks, with a second song. If the elephant was a male, the chief castrated it, wrapped its testicles in *Erythrophloeum* leaves, and carried them into the forest at some distance from the scene of death, to bury them with his men around him. This interment evoked a third song. These songs may be translated as follows.

[Chief places garland around elephant's neck.]

Our spear strayed from its course,
    O Father Elephant!
We didn't mean to kill you,
We didn't mean to hurt you,
    O Father Elephant!
It wasn't the warrior who took your life,
Your hour had come,
Don't come back to trample down our huts,
    O Father Elephant!

[Chief places another garland around elephant's tusks.]

Don't be angry with us,
From now on your life will be better,
You live in the land of the Spirits,
Our fathers will go with you to renew their bond,
You live in the land of the Spirits.

[After having castrated the elephant, the chief goes out with his men to bury the elephant's testicles.]

Here you will rest forever,
Rest in peace from now on,
Here are your children,
May your anger never fall back on them.

After having returned from the interment of the elephant's testicles, the chief mounted its body. On his leathery perch, he performed his special elephant dance with elaborate mimicry, and sang the same elephant song that he sang before leaving the camp. If the elephant was a female, he did this immediately after having decorated its tusks and sung his second song.

Once the chief had concluded his final performance the butchery and feasting began. The Pygmies cut off the elephant's head and trunk and removed its tusks. They dug a deep pit and built a fire of leaves in it, and there they smoked the trunk, the pièce de résistance. The women smoked other pieces to take home, and they all stayed as long as there was any meat left, although some of it may have drawn maggots toward the end, in which case they ate the maggots too. When the feast was over the women and children returned to their camp or camps, followed by the men. But in the event that more than one elephant had been killed, they might not go back for some time.

Elephant hunting: The Mbuti Pygmies

In the Ituri Forest, Mbuti Pygmies of both the bow-stalking and net-hunting bands kill elephants, but not in the organized way just described. Also they kill fewer, from none to three a year, most commonly just one. The Efe bowmen do it in a particularly clever way. When they know that elephants are about, and expect one of them to walk along a particular trail, several men who habitually hunt together conceal themselves on either side of it. When the elephant ambles up one man pops out of the bushes in front, and the elephant stops. A second man creeps out behind the elephant and slashes the tendons of one hind leg. The elephant turns around, but the assailant has disappeared, and another man hamstrings the other hind leg. As the elephant cannot go very far, the men can take their time killing it.

The net hunters of the Mbuti kill elephants in a different way. Some men like to kill elephants more than others do, as a matter of personal satisfaction and prestige. The hunter carries a special spear about four feet long, with a razor-sharp iron head. When he comes to a fresh elephant trail he smears some of the animal's dung all over his body so that the elephant will be unable to smell his own, distinctive odor. When he has drawn close enough to hear the elephant's bowels rumble, he moves in upwind, if there is any breeze, and jabs his spear into his victim's belly, just behind the ribs, and pulls it right out again.

When an Akoa hunter does this, his companions, like picadors in a bullfight, can distract the elephant enough to give the spearman a chance to escape, but not so with the lone Mbuti hunter. When the elephant turns he must stand stock still, and the Mbuti say that if you so much as blink you are a goner. Whenever the elephant is not looking at him the hunter keeps on jabbing, until the wounded elephant raises his trunk and charges off into the forest.

Spear in hand, the hunter now returns to camp, and if the other men have not yet arrived, he waits for them. Then he tells his story and exhibits his spear. Men, women, and children crowd around him to inspect the weapon, and may say: "Hmm, only that much of the blade is bloody. Probably he won't die. Let's let him go."

But if the blood reaches down the shaft to such and such a point, they will break camp and follow the elephant's trail until they come to the corpse, its belly blown up like a balloon from putrefaction. Once Patrick Putnam, who spent as much time with the Mbuti as Father Trilles did with the Akoa, came upon a group of Pygmies who had just reached a distended elephant, and witnessed the ensuing ceremony. A man other than the elephant hunter cuts a square of skin off the inflated area. He slices this into small bits and puts one into the mouth of everyone present. Then he removes another layer from inside the first rectangle, and passes this around, and then another layer, until he finally comes to a point where the body wall is thin enough to produce a small balloon of its own.

The man now picks up a child, supposedly the youngest son of the man who killed the elephant, or his youngest nephew; in any case the child must be the youngest one of those available of the hunter's kin who is old enough to bite through that bubble within a bubble. The man pushes the child's face into it and forces him to bite. The bubble bursts and the child's face is smeared with stinking putrescence. The child weeps and screams. This is an experience that he will never forget. The rest of the people did not enjoy eating the raw skin either, for they like it cooked.

Now a free-for-all takes place. Some of the men cut the elephant's flanks open, pull out the entrails, and climb inside to hack away at the meat. Having brought along kettles, they boil it, eat all they can, and dry the rest of the boiled meat on racks to carry to their patrons in the village. The tusks go to the special patron of the elephant hunter, who sells them to the Greek or Hindu trader, and gives the hunter a small share of what he receives.

Putnam did not attempt to explain the bubble-biting ceremony, but it obviously must have had some function, because it delayed the feast and was repugnant to all concerned. Let us go over its component elements. The master of ceremonies was not the elephant hunter, nor was he the chief, because the Mbuti have no chiefs. He must have been some respected individual who represented the entire band as a unit, because he gave each member a sacramental bit of raw skin to eat. So far, the rite may be interpreted as an assertion that the meat belonged to the band as a whole, and not just to the intrepid man who had slain the monumental beast.

Episode number two, the small boy's nauseous bubble-bath, was the climax of the rite. The boy had done nothing to warrant such treatment, but he served as a substitute for his father, or uncle, the killer. At this point we might conclude that this is just a way to deflate the killer's potentially puffed ego, actually a kind of what we call kidding. But it was not that alone, if that at all. The Pygmy hunter had placed his life in close jeopardy. A further element is added, insult.

Now it is virtually a standard rule among hunters that they should never mock or otherwise insult any wild creature whose life they have brought to an end. Their rationalization, if they do rationalize about it, is that such disrespect will offend the spirits that control the game supply. Subconsciously or on the threshold of consciousness (it is hard to say at what level) hunters sense the unity of nature and the combination of humility and responsibility of their role in it. This great and awesome feeling has just begun to return to us.

Thus the Pygmies could hardly have been making fun of the elephant by desecrating its corpse. They were staging a most dramatic climax to a rite of appeasement. If insult were intended, it was to the elephant's killer, through the agency of his junior representative. But the hunter's campmates could not have intended to humiliate him deeply, after having provided them with so much meat, and in the expectation that he would give them more later on. It is also possible that what the small boy was forced to do was a special kind of initiation rite to prepare him for a future career as an elephant hunter, but this is purely speculative.

The most reasonable explanation, following the rules of parsimony in logic, is that the Pygmies were putting on a wonderful show to persuade the elephant's spirit, still lingering around, that the hunter had made a mistake, or was at fault, and was being punished for his offense. Having received his apology, the spirit might then go away, and not witness the orgy that followed. This explanation, if correct, brings the Mbuti rite into general accord with that of the Akoa, whose ceremony is easier to understand because we know its lyrics as well as its stage directions. It also fits the fantasies of the

Ainu's annual bear ceremony, which will be described in Chapter 15.

Whale hunting: a rare and complicated enterprise

The only other animal hunted that is bigger than an elephant is a whale, not counting small species such as dolphins, porpoises, and blackfish. True whaling requires crews of hunters to go out onto salt water in seaworthy boats, and the kind of whales hunted are usually baleen or "right" whales. They are called right because they are the right kind of whales to hunt. When killed their bodies float because of their thick layers of blubber. There would be little point to kill a whale that would sink to the bottom, as the toothed whales do. Whaling is dangerous, not only because an angry whale could capsize a boat, but also because a harpooner might get his legs fouled in a line and be hauled overboard, and a whale might drag a crew far out to sea. Thus whaling requires strict discipline and careful preparation. As one whale can feed a whole community, more than one crew of five to eight men may participate, particularly in towing the prize home.

Few peoples with whom we are concerned in this book had the equipment needed to go whaling, or lived near whales' migration routes. They are thus limited to the Labrador Eskimo, the Eskimo of Alaska and Siberia, the Maritime Chukchi of Siberia, and the Nootka and Makah Indians of the Northwest Coast. During the nineteenth century commerical whaling greatly reduced the number of whales available to the peoples named.

In our discussion of trapping fur animals we have already mentioned the Eskimo of Tigara, a winter village situated on a rocky promontory, connected by a sandbar to Point Hope, Alaska, on the Chukchi Sea. Tigara is directly on the annual migration route of bowhead whales to their summer feeding grounds in the Beaufort Sea, north of Point Barrow. A bowhead is one of the two largest species of right whales, and a single animal carries up to three hundred plates of baleen in its mouth, and several tons of blubber.

The Tikerarmiut, as the Eskimo of Tigara call themselves, numbered some two hundred fifty persons in 1940, and were lucky if they killed three or four bowhead whales in a year. Before 1850, when the whalers from New Bedford and Nantucket began to arrive, their population was about one thousand, and their bag was fifteen to eighteen whales, or as many as they needed. Their descendants say that in those days they used to kill only the young, tender ones, and throw pieces of ice at the larger animals to drive them away.

Although they hunted other animals, both on land and at sea, no other activity in which the Tikerarmiut were engaged required as much preparation—both physical and psychological—and as much organization, as whale hunting. Whale hunting, therefore, greatly influenced their social structure and ritual life. The Tikerarmiut lived during most of the year in large, rectangular, semisubterranean houses holding a number of related families. The most prominent man in a household was usually a boat owner, and in effect, its captain. The tops of his boots were trimmed with bands of white fur, indicating his success to date in killing whales, and were thus in a sense comparable to the gold braid around naval officers' cuffs.

Besides the extended family dwellings, Tigara had, in the old days, six other, and larger buildings serving more or less as clubhouses. In 1940 only two remained. From January until the arrival of the snowbirds at the end of March or beginning of April, the members of the whaleboat crews sat in these houses getting their gear in shape for the coming season, and also taking part in or witnessing rituals, mostly performed by the shamans, one of whom served as what we might call the chaplain of each crew.

Now a man could inherit a whaleboat—a large umiak—from his father, but he could not become a captain unless he commanded the respect of other men and could persuade them to be his crew. During the time spent getting ready for the whale hunt the captain's wife fed the crew. She also played an important ceremonial part then, during the hunt and after a dead whale had been towed in to shore.

Although what immediately follows may seem extraneous to lay readers unversed in hunting magic, it was just as important to the Tikerarmiut as what we ourselves used to do before a declared war, with propaganda, fiery speeches, rallies, parades, and prayers to God to bring us victory.

One of the many duties of the captain's wife was to carry about with her a wooden vessel from which she was supposed to offer the dead whale a drink of water, and she wore a pair of magic mittens to insulate her hands from the water bucket. During this entire period she had to be a model of proper behavior in every respect, because the whales could see everything that was going on in Tigara, and were she to make the slightest slip, it might spoil the hunt. She had to be a genial, outgoing woman, like an American president's wife, one to whom a whale would be willing to give up its body. According to the Eskimo's belief, whales did not die. They simply took off their outside parkas, meaning their flesh. Their souls lived in their skulls, and after the butchery was over, the hunters threw the skulls back into the sea. Then a new whale was reincarnated, and the hunt would be good in another year.

One year in March, while the members of the crew were still working on their gear, the shaman and the captain's wife, who was carrying her whale's drinking pot, went to a spot on the north shore of Point Hope bar, where there are remains of former habitations, and where Froelich G. Rainey, the narrator of our account, was conducting an archaeological excavation. This was in 1940. By communicating with the former inhabitants of this site, the visitors hoped to obtain useful information.

The shaman beat his drum until he got his "power spirit" within his control, and "sent it down." In other words, his special spiritual helper, with which he had established a relationship earlier in his career by ritual means, sank invisibly through the stony ground to an underground house. There it found a manlike creature with long ears, "a kind of radio operator," as an informant soberly told Rainey, and this operator could hear every word said in Tigara, including anything that might adversely affect the forthcoming hunt.

But the underground house was crowded with spirits and full of confusion, so the shaman and the captain's wife moved on to a crack in the ice not far away, and the shaman sent his power spirit down that, this time successfully. There the shaman learned that the underground people had already killed a whale; a good augury. A man down there had a tail like a dog, and a wife. The man said that he would go up in the sky to change the wind to north, which is favorable for whaling, and that his wife would go down under the sea to the house of a "woman who feeds people" and ask her to make the sea calm.

After the shaman and the captain's wife had returned to the clubhouse, and the shaman had related these auspicious spiritual adventures, the men began to work over their harpoons.

When the time for the hunt drew near, old men, shamans, and captains put their heads together to decide which day to begin whaling. The decision had to be made by everyone in concert because all the boats had to set out together. It took only one boat crew to harpoon a whale, but they all had to have equal chances of sighting it, and eight boats were needed to haul it in afterward. The wind had to be from the north, and not too strong, and there had to be an open channel in the pack ice through which whales could swim northward.

Just before the moment had arrived to drag the boats on sleds down to the water's edge, each captain chose a special woman, other than his wife, to stand on the roof of his house, facing the hole in the top of the roof and holding a cord in her hands. Down below, the cord was attached to three deflated sealskin floats. Her job was to pull the floats through the roof, after which they would be blown up and joined to the men's harpoon heads by long thongs.

Now the choice of each such female assistant depended on a special circumstance, the kind of hunting charms that the captain wore to ensure his success. There were only two kinds, those associated with life, and those with death. In the former case, he chose a woman who had recently borne a child. In the latter, it would be one in whose family someone had recently died. The spirit, vital essence, or power, of the woman so selected would not cancel out the power of the captain's charms.

After numerous magical rites the crews walked to their boats, the captain last, accompanied by his wife. When the men were at their stations they shoved off, the harpooner at the ready. But the captain's wife now lay down on the ice, and the boatmen paddled back; the harpooner pretended to make ready to harpoon the captain's wife, and then dipped his harpoon into the water instead. The woman got up and went back to the village, and the crew took off.

In 1940, when the whale hunt began, some ten to fifteen crews were scattered on the edge of the ice for two or three miles, and a mile or two offshore. Each boat was drawn up on the ice with its bow pointing forward, and propped by pieces of ice in such a way that it could be launched at once when needed. The harpoon, with its line and floats attached, rested on a wooden fork on the bow. Much of the time the harpooner sat looking forward in case a whale should spout.

If a whale spouted right next to the boat, the harpooner stood up and held his weapon, while the other crew members shoved the boat out onto the whale's back, and the harpooner plunged his shaft into the whale, twisting it to free the head from the foreshaft, and then tossing overboard the three inflated sealskin floats. Then the harpooner paddled the boat back and the rest of the crew boarded, and paddled rapidly out again toward the spot where the whale had sounded. At that very moment, when the whale's body had sunk

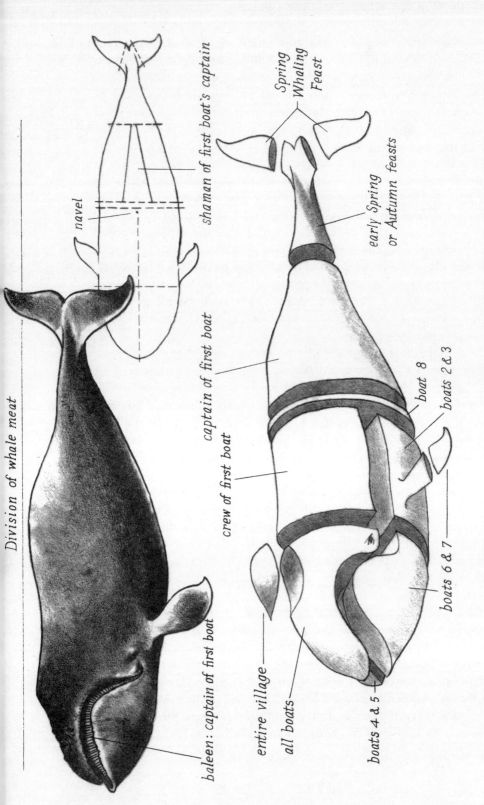

Division of whale meat

navel

shaman of first boat's captain

captain of first boat

crew of first boat

baleen: captain of first boat

entire village

all boats

boats 4 & 5

boats 6 & 7

boats 2 & 3

boat 8

Spring Whaling Feast

early Spring or Autumn feasts

21. How the Tigaran whalers divide the carcass of a bowhead whale. (After J. W. Van Stone, Point Hope, Seattle: University of Washington Press, 1962)

out of sight, the harpooner began singing a magic song of his own, and the captain had begun to sing his. This singing reached the ears of some of the other crews, who shoved off at once. As soon as the floats had risen to the surface, they paddled as fast as they could in that direction, for each crew was eager to stick a second harpoon into the whale.

Sometimes several boats were on hand when the whale rose, and some thrust in more harpoons, while others tried to reach vital parts with long, sharp-tipped spears. When the whale spouted blood, the men with the spears tried to reach its heart. Once dead, the whale rolled over and floated on its back. Then the captain of the first boat to strike the whale pierced its lower lip with a walrus harpoon, and hitched a rawhide towline to it.

The first eight boats to get there all made fast to the towline and dragged the body in together; their position on the line was the order in which they had joined the hunt. As the men paddled in they sang a triumphant song. Once they reached the edge of the ice they cut off the tail flukes, and loaded them into the first boat, to bring them in. Then two men from each crew got together to drag the carcass along the edge of the ice to where it could be hauled up for butchering, on land if possible.

The captain of the first boat sent a messenger up to Tigara, following the exact route over which the boat had been brought down, to give the captain's wife a piece of fluke, held up on the tip of a paddle, and one of her mittens, which had been taken along for luck.

Before towing the body in, the members of each crew had planted a harpoon in the part of the body to which it was entitled, and these rules were scrupulously followed, although there still might be vociferous arguments. Each captain got his traditional part of the body, which he shared in turn with his men. The captain of the first boat got the baleen, all of the body behind the navel down to the tail, except for a section as wide as a man's foot just behind the navel. This piece went to the eighth and last boat. A narrow strip cut from the belly between the eighth boat's strip and the genitals used to be given by the captain of the first boat to his shaman. The forepart of the body ahead of the navel was equally divided between the crews of the third and fourth boats, who also got the lower parts of the flippers. The lower side of the head went to the fourth and fifth boats, while the sixth and seventh boats got one lip each. The top of the head was cut up and eaten at once by everyone present, which meant the whole village. The flukes were saved for the spring whaling feast, and the tail portion for the early spring or autumn feasts.*

A Nootka whale hunt

Many other rites were performed, but for present purposes this is the end of the account as far as the Tikerarmiut are concerned. Let us leave them and fly, like one of their shamans, about eighteen hundred miles southeastward to Vancouver Island. There the Nootka Indians, whose woodworking skill we have admired, also hunted whales of a different kind, and under different conditions. Their principal whale was the California gray—also a baleen whale, but one with a mean disposition. At the end of the bowhead migration northward, a few of these grays sometimes come to Point Hope, but the Tikerarmiut scrupulously leave them alone.

The gray whales used to come in groups, like salmon jumping, as the Nootka would say. They liked to swim close to shore, to sport in the kelp beds, and to bask in shallow water. They have been known to attack people in and out of boats, but this habit did not prevent them from being exterminated on the Northwest Coast by Yankee whalers fairly late in the nineteenth century. None was seen after 1890, but they were rediscovered off the waters of Korea, where the Japanese hunt them, and some have returned from that side of the Pacific to California quite recently.

The waters off Vancouver Island are warmer than those at Point Hope, and ice free. The Nootka used to build excellent boats out of cedar logs, and could go farther out to sea than Eskimo in umiaks. They did not need eight boats to tow in a whale, but usually two went out together so that one could help if the other was in trouble. One member of each crew was the boat owner and captain, and usually a man of high social rank, a matter of importance to the Northwest Coast Indians.

Because whale hunting off Vancouver Island is every bit as dangerous as it is off Point Hope—perhaps more so—it requires just as much psychological preparation. In this case it is the captain himself who makes himself ready by a number of ordeals, wandering in the wilderness to receive spiritual inspiration, going to a magic

*This account is a combination of Froelich Rainey's published data and pages 49-52 of James W. Van Stone, *Point Hope*, (Seattle, University of Washington Press, 1962). Van Stone had access to Rainey's unpublished notes.

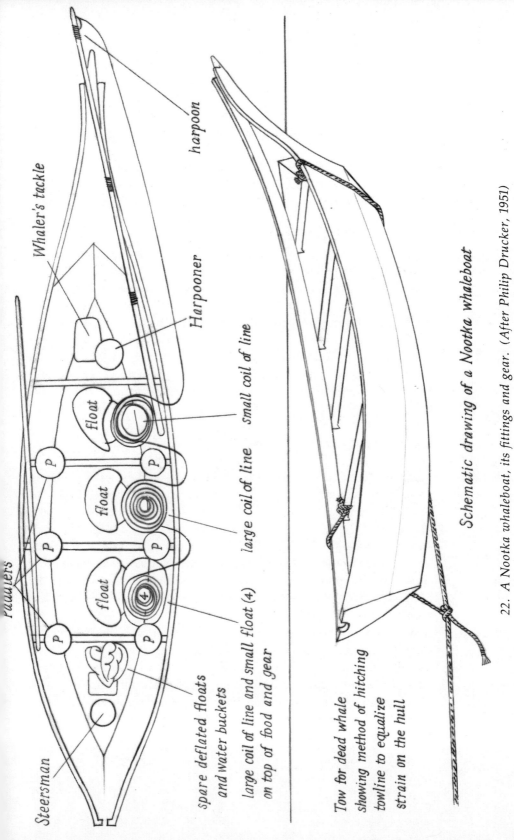

Whaler's tackle

harpoon

Harpooner

small coil of line

large coil of line

spare deflated floats
and water buckets

large coil of line and small float (4)
on top of food and gear

Steersman

paddlers

float

float

float

Tow for dead whale
showing method of hitching
towline to equalize
strain on the hull

Schematic drawing of a Nootka whaleboat

22. A Nootka whaleboat, its fittings and gear. (After Philip Drucker, 1951)

mountain to steal quartz crystals from ferocious guardians, taking many icy cold baths in streams, and scraping his skin with abrasives in an act of self-mortification to test his fortitude, and possibly to enhance his psychic sensitivity. While some of the events that transpired during his period of isolation would be hard to confirm, they were all real to him and symbolically as important as if they had really happened.

The Nootka boat crew consisted of eight men: the harpooner, who was the owner and a chief; six paddlers seated amidships on three thwarts; and a helmsman. The disposition of the crew and equipment may be seen in Figure 22. The Nootka used four floats instead of the three of the Tikerarmiut. The harpooner struck the whale off the starboard side of the boat, and then the boat sheered off sharp to port so that the line could pay off over the starboard side. For this reason the different members had different duties; the first and second starboard paddlers had to throw out the floats and see that the line payed out properly; the front paddler on the port side had to paddle with a deep, hard stroke to steady the canoe, and the other two portside paddlers had to back water to turn the boat to port as soon as the harpoon had struck. In other words, with a crew of eight, there were six different jobs to do, and in split-second synchronization.

Usually the chief-captain-harpooner took along a small seal-hunting boat with a crew of two paddlers to serve as a messenger-escort, and if he hit a whale they were to return to shore to notify the villagers. Also, one or two other whaleboats and crews went along to share the hunt, captained by younger relatives of the chief, and under his command. He had the right to strike first, no matter who had sighted the whale. At dawn the crews separated to cover a wide stretch of water, but in sight of each other. When a whale was sighted one member of the crew waved his paddle overhead to alert the other crews. The harpooner, who had been paddling with the others, let his paddle drop overboard, and it was the duty of the third and last regular starboard paddler to pick it up.

When the whale emerged after having sounded, the helmsman steered the boat so as to come up on the animal's left rear, and the harpooner could thus jab his weapon in by hand over the starboard side of the bow, into the whale's left flank. Then he dropped into a compartment to the rear of the bow to avoid getting tangled in the line which the starboard paddlers were paying out while those on the port side were turning the boat.

Some of the whales leaped clear of the water to shed the line, and others thrashed about with their flukes. Had any member of the crew been lax about his rituals beforehand, he would now be worried about his fate and that of his fellows. Sometimes a canoe was smashed; sometimes a man was caught in a loop in the line and dragged overboard. It was just as well to have another boat or two standing by. Sometimes a whale swam out to sea beyond sight of land, and then it was clear that one of the crew members had been negligent. When the crews finally caught up with the whale, the first thing to do was to cut the tendons of its flukes with long knives on poles, and to do the same with its flippers. Then the whale could swim no more, spouted blood, and died.

But once dead the whale could take in water through its mouth, and sink. So a crew member had to dive overboard and cut a hole through the upper jaw and through the lower lip and tie them together with a rope, and then two floats had to be tied to this fastening to hold up the whale's head, while the other floats were made fast around the body. As with the Tikerarmiut, the towline was hitched to the jaws, and its other end was passed lengthwise under the boat, and made fast to both sides (See Figure 22) in such a way that it might not capsize the boat.

Towing it in was backbreaking work, and sometimes the crew had to sleep at night while the helmsman kept the boat on its course. Sometimes the messengers in the smaller boat arrived in time to dispatch reinforcements — other boats to help with the towing. Once the whale was beached, the chief-captain distributed the meat, but he did it in terms of the relative ranks of the persons concerned. In other words, the social system of the Northwest Coast asserted itself at this point. It was based on wealth in fish and blankets, more than on what each individual had done. It was quite different from the Tikerarmiut way of slicing the whale, and whale meat meant more to the Eskimo than it did to the Northwest Coast Indians, from the standpoint of the food supply. But to both killing whales was great sport, a test of valor, and also a means of regulating behavior.

A Nootka chief calls a whale ashore

But the Nootka not only went out to sea to catch whales; sometimes they tried to call them out of the water to become stranded on the beach. In a somewhat grisly account, Philip Drucker tells how a chief fasted and exposed himself to the cold for four days, along with one or more assistants whose duties included seeing that he was kept alive. He did this in a special hut over a bluff where whales could be seen. Surreptitiously he obtained a human corpse, punched a hole through it from the back of its neck to its oral cavity, and put a tube through the hole so formed. Through this tube he called the whales, hiding behind the corpse. Whether or not he really knew how to call whales, as some Micronesians are able to call porpoises, we may never know.

6.

Fishing

Among people who hunt and fish for food, and not for sport, hunting is mostly men's work, and fishing is more often left to women, particularly if the fish are caught in traps and baskets. Most ways of fishing are less strenuous than hunting, and require less teamwork.

Because of the limitations of the aquatic medium, the equipment needed for fishing is technologically more advanced than are simple hunting weapons. It is not easy to spear or shoot fish in the water because its refraction angle makes aiming difficult, and its density reduces the weapon's velocity and impact force. The spears and arrows that some hunters use in fishing are even more complicated than the ones used for game.

On the other hand a fish does not need to be killed, except to keep it from flapping back into the water. Therefore the principal types of fishing gear are catching and holding devices — hooks and lines, nets, and traps. While land hunting is done on foot, much fishing is done out of boats, which, as we have seen in Chapter Three, take time and skill to build if they are to be of much use.

Quite naturally, fishing is concentrated along seacoasts and on permanently flowing rivers and lakes, and it may also be a seasonal occupation where rivers and lakes are frozen in winter, or where schools of fish swim upstream to spawn once a year. For geographical reasons, there are some hunters who have no fish to catch. They live mostly in deserts. There are other hunters who could catch and eat quantities of fish, but leave them undisturbed. The two outstanding examples of maritime ichthyophobes are the Tasmanians and the Alakaluf.*

The Tasmanians gathered as much shellfish as they could eat at low tide, and by diving, and the only time that they paid any attention to fish was when stingrays invaded the bays where the women were collecting molluscs. Then the men dashed into the breakers, brandishing spears, to drive the noxious stingrays away.

The Alakaluf also had too much shellfish easily available to warrant fishing expeditions. The time that they might have spent fishing

*There is archaeological evidence that fish were once eaten in northwestern Tasmania and in Alakaluf country.

23. *A fish gorge, as used by the Eskimo*

was more profitably used in hunting sea mammals. Both shellfish and sea mammals, in the cool maritime climates where the Tasmanians and Alakaluf lived, provide an abundance of animal fats, which both peoples needed. Most fish have more protein than fat, and both peoples got plenty of protein from other sources.

Methods of fishing: driving and hooking

Aside from picking them out of the water by hand, the simplest recorded technique of fishing seems to be one reported from Australia. There a group of women would walk across a shallow stream or water hole, hip to hip in a close line, and brandish branches torn

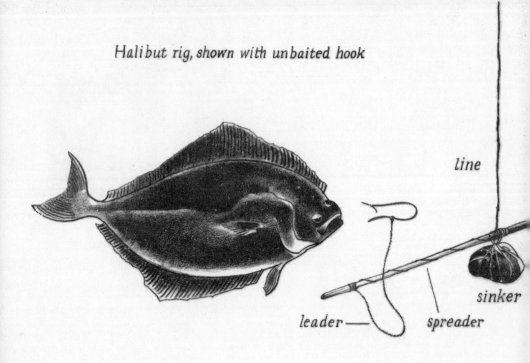

Halibut rig, shown with unbaited hook

line

leader — spreader

sinker

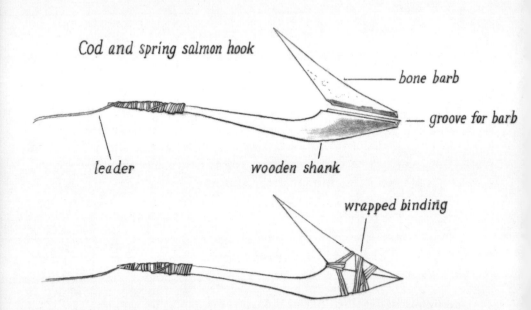

Cod and spring salmon hook

bone barb

groove for barb

leader

wooden shank

wrapped binding

24. Nootka fishhooks for halibut, cod, and spring salmon.
(After Philip Drucker, 1951)

from bushes in front of them. By scuffing their feet and moving the branches in the water, they drove whatever fish they encountered onto the bank.

Both the Andamanese and the Yaghans caught fish with hand lines, and without hooks. They simply tied bait to the end of a line baited with a sinker, and bobbed it up and down, leading the fish to the surface and grabbing it with the free hand. A simple, for them, Eskimo device for hand-line fishing is the fish-gorge, a piece of bone carved in the form of two cones of equal size, with a groove between them, and the line tied to the groove. The fish swallows the gorge end on, and then when the line is pulled, the points of the gorge stick in its throat. Such gorges were used by Upper Paleolithic hunters in Europe, who also made bone fishhooks; they drilled holes in a flat piece of bone and then cut grooves between the holes with flint chisels. Some of the aborigines of the east coast of Australia, and some of the California Indians, made one-piece fishhooks out of abalone shells, first grinding a shell to the shape of a disc, then cutting a hole in its center, and finally removing a section of the rim so formed. One of the fishing devices of the Penobscot Indians was simply a hook made of the wishbone of a bird, sharpened at one end by rubbing it on a stone, and the other end tied to a cord of basswood bark.

As might be expected, some of the fanciest fishhooks were made by various tribes of Northwest Coast Indians, and particularly for catching halibut, a large and succulent fish. The Nootka would steam a section of tough spruce over a fire in kelp bulbs until it was soft, and then bend it into a U-shape, with a narrow space between the two arms near the ends. One end was bent out a little, and the other end barbed on the inside. A leader of nettle fiber was tied to the center of the unbarbed arm, and also to a stick serving as a spreader, to keep the leader from fouling the kelp line reaching to the surface; a stone sinker held the device on the bottom where halibut, like other flatfish, swim about. Once a halibut took the bait, its head would spread the arms of the flexible spruce-root hook, and it had no chance of escape. Some of the northern tribes set out two such U-hooks, one at either end of a spreader.

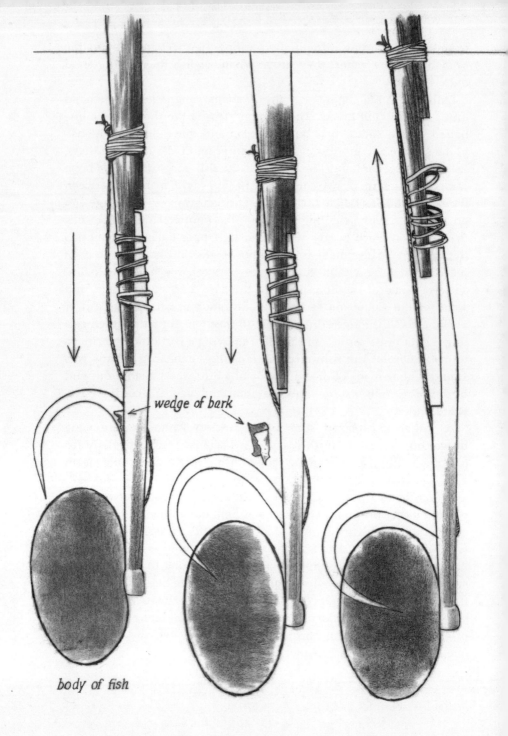

wedge of bark

body of fish

25. The Ainu **marek**, *a complicated device for spearing salmon*

Methods of fishing: raking and spearing

Next to dog-salmon, herring formed the principal staple food of the Northwest Coast Indians, and it appeared early in the year when food supplies were low. When shoals of herring appeared on the surface close to shore, the Indians went out in dugouts, two men to a canoe. One of them paddled and steered in the after part; the other knelt in the bow, holding a herring rake. This was a strip of yew-pole ten to twelve feet long, two or three inches wide, and a half inch thick. In the far third of the strip was set a row of sharp bone pegs. The man in the bow handled the rake as if he were paddling, taking long, deep sweeps, and then twisting the rake sidewise on the up-swing, and shaking the fish into the hull. In this way two men could fill the canoe with herring in a short time. The herring rake was apparently unique to the Northwest Coast Indians, and a most efficient device.

Spearing fish, on the other hand, is quite widely distributed, but commonest in the northern hemisphere and in Fuegian waters. The use of the fish spear has certain built-in limitations. It cannot be thrown, like hunting spears, because the fish may swim away with it, or it may float away. Thus it has to be retained in the hand, and usually needs to be quite long. Some are twelve feet or over, an awkward length to handle in water, particularly if a current or tide is flowing.

There is also the problem of refraction, which makes the fish seem to be where it isn't, unless the fisherman's hand and eye are directly over the fish, as when he is standing on the edge of a dam or weir, or sitting in a moored boat. The Yaghans speared fish from boats moored with lines of kelp, and their spear consisted of a simple wooden shaft with a fixed head of whale rib, and barbed, like the heads of their harpoons.

Northern hunters, including most of those in North America and northeastern Asia, use multiple-headed fish spears. The simplest is the leister, which has two divergent heads made of some springy substance like baleen, and each head is barbed on the inside. The fish is caught between the two, and usually there is a point in the middle to pin the fish to make sure that it cannot wriggle away.

The most complicated kind of fish spear we know of was the Ainu *marek*, so bizarre that Rube Goldberg or Roland Emmet might have invented it. It consisted of a wooden shaft six or seven feet long, a wooden foreshaft, a head, and a movable, pointed hook. The head was either a round knob—the end of the foreshaft, or a set-in piece of staghorn. Being blunt, its function was not to pierce the fish's body, but just to jolt it. The jolt would release an iron hook, pivoted in a hole through the foreshaft so that the point of the hook would swing through an arc toward the head of the spear and pierce the fish's flesh, pinning it to the head.

The shank of the hook, protruding through the hole on one side of the foreshaft, was held under tension by a stretched thong of sea-lion skin. On the other side, the hook was held in place between shreds of bark lining the slot in which it rested. When the head of the spear struck the fish, the impact was enough to jar the hook out of its slot and to let the thong contract.

Unfortunately for accurate study, these *mareks* have not been made for many years, and the only specimens that I have found in museum collections consist of the heads only. There can be no doubt that some *mareks* were activated by the elasticity of sea-lion skin, but for Ainu fishermen living along riverbanks far from salt water sea-lion skin was hard to get. Some of the museum specimens, and some old drawings, show that a cord was attached to the butt end of the shank, and the fisherman pulled the cord the moment the head of the *marek* struck a fish. This method required two simultaneous actions in addition to watching and aiming and striking the fish. The automatic type was easier to operate.

The Ainu got iron hooks by trade from Japanese who made them for trading purposes only, not using them themselves. It is quite probable that the Ainu had made similar ones of bone in earlier times.

However the hook was activated, a *marek* was a tricky weapon to handle. Boys practiced with it, and some grown men were better at using it than others. Being able to bring in a heavy catch of salmon with it was a matter of prestige and personal satisfaction. It could also be operated by elderly men who had not yet lost their manual dexterity, sitting after dark in little huts built over the stream, like smelt-fishing huts on the ice. In the floor of each hut was a hole, through which the old man peered by torchlight to spear smolt, three-year-old dog-salmon that had lost their markings and had become silvery-hued and shiny, and thus easy to see by torchlight. They ran at the end of the fishing season, the only time of year that the Ainu permitted torch fishing, when the darkness fell quite early in the afternoon.

In the spring the taimen swam rather sluggishly upstream in Ainu waters, keeping close to the bottom. The taimen is a large fish weighing up to 120 pounds, and related to the char. Its Linnaean name is *Hucho perryii*, and it is given many local names, e.g. mud trout, which it is not. Although not a great fighter, it is a big fish, and could be caught only with special spears. The Ainu made these spears with twelve-foot shafts, forked foreshafts, and two detachable bone heads like those of harpoons, one on each fork. Each head was tied to a cord lashed farther down the shaft, and when either or both heads became engaged they came loose and the fisherman pulled the taimen in by the shaft.

When an Ainu fisherman had brought in his salmon or taimen and taken out his hook or spearheads, the fish was far from being dead. To stun it, each man carried a two-foot club of willow wood with which he bashed it over the head. The club had to be made of willow, and not of any other kind of wood or of stone because, according to the Ainu creation myth, the backbone of the first man was made of willow, and they therefore considered it the noblest kind of wood. They believed that, if struck with any other kind of club, the fish would not run the following year.

Shooting fish with arrows

Under special circumstances, a number of different peoples shoot fish with bows and arrows, as, for example, the Andamanese, and particularly the inland tribes who had no access to shellfish. They would come down to inlets of the sea for this purpose, and also shoot them in freshwater streams. In both kinds of water the fishes' avenue of escape was so limited that the bowman had a good chance of retrieving his arrows. These arrows had detachable heads like harpoons and like the taimen spear, but in this case two cords led from the single head, one to each end of the arrow. Being longer than the arrow, the cords were wrapped around the shaft and held in place loosely enough so that when the head struck the fish and came loose from the shaft, the shaft would be dragged behind the fish at right angles to its course. Before long the shaft would strike a snag and the fish would be held.

The Akoa Pygmies of Gabon also shot fish under similar circumstances. Our old friend Father Trilles stated that the heads of some of these arrows were curved; being made of mollusc shells, they utilized the latter's natural curvature. Such an arrow was not easy to aim because the arrow curved in flight, and not all men had the skill to shoot fish with it. When the arrowhead struck the fish, it penetrated obliquely and cut a curved path in the fish's flesh. When it came out the other side, the crooked hole held the straight arrow shaft tight.

It would be easy to relegate this account to the Münchhausen file, but it must be borne in mind that Father Trilles was an exceptionally keen observer; and furthermore, he stated that he actually collected such an arrow and presented it to a museum in Paris, where it might be possible to find it.

Stunning fish with poison

The Akoa also caught fish by poisoning shallow, placid pools in streams. For this purpose they used at least seven vegetable substances, leaves, crushed seeds, or flowers, none of which was an ingredient in their arrow poison. The one most commonly used was the flowers of *Cassia reticulata*. After these substances had been thrown into the water, the stupefied fish would rise to the surface, from which they were easily removed. The Mbuti Pygmies of the Belgian Congo, who also had poison, did not do this because they did not usually eat fish.*

In Australia some of the aborigines used twenty different vegetable substances for fish poison, and they also caught emus in water holes in the same way with a special poison, the leaves of *Taphrosia purpurea*. But they never poisoned their weapons, or used poison on mammals, including human beings, although they employed magical "poisons" in warfare. Several Californian tribes poisoned fish with soaproot, squirting cucumbers, and horse chestnut pulp, grinding the ingredients in stone mortars before casting them into the water.

The wide and sporadic distribution of this practice can only mean that the peoples concerned lived in comparable environments where the water in streams and pools was relatively warm, where they ate

*A few were eaten by children. (Colin M. Turnbull, *Wayward Servants*, Garden City, Natural History Press, 1965, p. 166.)

many different kinds of wild plants, and had learned the special properties of inedible ones. In California the Indians who stunned fish with horse chestnut juice may have learned of its toxic qualities by chance, because they also ate the horse chestnuts after having extracted the bitter juice by leaching them in streams in bags.

Fishing with nets

Dip nets and landing nets are easy to make, because all that need be done is to make round or rectangular wooden frames and to fill in the enclosed space with cords or fine thongs by the same techniques used in making women's carrying bags. Most of the peoples who caught fish with hand lines made nets.

Large, unframed nets, like those into which the Mbuti Pygmies and the Birhors drove land animals, are as exceptional among fishermen as they are among hunters. It takes much cordage to construct one, and standard techniques of measuring the gauge with netting needles, and tying the interstices with simple, slip-proof knots. These nets also need floats and sinkers, and what is more important, the cooperation of large numbers of people to set them out and haul them in. Some of the coastal Indians of California are said to have used such seines, but this is the only recorded instance of seining, and it may have been learned from Europeans.

The turtle nets of the Andamanese were made of stiff cordage, and could have been copied from those of the Malay fishermen catching trepang along the coasts of the Andaman Islands. Also, in southeastern Australia, the same people who caught ducks flying over streams with tennislike nets also fished with them. Several men would hold a number of such nets vertically in the water, stretched with poles, and then they swam out in an arc, converging on the opposite bank.

Fishing with weirs, dams, and traps

In Chapter 4 we described methods of catching land animals by driving them into fences and pounds. These drives require large numbers of beaters, and sometimes the joint action of several territorial bands. Economically, to construct these barriers and enclosures is worth the effort only if the game moves about in herds. Though they operate on the same principle, fish weirs and underwater fences are much more profitable in terms of effort because schools of fish enter them under their own power, either with the rise and fall of the tides, or when the fish are swimming upstream to spawn. Fewer people are needed to build and to tend them, and they can be erected within a short distance of camps or villages.

Trapping fish is more efficient than trapping land animals. A hunter usually catches only one animal at a time. His traps are spaced far apart, it takes time and ingenuity to make them, and much walking to tend them. Fish traps can be set close together; they may be made by simple basketry techniques and can be tended by both men and women, and sometimes by children. In many cases, traps are combined with fences and dams, which guide the fish into them. The fences and dams also make it easier for men to spear fish.

In Gabon, the rivers near which the Akoa Pygmies live flood in the rainy season and fall in the dry season. When the water is low, men build walls of stone to form enclosures around pools, and the tops of the walls are under water during the rains. As the waters recede, fish are impounded between the walls, and women can collect them in baskets.

Along the shores of Arnhem Land in northern Australia, old stone weirs may still be seen along the coast where fish were caught at low tide. For both the Akoa and the Arnhem Land aborigines, building and repairing these stone weirs took much time and effort. The Akoa live close to Negro villagers, who catch many fish in the same streams. In Arnhem Land pottery found by archaeologists, and local traditions, suggest contact between the aborigines and otherwise unidentified Indonesians, even before the arrival of trepang fishermen from Halmahera, who actually took some of the aborigines to Macassar during the nineteenth century. In other words, it is unlikely that the stone weirs of either of these peoples were native inventions.

Catching fish in weirs in Gabon and Australia was a minor occupation providing a minor supplement to the protein diet of the Akoa Pygmies and the Arnhem Land aborigines. But salmon trapping was a major source of food to other hunters in cool, northern waters, and an activity that took much of their time in season and greatly influenced their entire way of life.

The waters of the North Atlantic and North Pacific Oceans, between latitudes of about forty and sixty degrees north, are the home of salmon, or used to be, and every year at different times various species of these fish, from spring to fall, commit suicide in vast numbers by swimming upstream in fresh water to procreate their kind and to die. On these runs the salmon age rapidly, as shown by changes in the configuration of their skulls and jaws, and their bones become cartilaginous, making them edible, like their flesh. Were the salmon not harvested, they would be wasted for human consumption.

The rise of industry has polluted many of the streams up which they used to run, and factory ships of various greedy nations capture them with gill nets before they can leave salt water.

In earlier times the rivers emptying into the North Sea were full of salmon in season, and the ancestors of many northwestern European peoples reaped this rich harvest. Salmon must have sustained considerable populations before the introduction of agriculture. The German word *lachs*, meaning salmon, was carried far eastward to India by Indo-European-speaking peoples, where Sanskrit-derived languages still retain the word *lakh*, as in a lakh of rupees, meaning 100,000, or, in effect, an infinite number.

Well into the last century two major groups of hunters still concentrated on salmon harvesting, the Ainu of Hokkaido and some of the Amur River peoples, and the Northwest Coast Indians of North America plus those of the Columbia River basin. All of them speared salmon, but caught many others in combinations of weirs and traps. I propose to conclude this chapter by describing the technical equipment of the Northwest Coast Indians, as exemplified by the Nootka, and presenting a synopsis of the Ainu annual fishing cycle and of the rites they performed to assure the continuity of the salmon runs from year to year. Whether or not these rituals worked is of less importance than the fact that they reduced the anxiety of the fishermen.

Nootka fish traps

Before the salmon began to run upstream, and after the people of each community had moved from their winter quarters to their

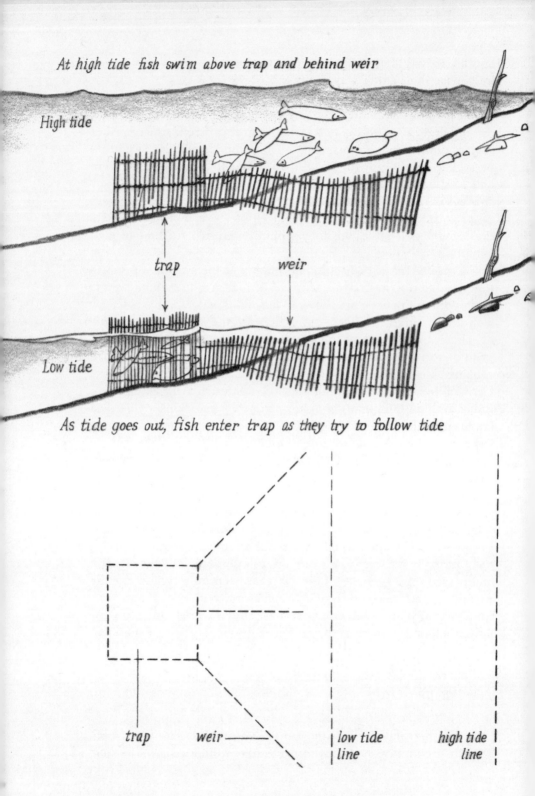

At high tide fish swim above trap and behind weir

High tide

trap   weir

Low tide

As tide goes out, fish enter trap as they try to follow tide

trap   weir   low tide   high tide
               line   line

26. Nootka salmon traps and weirs built in tidal water at the mouths of rivers. (After Philip Drucker, 1951)

summer villages on the shore, the men built tidewater traps. They had cut fir poles, and pounded them into the mud with large, flat stones. Each trap consisted of a rectangle about twelve feet long and six wide, and six to seven feet high, just high enough to be submerged at high tide, so that the fish could swim over them as the tide advanced. They covered the roof and sides with fir boughs twisted in and out between the poles like latticework or wattling, leaving gaps large enough to let water flow in and out while containing the fish (Figure 26). They also left two entrances on the shoreward side, wide enough for men to get through to collect the fish. To guide the fish into the entrances they constructed three fences of the same materials, the outer two being V-shaped and the middle one at right angles to the axis of the trap. These fences were of the same height as the trap itself, and low enough to be covered at high tide. They did not extend all the way to the high water mark on the shore. The salmon swam over them as the tide advanced, and were drawn into them as it retreated. At low tide the men entered the traps to throw the fish out toward the shore.

When the fish were about to swim upstream, the men made rectangular traps similar to the tidewater ones but smaller, with floors, and removable for emptying. They set these in pairs near the mouths of the rivers. The fish were guided into the narrow entrances of the traps by short, convergent fences forming parts of a longer weir across the stream.

Farther upstream, on the next stage of the salmon's journey, the men caught the fish in cylindrical basket traps, with one end of each trap closed and a door tied near the closed end of the cylinder, for removing the fish. To make such a trap they laid out parallel rods between twelve and eighteen feet long, laid four very flexible spruce branches horizontally across them, and lashed the branches to the rods. Then they bent the branches into hoops with the rods inside, and tied the ends of each branch together. These traps were set on shears, and in pairs, with their open ends upstream and the closed ends raised just out of the water. Various combinations of convergent wooden weirs were set upstream to turn the fish and to guide them into the traps, where the fish could not turn around and were held by the force of the current until they died.

They made other traps out of rods and branches by the same method, but in the form of a cone, with a wide mouth. The narrow end was closed by a movable door. Such a trap was also set out on shears, with the wide end well submerged and the narrow end completely above water. The purpose of this trap was to catch salmon that had already succeeded in swimming upstream. Men stationed above the trap drove the fish down into it, where they were held gasping in the raised end. The men opened the door and clubbed the salmon (Figure 27).

Conical fish trap

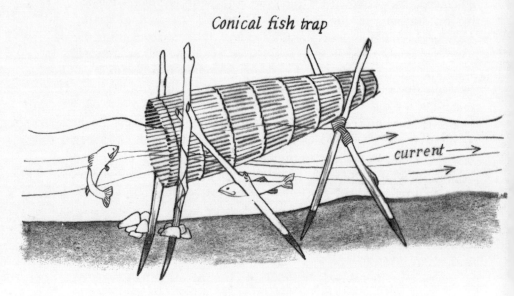

27. *A Nootka conical fish trap set in a stream. Salmon swimming upstream are deflected by weirs and carried by current into the trap. (After Philip Drucker, 1951)*

A fourth device that held the fish high and dry was for use still farther upstream, at the foot of falls. It was a shelf of poles with a backstop, both set at an angle. Salmon that failed to leap over the falls fell backward onto the shelf, where they remained until collected.

The Ainu Fishing Calendar

Unlike the Northwest Coast Indians, the Ainu were essentially an inland people. Hokkaido has no deep inlets, and the Ainu did little offshore fishing, except now and then for swordfish. Most of their fishing was done upstream, where the salmon spawned. Instead of sea mammals, they hunted principally deer and bear. With three seasons each for fishing, deer hunting, and bear hunting, they had a busy calendar, highlighted as follows:

Early March: bear hunters capture cubs.
Mid-March: deer hunting in snow.
Mid-April: bear hunters out again with set bows.
Late April: taimen start to run, fishing begins.
May: taimen and mixed fishing continues.
June: mostly collecting vegetable foods.
July: men set up weirs and cherry salmon appear.
August: cherry salmon fishing.
September: cherry salmon fishing ends, dog-salmon appear.
Early October: dog-salmon fishing begins.
Mid-October: deer fences are set up: deer drive.
    dog-salmon fishing continues.
Mid-November: younger men hunt bear in mountains, older men spear
    smolt by torchlight.
December: little activity.
January: deer hunting in mountains followed by bear sacrifices.
February: bear ritual ends.

The first fishing season did not begin until mid-April because the rivers had been frozen during the winter, and only then did the taimen begin to run. Food supplies were running low, and the people had been living mostly on preserved dog-salmon caught in November, and on winter venison. Fresh fish made a welcome change. Although very large fish, the taimen were also numerous, and dace, a member of the carp family, were running at the same time. The men caught the taimen with the long, double-headed spears described earlier, and set out basket traps for the dace.

The Ainu basket trap is a half cone of wickerwork fixed to a flat board floor. It is movable, and although it can be staked out at any suitable place in the river bed by men, it is tended by women. At the end of the fishing season these traps can be carried back to the Ainus' houses, and kept through the winter to be used again the following year. But the dams, weirs, platforms, and peep huts that they build have to be set up over again every year, because the ice floes in the river sweep them away in the spring.

When used for salmon later on in the year, the basket traps are set behind weirs, with their mouths pointing upstream, and the fish deflected into them are held by the force of the current. When the traps are set for dace there are no weirs to deflect the fish. The traps have to be set with their mouths facing downstream, and in order to keep the fish from being carried out again by the current, the rim of the opening is furnished with sharp, flexible sticks pointing inward like a shark's teeth. The dace get their gills caught in these barbs, and the women tending the nets have to extricate them. The barbs are removed at the end of the dace season.

While this dace-trapping is going on, some of the men are spearing taimen, but others are netting catfish. Although the catfish are not migratory, and are available whenever the river is free of ice, spring is the only season when it is profitable to take them. The device used for catching catfish is the bag net, which needs a team of three men. Two men hold poles in the stream, with both hands. When the net stretched between the poles is full, the third man pulls the cord that closes the net.*

When the cherry salmon began to run in July, the men speared them with the *marek*, previously described. For this purpose they used a relatively small *marek*; larger ones were reserved for dog-salmon, a larger and stronger fish. During the middle of the day the cherry salmon were often sluggish, and lazed idly in the quiet pools, hiding between rocks and under snags. Then the spearmen would coax them out by dragging a lure across the bottom. This decoy was nothing but a piece of iron wrapped in blue cloth — of the kind the women sewed on their coats — and tied on with white bark. At the end was a two-inch piece of white bone, tipped with a tail of bark and red cloth. When it was tugged at just the right speed, and with the right motion, the salmon found this enticing tidbit irresistible.

While the cherry salmon were running upstream and the men were spearing them from the banks or from dugout canoes, the women stood on platforms built over wooden weirs. The weirs themselves did not quite reach the surface of the water, and the fish were obliged to swim or leap over them. From the platforms, the women caught them on the upstream side in hand nets. Each net was made fast at its mouth to the two arms of a forked stick and a movable crossbar. A fisherwoman could close her net over a fish by pulling a string to draw the crossbar toward the crotch.

Later, when some of the salmon were moving downstream after spawning, the women caught them in unbarbed basket traps facing

*Watanabe (cf. Bibliography) says that only two men operated the bag net when catching catfish, but I find this hard to visualize.

upstream. Some of the men also speared them by daylight through the slits in the floors of their peep huts.

The third and most important round of the fishing season came with the arrival of the dog-salmon in October and November. This was the last run before the river froze, and the Ainu depended on dried and smoked dog-salmon for their staple food during the winter.

In the course of this third fishing season, the Ainu used different techniques in different parts of the river and phases of the run. In some times and places, they speared them at sunrise and sunset from the peep huts built for the cherry salmon, and lured and speared them from the banks during the middle of the day when the fish were sluggish. Toward the end of the season, elderly men speared them from their peep huts by torchlight, for the winter solstice was near, and at that latitude the days were short. These *marek*-wielders wore many coats one over the other, and warmed their hands by their torches. At the same time, the women worked on the weirs with bag nets, by torchlight.

Ainu fishing rites

The sequence of events that transpired during the three fishing seasons, as outlined and condensed above, seem matter-of-fact enough, but that is only part of the story. The Ainu were taking the chance that the dog-salmon run would fail, and dog-salmon were needed for survival during the winter. In one recorded instance, it failed in the Ishikari River in 1725. During the following winter and spring, over two hundred Ainu starved to death in that river valley.

The other part of the story is ritual, symbolic attempts to stave off such a disaster, as necessary as the rites of elephant hunters and whalers. In the Ainus' case, they needed supernatural assurance that nothing that they themselves could fail to do through carelessness or impiety would inadvertently bring about such a calamity.

The Ainu believed in a hierarchy of deities, with high gods and underlings to whom the former delegated some of their duties. Of top rank was Kamui Fuchi, the fire goddess and guardian of the hearth. Being invisibly present at all that was done and said indoors, she knew everything that went on in each household, and would report any breach of behavior to Petorun Kamui, the freshwater goddess stationed at the head of each river, and she would, in turn, relay this information to Chepatti Kamui, the owner of the dog-salmon. Chepatti Kamui lived, in human form, in an Ainu-like house in the open sea beyond the mouth of the river up which the dog-salmon ran, and if he were displeased at the treatment accorded his dog-salmon in any particular year, he would withhold them the following year.

Therefore when dog-salmon first began to appear at the local spawning grounds, the chief of the villagers to whom that part of the river belonged organized a ritual directed toward the Fire Goddess and the River Goddess, offering them both prayers and *inaus*, which are sticks of special kinds of wood so cut that undetached, curling shavings were left of various parts of them; each kind of stick was a special spirit-placing — a kind of perch for a different god or lesser spirit to rest on. Then the male head of each house in the settlement made his own *inaus*, and all the heads of households carried them to the riverbank and set them up near the spawning grounds of the dog-salmon.

The member of each settlement who caught the first dog-salmon sent it to his chief, and it was recognized as a sacrifice to the Fire Goddess. The same man also invited to his own house the other members of the community, to eat the rest of his first catch. The lower jaws of each dog-salmon from this catch were saved, as well as the lower jaws of those caught later on, and *inaus* were tied to them. At the end of the season the chief summoned all of the heads of households together again to conduct another ceremony, to bid good-bye and come-again to the salmon's spirits. They did this, with appropriate prayers, by casting back into the river the salmon's mandibles with *inaus*. Thus when the salmon's spirits returned to their master in his house under the sea, he would know that they had arrived safely after having been paid due respect by the people who had caught them. If no adverse report had been already forwarded to him from the Fire Goddess through the agents of the Goddess of Fresh Water, then the dog-salmon would be sent back the next year.

It may be added that the timing of events, the techniques of fishing, and the accompanying rites varied in detail from valley to valley and from one segment of a single river and its tributaries to another, owing to the distance of each fishing station from the sea, the way the fish ran, and local ritual procedures. Thus a routine learned in one place would have its local peculiarities. If a stranger were allowed to take part right away in the fishing in one headman's domain, he might make mistakes and thus imperil the next year's catch. This possibility served as a plausible rationalization for the local people to be wary of strangers and to keep their fishing rights to themselves. Even if it had served no other purpose, the complex of geography, technology, and ritual was a powerful force in assuring both maximum efficiency in fishing and the internal cohesion of the people of which each territorial group was composed.

7.

Gathering

This afternoon I picked, in twenty minutes, one and a half quarts of wild blackberries within ten feet of my study, and then read in the local newspaper that a lost twelve-year-old boy had lived alone, without harm, for eight days on a mountain in New Hampshire on berries and brook water. Our fields and woods are full of roots and other plants that the Indians used to eat. Gathering is the simplest way for people to get wild foods from their environment.

Our closest primate kin, the great apes, do not ordinarily gather food in the sense that we do, for they eat it on the spot, individually. The boy lost in New Hampshire did that too, and others who go out in groups to collect wild food may eat some of it in the same way, but they carry most of it home and share it, some raw, some cooked, with others.

As with game and fish, gathered foodstuffs are usually more abundant in some seasons than in others, and people have to know when and where to find them. This is easier than hunting because plants and slow game either do not move at all, or if they do, they do not have to be chased very far, and a woman or child can catch them. Furthermore it is easier to learn about the behavior of plants, molluscs, and the like than about that of animals and birds. One does not have to outwit a yam, clam, mussel, tortoise, or hillful of termites. Thus there is less of an element of chance in gathering than in hunting and fishing, and little danger except from snakes and bees.

Therefore not as much immediate ritual is needed in gathering or fishing, because the element of chance governing success or failure has been transferred from the vagaries of the hunt or run of fish to the general cycle of the weather. But if this cycle is subject to annual variation, anticipatory rites may be held, relieving doubts and anxiety over the rainfall, the growth of grass, and the swarming of locusts. Then when the fruits are ripe and the hives heavy with honey, simple first-fruit ceremonies may be held, comparable to the rites of spring among agriculturalists.

Implements need not be as well designed or as complicated for gathering as for hunting and fishing because fruits may be picked by hand or reached with a hooked pole. Roots, tubers, small animals, and some insects and their larvae may be dug from the ground, their nests, or rotten treetrunks with a simple pointed stick. Nuts and acorns may be picked off the trees or shaken to the ground; seeds may be beaten into containers with sticks, and shellfish pried from rocks with special sticks with spatulate ends. These are jobs that women can do as well as men, even if the women are accompanied by children.

Hunting requires much practice and skill, and freedom from household duties, including the constant care of young children — duties which normally fall to women. So men are usually the only hunters, with a few exceptions, as where women serve as beaters in net hunts and surrounds, or, as in Tasmania, where women climb trees after opossums, or among the Tiwi of Melville Island, northern Australia, where some women, members of polygynous households, kill wallabies to help feed their elderly husbands.

In cold, northern regions, where the temperature lies below freezing for many months and the ground is buried in snow, the fruits and berries are out of season and tubers and bulbs are unavailable. In such places women's work is concentrated on household duties, and particularly on making warm clothing. There the dietary balance between foodstuffs collected, and game and fish, is heavily weighted on the latter side, but there are some parts of the world where the ground never freezes, different fruits ripen in succession, trees are always in leaf, and game is scarce or little needed. There the scales tip in the other direction. The men too dig roots, and when the bees' nests are choked with honey, all other work ceases until it has been gathered.

A truce with tigers: the nonhunting Kadar

Root digging without hunting reaches its peak among the Kadar, a relict people living in the Cardamon Hills of southern India, located in the Western Ghats of Cochin, in Kerala State.

Over two thousand feet high although less than one hundred miles from the Arabian Sea, their country is one of softly rounded though steep granite mountains, scarred in places by high cliffs, but otherwise covered with rich, perennial forests, and subject to heavy storms during the southeast monsoon, and lighter ones during the northwest monsoon, with occasional showers in between.

The forest abounds in wild fruits, cardamon seeds, wild honey, and eight kinds of yams and other tubers and roots which used to form the staple food of the Kadar. Game is varied and plentiful, including the gaur (a wild ox which is incorrectly called "bison" in India), the tiger, the leopard, the Indian elephant, the spotted deer *(Cervus axis)*, the mouse deer or water chevrotain *(Hyemoschus aquaticus)*, the white-faced monkey (a macaque), and the black monkey (a langur), as well as many birds.

Having no hunting weapons, the Kadar do not kill the gaur nor even eat its flesh, which they regard with the horror which a Muslim feels about pork. Neither do they eat the white-faced monkey because they say it looks too human, nor the flesh of elephants, tigers, or leopards, because they consider these to be noble animals, and they would be unable to kill them anyhow. It may also be said that the Kadar have a truce with tigers, which in the old days left them strictly alone. Of all the peoples who ever went there, only Kadar could walk through the jungle without fear of tigers, and they say that when a tiger was staring at a Kadar from behind, he could sense its presence and walk quietly away. Now that the Kadar have been cozened by the contractors exploiting the lumber into eating rice and wearing sweaty clothing, they smell like plainsmen to the tigers, and are in danger, because by changing their odor, the Kadar have broken their truce. Indeed, the Kadar can still distinguish between the smell of the excrement of rice-eaters and that of yam-eaters.

During the late 1940s, when U. E. Ehrenfels (formerly Baron von) was doing his definitive fieldwork among the Kadar, he reported the following statements about the depredations of a man-eating tiger. It had killed and eaten two children at a time when the Kadar were eating rice and wearing clothing. Before each death an old woman shivered and shook for several days. When tigers had been near the camp earlier, she had done likewise, but the tigers had gone away.

After the first child had been eaten, and its remains found, its father went to the spot, fell on his hands and knees, and crawled to the putrid and scattered remnants of its body. He growled, and picked up the child's skull in his teeth and, still crawling, carried it to a pit that had been dug nearby and dropped it in, and then similarly transported the severed hands and feet. Finally he pinned these grisly objects to the bottom of the pit with stakes. During this ordeal the father was in a trancelike state, and those that had watched him said that he must have been possessed by the Hindu god Aiyappan, who rides on a tiger. But the old woman's warning may well

Digging sticks

trade iron tip

28. A Kadar digging yams. (After U. R. Ehrenfels, 1952)

have been a carryover from the time before the Hindus arrived, and the father's behavior, with or without Aiyappan's help, must have been an older, and presumably rarer, kind of performance too.

The Kadar like to recall the mythical days when their ancestors' life in the forest was idyllic. Delicious fruits hung low from the branches waiting to be picked, and fat black monkeys perched on the lower limbs with their long tails hanging down. All that the Kadar needed to do was to reach up and pull down mangoes and monkeys when they felt hungry. But one day some silly little boys and girls said: "Let us see if there isn't something else to eat under the ground." So they took some short sticks and began digging, and found succulent yams just under the surface.

Once the Kadar had begun to eat yams the fruit grew scarcer and harder to pick, and the monkeys' tails shortened so that they could not easily be reached. The yams too were now harder to get and sank deeper underground. Then the Kadar had to dig them with longer sticks, tipped with pieces of stone. Then they were obliged to walk about the forest digging, to get their food, covering more ground each day. Finally, in 1890, the contractors built their forest tramway and the Kadar needed still longer sticks shod with iron which the contractors gave them in exchange for cardamon seeds, honey, beeswax, and umbrella sticks. And the happy days were over.

In those days, when the Kadar wore only bark-cloth breechclouts or leaves, and bathed every day in the forest streams, they used to go out into the forest every morning to get their food. They went by families; a man, his wife, their children, and a dog. Most of the time they spent digging yams, but once in a while they would catch a tiny mouse deer in the brush along the streambed, and club him with their digging sticks. In the afternoon, after they had returned, a man might say quietly to his wife: "Let us go out and collect some firewood," and they would disappear into the forest to make love, and then bathe in a pool. Afterward they would cook and eat their yams, and when night fell the forest would become noisy, and the Kadar could tell each species by its calls and its rustlings. At night hosts of fireflies would flit about under the canopy of foliage. As far as our sources inform us — and they are good ones — the Kadar had no rituals concerning yams, which were constant factors in their lives.

The Chenchus: hunters forced into yam digging

Some four hundred miles north-northeast of the Kadar country lives another food-gathering people, the Chenchus, one of the many in southern India who also rely heavily on yams as their main source of food, although the men hunt deer with bows and arrows when they are able. The Chenchus had been pushed into hilly country north of the Kistna River, open parkland where game is relatively scarce, and furthermore, where hunting has been officially forbidden by local law. In winter they move about in the higher hills and in summer, when water is scarce and the heat oppressing, they camp in rock shelters along the banks of the Kistna.

They collect six species of yams and other roots, some of which are available the year round while others are seasonal. The most prized is a large, round, bulbous root that grows only during the rains. Each person, man or woman, takes along an iron-tipped digging stick and a basket, and while they are out digging they roast and eat some of the yams, bringing the surplus back to camp.

The women go out in groups each day and return before dark, whereas the men often stay away three or four days at a time, in order to exploit the corners of their territory that the women cannot reach in a single day's expedition. Unlike the Kadar, Chenchu men and women do not dig yams together. This division of labor in yam digging seems to be a recent adaptation to a reduction in the game supply, one that follows the hunting pattern.

The dry season, spent along the riverbanks, is a time of hunger, when the Chenchus live mostly on thick-shelled seeds that they crack with stones. The time of greatest abundance comes in April and May, when two kinds of wild figs and other fruits ripen, and the corollas (rings of petals) of the mohua tree (Bassia latifolia) fall to the ground. At this time they live in small villages in the middle of their territories, where they have permanent dwellings.

In anticipation of this event they may burn the grass under the trees, to make the corollas easier to pick up. Some they eat fresh; others they dry, boil, and ferment. According to old accounts they used to drink this brew, but more recently they have learned how to distill it in a simple still consisting of two pots and a bamboo tube, and they get very drunk on the raw spirits. As this operation is illegal they hide the stills in the woods, like moonshiners. At the end of May wild mangoes and a third species of fig ripen, and the people

G

become plump. During the rains many leafy vegetables spring up, and the Chenchus eat their leaves.

Because of their drunkenness, their disorderly conduct, and their occupation of land that others wanted, most of the Chenchus living north of the Kistna were forcibly evacuated by the police in 1950 and 1951 to the plains below, where they were made to live in agricultural villages.

Wild yams and honey bees in the Old World tropics

The Kadar and Chenchus were only two of a dozen or so nonagricultural peoples of India that depended much on wild yams for their basic food, and the same may be said for others in the Andaman Islands, Malay Peninsula, and parts of Australia, but not of Tasmania, where there were none. Wild yams belong to the family *Dioscoreacae*, of which the most suitable for human consumption belong to the genus *Dioscorea*, with over six hundred species distributed over the world's tropics and warm temperate zones.* Not a single species is common to the Old and New Worlds, and only one to Asia and Africa. In the New World only one species, dubiously documented, may have edible tubers, and that one is not found in hunting-gathering territory.

The African species are not numerous, but both Pygmies and Bushmen eat them. In South Africa *Dioscorea elephantipes* is a giant yam weighing up to seven hundred pounds. It is usually found lying between projecting rocks, the walls of which protect it from losing moisture into the surrounding earth. Among the Pygmies only women collect yams, but among the Bushmen both sexes do so. Mrs. Elizabeth Marshall Thomas, who lived among the Gikwe Bushmen, tells in passing of a Gikwe man who noticed a crack in the soil indicating the presence of a large yam. He kept this in mind for nearly a year and when the time came he went back there and unearthed it.

*I. H. Burkill, "The organography and the evolution of the Dioscoreaceae," London, Journal of the Linnaean Society, Botany, Vol. 56, 1960, pp. 323–412. N. I. Vavilov, *The Origin, Variation, Immunity and Breeding of Cultivated Plants*, (Selected Writings). Waltham, Mass., The Chronica Botanica Co., 1949/50.

In order to bear, yams have to be pollinated by flying insects, and particularly by bees. It may therefore be no coincidence that the geographical distribution of honey bees is much the same as that of yams, except that the bees' ranges are wider, as they pollinate many other species. In Tasmania there were neither yams nor bees, and neither yams nor honey were eaten by the surviving hunting and gathering peoples of the New World.

In Tasmania a minor substitute for honey was available in the sap of a tree, *Eucalyptus gunnii*, which was limited to the central part of the island between two thousand and thirty-five hundred feet of altitude, a relatively small part of Tasmania. It is a large tree, running up to twelve feet in diameter. Cockatoos attacked it and opossums tore holes in its bark, while ants swarmed over it.

The natives cut holes in the trunk a short distance from the ground, using sharp stones, and then carved out a basin at the foot of the tree into which the sap drained. In a large grove visited by G. A. Robinson, the man who removed the aborigines from Tasmania in the 1830s after the Black War, every tree had been so tapped, and he saw over a quart of juice each in some of these basins. The liquid was sweet, and tasted like cider. In some of the basins the sap had dried into a white paste which the natives ate.

Honey ants and honey bees

While there are native honey bees in parts of Australia, mostly in the relatively well-watered north and east, in some of the drier parts of the continent their place is taken on the aboriginal menu by a honey ant, a species of the genus *Myrmecocystus*. Workers of this species obtain sugar which exudes from galls on acacia trees. The galls are made by tiny wasps that irritate the twigs to the point of malformation. The worker ants ingest this sugar until their abdomens begin to swell, and then go back to their underground nests and regurgitate it into the mouths of sterile females, whose abdomens then swell up to over a half-inch in diameter, and weigh eight times as much as the ant herself. Immobilized by these burdens, the females hang by the claws of their tiny feet from the walls of their nests, until the time comes when the other ants are hungry, and come back to feed on their reserve. The aborigines know when the ant honey is ripe, and how to find the nests, and women and children especially, while on walkabouts after yams and other foods, dig them up and eat the shiny reddish ants like candy.

In the New World honey ants of the same genus behave in exactly the same way, all the way from Mexico City to southern Idaho, at altitudes of between five thousand and seven thousand feet, where the galls are formed on shin oaks, at least in Colorado. Only in brief rainy seasons in summer or early September do the galls ooze honey. Indians of the Southwest and of Mexico, mostly if not wholly agricultural, munch these honey capsules, and in Mexico some of the Indians make a drink of it, mixed with water. I have yet to find a reference to the nonagricultural Indians farther north eating them, and would welcome it.

True honey bees fall into two practical categories, stinging and stingless, and as one might ruefully expect, the hardest stingers pack away the most honey, and put it in the most difficult places to reach. Both kinds belong to the subfamily of Apini, social insects that build nests containing wax combs to hold grubs and honey. Of the Apini one genus, *Apis*, is by far the most productive of wax and honey, wild and domestic.*

In India, Southeast Asia, and Indonesia, the world's center of honey bees as well as of yams, three species are outstanding, *Apis dorsata, A. florea,* and *A. cerana. Apis dorsata* builds a large hive hanging from a branch of a tall tree or under an overhanging projection near the top of a cliff. I have seen such hives in the Kadar country, over a hundred feet up, full and bulging like giant breasts. The Kadar were looking at them too, for the honey season had almost arrived. Such a hive can contain up to seventy thousand cells and can be a yard long and thirty inches wide, yielding from fifty to two hundred pounds of honey in a season. In India, ninety percent of the honey and wax reaching the market comes from such *A. dorsata* hives.

Dorsata bees are very aggressive and sting like hornets, and sometimes their stings are fatal. New swarms are formed when some members leave a nest and build another one on the same branch, or another branch of the parent tree. As many as ninety-two such hives have been counted on a single tree. In the summer the bees leave their nests and migrate, sometimes crossing mountains up to six thousand feet high, and when they return they may or may not come back to their point of departure; some build new hives as far as seventy miles away. For this reason peoples to whom honey

*Remy Chauvin, *Traité de Biologie de l'Abeille,* Paris: Masson et Cie., 5 vols., 1968.

is an important source of food cannot be sure of finding *dorsata* hives in the same place each year.

More limited in range is *Apis florea*, which lives in the same regions but only on plains at altitudes below fifteen hundred feet. It builds large, globular nests on the limbs of trees, also stings, and also yields much honey.

Apis cerana nests in protected rock cavities, and can live at altitudes of over eight thousand feet, and also at higher latitudes than *dorsata* or *florea*. It yields less honey than the other two, but doesn't sting. Instead it clutches its victim and tries to bite. This is the most important honey bee sought by the Veddas in Ceylon, and it is more reliable than the others, because it does not move about very far.

In Africa south of the Sahara there is only one high-yielding honey bee, *Apis adansonii*. It ranges intermittently from the southern borders of the Sahara to the Kalahari, and is chiefly found in forests, savannas, and desert valleys, and is the principal source of honey for the Pygmies and Bushmen. There are also stingless bees in Africa who nest on the ground, but they produce much less honey.

Collecting honey from trees

Men who collect honey from tall trees or the faces of cliffs are faced with two principal problems, how to reach the hives and how to keep from being stung. It is a risky business, for a brave man may fall several hundred feet to an almost certain death. It is the only way of collecting food that is at all comparable in danger to hunting elephants or whales. But the reward is great, because whole families or groups of families can join in the feast.

If the bees' nest is in a tree, only one man is needed to climb it, but if it is on the side of a cliff, usually several men are needed, particularly when the honey gatherer has to climb down a rope from above. We have several accounts of both. Among the Akoa Pygmies of Gabon, the men watch the movements of the honey guide, a bird that also eats honey, and this bird leads them to the honey tree, where the best nests are located in the upper branches. Then one of the men, chosen to do the climbing, smears himself all over with a bee-repellent paste made from the juice of the crushed leaves of a species of *Aristolochus*, also used for snakebite, mixed with the sticky pulp of the fruit of an amomum tree, laying it particularly thickly over his face and hands.

He then climbs a neighboring tree, either with cords around his waist or via creepers, if the tree has any, cuts a liana, ties himself to it, and swings to the hive, clutches the trunk with his legs, and then plunges both hands into the hive and methodically tears it apart, comb after comb. He wraps the combs in leaves and lowers them to the spectators below with a second liana which he had brought with him. Each time he lowers a comb the people underneath tie more leaves to the liana to wrap the combs in, and he keeps this up, surrounded all the while by a cloud of bees, until the nest is empty, and then he climbs down.

Meanwhile neither he nor his companions on the ground have tasted the honey. Once he has joined them the bee-man looks behind him, spits on the ground, picks up a piece of honeycomb, removes the bees, if any, and lifts the piece in the air, reciting: "To right, to left, to thee I give, to right, to left, who glides, who flies, black and light, dark and shiny, to thee I give, this I offer thee; receive it, take it, master."

He now throws the piece of honeycomb behind him into the forest without looking, and no one will touch it. Then he spits again, and they all eat some of the honey, and the feast begins. Father Trilles witnessed this performance, and once while in a distant village among other Pygmies he saw a bee-dance acted out in the same way.

Among the Mbuti Pygmies of the Ituri Forest, during the honey season the net hunters, who live in bands of several families during the rest of the year, split up into smaller groups to collect honey, while those that hunt by stalking with bows and arrows combine into larger units both for their annual surround and for the honey season that follows it immediately. In either case the bee hunters either climb a tree with lianas about their waists, or climb a neighboring tree and swing to the honey tree by their arms. As most of the bees there do not sting much, no special repellent is needed, but the nests are usually built inside of rotten wood near the tops of the trees. The climbers have to chop them out either with hatchets or with fire-hardened pieces of hard wood. They carry torches up with them, and wooden tubes, through which they blow smoke to evict the bees. They too have bee-songs and bee-dances, details of which are not available.

The Italian anthropologist-explorer Lidio Cipriani once witnessed a bee hunt among the Önge of Little Andaman in the Andaman Islands, and there the men who climb the trees use another vegetable deterrent. A man who is about to climb a bee tree picks a handful of leaves from a plant which Cipriani was unable to identify, and crams them into his mouth. He chews them to a greenish pulp which he smears all over his body, especially in his hair. On the way up the tree he chews another mouthful, and spits the juice at the bees. Cipriani chewed some himself and found them without taste or odor. At the end of the bee hunt the Önges indulged in a long feast on the beach, eating many wooden bowls of honey, several pigs that the men had shot, and a heap of fish caught by the women, with much singing and dancing.

Collecting honey from cliffs in India and Ceylon

In India and Ceylon, where many bees build their hives on the faces of cliffs, another technique is necessary. This has been described in some detail for the Chenchu, but is mostly the same among other hunting peoples there. Two or three men go out together, carrying a stout rope and other equipment. Near the top edge of the cliff over the combs one man secures an end of the rope to a stake or tree, and leaves another man to guard it. This second man is usually a son-in-law or brother-in-law of the climber; the Chenchu say that they would not trust their own brothers to do this. The rope has a stick at the other end, for the honey collector to stand on. Before he climbs down he offers a prayer to one of his gods.

If the comb is attached to a flat surface, flush with the rim of the cliff, the man on the end of the rope first smokes the bees out with a torch of dry leaves, and then cuts the comb loose with a wooden sword, and puts it in his honey basket which is attached to another cord held by the man, or one of the men, above, and that man pulls it up and lowers it again for the next comb.

But if the comb is located under an overhang, the bee-man also takes down with him a bamboo pole with a spike in one end, and the man above holds a cord tied to the pole, just as he did with the cord attached to the basket in the previous instance. Like the Akoa Pygmy on his liana, the Chenchu bee-man swings on his rope in order to get close enough to the comb to thrust the spike into it and hold it fast. Then he keeps on swinging, until he is close enough to cut the comb free with his wooden sword, and the man above pulls up the pole with the comb attached.

If the comb is in a tree that has creepers running up the trunk a man may climb the tree, smoke out the bees, and cut out the comb, but if the tree has a thick, smooth trunk and no creepers, he may instead tie a light cord to an arrow, shoot the arrow into the comb, stretch the cord tight and make it fast to a stake, and let the honey run down the cord into a container. In Ceylon where the bees' nests are in crevices in rocks rather than on cliffs, the Veddas simply climb to them with ladders.

Collecting insects for food

While insects like honey ants and honey bees are exceptional in producing edible by-products, many others are themselves eaten, either as larvae or as adults. In Australia, observers of the aboriginal scene have long been intrigued by the partiality of the natives to witchetty grubs. They are the larvae of a number of species of moths, particularly those of the genus *Cossus.* They are white, four to six inches long, and are found among the roots of acacias. In collecting these grubs women have to compete with the marsupial mole, because they form the latter's principal food.

In the mountains of New South Wales, the adult *Argotis spina* provided an annual windfall. Many people would come together from considerable distances to harvest this windfall. They used to light fires under the rocks on which the moths collect, then spread them on the hot ground to singe off their wings and down, winnow them in baskets, and eat as many as they could. They pounded the rest in wooden troughs, and the paste would keep for a week. Sometimes they smoked them, in which case they would keep longer. These moths taste sweet and cause diarrhea for the first two days, but the people who ate them for a week or more grew fat on this diet.

In Africa the Pygmies collect and eat termites and colonial caterpillars. Our most detailed account comes from neither the Akoa nor the Mbuti but from another group in between.* As the termites tend to build their hills more or less in the same place each year, the Pygmies know where they are without search, and each man in the

*Paul Schebesta, *Among Congo Pygmies* (London: Hutchinson & Co., 1933), pp. 202 ff.

camp marks out his own hill. From time to time as the season approaches he goes to it and cuts into its side to see how high up the termites have risen, and thus can estimate how soon they will swarm out to fly away. The whole band may desert its huts for several days for the swarming. Because the insects begin to fly once they have come out, the people must be there beforehand. Near its hill each family sets up a windscreen, and they build a roof of leaves over the hill, and dig a deep trench around its base.

They build a fire in front of the windscreen, facing the hill, and dig a hole in front of the fire. At dusk the ants begin to fly. Striking the roof, they tumble into the trench, crawl toward the fire, and fall into the hole, out of which women scoop them up in baskets. Usually they roast the termites, although sometimes they eat them alive, pound them to a paste, or boil them. The Akoa Pygmies boil as many as they can, and scoop off the oil that rises to the surface of the water. They use this oil both in cooking and as a pomade, mixed with red wood-powder and applied to their bodies. It is this oil that gives the Akoa their strong odor which non-Pygmies find nauseating, if not intolerable. The Mbuti collect termites too. In the Ituri the insects swarm when the heavy rains begin in January and February, and thus provide the Pygmies with one of their two seasonal harvests, the other being the honey season, in May and June.

Locusts and other swarming, migratory grasshoppers, a plague to farmers and herdsmen in many parts of the world, are a boon to food gatherers living in arid regions where game is scarce. During the mid-1800s Maj. Howard Egan, a Mormon pioneer, described an Indian "cricket" hunt held near Deep Creek in northern Nevada. His "crickets" are large, dark-colored katydids, long-horned and flightless (*Anabrus simplex*).

He encountered a group of Indians who, for several days, had been digging five or six trenches, about a foot wide and a foot deep and thirty to forty feet long, joined together at the ends and facing uphill. The Indians covered the trenches with a layer of stiff, dry grass on which the insects were feeding. During the hottest time of day, the Indians split up into two groups, with men, women, and children in each, and each person holding a bunch of grass in each hand. Each party walked to a place some distance behind either end of the trenches, and then spread out in a single line. Swinging their bunches back and forth, they gradually drove the "crickets" toward the line of trenches. As they drew nearer they slackened their pace, to give the insects time to crawl between the grass stalks into the trenches. When all had been driven in, the Indians set fire to the grass held in their hands, and scattered it, burning, over the grass on the trenches, creating a big blaze and much smoke, through which the "crickets" could not crawl out. The squaws removed the toasted insects from the trenches, which were then half full of them, and transferred them to larger baskets, which they loaded on their backs, along with their babies in bent willow cradles. Major Egan saw one woman carry off some four bushels of the insects, along with her baby, to the camp three or four miles away. Unable to carry off all the insects in one trip, they returned several times until the trenches were empty.

From the dietary point of view, insects are prime sources of food because they are very rich in proteins, and when they are swarming in considerable numbers there is no need to hunt game. Insectivorous birds and mammals need little other food, nor do human beings on occasions like those just described.

Windfalls of wild fruits

A few instances may be noted of comparable windfalls provided by the vegetable kingdom. In a certain section of southern Queensland in Australia there grows a pine, *Araucaria bidwillii*, that bears the so-called bunya-bunya fruit, only once in three years. It is a seed about two inches long that tastes like a roasted chestnut. These pine trees are privately owned, but they grow close enough together so that when the fruit is ripe their owners and their families used to assemble there. Some five to six hundred persons would come there to eat the fruit as long as it lasted, which might be for several months.

The Indians of Lower California, long extinct, lived in a relatively barren environment where food was scarce, but prickly shrubs were fairly abundant in favored places. Among them is the pitahaya cactus, a member of the family that includes the tall and impressive saguaro of our own Southwest. The sweet pitahaya (there is also a sour variety) bears a fruit that is round, as large as a hen's egg, and covered with a green, prickly shell. Its pulp is white or red, juicy, and fairly sweet. Inside the pulp small black seeds are scattered. The fruit ripens in the middle of June and can be eaten for about eight weeks. During the eighteenth century the Indians used to come to the pitahaya clumps, where fruit could be picked in the hundreds. They would feast on it as long as it was available, and would grow fat. Then they would carefully pick the seeds out of their own accumulated excrement, roast them, grind them, and eat them. The Jesuit priest Father Jacob Baegert, who described this practice, called it a second harvest.

Collecting wild grass seeds

Collecting the seeds of wild grasses was undoubtedly a widespread practice, providing a major source of food to many of the world's peoples before the rise of agriculture. Indeed, it is widely believed that collecting wild grass seeds led to the beginning of cereal cultivation in West Asia, the Mediterranean, the Sudan, and Ethiopia, and probably China; and the same is true of the origin of maize cultivation in Mexico and Central America. That agriculture began where wild grasses grow is one of the principal reasons why so few of the hunting and gathering peoples still live where wild grasses are abundant enough to be a major factor in their food supply.

Another reason concerns a peculiarity of grains, as well as of legumes. When the seeds on wild grasses ripen, they have to have some way to reach the ground to germinate. Thus the glumes holding the seeds automatically open at just the right moment, spilling the grains or even ejecting them. The same is true of wild peas, beans, vetches, and other legumes that grow above ground. Anyone harvesting wild grains or pulse musr know when that time will come, and harvesters must congregate in sufficient numbers to collect the seeds, or they will be lost in the ground.

Now a fairly rare and lethal mutation removes from the plant its capacity for the glumes to open, or for the head or pod to shatter. When such a mutation is present, the seeds remain in their containers, and are unable to germinate. In the special case of maize, an even more drastic mutation occurs. By its means a single husk comes to enclose the entire ear, instead of the individual glumes found in the parent wild species. Both with the small grains and with maize, it must have required keen observation on the part of a few individual seedgatherers to visualize the potential advantage of these mutations. By selecting the mutant ears, husking them, and planting the grains, he (if not she) could raise a whole crop of shatterproof plants which could be set aside and husked or threshed later, instead of having to collect them all at once. This innovation would require the efforts of far fewer individuals and would increase the per capita yield. And by planting the seeds where they chose, they could reduce the element of chance as to where the plants would spring up next season.

California is the anthropologist's chief example of collecting wild seeds in great numbers without agriculture. Perhaps no California Indian both noticed and was able to act upon the observation of the mutation described, but another reason may be added in this special case. The parts of California where wild seeds grow in abundance have a Mediterranean climate, with winter rains and summer drought—just what wild grasses need. The Californians were not in contact with any other peoples growing comparable seeds, and the nearest place where any grain was cultivated lay to the southwest, beyond an arid country inhabited by other food gatherers. The second grain was maize, which unlike the Californian grasses needs rain in summer, the dry period in California when grasses ripen.

The technique of harvesting wild grains was very simple, and specifically women's work. They did not reap the grasses, but simply walked through the stand, each woman holding a basket in one hand and a stick in the other. She would place a handful of stalks against the edge of her basket, and beat the seeds into it with the stick.

Wild grass seeds were a particularly important item of diet in southern California, in the region near Los Angeles. Farther north, as in the Sacramento Valley, acorns yielded more food. At least twelve species of oaks were harvested. Men, women, and children turned out in the autumn to collect acorns. The men and large boys climbed the trees and beat the branches with long poles, knocking down the acorns which the women and other children collected in carrying baskets.

Pine nuts were also gathered, but in greater numbers in the foothills than in the valley. The hill people picked sugar-pine cones and then set them afire to burn off the pitch, which made them open, and the seeds fell out. Some of this crop they traded with the people of the valley for acorns and other goods.

These methods of harvesting apply specifically to the Maidu, whose methods of deer hunting have been described earlier. From these and other sources they were able to accumulate so much food that those living in the valley were relatively sedentary and achieved a population density of up to three persons per square mile, which is very high for food gatherers and equal to that of some agriculturalists.

This abundance of food, much of which could be obtained relatively easily and could be stored for winter consumption, gave the Maidu and many other California Indians enough leisure time to conduct many ceremonies, some of which were quite elaborate. But the principal rites were not those specifically linked to the succession of kinds of food obtained, but those concerned with human relations in general, and they were held in winter when there was little else to do, and people needed organized activities to keep them out of trouble.

Collecting molluscs for food

Let us return to the collection of molluscs, which has two overt purposes: to obtain food and to get shells. The Andaman Islanders living along the coast, as most of them did, collected Cyrena clams (resembling quahogs) and other shellfish at low tide. The women simply picked them up and put them in baskets. But the men went out in canoes to dive into deeper water to get Tridacna and Pinna. The Tridacna is the giant bivalve with toothed shells that has the evil reputation of closing on divers' legs and holding them to drown. The men took this chance because the Tridacna supplies much flesh. They also dived for Pinna, from the shells of which they made the adzes used in hewing out canoes. Cyrena shells served as all-purpose cutting and scraping tools.

In 1959, when I saw them doing it, the Alakaluf were still diving for mussels, clams, cockles, and other molluscs in the frigid waters of the Magellanic channels. It is the women who do this, and they are able to tolerate low water temperatures without ill effect. More than a century earlier the Tasmanian women were doing the same thing, also in cold water. As the farthest point in Tasmania from the sea is only sixty-odd miles, inland people were able to make periodic trips to special coves, inlets, and beaches for this purpose. The coast-dwellers did not always welcome the inlanders, and several instances have been cited in which fights took place.

Although the women did the diving, the men came along too, to eat their share of the shellfish and to guard the women from surprise attacks by enemies.

The women used to dive to considerable depths and pull themselves down, with baskets around their necks and wooden spatulas in hand, by grasping the stems of kelp plants that were anchored naturally to the rocks on the bottom. The deepest diving was for a local abalone (*Nothohaliotis*), the most prized shellfish of all and the hardest to dislodge from its grip on the rocks, as anyone who has tried to pry one off knows.

The abalone has a large, compact, and tough disc of muscle, as large as a tenderloin steak, or larger, and its flesh will keep longer, in a cool climate, than the soft parts of clams or mussels. Only abalone was carried into the interior to be eaten later. Also, the shells were useful. Beside a spring near the center of the island an early visitor once found an abalone shell, its holes plugged with clay. It had been left there by some thoughtful person to serve travelers as a drinking cup. The Andamanese use nautilus shells for the same purpose.

Shells used as ornaments and as currency

We have noted how many peoples who have access to suitable mollusc shells use them as tools, but they may also be used as ornaments and as currency. Some shells are hard, shiny, and highly colored. They are durable and do not decay. A string of shells about a woman's neck may be as valuable to people living away from the sea as a string of pearls is to those of us who can afford them.

One account has been published of a mortal battle between an inland band of Tasmanians having access to ochre, and a coastal band who had agreed to exchange seashells for the other's product. The inland people brought their ochre, but the coastal people arrived empty handed. Men were killed because of a breach of faith over the exchange of the two materials, neither of which was edible or of any other practical use. In other words, the Tasmanians were just as "human" as the rest of us.

As a rule, the only difference between collecting shells to be used for ornaments and currency and collecting those to be eaten is that the former need not be taken live; they can be simply picked up where they have been washed up by the tide. But there is an exception, that of dentalia shells. The dentalium, or tooth-shell, is a scaphopod, a tubular shell open at both ends and curved so that it looks like an incisor tooth. Throughout aboriginal northern California, the Northwest Coast, and even inland to the Plains, the Indians used to trade these shells, which grew in value the farther they were carried from their source. The dentalium is a deep-water, Pacific-coastal mollusc, and relatively few wash ashore. Only the Nootka Indians of Vancouver Island collected them, and most of them were apparently obtained at two places, one at Barkley Sound and the other off the village of Cahqos, northwest of Tachu Point. The chiefs of several Nootka tribes had the hereditary right to probe for the shells at the latter place.

The dentalia live on the ocean bottom in the mud at or near the surface, far below the low tide level and too deep for diving, but not too deep for Nootkan inventive ingenuity. They made a basically two-piece device to take them with. The first piece is a fir pole fifteen to twenty feet long, with a bundle of cedar splints lashed to one end, like a round-headed broom. The splints nearest the center were relatively thin; those on the outer periphery wider and springier. The head of the device is eight or nine inches wide, fully spread out.

The second piece is a narrow cedar board with a hole through the middle, and the diameter of the hole is a little greater than that of the broom-head, where it is lashed to the pole. At either end of the board is lashed a stone weight. The dentalia collector and his crew paddle out into the open water over the bed and one man drops this device overboard; he holds a cord tied to the pole just above the broom-lashing. In the canoe the crew have also brought along a few extra poles, for one is usually too short to reach the bottom. As each is lowered to almost its full length, another pole is lashed to it, and so on until the bottom has been reached. At this point the operator pulls upward on the cord—or on the top pole—thus drawing the broom-head part up through the hole in the board, thus pulling the cedar splints together. Once he has brought the broom-head back aboard, he pulls back the board and removes whatever dentalia are held in it.

Although this is hard work, a catch of one or two dentalia was considered profitable. If they failed in the first casting, the crew could paddle the boat back to the same position or near it, for the boat would have drifted off the bed by that time, the water being too deep for anchoring.

Once dentalia shells had been replaced by dollars, it became no longer worthwhile to probe for them with so awkward if ingenious a device, and little is remembered about the technique by the contemporary Nootkans. Like that of the Ainu *marek*, or spring-hooking salmon spear, the circumstances of the invention of the dentalium-collector will probably remain a sealed mystery.

8.

Food and Drugs

In any well-regulated society, there is more to eating than the simple ingestion of food. Eating is a pleasant activity, and most people enjoy eating together. When the day's work is done, the fire is glowing, and the smell of meat cooking makes hungry men's stomachs rumble in anticipation, people sit down on their haunches to join together in a meal. Most hunters live off the wild produce of their territories, and they are well fed. They have to be, in order to lead their normal, active, out-of-door lives.

Within his community and under ordinary circumstances, no one usually goes hungry, because food is shared. Thus an equitable food distribution strengthens the bonds that unite the members of territorial groups. As a prelude to our forthcoming study of the ways in which hunting peoples are socially organized, we need to know who divides the food, who eats with whom, who prepares the food, and how it is preserved.

How food is shared

As a rule vegetable foods and slow game, collected mostly by women, belong to those women's family households and are shared with other families only if some of them are hungry, and the same is true of shellfish, most finfish, and of birds' eggs and turtles' eggs. But the distribution of game is another matter.

If every man who killed an animal or bird were to keep it for his own family, some would have more than they could eat and others would go hungry. Besides, more than one man usually takes part in a hunt and success is frequently the result of cooperative action. If men were greedy about what they killed, the conflict between men and between their families would weaken or dissolve the familial as well as economic ties that hold the social unit together, and people need each other's company as much as they need food. A division of meat is therefore basic to the continued association of families in any human group that hunts, and rigid procedural rules must

Dividing a kangaroo into shares

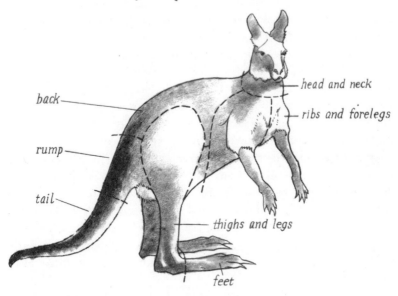

back

rump

tail

head and neck

ribs and forelegs

thighs and legs

feet

29. *How the body of a kangaroo is divided into shares for distribution among hunters and their kin. (After Richard A. Gould, 1969)*

be followed in order to keep the peace, particularly when some parts of an animal's carcass are preferable to others.

In whales, as we have already seen from the example of the Tigara whale hunter, the choice portion is the solid muscle meat that lies more than one foot's breadth aft of the leviathan's navel. In kangaroos, it is the tail. In elephants it is the trunk. In bison it may be the tongue. These butchering specifications do not always include some parts of the animal that may be eaten on the spot of the kill or shortly afterward, like the eyeball fat of guanacos among the Ona, or the meat at the top of the whale's head and its flukes among the Tigarans.

As for who takes charge of the division, this varies in terms of the organization of the hunt and the social structure of the people concerned. In the case of the Tigarans, it is the captain of the first boat. Among some of the South African Bushmen it is the chief of the band who cuts the meat up under a sacred tree in the center of a camp.

Among the Birhors, after a monkey hunt, once a chief has roasted a little of the meat and offered it to the spirits of the chase, the entrails, tails, and feet of the monkeys are divided equally among the men and the women who served as beaters. Each man who provided a net also gets a hind leg. The two flankers each receive a hind leg as dividend, and the chief gets the neck and half of the back meat of each animal killed, in addition to his hunter's share. If some meat is left after this distribution, it is divided into as many portions as there are eligible persons, plus an extra share for the chief. Men who stayed home are given none in the formal distribution, but they may get some from their wives and close male kin.

After an annual deerhunt the men carry all of the carcasses back to camp and dismember them with axes. They roast the heads, and all of the men eat them, except those whose wives are pregnant. Then the chief gets all of the necks and one side of each back; each net owner gets the other side of the back of each deer caught in his net, each flanker gets a foreleg, and the herald is given a knee-joint of each animal. The rest is divided up by families, even those of men who stayed in the camp.

Among the Mbuti Pygmies of the Ituri Forest, there seem to be as many ways of distributing meat as there are territorial hunting groups, each group being composed of a number of bands. Colin Turnbull gives details of three systems among net hunters and three more among bow hunters. Each is different, but the main element in common is that the men do the distributing themselves, with the older men settling any disputes. Among these six groups the carcasses are butchered into between five and eight cuts of meat, according to local usage. All together these cuts are: head, back, liver, shoulder, chest, rump, stomach, foreleg, hind leg, and genitals.

The cuts are given to between five and eight categories of recipients. Among the six groups the recipients are: older people, active male hunters, women who were beaters, women who also carried the meat, children, net owners, helpers of net owners, spear owners, owners of dogs that helped with each particular animal, fathers of such dog owners, sisters or sisters-in-law of the killer, anyone who went ahead and put up the first game, everyone concerned, and the dogs themselves.

In three cases the older people got the stomachs; in one the heads; and in one the rumps, these being relatively soft parts requiring little mastication. The back of an animal may go to the owner of the dog that drove it, to the male hunters, or to everyone, by equal division. The genitals may be given to the children to make them grow, or to a dog. In the event that members of different territorial groups are hunting together, the regional differences of protocol may cause disputes, but theoretically the local ground rules hold.

How people with graded ranks divide the meat

At the opposite end of the spectrum stands the intricate protocol of food distribution practiced by the Northwest Coast Indians, of whom the Nootka will again serve as an example. Here the guiding principle is not so much who did what in getting the meat, as who has inherited what rights to which piece. The Nootka recognized chiefs of graded rank; house chiefs, tribal chiefs (a tribe being the people who shared a winter village), and, in some cases, a head chief of a confederacy, the latter being the sum total of the people inhabiting a summer village when more than one tribe lived together during that season.

In one instance cited by Drucker, a man killed a hair seal, a large and much-prized pinniped. Then he either had to give a feast to which the six tribal chiefs of his confederacy were invited, or turn over the seal to his chief to give the feast, and receive a present in return. It may be noted that even if the chiefs were out fishing they would be called in for this occasion. The top-ranking chief got the seal's breast; chief number two got the right front flipper; number three the left front flipper, number four the right rear flipper, number five the left rear flipper, and number six a wide strip of fat cut from the back of the neck to the tip of the tail. The rest of the fat was then cut off in similar long strips and given to other chiefs of lesser rank. Each chief did not have to eat his entire portion at the feast; he could take home as much of it as he liked. If two or three seals had been caught, the take-home portions would be correspondingly greater.

Only the hair seal drew the six chiefs to such a feast. A man who killed any other sea mammal was supposed to give a feast with it, but he could divide the meat as he liked, and the same was true when deer or bear were killed, unless the hunter's chief wanted to give a feast, in which case he would compensate the hunter.

The division of fish followed a different schedule. The chief who owned the rights to a certain fishing ground would open the fishing season by sending out some of his men to make the first catch, or first two catches, for him, after which his subjects were free to go fishing on their own. Later on, after the fish had been dried, the chief would send some of his men around to collect portions of it as tribute. No definite percentage was used in assessment; each man gave as much fish as he thought proper, knowing that it would be served up later in a feast given by the chief, to which he himself would be invited, and where he would eat his share. He would not go hungry, for there was more than enough fish for everyone.

As with fish, so also with berries and edible roots. The chief would send groups of women out to pick or dig them in patches that he owned. He would pay the women with some of their produce, and give a feast with some of the rest. Then anyone else that wanted to could go out after these vegetable foods.

Trading food

As a rule hunters and gatherers do not trade food in any quantity because they have all they need on their own property. But there are a few exceptions, particularly among the wealthy Indians of the Northwest Coast. There, where the Nootka have a near monopoly on whale hunting, they preserve more whale fat than they need, in the form of oil, kept in bladders and skins. Members of the more northerly tribes come by boat to Nootka villages to obtain this oil in return for more durable goods. In a cool, dry climate, where little vegetable food is available, animal fats such as whale oil provide much needed energy and vitamins.

The examples given above, except for the unusual instance of trading whale oil, may serve as a generalization, for they apply to every group of hunters that we know about who deliberately and regularly kill animals for food. But there are a few exceptions, particularly that of the Kadar of the Cardamon Hills of India, who go out in single family units to dig yams. If they chance to kill an animal, this act is incidental to other activities, and there is no hunting in groups. As far as we know they do not divide the meat so obtained with other families, nor is there any particular reason why they should. This exception helps to prove the rule.

Eating food raw and cooking it

When our own ancestors were still hunters, ample evidence shows that they ate much of their food after it had been cooked. We still eat fruits, lettuce, oysters, and the like raw, and the Japanese eat raw fish. In these respects we and the Japanese do not differ from most hunters. Among the latter the Eskimo have a reputation for eating an unusual quantity of raw meat. In fact, the word Eskimo means raw-meat eaters in cree, an Algonkian language.

In view of their poor supply of vegetable foods this culinary habit is partly responsible for keeping Eskimo healthy. Among the Caribou Eskimo of the Canadian Barren Lands west of Hudson Bay, it is difficult to cook at all because of the local paucity of firewood and of their distance from the sea. Unlike their relatives on the coast they have no whale or seal fat to burn, and they need to eat caribou fat to preserve body heat in their fireless tents and igloos. But still, like everyone else, all the Eskimo cook, and with an advanced technique — boiling. Most hunters cook by simpler methods, as we shall presently see.

Roasting food, as practiced by the Tasmanians

Let us now assume that the afternoon shadows are lengthening. The men have returned from their hunt and the women from gathering firewood. The fires are burning down to coals. Some people's stomachs are rumbling a bit with the anticipation of a meal, and young children are fractious. The time has come to cook whatever food is at hand and to eat.

Let us also record what happened at such a time. The scene is somewhere in Tasmania; the date Sunday, 11 December 1831; the narrator George Augustus Robinson. Between 1829 and 1832, Robinson, a small, sandy-haired, soft-spoken man, walked fearlessly all over the island, unarmed, persuading the hostile natives to come with him into exile on the offshore islands. Someone had brought a wallaby into the camp of Mannalargenna of the Oyster Bay Tribe. The chief was traveling with Robinson, who wrote in his diary: "This animal is first thrown on the fire whole as is their custom with all animals, and when the hair is singed they take the carcass off the fire and rub off the scorched hair with their hands. This practice is tenaciously observed with all animals except the opossum; the fur of this animal is first pulled off previous to its being placed on the fire. After the chief had rubbed the hair off the wallaby, he broke the foreleg by twisting it with his hands, this practice is also observed with the other animals. He then cut the hind legs, after which he made a hole in the belly with his fingers and pulled out the entrails and then thrust in some hot ashes, the animal being previously roasted outside. The animal was then ready for eating."*

Having cooked the wallaby, the chief distributed its meat to those present, who ate everything half raw except the bones, gristle, skin, and the intestines which he had drawn out. Larger animals, like seals and the gray kangaroo, had to be cut up to be brought in. Ducks and penguins were slit ventrally after a preliminary roasting and then cooked again with their insides against the fire. Roots, most fungi, and other vegetables not eaten raw were roasted whole in the ashes after the fire had begun to die down, and fern roots too large to be carried in whole were cut up where found and roasted in pieces. The latter were usually eaten with strips of roasted kangaroo skin. Shellfish were also simply roasted, on the beach, or after they had been carried inland.

Australian cooking techniques

It would be hard to find any simpler cooking techniques than those just described. Roasting was also the principal method of the Australians, but not the only one. Sometimes, before cooking a bird, they encased it in mud, which hardened in the fire. When the mud crust was broken off, the feathers came with it, and the natural juices of the bird were retained. This method is thus a form of baking. In a recent account Richard Gould describes how he watched two men who had been hunting in the western desert, and had caught two monitor lizards. They roasted them whole, then pounded them—skin, bones, and all—into a paste which they ate by licking it off their fingers.

In Queensland a more sophisticated method than ordinary roasting was sometimes followed. Whoever was doing the cooking

*N. J. B. Plomley, ed., *Friendly Mission, the Tasmanian Journal and Papers of George Augustus Robinson,* 1829–1834 (Hobart, Tasmania, 1966), pp. 548–49.

cleaned the body, filled its cavity with hot stones, and dislocated the limbs to make a compact package. Then he wrapped it in bark and buried it in a hole over hot ashes, piled on some sand, and built a slow fire on top. But in Victoria, some of the more sedentary tribes

30. *Roasting a kangaroo in live coals. (After Richard A. Gould, 1969)*

used a true Polynesian-style earth oven for cooking all kinds of food. They put hot stones in a hole, laid the food over them wrapped in leaves, then more hot stones, then earth on top. Sometimes they put wet grass with the stones, leaving some holes to pour water in from time to time, to create steam. The product was tender and juicy.

Broiling, boiling, and pottery

The South African Bushmen roast much of their food, but they also broil meat, in a sense, by hanging strips of meat over the fire from sticks thrust into the ground. The Fuegian Indians follow the same practice, and the Indians of the North American forests grill fish on wooden grids.

Somewhat surprisingly, the Andamanese of Great Andaman boiled turtle and wild pig meat in pots of their own making. These are crude, hand-shaped, untempered vessels of local clay, fired at the low temperatures of ordinary campfires. Until Lidio Cipriani excavated some of the Andamanese shellheaps and got carbon 14 dates from charcoal preserved in them, the presence of pottery among people otherwise so simple in other technological respects was a mystery. Cipriani found that the earliest pots in the deposits dated from after A.D. 1500 and were better made than the later ones. Also, there were no pig bones before the arrival of pottery; the pigs hunted by the Andamanese were domestic ones gone wild, and introduced by the same seafaring visitors that taught the islanders to make pottery.

It used to be customary in anthropology to associate pottery with agriculture as parts of a single, inseparable complex, but there is no basis in fact for this linkage. Some agricultural peoples do not make pots, and some hunters and gatherers do. The reason why pottery and hunting are usually incompatible is that pots are fragile and most hunters have to move about, carrying their gear with them. The Ainu used to make pots, and so did some of the Alaskan Eskimo. Both were nearly sedentary.

Boiling without pottery

The Eskimo and the Ainu are not the only hunters who boil food; others have found ways of doing it in less friable containers. One is by cutting vessels in which water can be boiled out of some soft stone, like soapstone. This is a well-known Arctic Eskimo trait, and they used to travel long distances to find suitable outcrops. Some of them also melt snow in these stone kettles to obtain drinking water in winter. They suspend the kettle from a wooden frame over a blubber-burning lamp of the same material. The Chumash Indians of the coastal region of southern California also made soapstone vessels, and when they broke them they used the bottom pieces to fry food on.

A second way is to boil food in a watertight kettle of birchbark or some other kind of bark, preferably wild cherry, because its bark is thick and tough. The kettle must be held near enough the fire to boil the water, and far enough from flames to keep it from burning. This is a common method throughout the forested regions occupied by Indian hunters in North America, and was also used in northeastern Asia.

A third technique is stoneboiling. An otherwise perishable container, of wood or basketry, which is also waterproof, is partly filled with water, and hot stones taken from a fire with tongs are dropped in, in succession, until the water boils and the food is cooked. In California the Indians boiled in baskets. The hot stones had to be stirred in the basket so that the food would be cooked evenly and so that they would not burn holes. By this method they cooked the acorn mush that formed the staple food of about three-fourths of the Indian population.

In the Northwest Coast region most of the meat was boiled in the same fashion, but in cleverly made boxes of cedar wood. These boxes had all four sides made of one piece, which was slotted at the corners on the inside, steamed, and bent. Northwest Coast Indians seem to have been the gourmets of the hunting world. Franz Boas collected about 150 recipes from a Kwakiutl woman, the wife of Boas's collaborator George Hunt, who was himself half Scot and half Tlingit. Besides boiling food in boxes the Nootka, neighbors of the Kwakiutl to the south, broiled it over coals, roasted it in ashes, and steamed it under mats. This last technique was used mostly for fern roots which were not very often eaten. In the large feasts, anywhere from four to ten courses were served. Young men did most of the cooking when there was much food to be served. Otherwise, the women were the cooks.

As every cook knows, there is more to preparing food than simply exposing it to heat. Preliminary processing may be needed to make it palatable or even edible. To cite a simple example we may return to the Nootka, who now and then eat raccoon meat, although they do not like it very much because of its rank odor. Before cooking it they soak it overnight in a box of fresh water.

A number of vegetable foods have bitter or even poisonous substances that have to be leached out before they can be eaten. In parts of northern Australia, particularly in Arnhem Land, the edible fruit or nut of the cycad palm receives this treatment. The women crack the shells, remove the kernels, pound them on stones, and then soak the pulp for three to five days in a trenchful of water. Then they mold the pulp into cakes or loaves, wrap them in paperbark, and bake them in hot ashes.

In Central California acorns, horse chestnuts, and wild nutmeg were all treated in the same way; they were pulverized and leached before cooking. Most acorns were stored in small twig granaries of basketry set on posts, and when they needed them, the women would draw the acorns out by poking a stick into the side of the basket to enlarge a hole to the right diameter. Other acorns, and the other seeds, were kept in baskets inside the house. The women would shell them and then pound them in a mortar, and some of the mortars were stationary mills — i.e., depressions in outcrops of stone where several women could work together. A woman would spread out her pulp on a circle of sand and pour water over it. After doing this several times she would remove the pulp from the sand, and sift it. It was then ready to be stoneboiled in baskets, or sometimes made into heavy cakes of unleavened bread. They also pounded dried meat, salmon bones, and deer vertebrae, and stored them in baskets.

Preserving food

The Ainu used to dry and smoke split salmon by hanging the fish on racks under the eaves of their houses, which had no chimneys, and the Northwest Coast Indians amassed large quantities of this nutritious preserved fish by the same means. Preserving salmon placed them in an economic bracket comparable to that of many farmers, and allowed them to devote the winter months to ceremonial activities.

On the chilly shores of Tierra del Fuego and the Magellanic channels, fat used to be preserved in intestines, bladders, and skins. The Yaghans used to make sausages. They would turn a length of seal or sea-lion intestine inside out, clean it, tie it at one end, and blow it up like a balloon, and then tie the other end. They would hang it up to let it dry, and then fill it with toasted blubber and with oil extracted from fat hung over a fire and allowed to drip into a shell. Next they would tie wooden plugs into each end, and draw some out to drink from time to time. In a similar way they made blood sausages, and roasted some of them.

The Alakaluf would similarly pack fat into a piece of skin, making a balloon about a foot or so in diameter. Then they would bury it in a bog for a while, and after it had fermented they would dig it up again, hang it up in a hut, and when anyone felt so inclined he could pour some into the palm of his hand and lick it. This fat was of course rancid, but it may have smelled no more strongly than overripe Limburger cheese. Both the Alakaluf and the Yaghans also ate rancid fat after a whale had been stranded and had died. Fat is an important element in the diets of peoples who live in cold climates and who have few vegetable foods rich in carbohydrates. Just as the Caribou Eskimo depends on a heavy ingestion of fat to keep warm in their unheated igloos, so there must also have been some compelling dietary reason to explain the craving for rancid fat among the maritime Fuegians.

The unimportance of drugs among hunters

Before outsiders began bothering them the vast majority of hunting and gathering peoples were notably free from the use of habit-forming drugs. Otherwise they would not have been able to go about their work of living off the land as efficiently as they did.

First of all, they had no alcohol, except for the Ainu, and the Ainu had it only after they had begun to grow millet in order to brew beer for ceremonial use. The Plains Indians did not get peyote from the south until after they had been shattered by the whites. The Congo Pygmies could not have had marijuana, which they now smoke, until their Negro hosts had obtained it from Arabs, and the Gabon Pygmies could not have made banana wine until they had been able to obtain bananas from abandoned plantations and by theft.

This leaves us with a few other drugs to discuss, namely jimsonweed, agaric, *pituri*, and tobacco. Jimsonweed (*Datura stramonium*), was used in southern California in initiations of young men, but botanists are not even sure that it was a native American plant. Agaric is a poisonous mushroom that gives hallucinations, somewhat as LSD does. It was chewed by Chukchi living on the peninsula named for them in eastern Siberia, and, like the pitahaya seeds of the Indians of southern California, it went into a "second harvest"; persons wanting visions would drink the urine of those who had chewed it.

The Australian aborigines had a native drug, *pituri*, made from the bark and leaves of a bush, *Duboisia hopwoodii*. They roasted these plant materials until they were soft and pliable, chewed them, and mixed the product with acacia ashes into cakes, which were widely traded because the plants grew only in limited areas. Men who chewed them carried the cakes behind their ears. The *pituri* gave them a dreamy, devil-may-care feeling before tense occasions, such as fights. They also used two species of native tobacco, *Nicotiana gossei* and *N. excelsior*, which they treated and traded in the same way. They did not begin smoking tobacco until taught to by Indonesian fishermen in the sixteenth century, the same time that the Andamanese also learned this habit.

Among the hunting peoples of North America tobacco smoking was marginally diffused from agricultural tribes to the south and east. The California Indians picked it wild, and the Tlingit of the Northwest Coast grew it, their only crop. Among all these peoples it was used ceremonially and not as a daily habit. The Eskimo learned to smoke it from the Russians, directly or indirectly. Drugs, along with new diseases and new foods such as flour and rice, share the principal honors for the decline of hunting populations throughout the world, plus the social disturbances caused by the presence of traders and colonists in recent times.

9.

*The Social Organization
of Hunters: Territories,
Bands, and Kinship*

Introduction

With this chapter we move from material culture to social organization. In Chapters 2 through 8 we have concentrated on the techniques by which hunters and gatherers make a living, and in the rest of the book we shall pay primary attention to their ways of getting along as individuals, in groups, and in intergroup relations. In order to describe material culture realistically, we had to mention some aspects of social organization, such as the role of the chief and the division of meat, and to cite a few examples of hunting rites. A hunt must be organized if it is to succeed, and ritual is needed to allay anxieties over the outcome of the chase and to ensure the most efficient procedure during it.

In the following chapters the emphasis will be on social structure and ritual, but technology cannot be taken for granted. The lives of hunters are complete entities, and cannot be broken down into artificial categories in order to conform to a methodological scheme of which the participants are unaware. In other words, we cannot split them up into the economic, political, religious, and other compartments of behavior visible in our own societies.

Hunters have no jails, no uniformed police, no law courts operating the year round, no civil service, and no priestly hierarchies. They have their own equally effective mechanisms of keeping a tolerable degree of peace, but these mechanisms are usually merged. In combination they manage to keep what we call the crime rate down to the level of our own, or lower, if we consider organized warfare as a sanctioned form of crime, among both hunters and ourselves.

Viewed separately for the sake of clarity in exposition, the hunters' ways of maintaining order include the organization of individuals into territorial bands, the relationships between such bands, kinship, the incest tabu and its ramifications, age grading, and ritual procedures that reduce friction to a minimum in the function of these other elements of social behavior.

There are two ways in which the subject of human relations can be approached. We can start with the individual, move on to his family, and then work outward through the web of his relationships in dealing with everyone he has to deal with, until we reach the outer limits of the society of which he is a member. Or we can start with the group itself, bound it, define it, and cope with the details later. This second way makes good sense from an historical as well as a functional point of view because the territorial band is probably older than the family and may even antedate the species *Homo sapiens*, to which we all, hunters and nonhunters, belong.

Space, territories, and bands

An essential point about a group of people, however organized, is that they occupy space, both corporately and individually. The position of a group in space tells us something about its relationships to other groups, and the position of individuals vis-à-vis each other gives us further information about the group's internal structure.

Most of the hunting peoples of the world live in bands. A band is a group of somewhere between thirty and a little over one hundred individuals who own and occupy a single territory, and share food. As the population density of a band's territory is rarely more than one person per square mile, a territory may cover anywhere from about thirty to several hundred square miles, and it may include water rights to lakes, streams, and coastline, which are just as important as land in providing food.

Among hunting peoples undisturbed by modern contacts the normal composition of a band would be a number of families, each consisting of a husband, wife or wives, and children, plus a few elderly couples, widowers, and widows, and sometimes a bachelor who had not been successful enough at the chase to acquire a spouse. A few visitors might occasionally be present, and the band might split into smaller units seasonally and later regroup, but there is normally no question as to who owns the land.

In many societies, but not in all of them, the men do not marry within their own bands, but take their wives from neighboring ones, and give their daughters or sisters to men of the groups from which they obtained their own wives. Usually the groom will give his

H

proposed in-laws a modest present, including meat that he has secured by his own prowess as a huntsman. Sometimes he will stay with his in-laws for a while and help them before leading his bride back to his own people. When she gets there she may find aunts and cousins who had been imported earlier, including perhaps her mother-in-law. She will go out collecting food with the other women, and under normal circumstances she should not remain lonely very long.

The virtues of this system are obvious. The men have lived on their land since birth, and know every rock and tree. They know the schedule of seasonal changes in vegetation, where the deer browse, where the bees are likely to build their hives, and all the other details needed in their daily and yearly rounds. The women need rather to know where to find foodstuffs that do not move, like berries, mushrooms, yams, and mussels.

The men hunt together because it is more efficient for them to do so than to hunt singly, which is, after all, lonely work. The women work in groups mostly for companionship. The men divide the meat as a matter of course, while the women share vegetable food (which tends not to spoil so fast) with other families only when the latter are hungry. It is clear enough then, why men should stay on their own land when they can. Conversely, several good reasons may be advanced as to why it is a good idea to import wives. Through the mechanism of the incest concept and its extensions to classes of kin, interband exogamy (marriage outside the community) helps considerably to ease relationships between neighboring groups of people and thus reduces the chance of serious conflict in case of trespass. A man who hunts on his neighbors' territory without permission risks being killed, but if he has a brother-in-law in the next camp he stands a chance of getting permission to hunt there if he needs to, and by having hunted with his father-in-law on his postnuptial visit, he knows where to look for game in it.

If a man in one band makes off with the wife of a man in the next band, the chiefs or elders of the two bands may call a meeting to discuss the matter and find some solution other than bloodshed and a lengthy feud. Also, if a man dies of a mysterious ailment and a shaman accuses a man in a neighboring band of sorcery, a similar meeting may ease matters. These are four good reasons why it is advantageous to have in-laws in the next camp. The only way to get them is to marry outside, and if a man has two or three wives from different bands, so much the better.

Relations within bands

Spatial position is also of prime importance in interpersonal relations between individuals within groups. Protocol dictates who shall sit, eat, and sleep where, who shall enter a building or an enclosure first, the entrance order of everyone else in the line, and who shall speak when; consequently, time is combined with space to provide a habitual framework of human interaction that prevents confusion and keeps order. The location that an individual takes on such occasions reflects, of course, his role and his status in the group as a whole.

The men who share a camp at night have usually been out of doors, i.e., during daytime, covering much ground, seeing few other persons, and not talking much, particularly if they have been hunting. The women, in or near camp, have seen more persons and done more talking. By now the men need a chance to talk and sing and perhaps to dance, in order to make up for their relative silence and comparative solitude during the day. Space is important for this, because everyone needs to be close enough to each other so that all can see and hear what is going on, including the children.

This way the children automatically learn the local rules of behavior. By the time they are grown up they will know exactly what to do to or for every category of person they are likely to encounter. These nightly events not only provide a painless, automatic education, but an education that is also dramatic and exciting. The children see before their very eyes hunts acted out, men parading around in masks, and shamans pulling magical objects out of the air. They may hear tales with a moral flavor, such as, what evil fate befell a greedy man, or how a strong man did foolish things to please a pretty woman.

Such stories seem to be found in all cultures, in one form or another. We have them too, in fairy tales, and in such admonitory rhymes as *Rockaby baby, in the tree top. When the wind blows the cradle will rock. When the bough breaks the cradle will fall, and down will come baby, cradle, and all.* Any young mother brought up on this jingle would be careful where she hung her baby in its cradle. If she had also been brought up to believe that an evil old ogress flits around the camp looking for children's excrement, by means of which she can eat souls of babies and thus cause them to sicken and die, the young mother will institute toilet training as soon as she can, and the camp will be clean.

Symbolic ties to the land

Within an exogamous, territorial band, the men live on the land where they were born, and which they collectively own. Such a band seems to be the least common denominator in human society; however, where food is particularly abundant, individuals may inherit or stake out rights to special fruit trees, bee trees, or rich fishing grounds, and wealth may become a source of social differentiation, particularly, as among the Northwest Coast Indians, with fishing grounds.

In any case, the ties of the men to their land are often reinforced by the personification of such outstanding features of the landscape as huge rocks, caves, tall trees, and water holes and streams. These may be conceived of as the abodes of their ancestors to which the latter have returned after death and from which newborn babies get their souls. Or (as in Australia, parts of India, and in a few other places) rocks may be called petrified ancestors, who passed that way in the dreamtime. This concept may not always be as clear-cut as implied. An individual, when questioned on the subject, may express it more generally by saying: "You see that rock? It has *power.*"*

As the members of such bands take most or all of their wives from neighboring bands, a web of broader units may spread out across the countryside. A range of mountains or a broad river or some other natural barrier may separate clusters of intermarrying bands. As we move outward from a given center, differences in spoken dialects begin to appear, until finally we reach a linguistic frontier. At least nine distinct languages were spoken in Tasmania, in Australia perhaps five hundred, and in California over thirty. For want of a more suitable term, anthropologists are accustomed to label such linguistic units as tribes, but at the linguistic level they lack tribal organization. Among a few hunters there are true tribes in the political sense, and even confederations of tribes, but these depend for their existence on a combination of an abundance of food and superior transportation, otherwise usually limited to cultivators and pastoralists.

Each simple territorial band is essentially an independent, sovereign state, at least from our point of view. But when the proper arrangements have been made, bands may join forces, as when two bands of Akoa Pygmies get together for an elephant hunt, and when Birhor bands combine for an annual deer drive.

*W. E. H. Stanner, "Religion, Totemism, and Symbolism," in R. M. and C. H. Berndt, eds., *Aboriginal Man in Australia* (Sydney, Angus and Robertson, 1965), p. 231.

What we have outlined above is more or less the standard situation among hunters, but before we go on to examine the variations in kinship structure and political organization, it may clear the air to discuss two kinds of exceptions, the apparent absence of territorial bands, and the presence of mixed bands composed of persons of different territorial origins.

The Yaghans, a decimated and disrupted people

Having been in contact with European navigators and their crews from the early sixteenth century onward, the Yaghans had been decimated by imported diseases by 1884, when the Reverend Thomas Bridges established his mission among them at Ushuaia on the Argentine side of Beagle Channel in Tierra del Fuego. At that time the Yaghans were moving about along the coast in single family groups, or in pairs of families, one of which contained a marriageable boy and the other a marriageable girl. When these two were married, the parental families again might separate.

The situation just described might seem like a rudimentary and chaotic form of social organization without a knowledge of the historical background. Thomas Bridges gathered the surviving Yaghans together at Ushuaia, where they told him about their previous social structure, confirmed by Hyades, another contemporary observer.

The Yaghans had lived along the coast and island shores in five separate major territories, separated by natural barriers, each group speaking its own dialect. Inside each of these five regions were smaller territories, located on bays, sounds, and groups of small islands. These units bore the names of the places where their inhabitants lived. The term for this smaller population unit was the Yaghan word for house. The families that composed each "house" were deeply attached to their own miniature countries and in each case shared its supplies of food and other raw materials. Yet the members of one band were free to drag their canoes across narrow isthmuses belonging to others, and to cross each other's territories in search of rare materials, such as pyrites for firemaking and ochre, provided that they did not tarry on the way. They also came together to feast on the flesh of stranded whales, at which time they would hold ceremonies together. Above the family level their organization was informal, although in each "house" there were generally one or more men with a reputation for sound judgment whose advice was sought.

The Alakaluf, the Western Shoshone, and the nonhunting Kadar

In recent times the Alakaluf, numbering about forty in 1959, rowed up and down the Magellanic channels from one end to the other, hunting sea lions and collecting mussels. But anciently there were regional differences in canoe types, and probably regional territories. The western Shoshone of Nevada, whom Major Egan saw harvesting katydids a century ago, had neither bands nor territories by that time, but they had been raided by their relatives, the horse-riding Utes, and forced to live in hiding. The Yaghans and the Alakalufs lost their social structure because they had been decimated by diseases; the western Shoshone had been reduced and scattered by the invasion of more powerful neighbors.

Still other examples of the same process may be cited, but there is at least one other of perhaps a different nature, that of the Kadar in the Cardamon Hills of India, who go out in husband-and-wife teams to dig yams. It has been specifically stated by Ehrenfels, who studied them carefully, that they have no territories, but the total land area in which they live is little more than one hundred miles square, and their population, 1,238 in 1911, had been reduced to 565 in 1941. Individuals and families move about in this territory freely, combining and separating as they see fit, but all Kadar recognize two holy mountains in the middle of their country as the ancestral couple from which they are all supposedly descended. Thus they are a single people, and their country is their territory, although they are not organized in specific local groups. It may be recalled that they do not hunt deliberately, but kill a small animal only occasionally when it is easy to do so, and with their digging sticks. The problem of who divides the meat and who gets what scarcely exists, and hunting in groups and dividing the meat are key factors in band structure. It is an open question as to how the Kadar got their food and how they were organized before they were driven up into their yam-filled hills.

Composite bands in Canada, India, and Australia

The second anomalous type of organization is the composite band. Such a group is formed when members of two or more different territorial bands join up on the land of one of them. We are not referring to seasonal or occasional events when members of two or more groups come together for an elephant hunt, a caribou surround, or to feast on argotis moths, pitahaya fruit, or the carcass of a stranded whale, for after these gatherings the people go back to their own lands. In northern Canada and inland parts of Alaska, both Algonkian-speaking and Athabascan-speaking Indians have been living in composite groups for some time, but they are no longer strictly hunters because for several centuries they have been fur trappers for white traders. Before that, old accounts and linguistic analysis indicate that they were organized like most other hunters.

The Chenchu of southern India (who are also symbiotic) say that they were originally descended from a brother and sister who lived alone in the jungle and produced offspring, and that their children gave birth to other boys and girls who married in the same fashion, until their descendants became more numerous and decided to split up into exogamous bands, each with its own territory. But by the time they were pushed up into the hills, the bands united into composite villages near the mohua trees from which they made their favorite drink, although at other times they still got food from their individual territories.

Composite bands existed in the late nineteenth and present centuries in North Central Australia, but we do not know how long these people had lived in that fashion. In the better-watered parts of the continent, particularly in the south and east, the usual territorial bands were found when the first settlers arrived, as in Tasmania. In the part of Australia that had composite bands, the rainfall is fickle, and people living in one territory may find little to eat one year, while their neighbors have had rain, the grass has grown green, and more game is available. Shifting from territory to territory is a normal thing to do, and elaborate kinship and ceremonial ties make coexistence possible without undue friction.

In the earlier times, before European colonization, each band may have had more land, and the pressure of tribes from the occupied areas may have had a compressing influence. Nowadays, of course, the aborigines who cluster around cattle stations and missions are refugees from many bands, just as the Indians on many of our reservations come from different tribes. It is hard today to find an example of a composite band fully divorced from symbiosis or from the effects of contact with agriculturalists, traders, whalers, and colonists; these are just as rare as bandless peoples, and probably for the same reason. Instead of having too much space, they have too little.

Boundaries

Obviously, people who live in territorial bands have to have some way of meeting each other without fighting on first sight, not only to arrange marriages and communal hunts, but also to reach rare sources of special foods and materials, and to invite each other to ceremonies. One way was recorded a century and a half ago among the Tasmanians, and it has been confirmed by archaeologists. The latter have found at least nine sources of ochre that had been worked, and eleven places where people had quarried stone for implements. There were doubtless more. We have also discovered routes marked by campsites containing, among other things, abalone shells. These routes not only linked the ochre and quarry sites to each other, and both to beaches where abalones were collected; but the routes also seem to have coincided (at least the inland ones) with tribal boundaries. These "roads" were kept burnt over, and thus served in a sense as international boundaries over which bands could travel to obtain the materials mentioned with a fair chance of avoiding armed conflict.

In some other places, as with the Yaghans, travelers were permitted to cross through territories rather than between them. Among the Vedda of Ceylon, some frontiers ran along well-recognized ridges and streams, but where they passed through forests they were marked by figures of a man holding a drawn bow and arrow, cut in the bark, an easily recognizable STOP sign. In 1630 a Portuguese made a journey through the forest of Ceylon. When he came to a boundary he would find a group of bowmen standing under such a tree. The men made him wait while they sent a messenger to ask permission from their "elder" to let the traveler pass, and when the permission had been granted one of the archers escorted the stranger to the next boundary, where the procedure was repeated. In seven days the traveler had twelve guides, and had crossed as many territories.

In Australia, heralds were sent out to deliver invitations to members of a band some distance away, across tribal boundaries. The man chosen for this purpose was painted and otherwise decorated in a distinctive way; in effect, he wore an easily recognized uniform that insured his safety. He also carried with him a message stick so carved and otherwise decorated as to indicate the nature of the proposed visit, and notches on it to show the number of days before the meeting was to take place. While the herald might be able to deliver his message orally if the two groups spoke the same language, there were occasions when they did not. In any case the stick itself made the invitation formal and official.

In California and elsewhere in North America messages of the same nature were conveyed, but — at least in California — instead of a message stick the date was indicated by knots on a string, a prototype of the Peruvian *quipu* used by the Incas for more complicated records. The use of such mnemotic devices does not imply that the people concerned had elaborate numerical systems and could count in large numbers. Few of them could. All they needed to do was to touch the notches or knots with their fingers.

The troublesome subject of kinship terms

Any territorial band of hunters contains a number of families. Many of these families are, by force of circumstance, related to each other, and each family may have relatives in other bands. When people refer to their relatives they have special words to make clear to the listener what the relationships are, and these words are kinship terms. These terms are much more important to hunters than they are to us because most of the other persons that a hunter sees and does things with are relatives. In our society, the reverse may be true. If we have first cousins, we may see them only at weddings and funerals. Some may be rich, others poor, some in *Who's Who* and others in mental institutions. We often do not know the names of some of our cousins' children, who may live over a thousand miles away.

H*

Most of the people we work with or share our leisure hours with today may not be relatives. Because kinship beyond the bounds of the immediate family plays so small a part in our lives, we have a blind spot about it, and when we read about kinship terms in anthropological publications, that blind spot may be enlarged by obscure academic jargon. The whole subject is troublesome, but it doesn't need to be. If the hunters themselves understand it, there is no reason why we shouldn't try to, at least in a rudimentary way.

As we look through the lists of kinship terms used by various groups of hunters, we notice at once that, in most cases (the Mbuti Pygmies being an exception), they are more numerous than ours, and draw finer lines of distinction than ours do. In Andamanese there are separate terms for older brother, younger brother, older sister, and younger sister. When a mother is referring to her children she uses different words for each child, depending on its relative age. Yaghan also has a proliferation of such terms, extended to the relative ages of uncles and cousins.

Relative age clearly is important to these and other hunting peoples, not only within individual families, but also between the members of the band as a whole, the reason being that sets of brothers and sisters may span several of the age grades of which the band is composed. This happens because hunters' wives marry young (at least for the first time), and may produce children from menarchy to menopause. But they usually space them at least three years apart, so that child number two will not have been begotten until after number one has been weaned. Usually twins are not kept, and many children die in infancy, widening the gaps. This spacing of children may help reduce the amount of sibling rivalry below that seen in some other societies in which children are born closer together, and the differences in kinship terminology designating older and younger siblings reenforces the feeling of separation.

Brothers and sisters thus may not be close companions. Their companions are other children of like age that they grew up with. An older sister may carry a baby brother or sister on her back, but she does so more as a deputy mother than as an equal. Her peers are her age mates. They all go through puberty rites together and remain friends throughout life. An older brother is, in the same way, a deputy father or uncle in his attitude toward his younger brother, and their being of different age grades may separate them until death or senility.

The three primary incest tabus

Before we proceed in our general coverage of kinship to the question of how it affects who may marry whom, let us try to simplify matters by first stating who should not. In human societies as a whole, this is a complicated matter depending on many factors, such as differences in social class, religion, and even race. But in most hunting societies it is to a considerable extent associated with the so-called incest tabu, which dictates who is forbidden to have sexual intercourse with whom, because in most cases marriage implies the possibility of sexual relations between man and wife, and childbearing.

While under certain circumstances, in some societies, a young man may marry a woman past menopause, he may manage to have sexual relations with other women, and may eventually get a nubile second wife. In any event, the incest tabus recognized in any given hunting society bear some relationship to his choice (or to his and/or her parents' choice) of a marital partner. Of these prohibitions there are three basic and quite different incest tabus, prohibiting intercourse between father and daughter, mother and son, and brother and sister. These prohibitions are not based on instinct or the inductive experience of the genetic consequences that sometimes result. Some individuals violate them, but if so the violations do not result in marriage.

To a considerable extent these primary incest tabus are based on two kinds of antisocial results. Parent-child intercourse would disrupt the lines of authority between generations, lines that hold the family together. Brother-sister intercourse during adolescence would inhibit intermarriage between families, reducing their interdependence. Were a married woman to have intercourse with her brother, it would create a state of serious conflict between her husband and his brother-in-law, two kinsmen by marriage who, in certain cultures, might need each other's confidence and help (as, for example, in the case of the Chenchu who collected honey from a cliff, and would trust only his brother-in-law to guard the rope). Because of the frequency of interband exogamy among hunters, two brothers-in-law might belong to different bands, and incest of this kind would jeopardize peaceful relations between those bands.

In certain cultures the prohibition against marriage between brothers and sisters may be extended to the children of men who have made pacts of blood-brotherhood together, as in some parts of Australia, or to the children of two men who habitually hunt together alone, as among the G/wi Bushmen of the Central Kalahari Game Preserve in Botswana. The association of the two partners may last a lifetime, and they and their families may be alone in the bush for six months out of every year. The sons and daughters of the two families have been brought up with the intimacy of brothers and sisters, and marriage between them is forbidden.

These and other considerations suggest that the yearnings for sexual intimacy between brothers and sisters who have lived together during childhood may be weaker than those that attract fathers and daughters and mothers and sons. Many origin myths tell of brother-sister mating in a matter-of-fact way, apparently because of the need to derive a whole people from the offspring of a single couple. In these accounts, the first brother and sister couple had not been brought up together, and had no one else to marry; as soon as their offspring had multiplied enough to permit it, the brother-sister prohibition arose. Oedipus-like myths of mother-son matings are rarer, but there are many referring to fathers violating their daughters, or even just trying to, followed by natural catastrophes of a cosmic nature as exemplified by the story of Manbuk the Young Hunter and the Seven Water Maidens, to be given in Chapter 13.

Hunting peoples extend the brother-sister marriage prohibition to first cousins related bilaterally (on both sides of the family), or unilaterally (on one side only). Here I refer to actual first cousins as well as to those individuals who have come to be so considered through adoption or other means. (In some hunting societies the word for "cousin" may be applied to cousins of various degrees, but the people concerned know whether "close up cousins" or "far away cousins" are meant. In fact, the words for brother and sister may actually be applied to these various cousins). If the extension is bilateral, marriage is forbidden between all such first cousins, all first and second cousins, or, in extreme cases, between all persons believed to be descended from a common ancestor on either side. This ultimate prohibition is seldom more inclusive than the second-cousin tabu because people who have to remember the names of all their ancestors seldom can name all of them more than two generations away.

If the prohibition is extended unilaterally to first cousins, that means that only the first cousins on one side of the family are affected. The children of two brothers or two sisters are called parallel cousins; those of father's sister and mother's brother are cross cousins. With few exceptions among those hunters tracing unilateral descent, cross cousins may marry but parallel cousins may not.

Unilateral restrictions are easier to extend than bilateral ones, because only the ancestors on one side of the family need to be remembered. Thus while bilateral prohibitions rarely stretch beyond second cousins, unilateral ones may be spread out more or less indefinitely on one side of the family, through a belief in a remote common ancestor, perpetuated in a myth.

When boys and girls who are related in this remote and often fictitious way first meet, they may feel just as much attracted to each other as if they were not supposed to be related, and they may find the prevailing incest tabu hard to keep. They may discover ways of evading it, within or without the ties of marriage, if necessary by elopement. We shall see some examples of this as we proceed.

10.

Marriage

The ideal choice of spouses

Having learned who is forbidden to marry whom in hunting societies, we may now consider who is not only allowed, but expected, if possible, to marry whom. The answer is simple. *The ideal choice of marital partners will bring together a man and a woman whose relationship to each other lies just beyond the outer limits of the extended brother-sister incest tabu.*

In another sense, the ideal or preferred mating (not always achieved) is one which will create a minimum of disturbance to all persons in any way affected by it. These persons include the parents of the couple, their other close kin, and their habitual associates. But a man must not be led too far afield for a wife. If possible she must have been brought up speaking the same language and following the same set of customs as the groom's sisters, and ideally the two families should already know each other. Otherwise the presence of a stranger may cause too much disturbance for easy tolerance in the group into which the newcomer, bride or groom, is introduced.

In our own societies the least disturbance to all persons concerned will be created if we marry within our own ethnic group, religion, social class, and educational level, with little regard for kinship beyond the reach of our relatively limited incest restrictions. But among most hunters, except to a certain extent for those that have developed class systems, kinship is the key consideration.

When the kinship term for "cousins" is the same on both sides of the family, we call the system "bilateral." A boy is supposed to marry a girl beyond the range of first or second cousins, on either side of the family, or beyond any known relationship.

With few exceptions among hunters, descent is reckoned patrilineally because it is the men of a band that own its territory and hunt on it. Therefore, when the system is "unilateral," the bride should ideally be a first cousin on the side of the family through which descent is not traced. For this reason there can be two kinds of kinship terms for "cousins." A boy might be expected to marry his mother's brother's daughter or his father's sister's daughter, since either of these would belong to a patrilineage different from his own.

If this statement causes any initial confusion in the reader's mind, the simplest way to make it clear is to sit down with pencil and paper and write out the names of your parents, brothers and sisters, uncles and aunts by blood and by marriage on both sides of the family, and all first cousins. If you are a male, underline the names of all your father's sisters' daughters and mother's brothers' daughters. If you are a female, underline those of your father's sisters' sons and mother's brothers' sons. Those whose names are underlined would have been eligible for you to marry if you had been born into a hunting band with unilateral kinship and patrilineal descent. In either case you will probably be glad that you weren't.

Every young man does not have an ideal marital partner awaiting him, according to this system. There may have been no eligible girls on either side, and had there been, his older brothers might have married them already. If a boy's parents cannot find him an acceptable marital partner of an appropriate age, he may have to become betrothed to a girl who is still a baby. Then he will have to bide his time until she comes to puberty before he can have sexual relations with her, even if he has already married her. In the meantime, he may have made shift with a widow older than himself, which has certain well-known advantages.

If we review the principal hunting peoples chosen as examples in the preceding chapters, we will find that the following have *bilateral* kinship and marital systems: most of the Bushmen, most of the Pygmies, the Andamanese, the Yaghans, the Indians of Central and northern California, the Nootka, Salish, and Kwakiutl of the American Northwest Coast, most of the Northern Athabascan Indians, and the Arctic and Eastern Eskimo. *Unilateral* systems are found among the Australian aborigines and probably the Tasmanians, most of the hunters of India, the Vedda of Ceylon, the Northern Algonkians, and the northern tribes of the Northwest Coast Indians.

Further complications are provided by what might be called *mixed* or *transitional* systems, in which the marital prohibition is bilateral but with a tendency to trace descent principally through one line, particularly the father's. This is the easiest of all to explain because it falls closest to our own. We do not ordinarily marry first cousins on either side; we take our father's surnames; and a woman's married name is her husband's. Examples are those of the Ona and Bering Sea Eskimo. The Ainu have a double descent system to be described presently, and the nonhunting Kadar of India, apparently uniquely, permit marriage with first cousins of all categories.

Neither of the two most clear-cut systems, the bilateral and the unilateral, is necessarily older or more archaic than the other. They are simply two possible ways of matchmaking in societies where everyone is more or less related to each other in fact or fiction. They exist because, by dividing us into males and females nature has provided us with two principal choices. Both are found among the technologically simplest and most advanced of hunting societies.

Whatever the kinship system may be, there are three principal ways of getting a wife: by an exchange of women, by capture, and by "purchase," often really an exchange of property. The first is the commonest. Marriage by capture is often simulated in hunters' wedding ceremonies, but as a real thing it seems to have been limited to the Tasmanians and the Ona. Marriage by "purchase" is found where some men are richer than others, as on the Northwest Coast.

The so-called "joking" relationship

No matter how the men of any given people may get their wives, every individual usually has to divide the persons whom he or she knows into two mutually exclusive categories, those to be treated with respect and a certain amount of formality, or even avoided, and those that can be dealt with in a relaxed, informal way. The former category characteristically includes all older persons of both sexes whether closely related to the individual concerned or not, and members of the opposite sex unavailable to each other in marriage.

The second category includes two kinds of people; all members of his or her own sex and age grade that he or she sees and does things with frequently, like group hunting companions and women that collect yams or pound acorns together, and members of the opposite sex that might have married each other if they had not married somebody else. Joking between members of the same sex tends to preserve a balance of personalities, and thus to reduce arrogance or boasting. Joking between men and women who fall into this relationship allows them, in some cases, to work off their residues of sexual impulses left over from, or in lieu of, marriage by talking freely about sex in a kidding kind of way, making believe to insult each other, and playing humorous tricks on each other. In anthropological jargon this kind of behavior is called *the joking relationship*. Jokes are not always funny and sometimes they go too far, leading to adultery and fighting.

The question as to who may "joke" with whom in different societies depends on the structures of their marriage systems. For example, in unilaterally organized bands in which all males are believed to be descended from a common ancestor, the boys must treat all girls of their band as their sisters. They therefore view the prospects of interband meetings with the same keen anticipation as boys and girls immured in unisexual boarding schools regard going home for vacation, and taking their roommates with them.

Marriage among the Kadar

In the rest of this chapter we shall choose a few examples of marriage systems among hunting peoples, picking the ones that together show the range of extremes. None is more unusual than that of the Kadar, who have no tribes, clans, or totems; and no social unit larger than the extended family and the collection of families that may happen to be camping together. The Kadar marry when both partners are about eighteen. Before marriage boys and girls have much freedom, and many matches are love affairs, although some are prearranged.

Like the other nonagricultural and nonpastoral peoples of India, they have unilineal kinship terms, but their choices of marital partners are different from the others. Over half of the Kadar matches recorded in the 1940s were between a boy and his real or classificatory father's brother's daughter. This is one form of what is called *parallel cousin* marriage, and it may well be the only case of its kind known among food-gathering peoples. Most of the other Kadar matches were *cross cousin*; usually between a boy and his mother's brother's daughter.

Divorce is frequent among the Kadar. Most middle-aged persons have been married two or three times, and sometimes remarried to a former spouse. Ehrenfels, who studied them, recorded two cases of polyandry, in each of which two men, who were not brothers, shared a wife. In one case, one husband later married another wife in a different settlement and was supposed to leave his first, poly-androus wife alone thereafter; but he continued to visit wife number one from time to time, until wife number two made so much trouble that he desisted. A few men had two wives at once.

As the Kadar have no bands and do not hunt, each family is self-supporting. With no meat to share and a constant supply of yams, they need no social structure more inclusive than the family, and if their ancestors hunted before being driven up into the forest where yams are abundant, they presumably once had unilateral bands as the Birhors, Chenchu, and Veddas do. Lacking historical information, we cannot be sure.

The !Kung Bushmen and their same-name tabu

Another people having what seems to be a unique system of regulating marriage are the !Kung Bushmen of the Nyae Nyae country of the Kalahari Desert, centered around the Gautscha water hole in northeastern Southwest Africa and overlapping the border of Botswana. They are divided into thirty-six intermarrying bands ranging in size from eight to fifty-seven persons but averaging twenty-five. Each band has a headman or chief who decides who shall go where and when on collecting expeditions, because the timing of the yearly round is critical to ensure the food supply. The headmanship is hereditary by primogeniture.

The !Kung bands are composite, in the sense that a young man will go to live with his wife's band until she has borne him two or three children. Then he will bring his family back to his own band unless he chooses to stay on. If he has inherited a headmanship he cannot exercise it until his return, in which case a younger brother may act as regent.

Marriage is theoretically forbidden between a young man and any first, second, or third female cousin on either side, and also between certain relatives by marriage, including step-relatives. In all there are seven categories of persons whom a man cannot marry, and seven forbidden to a woman. All are designated by special kinship terms. Mrs. Lorna Marshall, who collected this information in great detail, found only three instances in which these rules had been broken. Two men had married some kind of cousins, and a third had married his stepdaughter as well as her mother. For this he was considered insane and was so harassed that he left his band permanently, along with his younger wife.

Besides the seven categories of persons whom a !Kung may not marry because of known kinship, the prohibition is further extended to include all other persons of the opposite sex who bear the same given name as any one of the persons included in those seven categories. In other words, if my mother is named Alice, I cannot marry any girl named Alice. Among some six hundred Nyae Nyae !Kung whose names Mrs. Marshall recorded, she found forty-six male and forty-one female given names, with an average of a dozen to fifteen persons bearing each of them. This name tabu subtracted another fifteen percent or so of the otherwise available potential spouses left over after the elimination of the members of the seven forbidden categories, thus considerably reducing the field.

The apparent justification for this same-name tabu is that, if two persons bear the same name, they must be distantly related, because given names are inherited, as follows. A father names his firstborn son after his father, and if he has more than one wife, the father will give the same name to the firstborn son of each wife. This duplication will cause no confusion because each individual has a nickname as well. The father names his first daughter after his own mother, his second son after the father of the child's mother, and a second daughter after her mother's mother. If a wife bears him more than two sons and/or two daughters, the father may name subsequently born children after his own brothers and sisters.

Like any other regulation, this same-name tabu is subject to some flexibility, for a person's bestowed name may be changed before reaching maturity. In one recorded case, her father changed a girl's name because he wanted it for another daughter. However, this change might not make much difference in her marital prospects because her new name would be taken from the same name pool as her old one.

The same-name tabu has this effect upon the joking relationship among the Nyae Nyae !Kung. No two persons share exactly the same roster of joking partners of the opposite sex. One brother may be allowed to joke with some women that another brother must avoid, and vice versa. It thus prevents the formation of cozy bisexual groups, and limits chances for adultery, a very real source of potential strife because these people are very strict about sex, what with long periods of continence during pregnancy and lactation.

Directly or indirectly sex is their dominant joking theme, like money among the Scots, excrement among Germanic peoples, and the police among hippies. When men are alone together, one may tease another by saying that the latter has oversized testicles, and in mixed company, a man may tease a beautiful woman by telling her, with a straight face, how ugly she is.

According to Mrs. Marshall, her Bushmen copulate only in the strict privacy of their huts, lying on their sides, and from the rear. The husband pulls his wife's labiae minorae first to excite her. The labiae hang several inches down the thighs. Many physical anthropologists have debated whether or not this trait is genetic. Mrs. Marshall also found out that when a man has two wives, he lies in the middle, with one on either side; thus each wife is a close witness to what happens to the other. It may be added that such cozy nocturnal life at close quarters is a rare thing among polygynists, for in other cultures each wife usually has a sleeping place of her own. Among the Australian aborigines, when camping out in the open, the husband will have but one wife sleeping with him at a time. He will also approach her from behind, not necessarily from preference but because copulating in that position attracts the least attention when everyone who is awake can see, by wavering firelight, more or less what everyone else within eyeshot is doing.

Australian marriage classes

In Chapter 9 we discussed the problem of composite bands in north-central Australia. This is also the part of the continent in which marriage systems reach their peak of complexity, not only in Australia but perhaps also in the world. It is a land of unstable and unpredictable rainfall, with irregular alternations of feast and famine. If a man takes a wife from a distant band he may thus establish friendly bonds with people with whom his own group may need to share resources when the land of one is more favored than that of the other, both fully knowing that the situation may be reversed during the next year. In other words, by force of circumstances, they temporarily fall into the relationship of contiguous bands living in stabler environments, and they need to establish or to reinforce comparable ties for the same reason, mutual survival. But as many of them do not

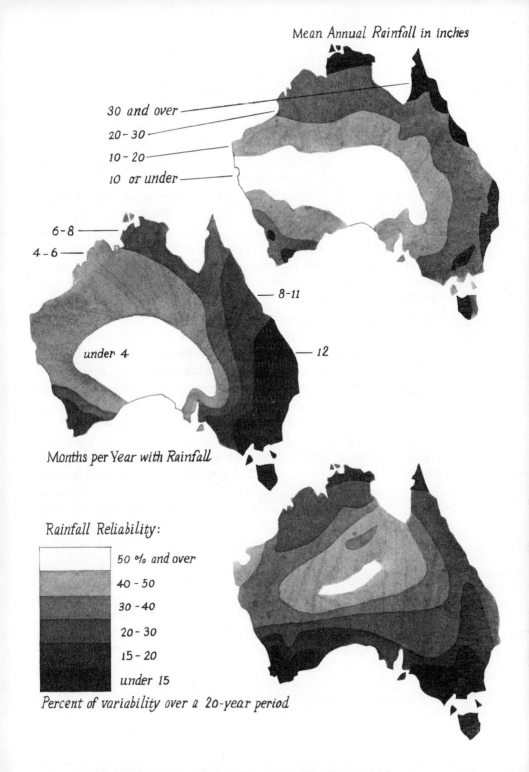

Mean Annual Rainfall in inches

30 and over
20 - 30
10 - 20
10 or under

6 - 8
4 - 6

8 - 11

under 4

12

Months per Year with Rainfall

Rainfall Reliability:

50 % and over
40 - 50
30 - 40
20 - 30
15 - 20
under 15

Percent of variability over a 20-year period

1. Rainfall in Australia and Tasmania. The densest and
stablest aboriginal populations were found where the rainfall
was greatest, least seasonal, and least variable; social organization
was most complex where the rainfall was lightest, most seasonal,
and least reliable

know each other very well, if at all, they may not be sure what their relationships to each other may be. But as meetings like this are prime occasions for matchmaking, something must be done about it, and it is.

In Central Australia, where we find our classic example of this situation, the people are divided into a number of marriage classes, usually four or eight. Each of them bears a totemic name. A flying fox man, for example, need know only that he may marry only a rain woman, and in an eight-class system seven other categories of women would be unavailable to him, including those of his own class. But there is more to it than this. His son will not be a flying fox man at all, but let us say a cockatoo man, for cockatoo men are the offspring of flying fox-rain unions. Their son will not marry a rain woman like his mother, but a fringed lizard woman, and their children will belong to a fifth class and marry into a sixth, until the eighth time around, when it will be flying fox with rain again.

This sounds very complicated to us but it is not to the Australians who are born and die with it. Because many bands may participate in it, it need not create any greater shortage of marriageable women than would occur in a two-band exchange with cousin marriage preferred. The total number of individuals is relatively great, containing two or three hundred persons in some cases, with forty to fifty persons in each class. It is really quite exciting—it mixes people around, and it creates close relationships between persons living far apart. A man traveling far afield may meet a stranger, and wonder how to deal with him according to kinship etiquette. Instead of sitting down like two old ladies from Boston and counting back ancestors until they get to, let us say, Governor Bradford, one of them says: "I am a flying fox man." The other may reply: "Why, so am I," or else, "My father was," or, "My son is. I am a cockatoo myself." A marriage class is more than a matrimonial unit, it is a kind of club.

The system is a unifying device, one which has spread relatively recently in Australia, and it may simply be one of the several effects of pressure by the white men. It is unwittingly promoted by the missionaries and station owners, because they both give handouts of food and thus draw large (for them) groups of aborigines from considerable distances. To what extent the members of Australian marriage classes are *really* related is an academic matter, of less importance than the fact that the system works. It has many local elaborations and manifestations, some of which are not yet fully understood, or agreed on, by social anthropologists.

Marriage and wooing among the Tasmanians

We know very little about the marriage system that existed among the Tasmanians, but it seems to have been a simple exchange of women between bands occupying adjacent territories, as among the aborigines of the forested regions of southeastern Australia. This exchange was not always equal or necessarily peaceful. In one account we are told that a band living near Hobart Town before the colonists' arrival was raided by neighbors who killed the men who tried to stop them and took away their women. And there are other accounts of individual cases of marriage by capture. Sometimes when a man from a neighboring band had the right to marry a girl, but neither she nor her parents liked him, it is said that they killed the girl rather than give her up.

The Tasmanian wooing technique could also be violent. G. A. Robinson described how an Oyster Bay man named Woorrady won his bride, a Bruny Island woman named Trugernanna. Both were members of Robinson's retinue, and Trugernanna was the last full-blooded Tasmanian to die, in 1876.

At night when Trugernanna had retired Woorrady would creep over and lie next to her, and he would keep her from sleeping by pricking her breasts with a sharp-pointed stick. When Trugernanna tried to move away, Woorrady either held her or moved with her. Although she resisted for some time and made uncomplimentary remarks about her suitor, she finally gave in, and the couple remained together until Woorrady's death.

Incipient clans and marriage among the Ona

The Ona, who occupied the grassy northern portion of Tierra del Fuego, owned thirty-nine named and clearly bounded hunting territories. Some of the latter ran from the mountains to the sea, while others were confined to the mountains. Each territory was inhabited by between 40 and 120 persons, and the total Ona population was 3,000 to 4,000. The Ona forbade marriage with first cousins on either side, but they also had separate terms for father's and mother's kin, and the men of each territory felt themselves linked to the land through their paternal ancestors. Thus the men of each territory formed an incipient patrilineal clan.

As with the Tasmanians, one form of marriage was by capture. This statement is not a traveler's tale but a fact observed by Lucas Bridges, the missionary's son, and documented with case histories. A man seeking a wife would cross the ridge separating his country from the next one, find a girl who was tarrying behind the others in one of their frequent moves from camp to camp, threaten her with drawn arrow, and herd her across the border.*

Lucas Bridges tells of one event in which some Onas from the mountains met another group from the Cape San Pablo region. The mountain men greeted the others warmly and invited them to camp with them. When everyone was having a good time, with much hilarity, the hosts arose and shot the San Pablo men and took their women. If a captive woman tried to run away, either in such a massacre or otherwise, her husband would shoot her in the legs with unbarbed arrows or, if he could reach her, he would beat her. A man who captured a mother and a daughter as fair prize could keep and sleep with both of them. The situation among the Ona was different from that of the Bushman who married a mother and daughter and was driven from his camp with the younger female. Whereas in the case of the Bushman marriage was a reciprocal affair, with many categories of relatives excluded, the Ona excluded only first cousins, and marriage by capture from a hostile band was another matter.

There were also gentler ways of getting a wife. Once Bridges saw a young Ona standing under a tree where a girl and her parents and younger brother were camped. The girl was holding the young man's bow and arrows, which he had handed to her. She toyed with them for a little while and then gave them to her brother, who took them back to their owner. This was a proposal that the girl had declined, but the young man repeated the performance on several occasions until the girl finally stood up and carried the bow and arrows to the boy herself. She had given in.

*Marriage by capture was also practiced by the Kutchin Indians of Alaska.

Double descent among the Ainu

The Bushmen, Australians, Tasmanians, and Ona are or were nomadic in their movements. Whole families or groups of families moved about together in their territories on their seasonal rounds of hunting and collecting. But there are other hunters whose women stayed home most of the time while the men went out hunting, by land or sea. In this respect these people resembled garden cultivators like the Iroquois, whose women grew the maize, beans, and squash that provided the staple foods, and whose men went out on seasonal hunts and warlike raids. The Iroquois had a matrilineal organization. Among hunters whose women stay home, some form of mother right may assert itself, or at least some recognition of the importance of the maternal line of descent. People who have fixed residences do not have to carry all of their equipment with them. They can accumulate property, and property breeds differences in wealth, rank, and social classes. The most likely combination of circumstances that keeps women at home and allows the accumulation of wealth and rank (outside of agriculture), is a seasonal abundance of fish, particularly salmon. For maize, beans, and squash, read *salmon*.

Each Ainu settlement consisted of a string of houses and outbuildings along the bank or banks of a segment of a river. There were seldom more than three households in a settlement, and three was the number whose inhabitants helped each other in house building and fishing, and who shared food. If there were more than three, there was more than one sharing unit and the settlement was thus composite.

The men of each Ainu settlement belonged to one or more patrilineal units based on common descent over as many generations as the men could remember. These patrilineages were totemic. The names of only six are known, and six may have been all that there were. Each one bore the name of the spiritual owner of an animal or bird. The six named were bear, fox, wolf, eagle, hawk, and eagle-owl, the last named being a species of horned owl. The ancestor of each lineage was supposed to have been descended from the spiritual owner of the animal in question, as in the case of the bear. According to their legend, a lonely woman was once visited by a strange man who impregnated her, and then turned into a bear, and her son was the founder of the bear lineage.

Members of these six totemic units ranged up and down the valleys, some of them more concentrated in certain settlements than in others, and the common affiliation in different settlements gave a kind of cohesion to neighboring settlements in the old, pre-Japanese days when men from different major segments of a valley, or from different valleys, fought each other. It may be added that among the Ainu six was a sacred number and the prime unit of counting.

On the other hand the Ainu women traced their descent through their mothers to any one of eight totemic creatures, four of which duplicated those of the men. The eight were: Goddess of Fresh Water, bear, grampus, fox, wolf, eagle, wild dog,* and hare. Now the women recognized only four generations of descent as a unit of exogamy—the woman in question, her mother, mother's mother, and the latter's mother. Even if a woman knew the name of her matrilineal great-great grandmother, it did not matter as far as marriage was concerned.

Each woman wore around her waist a secret girdle plaited from wild-flax fiber in such a way as to symbolize abstractly the female lineage of her mother. Being extremely modest about showing their bodies, the women did not let men see their girdles. Although the men knew that they could not marry a woman who was descended from their mother's maternal grandmothers, they were kept in ignorance of the names and meanings of the designs on the girdles. All that they knew, apparently, if they knew it at all, was that their wives wore them.

Now and then it might happen that a young man wished to marry a girl who was not descended from his mother's maternal grandmother but who, unknown to him, wore a secret girdle of the same pattern as his own mother's. In such a situation the local women would go into conference, agree that the match was permissible, obtain the consent of the girl's own mother, and then simply give the girl a new girdle with a different design, and neither the groom nor the other men would be aware that anything unusual had happened.

So closely was this secret of the girdles kept that no student of Ainu culture, as far as we know, had been aware of their existence until, as late as 1934, a Scottish physician who lived among them, Dr. Neil G. Munro, gained the confidence of two of his female pa-

*Called raccoon in the literature, because some of them have black lines on their faces. They are really a local species of canid, *Nycteutes procyonides viverinus* Temminck, that live in rock cavities near the holes where bears hibernate, and are considered by the Ainu to be servants of bears.

tients whom he had persuaded to undress in his presence in the course of his work. They gave away the secret, and explained the system to him. They told him that long ago the women had received the designs from Kamui Fuchi, the Fire Goddess, who had also given them secret powers, including the ability to put out fires. Once when his straw-roofed house was on fire Dr. Munro saw a group of women waving branches in the direction of his house, with the intention of extinguishing the flames through the power conferred on them by their secret girdles.

In view of the small size of the Ainu communities, these marriage regulations fostered a circulation of women up and down each valley and kept the people of its settlements in touch with each other even more closely, it would appear, than did the patrilineal affiliations of the men. In most cases the men resided where they had been born, and visited each other mainly on ceremonial occasions, notably on the winter round of bear sacrifices, the most spectacular and widely known item of Ainu culture.

The six male and eight female lineages were not all thought to be equal in rank. The masculine bear lineage was thought to be a cut above the others, and two of the female lineages, ones not found among the men, occupied an inferior status in one way or another.

The wild dog lineage had no spiritual owner, like those of the other animals and birds named, but it may have come under the protection of the owner of the bears, because the wild dogs were believed to be the bears' servants. The hare lineage, ranked at the foot of the list, was said to be descended from a beautiful young woman who inadvertently let a young man see her plaiting a secret girdle in the forest. She was therefore obliged to marry him, and eventually she turned into a goddess who protects her female descendants and prevents their children from being born with harelips. The low rank of this lineage is attributed to its ancestress's inadvertent immodesty.

Variations among the Eskimo

We now move on to the top of the New World, the lands inhabited by the Eskimo, all the way from the Chukchi Peninsula in Siberia to East Greenland, and as far south as Kodiak Island in the west and Labrador in the east. Every schoolchild, presumably, knows about

2. *Distribution of the Eskimo. (After Hans-Georg Bandi,* Eskimo
Prehistory, *College, Alaska: University of Alaska Press, 1969)*

Polar
Eskimos

West Greenlanders

East Greenlanders

Iglulik Eskimos

Baffinland Eskimos

Netsilik

ibou
mos

Hudson Bay

Labrador Eskimos

Eskimo culture and most of them consider it to be uniform wherever Eskimo live. However, as we have seen in previous discussions of material culture, all Eskimo do not go whaling, few of them make or made snow houses, not all of them drive dogsleds, nor do they all burn blubber in lamps. A comparable diversity is seen in many aspects of social and spiritual culture, and even in language.

Today about 16,000 Eskimo live in Alaska, more or less 1,300 in the USSR (as of 1927), 11,000 in Canada, and 25,000 in Greenland — the last figure including many persons of mixed ancestry — and most Eskimo live below the Arctic Circle. At the time of European contact they may have totaled about 50,000, with 26,000 in Alaska, where they are believed to have arisen, according to both linguistic and archaeological information, before 3000 B.C.

Eskimoan is most closely related to the language of the Aleuts, more remotely to those of the Chukchi, Koryaks, and Kamchadals in Siberia, and possibly, but not certainly, to Indo-European. They are an Asiatic people and differ from the American Indians in several genetic respects, most conspicuously in having, in all groups tested, the gene for Blood Group B. In Alaska there are two Eskimo languages, one north of Norton Sound and the other south of it. The North Alaskan language extends eastward, in various dialects, as far as Greenland, where the Eskimo arrived during the fourteenth century A.D. after the extinction of the European colony there. The South Alaskan language is split into four dialects, one spoken by the Siberian Eskimo, one on Nunivak Island, one on the Alaskan mainland from Norton Sound to the Aleutian Peninsula, and one on Kodiak Island and around Prince William Sound. To a certain extent these linguistic differences mirror cultural differences, including kinship and rules of marriage.

The classic "Eskimo" type of kinship, widely cited in anthropological writings, is a simple bilateral one like our own, which we have also encountered elsewhere. In it brothers and sisters are distinguished from cousins on either side, the terms for which are lumped. One is not supposed to marry a cousin on either side. This system is found in northern Canada and Greenland. In most of Alaska, while descent on both sides is recognized, the terms for paternal or parallel cousins are the same as those for brother and sister, with the implication that parallel cousins may not marry, while in some groups cross cousins may do so.

Sex relations between unmarried persons are free. Wife-lending to trading partners is usual, although often the wives lent say that they do not enjoy this. Unless potential spouses are unavailable locally, marriage is usually within the community, especially in Alaska where the Eskimo live in fairly large villages. As a rule the newlyweds go to live with the girls' parents, at least until they are able to obtain a house of their own.

The men's clubhouses, which we have mentioned in the community of Tigara at Point Hope in connection with whaling, are found among most Alaskan Eskimo and also in Greenland. A young man usually belongs to the same men's house as his father, but changes are possible. Young boys often sleep there, and some married men do at times. (Their wives bring them their food.) During the winter the members of one men's house invite members of others to visit them and at that time put on elaborate ceremonies, and exchange gifts.

The Eskimo in general are well known for their free camaraderie, sharing food and other belongings, and for their permissive attitude which avoids conflict except in cases of serious antisocial acts. But in the relatively large villages in Alaska, the position of whaling captain lends prestige, and traders also may acquire wealth which is not fully shared, and which becomes a vehicle of differentiation between men. The Chugash of Prince William Sound, whose marital rules are poorly documented, actually had chiefs and slaves, like their neighbors the Indians of the Northwest Coast. These latter include one tribe, the Eyak, whose territory the Chugash surround.

The Bering Sea Culture, based on whaling, arose in the northern part of the Bering seacoast of Alaska about 1800 B.C., and was also extant on St. Lawrence Island and the Siberian coast. It was characterized, among other things, by an efflorescence of art in carving walrus ivory. In one form or another, it lasted until the period of modern contact, as exemplified by the culture of the people of Tigara. Thus it had been in full flower long before Eskimos had spread across the north of Canada to Greenland.

This excursion into archaeology and chronology has a bearing on the modern differences in social complexity and marital norms among the living Eskimo. In this light the classic simplicity of the social arrangements among Canadian and Greenland Eskimo may be considered to be a relatively modern effect of the decline of whaling in the latter regions, and of the movement of some of the Eskimo inland to hunt caribou.

I

3. *Eskimoan languages and Eskimo trading places in Alaska. Eskimoan includes Eskimo and Aleut. Eskimo is divided into a northern and a southern language. Northern Eskimo is spoken from north of Norton Sound in Alaska to East Greenland. Southern Eskimo is divided into four dialects spoken in: (1) Siberia and St. Lawrence Island; (2) Nunivak Island; (3) the area from Norton Sound to the Alaska Peninsula; (4) Kodiak Island and the southeastern coast, as indicated. Trading places include Nelson Island, Hooper Bay, and Hotham Inlet on Kotzebue Sound*

The American Northwest Coast:
marriage, wealth, and rank

Let us now take a closer look at the Northwest Coast Indians, whose advanced technology we have referred to frequently, and who had as complicated a social structure as any other found among hunters, the reasons being that they were virtually sedentary, had ample food, and superior transportation by sea. They extended along 1,500 miles of Pacific coastline and on many islands, all the way from Prince William Sound in Alaska to northern California.

They included eight major groups, the Tlingit, Haida, Tsimshian, Bella Coola, Kwakiutl, Nootka, Coastal Salish, and Chinook, and many smaller ones, most of the latter being within the continental United States. They spoke different languages, each of which was divided into dialects. The Tlingit and Haida languages in the north are remotely related to Athabascan. Bella Coola, Kwakiutl, Nootka, and Salish belong to Algonkian-Ritwan, the same superfamily as Algonkian, and Tsimshian and Chinook are Penutian, a family concentrated in Central California and including that of the Maidu, of whom we have spoken earlier. It is most probable that some of these peoples were descended from inland tribes that had crossed the mountains or come down the river valleys to harvest the rich marine life of the coastal waters and inlets, while others may have been there longer and had no perceptible eastern connections. This listing of languages spoken by the Northwest Coast Indians is not an academic indulgence. It is pertinent to the study of the social structures of the Northwest Coast tribes, because their structural differences follow linguistic lines.

In these respects the tribes divide themselves into a northern and a southern tier. The northern ones include the Tlingit and Haida, both Athabascan speakers; and the Tsimshian, Penutian speakers; as well as the Haisla, a geographically separated northern branch of the Kwakiutl living cheek-by-jowl with the Tshimshians, and subject to their cultural influence. The members of the southern tier include the Bella Coola, the majority of the Kwakiutl, the Nootka, the Coastal Salish, and most of the small groups farther south.

The main differences are that the northerners have unilineal descent, are strongly matrilineal, and incline to build up rather complex social groups, while the southerners favor the father as the head of the lineage, while tracing descent from both sides of the family. Among the northerners a newly married couple lives in the groom's maternal uncle's house, while among the southerners they live in the groom's father's house. The northerners forbid parallel-cousin marriage (i.e., a boy cannot marry his father's brother's daughter or a girl her mother's sister's son), but prefer cross-cousin marriage. The Tlingit and Haida permit marriage with the paternal cross cousins only (i.e., the groom's father's sister's daughter), while the Tsimshian prefer it between maternal cross cousins (i.e., mother's brother's daughter). While these details may seem trivial to us and even boring, we have to mention them if we are to understand the next step, the nature of social structures more complicated than the individual family and the band, both of which units seem to have been overshadowed in the lives of the northern West Coast Indians. The matrilineal tendency of these tribes is a rare thing among hunters in general and is most commonly found among sedentary agricultural peoples, as stated on page 217.

Among the southern tribes, from the Kwakiutl and Bella Coola southward, where marriage is concerned no choice is made between father's and mother's kin. The Kwakiutl prefer marriage between second cousins whereas the Nootka and most of the tribes south of them forbid marriage with first or second cousins; but from the third cousin level on, the field is free, subject to other considerations, such as wealth and rank. In other words, don't marry for money necessarily, but marry where money is, and a good lot of maternal names and privileges from one's wife's family will do the children no harm. These ideas are not hard to understand for people brought up in our own culture — at least, if we are over thirty. If we are over sixty it is even easier.

When it comes to organization above the level of families and extended households, the northerners were more complicated than the southerners, who made up for the relative simplicity of their kinship structure by a meticulous emphasis on rank. The Tlingit and Haida were each divided into two moieties, called Raven and Wolf among the Tlingit and Raven and Eagle among the Haida. These moieties were exogamous — every man had to take a wife from the opposite one, as the marital rules suggest, and every man got his rank from his mother. These moieties had no political power, which was vested in the smaller groups — extended lineages, clans almost — of which each moiety was composed. Each lineage traced its descent

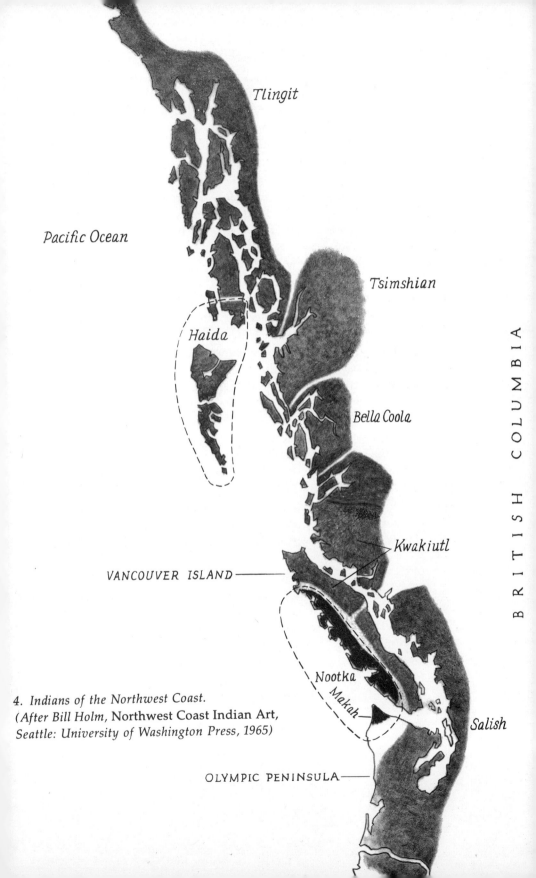

Tlingit

Pacific Ocean

Tsimshian

Haida

Bella Coola

B R I T I S H   C O L U M B I A

Kwakiutl

VANCOUVER ISLAND——

4. *Indians of the Northwest Coast.*
(After Bill Holm, Northwest Coast Indian Art,
Seattle: University of Washington Press, 1965)

Nootka

Makah

Salish

OLYMPIC PENINSULA——

through one matrilineal ancestress.* Both moieties and lineages had crests; i.e., representations of animals or supernatural beings that, they believed, had either been their actual ancestors or had helped their ancestors in some way.

Although called totems, these crests were more like European heraldic devices combined into coats of arms and serving the same purpose, to show how noble a person might be through descent on both sides of the family. Originally these crests were painted on houses, boxes, and other objects before the invention of totem poles by the Haida after the introduction of metal tools by trade. Once they had these tools the Haida traveled up and down the coast carving totem poles for others, a well-rewarded service.

The Tsimshians, who were Penutian, not Athabascan, speakers, had no moieties. Those living on the coast were divided into four matrilineal clans—Eagle, Raven, Wolf, and Blackfish. These clans were exogamous, and a branch of each one formed part of each of the fourteen so-called tribes, each tribe being a unit that wintered together, as previously stated in reference to the Nootka.

We have also mentioned the Nootkans' way of organizing their families into patrilocal households, with patrilineal chiefs of various degrees of importance. A child inherited his rights and privileges from both sides of the family, and the same was true in the case of the Kwakiutl—the best known of all the Northwest Coast Indians, thanks to the work of the late Franz Boas. During the potlatch period, from 1849 to about 1930, Kwakiutl culture reached a climax and declined, the two guiding factors being the introduction of Hudson Bay trade blankets which served as wealth and currency, and the decimation of the population owing to the white man's diseases. (We know little about what went on among the Kwakiutl before 1849.)

The Kwakiutl were divided into seventeen or more tribes, as defined above, and each tribe was subdivided into a number of units known as *numima*, each with its collection of related families. Every tribe was ranked in order of social importance, the Kwakiutl proper being Number One. Within each tribe, the numima were also graded, and so were all of the individuals within the numima. Thus everyone had his or her position in Kwakiutl society, but he or she did not necessarily get it at birth. The chief, who was Number One in

*Matrilineal descent may also be connected with slavery, as among the Tuareg of the Sahara. No matter how many children a Tuareg nobleman may have by black concubines, only those borne by his wife will have rank.

his tribe, gradually conferred on an individual the rights and privileges that the latter had inherited, and if he wished to, he might bestow on a favored person additional rights and privileges that were then without owners because of the many deaths that had occurred owing to new diseases.

These rights included titles, the privileges of singing certain songs, of wearing specific ceremonial masks, performing certain dances, sitting in a certain place during a potlatch, having one's name called in a certain order during ceremonies, and the right to fish in certain places where the fishing was good. Rights were inherited on both sides of the family and everyone except slaves held some of them. But some of the people had many and others very few. Since a chief's son could acquire high rank early in life, rank far overshadowed age grading in Kwakiutl society.

The Indians themselves recognized each person's position in society (and no two people were exactly the same in this respect), but they also recognized that some people were more important than others, and had words for what we call nobles and commoners. Nobles married among themselves, and their children were not allowed to play among commoner children. It is hard to find a cutoff line between these categories but one has been suggested: between those persons who had inherited the rights to take part in the performances of the winter dance societies, and those who might only watch them. The winter dances were elaborate productions in which scenery was changed in utter darkness when the fire was quenched. Prop men hidden above the crossbeams pulled strings to make wooden birds fly across the room, and to make jointed masks work. A series of tunnels and speaking tubes let actors appear and disappear, and mysterious voices boomed out of the ground.

Still there was a little mobility in the Kwakiutl system. A man who was an especially fine woodcarver or boatmaker might be given a few rights by a chief who appreciated his services, or the man's children might be given them. A chief could adopt his own grandson to raise the younger man's status ahead of time, so to speak, and an antisocial person might not get as many rights as he was entitled to.

As for slaves, they were Indians captured in war from other tribes. Many of them were Indians from the interior of northern California whom the Chinook traders brought north to sell in return for dentalia shells and Nootka canoes. A chief could kill his slaves if he wished. Sometimes they were buried as sacrifices under houseposts when a new house was being built, and sometimes they were tied up and laid on the beach as rollers for a visiting chief's canoe. With such a fate in mind you'd think that a slave would try to run away, but he had no place to go. His place of servitude was far from his home, which could be reached only by boat. Prisoners taken from neighboring tribes had a better chance of escaping, and for that reason they were usually ransomed or exchanged.

As we move down the coast toward the country the slaves came from, we find, as previously mentioned, a number of small groups whose culture resembles that of the Northwest Coast tribes in an attenuated way. In northwestern California the Yurok and Wiyot were primarily interested in wealth, particularly in shell money, and displayed their family treasures at annual ceremonies, but did not give them away, as in potlatches.

The Yurok believed wealth and sex to be incompatible and would not have intercourse in their houses, in which they stored their treasures. In fact, a rich man would abstain from sex during the winter, which was the ceremonial season, and had intercourse with his wife or wives only in the summer and out of doors. Wealth also included fishing rights and rights to hunting along the riverbanks, but inland hunting rights were communal.

There was much feuding and paying of blood money, and a rich man could draw henchmen from among his kinsfolk by paying their debts. In this way he could built up a retinue of followers. He could also stop a war by paying out shell money and thus add to his renown. The Yurok also had slaves, not captives but men who had incurred debts which they could not pay; but the children of such slaves were free.

Marriage was forbidden only between first and second cousins, on either side, and the groom or his parents had to pay a bride price. As the villages in which they lived were small, it was usually necessary to seek a bride from outside. These customs were not limited to the tribes in question, but were common in northern and central California, as among the Maidu, whose economic activities we have described earlier. In southern California the picture changed. In many tribes there were exogamous moieties whose activities included much ritual, and the situation was comparable to that in North Central Australia. We will come to these later on in Chapter 15.

Moieties among the Penobscot Indians

Most of the Northern Algonkian Indians, before becoming commercial fur trappers, used to differentiate between paternal and maternal cousins. They forbade parallel-cousin marriage and permitted, or even preferred, cross-cousin marriage. This type of marriage fostered the rise of incipient patrilineages, as among the Ona.

But the Penobscot Indians of Maine carried matters a step further. They had permanent winter villages from which the men went out hunting, and they were organized into twenty-four patrilineages, among a population of between six hundred and one thousand persons, ranging from twenty-four to sixty in each patrilineage, which was really an extended family. They were given the names of animals, including fish, and divided into two categories, land creatures and water creatures. Each lineage marked off its hunting territories by blazing pictorial symbols of its totem on trees. Each also had an origin myth. The land people had separate myths, but the water people had one in common, as follows. Once upon a time a giant frog swallowed all of the water in the world, creating a drought, and everyone was thirsty. The culture hero Gluskabe killed the frog, releasing the water, which rushed down the rivers to the sea. During the flood some of the people were washed off the banks and turned into water creatures. Their relatives who had been lucky enough to remain on land and to keep their human form took the names of the water creatures into which the others had been transformed. The bear people were descended from a girl who had been stolen by a bear and had lived among the bears until she escaped.

These lineages were ranked in both divisions. The frog folk were at the top of the list among the water people, the squirrel folk among the land people. The Penobscot chiefs were usually selected from among the frogs or the squirrels, although now and then the honor went to a bear. The Penobscots did not choose their own chiefs; they were chosen by the chiefs of the other tribes of the Wabanaki Confederacy meeting in Oldtown, Maine, including the Passamaquoddys and Malecites.

The land versus water division of the lineages was, in effect, a moiety system. It was reflected in the grouping of houses in the village. Each side lived together, and they competed with each other in games. Rare among hunters, the moiety system was common enough

I*

among the agricultural Indians south of the Merrimack, from whom the Penobscot had already begun to take over garden cultivation.

Bride selection among the Akoa Pygmies

In the case of the Northwest Coast Indians we have seen that wealth made rank and permitted the purchase of brides. The same principle applied to the elephant-hunting Akoa Pygmies around the turn of the century. Elephant hunting gave them ivory which they traded with the Fang for other goods, including cheap jewelry beloved of brides. The women also had a quid-pro-quo in that they caught fish. Marriage was exogamous between Akoa "villages," as the two following tales recorded by Father Trilles will illustrate.

The first is called *"Turtle Dove and Her Three Suitors,"* and it may be summarized as follows.

In a camp near the Ebe River once lived a girl named Kukulu, the Turtle-Dove. Her father was Kolélé, He Who Lies Hidden. She was strong, shapely, and her skin was shiny and red, for she rubbed it with lots of oil and red wood-powder, and she wore many necklaces. She was good at fishing and cooking, and when she danced she writhed like a snake. Her bottom wiggled so much that one would think she had two bottoms. Her hair was always well plaited and oiled. It was time for her to get married, and all the young men wanted her.

Her father had accepted payments in advance from three of the suitors, and the others had given up. The first of the three was Sekhu, the Chimpanzee. He was strong and hairy, and had a big head and big arms and legs. He could beat anyone fighting and he could run through the trees faster than the monkeys and catch them. His arrows felled all game, and he had already killed two elephants and he wore a necklace of hairs from their tails. All the women ran after him.

The second was Bélébili, Arrow of the Forest. He had paid the most. He was small and thin, gay, happy, always singing and dancing. He brought in the animals by whistling and talking like them. His hut was always full of meat. He knew how to talk with girls, and already had children in several camps. He ran after all the girls.

The third was named Okuta, Poisonous Mushroom, because on the day he was born his mother had fed his father a great meal of mushrooms. Among them was a bad one. His father had colic, his bowels turned over, and he died. Poisonous Mushroom hadn't paid much to Turtle-Dove's father, who wished he hadn't paid anything. Poisonous Mushroom never hunted or fished, but his hut too was always full of meat, because others brought it to him. He was a great shaman, a great healer, and some said that he was also a sorcerer at night. He had blood in a corner of one eye, a tooth that stuck out, and one shoulder higher than the other. He never looked anyone in the eye, and the girls ran away when he came.

The time for Turtle-Dove's marriage arrived. All three men went to her father's camp to claim her. Chimpanzee said: "She is for me." Forest Arrow said: "I will not yield her to anyone." Poisonous Mushroom said: "I will kill anyone who takes her from me."

At this point the bard who was telling the story to a rapt audience asked his question: "Who got her? Which one?" During the rest of the evening men, women, and children screamed and argued, each with a different reason for a particular choice, and the clamor went on long into the night.

Now comes the other story, called *"The Young Man and the Three Girls."*

Once a young man wanted to get married. His father had made proposals to the fathers of three girls, living in different camps. The young man's name was Ephra. He was a good hunter. He covered his body with oil and red wood-powder, and wore a wreath made of a liana, the sign of a young man seeking a wife. He started out for the first camp. It was a long way. When he came to a crossing path, he saw a chameleon on his left. It was a good sign.

He arrived at the first camp, seated himself in the middle, and said: "May you grow to be old, and be in good health." It was the conventional greeting. And he spoke with the men. Ekhüi, the girl in question, was out fishing. When she returned her basket was full of good fish.

Ehküi threw her basket into the hut and said to her mother: "You have been sitting here resting. I am tired. You cook the fish."

And her mother did, and they all ate it, on a piece of bark. Ephra ate very much and said: "My belly is full," the habitual way of thanking one's host at the end of a meal.

Next day Ephra walked to the second camp, a long way. He shot a flying squirrel in the air, a good shot. Near a deep river, beyond a marsh, he saw a thin wisp of blue smoke. That was the camp. He went in and sat down and said: "Grow old, all you men, and be of good health." And the men replied accordingly.

But Pamo, the girl he had come to see, was not there. She was out fishing with her mother and friends. When she came back her basket was only half full. She was not a good fisherwoman, and poor at plaiting baskets and making fish traps. Her mother had never taught her. Her mother said: "I am tired. Prepare the meal."

So Pamo scaled the fish and cooked them, with delicious-smelling herbs, wild pepper, and salt. Ephra ate a lot, and it was very good. He ate some more, and then he said: "My stomach is bad and I am tired." So he went out into the forest, relieved himself, came back, cleaned his teeth as Pygmies always do after a meal, and said: "My belly is full." He drank a hot infusion and fell asleep.

The next day he took up his bow and walked to the third camp, where the remaining girl lived. Her name was Mo-To, Clever Hand. Ephra found his own father there, for his father had come ahead of him to announce the purpose of Ephra's visit. After an exchange of greetings with the men, Ephra's father said: "There is Mo-To."

"Yes," said Ephra, "Mo-To is there."

She was there because her father, the chief, had brought her out. Ephra looked at her and counted her necklaces. She was young and strong, with well-developed breasts, and her nipples stuck straight out in front. She had already had a baby, which was a sign of fecundity and of a happy marriage. Ephra looked at her and said: "It is good."

Then the chief said: "My daughter is a good girl. She knows how to make love. You will be a happy man."

Ephra asked: "Is she a good fisherwoman?"

Said the chief: "She doesn't like to put her feet in cold water to catch fish. Her husband will bring in plenty of meat. I hear that you are a good hunter."

Asked Ephra: "Is she a good cook?"

Said the chief: "She is afraid to go into the forest to collect dry firewood, but you can collect it for her."

Asked Ephra: "Does she know how to cook meat?"

Said the chief: "She doesn't like to burn herself at the hearth, but she knows very well how to make love. You will have many children. You will be happy."

Ephra said that he would think about it, and he went back to his camp and thought. A few days later he got married, but which one did he choose? Mo-To who knew how to make love, Pamo the good cook, or Ekhüi the good fisherwoman?

The usual clamor arose in the camp, but the bard wouldn't give the answer. The next day the bard told Father Trilles privately that Ephra married all three—not all at once, which he would have preferred to do had he been able to, but one at a time. First he got love when he was young, then good cooking when he was older, and finally good providing after he had grown too old to hunt.

It is unlikely that these glamorous tales fully represent the normal range of procedures in Akoa culture as of seventy or eighty years ago, but why should they? Their dramatis personae were heroes and heroines, and in addition to their moral overtones, these tales were part of the Pygmies' Hollywood.

11.

Government and Fighting

Keeping internal and external peace

The purpose of this chapter is to focus our attention on a subject to which we have already referred in passing many times. It is to explain how groups of hunting and gathering peoples who have no codified legal systems, professional police, or standing armies keep law and order among themselves and between each other; i.e., internally and externally.

There are many mechanisms by which internal order is maintained, some of them less deliberate and more automatic than others. They include the need of domestic harmony within and between families; a respect for the wisdom of mature men; the gradual education of the young by their observation and imitation of their elders, by the give and take of play activities among peer groups between the ages of weaning and puberty, by the telling of moral tales of an exciting nature, and by rites and ceremonies held both at critical periods of life and during the slack seasons in the annual cycle of food-getting.

Sometimes these mechanisms are almost enough to keep internal peace, providing that the social structure is simple enough, the groups themselves small and uncomplicated, the seasonal round of activities varies little, and distinctions between individuals are unrelated to differences in wealth. But they are rarely sufficient if the groups are large and internally segmented on lines of kinship, rank, and property. In the latter cases a clear-cut political structure may emerge, with recognized political leaders, followers, and a chain of command.

Keeping the peace between geographically separated, autonomous groups is more critical and more difficult to achieve than internal order because the members of the groups concerned see each other less often than they do their fellow members, and the neighboring groups may speak different languages or dialects and may follow different customs and rules of behavior. In such cases the auxiliary mechanisms that help to keep the peace internally may be less effective, and a more formal degree of political organization may be necessary. Thus chieftainships may arise in groups who do not need them for internal affairs alone, but also for war and for trade.

Now the actions and conditions that cause disturbances, both within and between autonomous groups, are: inequities in the food supply; a failure to share with others; marital quarrels, especially over adultery; mysterious, sudden deaths that cannot be explained easily without being attributed to sorcery; and violation of territories. In some of the most simply organized groups general arrogance and antisocial behavior may be enough to warrant the expulsion or execution of the person concerned, usually but not always a man. While murder is usually the business of the kinsmen of the deceased alone, and may be followed by feuds, expulsion and execution — which often amount to the same thing — are done by common consent, and no vengeance is taken. There are no jails and, with a few exceptions, no trials, but in the case of a death attributed to sorcery, inquests may be held to determine the identity of the sorcerer. If it is suspected that the sorcerer is someone who belongs to a different band from that of the victim, the inquest may take place at an interband meeting, in which case the matter may be settled by mutual consent, and warfare avoided.

The belligerent Bushmen

The G/wi Bushmen of Botswana have no chiefs, but in each band the elderly men and women of the families longest in residence advise the others where to hunt on various parts of their territories. Fighting occurs within a band on account of adultery when detected. The injured husband and his wife may beat each other, but without serious injury, and if they do not make up afterward they may separate in divorce. Then the husband will berate his wife's lover and the two will scream at each other, exchanging insults, but they seldom come to blows. When the other members of the band become tired of the noise they will try to calm the two men down and bring about a reconciliation. If this fails, one of the two men will leave the band.

Among the !Kung Bushmen of the Dobe region recently studied by Richard B. Lee, there are no chiefs, but there is seldom any quarreling during the seasons when small bands are out seeking food alone. When they get together in numbers of forty or more persons around a water hole, fights sometimes break out, and usually on account of adultery. Men fight their wives, women fight women, and men fight other men, all in the presence of the entire assembly.

The fights are really duels, or at least start out as such, and begin with very vociferous verbal battles. The opponents hurl at each other sexual insults, the same ones used in their most intimate joking relationships, but now uttered seriously. After a while the protagonists either calm down, or pass a point of no return beyond which they must fight, as when a woman is told that her labiae minorae are black, or a man is told that his penis is bare like that of a dead man, for they do not circumcise.

When men are fighting women, or women fighting women, they use no weapons, for women have none. These combats are a combination of wrestling and hitting, trying to get deadlocks on each other, and end when one gets the other on the ground. When men fight each other, they are usually neither close kin nor totally unrelated, but men in an intermediate kinship category. Instead of wrestling they shoot at each other with poisoned arrows or hurl poisoned spears. They fight face to face, dodging the missiles, and do not shoot as accurately as they do when hunting, scoring frequent misses. Now and then bystanders are hit by mistake and killed, including women and boys. Their poison takes about six hours to kill a man, and when one is hit others may cut the wound to make it bleed, and try to suck the poison out, but still the wound is often fatal. After a fight with or without weapons the relatives and supporters of each participant join together with much conversation, in order to make up, but the duelists, one of whom may be dying, do not take part in it. When it is all over everyone present usually joins in a trance dance, a kind of ritual concerned with healing, in which men and women pass into a semiconscious state through hyperventilation, thus smoothing things over and bringing the relations of all parties more or less back to normal.

Lee also stated that when a man had killed too many others, the other men would get together and decide to kill him. They would follow him when others were not present, and execute him by a battery of missiles, but this was dangerous work because he might detect them and shoot back, with losses on the executioners' side before they had succeeded in their mission.*

Variations among the Pygmies

The Pygmies present a wide range of political organization and much variation as to whether or not they fight and if so, how. The Akoa of Gabon live in camps permanent enough to merit the name of villages, and have chiefs. As previously stated, their chiefs arrange the elephant hunts and they also lead their men in combat when their enemies, the Fang Negroes, discover their hideouts and attack them. If they do not have time to abandon camp, the Akoa climb trees and shoot the Fang with poisoned arrows, but there is no evidence that they fought each other, either within or between camps, although in one tale a woman unsuccessfully tried to persuade her husband's brother to kill her husband. In one camp there was also a second chief, so-called, whose job it was to trade with the Fang, at best a risky business.

The Mbuti live in definite territories bounded by streams and ridges, and each territory belongs to a band. As previously stated the number of persons living together fluctuates when the honey season arrives for the net hunters, and during the annual surround for the archers. But it also fluctuates regardless of the seasons when individual families go to visit kinsfolk in other bands. They do this partly to stay with the wife's family and partly because they simply want to see other people. Thus each camp may contain a number of visitors staying for periods of varying length.

Like that of the !Kung, their kinship system is bilateral and a young man may not marry a girl to whom he is believed to be related. But as they have no special way of bestowing names and no name-matching system, and because their memories of their deceased

*The foregoing account is based on my memory of a colloquium given by Richard B. Lee at Harvard on March 5, 1970. In their publications on the Nyae Nyae !Kung Bushmen, Mrs. Lorna Marshall and her daughter Mrs. Elizabeth Marshall Thomas made no mention of fighting, but Mrs. Marshall has stated privately that she had heard of such combats having taken place in former times. Five earlier accounts of the !Kung and of the Cape Bushmen reported fighting between bands, with both bows and spears. (I. Schapera, *The Khoisan Peoples of South Africa* [London, Routledge and Kegan Paul, 1930], pp. 157–59.)

ancestors are short, the prohibition against marriage rarely extends far beyond first cousinhood.

Their social fabric is far less dependent on kinship than it is on age grading, with the older men and women making the final decisions as to when and where the camp should be moved. This decision may be preceded by heated debate. When the shouting has grown too loud, an older man whom everyone respects may take the center of the stage and demand silence, on the grounds that the noise is offending the forest, which they personify in a general way as their father and mother, their protector, and their supplier of food. Then a decision is made.

Besides such older men of prestige, the band may contain at least one man who is a troublemaker, and he may choose to camp a short distance away from the others, but he is tolerated because he is a buffoon, or a good storyteller, or both.

If the tension grows too great, the whole band may decide that it is time to visit a village of their Negro trading partners, if that term may be used to designate a less formal relationship from the Mbuti point of view than the Negroes consider it to be. The Mbuti will carry in some meat and perhaps a tusk or two of ivory, and they may be persuaded to do a little work, as in roofing houses. In exchange they eat the villagers' bananas and drink their banana wine, as well as cadging a few pots and some arrowheads and knives. For the most part the transaction is not one of formal exchange. The Pygmies make gifts of the meat, and wheedle or "liberate" some of the villagers' portable goods, or "borrow" dogs. The Pygmies say that they "eat" their hosts, who treat the Pygmies in a familiar if patronizing way.

In the village the Pygmies entertain their hosts with songs and dances, but these are not the songs and dances of the forest. Also there may be one man whom the Negroes call "chief" because he seems to be the most facile mediator between themselves and the Pygmy band as a whole, but back in the forest his authority quickly evaporates. The Negroes may stage wedding ceremonies between Pygmy couples united since the previous visit, but the Pygmies themselves have no formal weddings.

In addition to the fiction of chieftainship the villagers create personal bonds between Negro lineages, which are unilateral, and individual Pygmy families, which are not. These bonds are symbolized by circumcising boys of both peoples in a common puberty ceremony. While in the village the Pygmies adopt a joking relationship between these lineages and families on the basis of who was circumcised with whom, but back in the forest the relationship becomes one of derision.

There, where the Pygmies are alone, a free exchange of personal remarks seems to include nearly everyone of an age grade. Except for a respect for one's elders the band structure appears to be almost anarchic, but a seemingly uninhibited exchange of views provides a balance that usually falls short of violence, except for occasional wife-beating. Here again the concept that noise offends the forest supplies the symbolic mechanism of keeping domestic order.

To the east of the Mbuti country in the far west of Uganda live two other bands of Pygmies, hitherto unmentioned in this book. They number only about twenty to thirty individuals each, and each is attached to a lineage of the Amba Negroes, who used to fight each other. When this happened the Pygmies joined the forces of their overlords and took part in the battles, fighting each other as well as the Amba on the opposite side, and they are said to have fought very well, particularly when in deep forest. All of which goes to show, and more than three examples could be cited, that in a symbiotic situation, or one of hostile outside contact, the political structures and fighting habit of Pygmies are locally variable and dependent on local circumstances, as with the Bushmen.

The Andamanese

In the Andaman Islands we also find regional diversity principally between the Great Andamanese and the Little Andamanese. The Great Andamanese were divided into two regional subgroups, a northern and a southern — the former with three tribes (using the word in the geographical and linguistic sense), the latter with five. The Little Andamanese had three — the Önge of Little Andaman Island, the inhabitants of North Sentinel Island, and the Jarawa of the interior of South Andaman.

Most, but not all, of the Great Andamanese tribes were further divided into coastal and inland bands, each with its own territory and numbering about forty to fifty people. Like the !Kung Bushmen and Pygmies they had unilateral kinship systems and forbade cousin

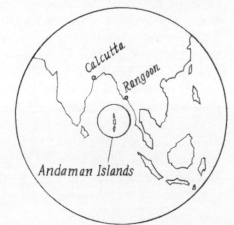

5. The Andaman Islanders

NORTH ANDAMAN I.

MIDDLE ANDAMAN I.

North Andamanese

South Andamanese

SOUTH ANDAMAN ISLAND

Aka-Béa

Port Blair

Jarawa

North Sentinelese

LITTLE ANDAMAN I.

Önge

Scale of miles

50

Calcutta

Rangoon

Andaman Islands

marriage. Early accounts definitely stated that each band was politically autonomous and was headed by a man of superior judgment who decided when to move camp, often directed the hunt, divided the meat brought in by unmarried members of the hunting parties, and tried to settle quarrels between the men. His wife played a similar role among the women. In each tribe that included both coastal and inland bands there was usually a superior chief for the coastal bands and another one for the inland bands.

The role of the superior chief was to try to keep the peace at times when different bands of the same tribe came together once a year by prearrangement, at the superior chief's camp, to dance and feast together and to exchange goods in the form of gifts. His job was not an easy one, and despite his efforts, fights sometimes arose. In meetings between coastal and inland bands, two superior chiefs would be better than one because of the mutual contempt and hostility between the coastal people and the inlanders.*

In the old days, a potential Andamanese chief was a young adult in the camp who possessed the virtues that attract even younger men to seek his company. He was usually a good hunter, generous, and, above all, even-tempered. Unmarried young men were eager to go hunting with him, and to help him build his canoe. Such a natural leader might attract young men from other bands to change their residence and join him, and his wife was usually a leader among the women. It was these influential men who eventually became chiefs, and arranged the annual intergroup meetings. Both the mobility of the young men who changed their bands to be with him, and the matings and adoptions initiated during the intergroup meetings enhanced a tendency toward exogamy, concerning which there was no fast rule.

During the annual interband meetings, the presence of the superior chief and the band chiefs usually prevented serious bloodshed at that time and place, but grievances were remembered, and revenge might be taken later. Before setting out the men of the attacking party painted their bodies with red ochre and pipe clay, put on all their ornaments, and whittled some shaved sticks, which they thrust in their belts and headbands. They also rubbed their

*By the turn of the century, the Great Andamanese population had become so reduced that there were no longer enough bands to warrant these exchanges and no one left to fight, except the Jarawa, whose principal enemies were the convicts and other settlers sent in by the government of India. By 1911 the chieftainships at both levels had disappeared, leading A. R. Brown to imply in his much-quoted monograph that the Great Andamanese society was one lacking political structure (see Bibliography).

bows with these sticks to make them shoot well, and just before leaving, the men danced.

At dawn, while everyone was still asleep, or late in the afternoon when they were busy cooking and eating, the camp of the victims might be attacked. The raiders either crept through the jungle or approached in canoes. They leaped on their victims by surprise, quickly shot all the men and women unable to escape, and took away any uninjured children, to adopt them. They also made off with all the food and equipment they could carry, and spoiled or broke the rest.

If enough members of the group survived to reconstitute the band, they might eventually grow numerous enough to seek revenge, and a lengthy feud might arise. In North Andaman, if not elsewhere, feuds were resolved by a special peace-making ceremony. This was initiated by the women because it was they who had kept the hostility alive, egging on their men, and once they were ready to call quits they had no trouble winning over their husbands.

One or two of the women of the group that wanted peace would be sent by their chief to speak to the women of the other band to see if a meeting could be arranged. If so, the band that had made the last raid would invite the others to their camp, where the men had already set up a fence across the dance floor. This fence was a row of posts sunk in the ground, with a rail of canes lashed across their tops, and a screen of shredded leaves hanging from the rail.

When the right moment had come, the men of Group A, the local band, stood behind this fence, leaning their shoulders on it, with their arms outstretched along the rail. Now the Group B men, the visitors, entered and danced in front of the A men. Then each man of B shook each man of A, and each woman of B shook each woman of A, and they all sat down and wept, which is their usual form of friendly greeting. For two days or so the combined group would dance and hunt together.

So much for fights and feuds between bands. In addition, as expected, trouble sometimes arose within the camp. Each band usually included one or more men too lazy to go out hunting with the others, some who were adulterous, a few who failed to show proper respect for their elders, men who didn't like to share their food and other possessions with others, and quick-tempered men. Such individuals were usually tolerated and, if improvident, fed, but they were unpopular. Their only punishment was a loss of esteem by the rest of the band, but that was a serious matter in view of the small numbers and social coherence of the group.

There was little theft because everyone knew what everyone else owned, and detection would be instantaneous. Adultery was also hard to conceal because there was little privacy. If a cuckold started to beat his wife her relatives would stop him, and he couldn't kill the adulterer without risking vengeance. So he simply cursed and abused his rival. Adultery was rarely repeated, because it would lead to murder.

Killings within the band were rare. Men grew angry with one another, berated their opponents, and broke things to vent their wrath. Now and then two men would shoot at each other, usually aiming wide of the mark, and the rest of the people would disappear into the forest, except for the chief. He stayed behind and tried to break it up, for few if any would dare to shoot at him.

If one man actually killed another with his arrows the murderer dashed out into the forest and stayed away for a few weeks until the others had simmered down. Staying out alone at night was punishment enough because of his fear of jungle spirits. While hiding out the murderer also had to take steps to keep his victim's ghost from harming him. He had to wear red paint. He attached to his body many shredded sticks made, if possible, of mangrove wood. He dared not touch a weapon or feed himself. As a rule his wife and close friends brought him food and put it in his mouth.

When told that it was safe to go back he did so, underwent a purification rite, and could then resume a normal life, except that he had to continue wearing shredded sticks for a year or so. Revenge was rarely taken, either in the forest or in camp, but if it was it was the immediate family of the victim that took it, and the rest of the camp had no responsibility.*

---

*The above account of the political structure, warfare, and in-group fighting among the Great Andamanese is a composite of data from more than one tribe, and there may have been local variations of which we may never be aware. As for the Önges, North Sentinelese, and Jarawa, we know almost nothing, not because they are virtually extinct like the Great Andamanese, for they are not, but because the government of India excludes visitors, including cultural anthropologists.

The Önge live in independent villages along the coast, each with its local chief, but there is no mention in the meager literature of regional chiefs, possibly because the interior is uninhabited and there is little reason for interband meetings. The only reference to fighting is that in former times the Önge used to travel by canoe to the Nicobar Islands to raid their agricultural neighbors. The Great Andamanese did not venture onto the open sea. We know next to nothing about the North Sentinelese, and as for the Jarawa, they are said to live in bands with their own chiefs, and have long been at war with everyone else on their island; they do not keep dogs lest the latter bark and reveal their presence to enemies. And that is just about all we know.

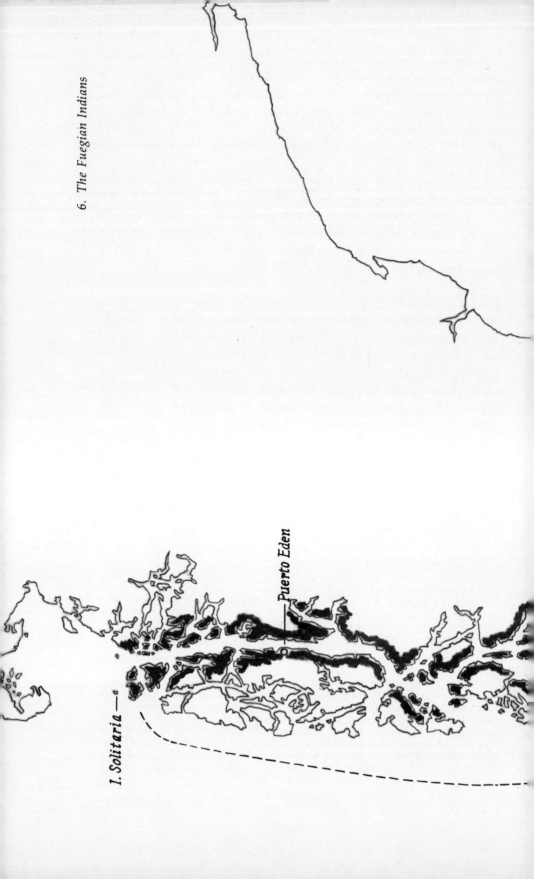

6. The Fuegian Indians

I. Solitaria —

Puerto Eden

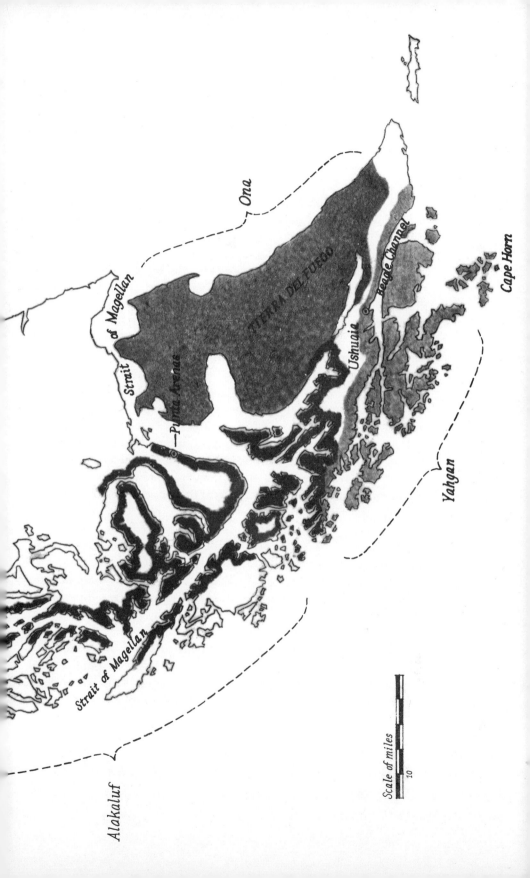

Ona

Strait of Magellan

Cape Horn

Beagle Channel

TIERRA DEL FUEGO

Ushuaia

—Punta Arenas

Yahgan

Strait of Magellan

Alakaluf

Scale of miles

10

The Yaghans

The Yaghans were as simply organized as the Great Andamanese. Like them, the Yaghans were boatmen. Their small, territorial bands had neither councils nor official chiefs, but in each band one elder exercised informal authority, and his position was not hereditary. He was a man of sound judgment who gave advice to his kinsfolk, and they usually followed it, although he had no means of compulsion. His words of wisdom were not orders. At times he would make arrangements with the corresponding men of other bands for their peoples to come together for ceremonies.

If anyone within the band were behaving antisocially, one of his close relatives, and not necessarily the elder mentioned above, would first consult with others of the offender's kin and then go to the offender and warn him to mend his ways, in an attempt to prevent fighting; but this admonitory maneuver did not always succeed. In fact, internal brawls were rather frequent, as the Yaghans were quite sensitive to insults real or surmised, and angered quickly. As with the Bushmen, fights began between two persons rather than between bands as a whole, although they might spread to groups of kin.

Women angry at each other punched, bit, and pulled hair, and if the action took place in front of others, other women or eventually men tried to separate them. But if the women really wanted to have it out, the hostile pair would retire to the woods or to the beach to continue the fight, although as far as we know they never killed each other.

Men fought over insults and sneers made in general conversation, and even over imaginary slurs incident to such conversation, as when one man would see another man glancing in his direction and passing inaudible remarks to a third person. Grudges thus begun might be held in restraint for years before the hostility broke into action, for the Yaghans were too busy most of the time getting food, and the grudge-holder awaited a suitable occasion. A weaker man who felt himself insulted might lack the courage to retaliate and would, instead, lead his family away for a year or so to live alone.

The Reverend Thomas Bridges reported at his mission at Ushuaia that two men once fought, and a week later one of them died. Shortly afterward six canoeloads of the victim's kin arrived to avenge the murder. Both sides wore war paint, the pattern for murder being red stripes running down and outward over the cheeks from semi-circles under the eyes. Meanwhile the killer had escaped, and after much turmoil and fierce threats and gestures, a nephew of the slayer on the latter's mother's side had to surrender most of his possessions to the avengers to be spared. The slayer himself, whose hideout was discovered by a cousin of the victim, was badly beaten by the latter.

The cause of this antipodal donnybrook was a suspicion of adultery, the spark that ignited most murders. Also, a man who left his wife for no good reason might be killed by her relatives, and thus a feud could begin. But if one man attempted to kill another for a trivial reason, such as a fancied insult, the assailant's kinfolk would try to stop him for fear of the consequences to themselves. Between 1871 and 1884, Thomas Bridges was aware of twenty-two murders, but the Reverend Martin Gusinde, the principal authority on the Yaghans, would double the figure.

Leadership and fighting in unilaterally organized societies

So far we have cited examples of leadership and fighting among simply organized societies. In most, the descent was traced bilaterally, the G/wi Bushmen and the Amba Pygmies being exceptions. Among some the rate of violence was higher than among others, but the principle seems to be the same, that with descent traced on both sides each person, aside from sets of brothers, has a different roster of kinsfolk, and not very many at that. Fights arise characteristically within a band rather than between bands, there being little if any firm authority to stop them. More organized and more externalized fighting occurs among peoples with unilateral kinship ties, via lineages, clans, formal leaders, and the like; or with bilaterally organized societies having some basis of organization other than kinship, such as rank, class, and differences of wealth.

The Ona

The Ona, northern neighbors of the Yaghans, may serve as an example of a unilaterally organized society, although it was a nascent one. As stated in the last chapter, they differentiated between paternal and maternal cousins, aunts, and uncles, but forbade marriage between cousins of either side and thus lacked the ties which interband cousin exchange fosters in other, more fully patrilineal societies. Each of their thirty-nine territories was inhabited by bands organized primarily around patrilineal descent, and members of neighboring bands got together when a whale was stranded or when wrestling matches were held. Each band had a leader, a man whose authority was most manifest in times of war and other interband confrontations.

The usual causes of conflict were trespass in search of game, and the theft of women — and either could lead to feuds — but they were feuds between bands rather than inside them. Because the guanaco did not observe territorial boundaries, it was tempting to pursue one over the ridge which separated most territories, and even if a dog chased a guanaco over the frontier, it might give rise to retaliation. As the game was shared by adjacent bands, the human population in general needed to be kept at a constant level, and some raids were motivated by an attempt to reduce the population in the next band.

During such a raid the men wore no ceremonial garb or war paint. As many men as could be brought together crossed the border and jumped the enemy by surprise. The enemy fled and gathered as many of their own men as possible to return the attack. The Onas did not torture their captives, but they killed the men and kept the women and children to incorporate into their own group, unless a few got killed in the excitement.

If one band had been attacked and could not reply in kind, it would send out a wrestling challenge by an old woman, too old to be worth capturing. Both parties met at the proper time and formed a semicircle facing each other. An old man of the aggrieved group would stand out and make a long speech telling the other side why his group was angry, and then one of the challengers would stand out and, with a hand extended, draw one of the others into the ring. They wrestled standing up, and tried to throw each other to the ground. They quit only when one of them was exhausted, and his place was taken by another of the latter's side, and so on until there were no challengers left. During the bouts men of each group praised the other side, and after it was over they would announce their intentions to each other, and the challengers would go home.

If neither war nor wrestling would satisfy a man, he challenged his enemy to single combat. The challenger appeared naked outside the enemy camp, and his enemy shot six arrows at him, the challenger dodging, and advancing with each step. If he survived, the challenger shot at his enemy in a similar fashion, or at a relative of his enemy if the latter was a poor dodger. To retreat during this ordeal was a great disgrace. In many cases one of the men was killed or wounded.

Eventually peace might be made. It was arranged by a third party. Each man on each side made five headless arrows, but with a wrapped rawhide disc near the point, intended to wound but not to kill. Each man gave his five arrows to his worst enemy, and the enemy shot the five at him rapidly while he ran toward the shooter. Thus most of the participants were wounded to some extent, and by their own arrows, and each man had a crack at his favorite antagonist. This painful but nonlethal performance terminated the feud.

The political situation of the Ona marks a transition between a bilateral, loosely organized system which lacked firm authority to a unilateral one in which leadership was more nearly crystallized. It also marks a change from disorganized brawls and fights starting with individuals to concerted raids and ordeals between groups. For a continuation of the latter theme, we turn to Tasmania and Australia.

The Tasmanians

As for the Tasmanians, despite our ignorance of their kinship rules, we know from contemporary evidence that they lived in exogamous, patrilocal bands, and we also have accounts of several rather stirring events. From these we gather that they had territorial chiefs of considerable power, and that in some cases at least their office was hereditary. The chief of the Oyster Bay Tribe, for example, was a tall, powerful man, a good fighter using extra long war spears. He claimed to have a resident spirit inside his chest that gave him special information, including the whereabouts of enemies, and warnings of impending attacks.

In one fight in the northern part of the island, one band found itself hopelessly outnumbered. Two young men who were ashamed to run away volunteered to stay behind, and refused to leave while the others fled. They bravely sacrificed their lives to cover the retreat.

To settle differences between two men of the same band, the antagonists would fight a nonlethal duel without involving others. Each man was armed with a hunting club, a waddy. Each in turn would wave his waddy over his head and orate for some time, before whacking his opponent over the head, while the latter would receive the blow with evasive tactics. When one of them had had enough, they quit.

Woorrady rapes and kills his sister-in-law

Woorrady, G. A. Robinson's faithful helper who vigorously wooed Trugernanna as described in Chapter 10, had previously, by his own account, raped and killed a sister-in-law, for the following reason. One of Woorrady's brothers had married a woman from a distant band. Although he was very fond of her, his wife left him and returned to her own people. Setting out alone in search of her, the husband crossed through many territories and asked many persons if they had seen her. Finally he saw her with two men and several other women. He stopped to sharpen his spears, and then attacked the men, but one of them pretended to run away, doubled and came up behind Woorrady's brother, and speared him in the back. The five then closed in on their victim and attacked him vigorously, and his own wife beat him over the head with a spike. Woorrady's brother thus died.

Back at home, his own people kept a constant watch for him, but after much time had passed one man volunteered to go to look for him. After another long search he found the body in a hollow tree and brought the bones home. Still later some of the assailants' people, including the ex-wife who had wielded the spike, came to a river in Woorrady's country to collect eggs. The local people fell on the visitors and killed many, and that was when Woorrady raped and killed his sister-in-law. Of his brother Woorrady remarked at the end of this tale, "He was a big man and a great fighter."

The Australians

In considering the political structure of the native Australians we must remember that Australia is a continent, and the only one that was inhabited exclusively by hunters and gatherers. We have seen considerable diversity in the regional distribution of items of material culture, and there was even more continental variation in the use of territories and in marital arrangements. Australian systems of government were equally varied.

In the better-watered parts of the continent, particularly Victoria and the Murray River country, the first British colonists found relatively sedentary populations, with patrilineal clans living in their own territories and governed by powerful chiefs, whom the settlers called kings. In 1803 a party of colonists was surveying at the northwest point of Port Phillip Bay, at the foot of which lies the present city of Melbourne. According to an early account "they were met by a number of natives who, on a shot being fired over their heads, ran a small distance but soon approached again with the king, who wore a very elaborate turban crown and was always carried on the shoulders of the men. Whenever he desired them to halt, or to approach, they did it immediately."*

Probably the most formal and the most complex kind of chieftainship recorded in Australia was that of the Jaraldi people in the Lower Murray River country, one of the continent's most populous regions. In the middle of the last century, each territorial clan had its own headman and council, and there was also a paramount chief for the entire tribe. The council members of each clan were elected in a meeting between the middle-aged and elderly men, and a few of the outstanding younger ones as well. In a few cases women were also elected.

The council of the whole tribe met to deal with inquests over the causes of deaths, cases of adultery and elopement, and accusations of sorcery, to send out trading parties, to arrange for the reception of guests from other tribes, to choose men to send out on revenge expeditions, and to decide on the time and place of a ceremony, and on whom to invite.

The tribal chief was traditionally chosen from one clan, the Mangguruba. He had to be firm but amiable, well versed in tradi-

*J. Shillingshaw (1870), cited by A. W. Howitt, *Native Tribes of Southeast Australia* (London, 1904).

tion, and free from all suspicion of practicing sorcery. A second clan, the Manangga, supplied the chief's principal adviser, and he was also chosen by election. A third, the Lindingsjara, gave the chief his first wife, and a fourth, the Liwurindjara, gave him his second wife.

The last great headman was Bulami, who took office from his father between 1856 and 1859. Bulami, the clan chiefs, and certain councillors wore cloaks of squares of opossum skins stitched together; Bulami's cloak was made of the finest fur and had a fringed hem of mallee bark tassels (*Eucalyptus domosa* or *oleosa*). The other men, besides these officials, wore cloaks made of similar squares of plaited rushes and bark fibers.

One of Bulami's chief advisers was Daramindjeri, his mother's brother, who was not only a great orator but also an expert at detecting hidden sorcerer's paraphernalia among the effects of the persons present at inquests. Daramindjeri acted as attorney for the defense, in the trial of an accused person unable to present his own case skillfully. If anyone threatened the accused, Daramindjeri would warn the others: "Before you hit him, you will have to strike me first." Daramindjeri's sister, a powerful sorceress, had much to say in sorcery cases, and at times her brother had to restrain her.*

The majority of these cases were over trouble with women and over accusations of sorcery following inquests. In both kinds of trial special seating arrangements were followed, with the accusers on the chief's right and the accused on his left, with their own clans, including women, backing up each side. The chief opened the session by asking the people why they had come there, bidding them to speak up and hide nothing. Then the older men spoke first, followed by the younger men, with the women talking together. If the discussion became too loud, and feelings were running high, some man would stand up and take the role of a clown, distracting attention and making his audience laugh. At a suitable moment the chief would bid them to be silent, and then he would review the discussion. After that, direct accusations and denials were in order, and finally the chief demanded silence again, and pronounced the accused guilty or innocent.

In some cases which did not involve sorcery the punishment was

*Ronald M. Berndt, "Law and Order in Aboriginal Australia," in R. M. and C. H. Berndt, eds., *Aboriginal Man in Australia* (Sydney, Angus and Robertson, 1965), p. 179.

administered on the spot. A member of the court would beat the convicted person with a club, inflicting a stated number of blows on his head. Or instead, he might be banished from his clan and have to go live with his mother's people, where he had limited hunting and fishing rights. If the accused was convicted of sorcery, he was not touched, but he was magically outlawed. Anyone could now work sorcery against him, and when he died, there would be no inquest. Under the circumstances he might not be expected to live very long.

Farther north and west there was no chieftainship, nor was any needed. Four different kinds of human aggregations, the landowning clan, the food-getting mixed band, the complicated marriage classes, and the totem-reinforcing fraternities, along with the initiation system, provided a substitute for formal leadership.

Perceptible power lay in the hands of the mature, fully initiated, and usually polygynous men of the age group from thirty to fifty, and the control over the women and younger males was shared between them. While rivalries between individuals with powerful personalities inevitably arose, they did so chiefly over women, accusations of magic, or both, and individual fights occurred. Yet a thorough indoctrination in ancient procedures of behavior stopped or abated most conflicts. Otherwise too much fighting would break up the tribal networks of mutual aid needed to live off a climatically unstable land.

Anthropologists usually refer to this system of collective responsibility as *gerontocracy*, which is a misnomer, because the Greek word *geron* means a senile man, and these men were in the prime of life. They may have looked old because aborigines gray early, and it is possible that gray hair was a symbol of authority. A better word, if one is needed, would be *poliocracy*, from the Greek *polios*, a grayhaired man.

These poliocrats ruled mostly by example, but when crises arose the ones who were present and concerned met beside a fire to talk things over until they reached a common decision. Then, if steps needed to be taken, they would act. When a man had created some intolerable disturbance they went out together on a dark night wearing slippers made of human-hair netting covered with emu feathers, stuck onto the cords with human blood. The tracks that they left which led to the body were individually unidentifiable, and anyone else would be ill-advised to follow them.

Killing a man with a sliver

One way of killing a man without detection, if the assassin was lucky, and one not necessarily used in executions, was by sticking a thin sliver of bone or hard wood into the victim's body while the latter slept. It is well known that there are certain parts of the human skin that are less sensitive than others, and many of us have probably seen people stick needles into themselves to show off. If the victim is out of doors, naked, sleeping soundly, and his skin is cold, so much the easier, particularly if the sliver-man blows on the spot first. Once the sliver is entirely past the skin he can rub it gently and it may leave no conspicuous mark. As the man wakes up, arises, and moves about, the sliver may also change its position until it hits a vital organ, in which case it may cause death, not to mention the possibility of infection.

Some field workers have stated their disbelief that this has ever happened, and that when a man feels sharp internal pains he may think that someone must have slivered him, and worry and frighten himself to death. Other field workers swear that it really has happened, but because no conscientious anthropologist would let it be done to a sleeping man in his presence, even if any aboriginal sliver-man would consent, we may never know. At any rate it lies outside the realm of sorcery, according to our way of thinking.

But in the aborigines' minds such a distinction would be unlikely. Sorcery rose to a high peak in Australia, and enough recipes have been recorded to fill a witches' cookbook. Most of them involve the use of material from the intended victim's body, decayed corpse material, and special sticks and bones. For example, a rejected lover may search for and find a place where his would-be girl friend has urinated on the ground, and then thrust a magic stick into it, to make her bleed excessively during menstruation and eventually die.

Bone pointing

The best-known of these devices, and one widely used throughout Australia, is the pointing bone. It consists of three parts; the bone itself, a string attached to it, and a cup of some kind. When a sorcerer points his bone at his victim from a distance of, let us say, forty yards, or at any rate far enough away not to be detected, the latter's blood then moves invisibly through the air into the bone and along the string into the cup, and at the same time a magical bone or pebble in the sorcerer's possession moves in the opposite direction to lodge in the victim's body and make him ill.

Then the victim's soul may follow his blood into the cup, where it is sealed off from escaping by a lump of wax. Once the soul has been captured, the sorcerer wraps his kit in emu feathers and buries it. Meanwhile the victim is supposed to continue to be ill. After several months the sorcerer digs up his cache and burns it, and the victim dies. Or so the shaman may say at the inquest, and the man convicted of having pointed the bone will be out of luck. There is no question about bone pointing; we have genuine photographs of men doing it.

The double duel at Mungeranie

Let us get down to actual fighting. As previously stated, the principal reasons for it were jealousy over women and suspicion that an otherwise inexplicable death had been caused by sorcery. Sometimes the two were combined in a single case, as illustrated by a four-man double duel fought early in the present century at Mungeranie, a station some forty-five miles east of Lake Eyre in South Australia. The cause was also a double boning, in which first a man's daughter and then his wife died. A physician who saw the first body said: "Had I been asked for a death certificate I would have called her complaint by quite a different name."*

The man's name was Mulka Bill. He lived to the south of Mungeranie, the scene of his daughter Polly's death, but when he heard of it he came north to find out who had boned her. He was a disagreeable man and always picking fights. The headman and shaman of the Mungeranie clan received him coldly. So Mulka Bill moved about from one place to another in his search, making mischief everywhere, his wife Alice with him. Having failed to find the bone-pointer, the couple returned to Mungeranie. One day a band of people from a place called Kanowa came down on the other side of the creek from the station, and Alice's son was with them. Although

*G. Horne and G. Aiston, *Savage Life in Central Australia* (London, 1924), pp. 13–15. Horne was the physician, Aiston a mounted police officer.

the creek was in flood, she swam across to visit with the boy, and back again. The water was very cold. Alice died.

Now Mulka Bill accused the Mungeranie men of having boned his wife and daughter, and Mulka's mother's brother, named General, backed up Mulka Bill and demanded vengeance. The Mungeranie headman called a council meeting and two local men were appointed to fight the two accusers. Because Mulka Bill had one disabled arm, he was pitted against Dinnabillie, who had lost his left hand. General, a powerful man and a famed fighter, was matched with Carunta, Dinnabillie's sister's son, a slender youth. The fight was held at the Seven Sandhills, halfway between the camps of the two groups.

Each man was armed with six regular boomerangs, three stuck through his hair-belt at either side, and a four-foot war boomerang was thrust through the belt behind, with one arm of the weapon over his head so that he could reach up and draw it when needed. Dinnabillie also had a revolver for shooting diseased cattle, but before the fight he handed it to another man who could keep it in case of Dinnabillie's death.

Carunta was left-handed. When he cast a boomerang at General it came in from the wrong side, glanced off General's boomerang held up as a guard, sheared through General's heavy browridge and smashed his eye.

Now Dinnabillie ran in toward Mulka Bill, casting his boomerangs one after the other with his only hand, and then seizing his long war boomerang with the same hand, he whirled it around his head and crashed it into Mulka Bill's chest. "Enough," said the umpire, whose affiliation was not stated, and the fight was over.

Mass combats in northern Queensland

The double duel held at Mungeranie was a minor event compared to a mass combat that took place near the headwaters of the Herbert River in northern Queensland, in the 1880s. It was witnessed by about three hundred spectators, including a Danish zoologist, Carl Lumholtz, who described it.*

The fight was one of a series of three or four that took place during the hot season, from November to February. The people who took

*Carl Lumholtz, *Among Cannibals* (New York, Scribner's, 1889), pp. 119–127.

part were members of several patrilineal totemic lineages whose territories lay within reasonable walking distance of the fighting ground, a grassy glade beside the Herbert River. Most of the rest of the countryside was hilly and heavily forested. Game was scarce, and wife-stealing prevalent. During the rest of the year the men had been saving up their grievances for the hot weather, the usual time for riots and fights everywhere.

Whole bands—men, women, and children—converged on the glade for this event, camping by night along the way. Menstruating women came along too, but they were not allowed on the battle ground. Instead they had to stay near the stream. For several days both men and women busied themselves roaming the neighborhood in search of cosmetic materials, such as ochre, white clay, and beeswax from honeycombs, and all that they found they turned over to their chiefs, who rationed them out on the morning of the fight. Then they all busily painted themselves and each other, some only their faces, others their whole bodies, in bold, startling, and individual designs, except for two men who were bright yellow from head to foot. Like other natives of northeastern Queensland, many of these men had frizzly, Papuan-like hair, which they teased out into "Afro"-style mops. Before fighting they saturated their hair with beeswax in one of two styles, separate spikes or a solid cake, not only striking in appearance but also serving as helmets.

The men were armed with spears, bundles of boomerangs and throwing sticks, and long, heavy, wooden slashing swords. Each man also carried an oval shield of soft wood, its front painted with individual designs in red, yellow, and white. A combatant ready to fight held his sword straight out in front of him with one hand, a considerable feat because of the weight.

Getting themselves decorated and armed took the men most of the day, and by the time they were ready to fight it was late afternoon, and, incidentally, a little cooler. The men of one band, whom Lumholtz accompanied, lined up on one side of the field, with much leaping and screaming, loud war cries and fierce gestures and glances, and much brandishing of weapons. Then they marched across the field in line, followed by their women, to the place where their particular enemies were also lined up, shields in their left hands and wooden swords in their right. These enemies all wore thirty or forty yellow and white cockatoo topknots in their hair.

As soon as the challengers halted, three of the cockatoo-crested men ran forward with long leaps. When they came to tall grass they jumped up high above it and as they landed crouched down so that their heads could barely be seen. Having arrived about twenty yards from Lumholtz's group the three stood, ready to fight.

Then three men of the other side advanced and took their positions, and three duels were fought at once, each man slashing at the other with his sword, and they kept on until one man gave up, or until his shield was split by a blow. Not one of the six seems to have been seriously injured. But while they were sparring their companions grew increasingly excited, and began attacking each other with spears, boomerangs, and waddies, and some were hurt.

Even in these apparently informal melees rules were followed, for if a spearpoint passed through a man's shield and grazed him, he was then disqualified. Meanwhile the older women collected fallen weapons and handed them to their men, and when a man was on the ground his women stood over him, shielding him and striking any would-be attackers with their digging sticks.

Not one, but several sets of opponents fought that day until sunset, which fell only about a half hour after the contest began. As they had not finished, they resumed it the next morning for about an hour, after which they quit and went home. In this series of fights no one was killed, but some were injured. In the next combat that followed a few weeks later, one man received a barbed spear through his body and died several days later.

Killing was obviously not the main purpose of this massive encounter, and it was probably not entirely a mechanism for blowing off pent-up steam, although that it did. The possession of women seems to have been a motive, for Lumholtz stated: "Many a one changes husbands on that night. As the natives frequently rob each other of their wives, the conflicts arising from this cause are settled by borbory (the combat), the victor retaining the woman (p. 124)." And: "As a result of the borbory several family revolutions had already taken place, men had lost their wives and women had acquired new husbands (p. 127)."

Fighting over women was particularly frequent in Australia, because of the age inequities of the marital system, because a woman might be given to a man repugnant to her, one with "boomerang legs" or some other physical defect, and because of the prevalent "sweetheart" relationship. This was a semitolerance of extramarital intercourse overstimulated by magic love songs. While it took care of some persons' extramarital sexual requirements, it did so only at the risk of violence. Australian aboriginal sex life was, in a sense, like an endless French comedy, and why not? Hunting was no great stimulus to the Australians, for the marsupials are not clever animals. There were no elephants, tigers, or bears to challenge the men's virility. Only women, and a chance to fight other men for women's favors.

The Alaskan Eskimo

On Nunivak Island and at Tigara, the Eskimo lived in permanent villages, each of which was politically independent and none of which had a central government or chiefs. Each family was autonomous, and the principal focal points were the men's houses. Such leadership as there was was exercised informally by traders (Nunivak) and whaleboat owners (Tigara).

No mention has been made of fighting and killing on Nunivak, but at Tigara accounts have been given of a few murders in earlier times. These were avenged by relatives of the deceased without any corporate action. The Nunivak men used to join their trading partners at Hooper Bay and on Nelson Island to fight the inland Eskimo when their help was needed. There are also accounts of inland Eskimo coming across in their boats to raid on Nunivak Island, and of the battles that the Nunivak men fought to repulse them.

The same thing took place now and then at Tigara. On the occasion of the last attack, a woman who, according to local custom, was holding her baby up to watch the sun rise on the eastern edge of the village at dawn, saw an attacking party and gave the alarm. When the Tigara men rushed out to repel the attack, they found their barefoot invaders already in rout. Their feet had been impaled in the dim light on a barrier of sharpened caribou and walrus bones which the villagers had set up across the narrow spit of land connecting Tigara with the mainland.

Political structure and internal peace-keeping among the Northwest Coast Indians

As previously stated, the three major northernmost tribes were organized into matrilineal clans (more accurately lineages) and the clans were grouped into nonresidential phratries (groups of clans), while the Kwakiutl and Nootka recognized bilateral kinship and were organized into extended-family house units in their villages, under ranked chiefs. Although called "tribes," or "nations," the Tlingit, Nootka, etc., were really linguistic units and had no formal political status.

The basic unit of government consisted of the inhabitants of the two or more houses, numbering about forty persons each, in a winter village. Each house had its chief, and one of them outranked the other or others. Each village was politically independent and could wage war on other ones. In the fishing season a number of winter villages might be combined into summer villages, but the component units were still autonomous, although they might act together as loose confederations.

Owing to their different kinds of kinship organization the northerners and the southerners had different ways of maintaining internal order. The Nootka men quarreled over women, and polygynous women quarreled over the favors of their husbands, as elsewhere in the world. Other disturbances were caused by accusations of witchcraft to explain otherwise inexplicable deaths. Such confrontations began with loud cursing matches and hair pulling, but seldom reached the level of violence, for others separated the contestants. A well-bred nobleman was trained never to show anger at a slight or insult, but simply to turn his back and walk away.

As the contestants were related to the witnesses on both sides of the family, it was not easy for the latter to take sides, but easier for them to play the role of impartial peacemakers, and men of substance and rank did not wish to risk losing prestige and rank through fighting. Philip Drucker reported only two examples of murder and one of suicide among the Central Nootkans that he studied, and both were undoubtedly rare among the southern tribes.

Among the Tlingit the situation was quite different.* There was no such thing as a crime against the individual, only against his clan. Owing to their unilateral organization it was easier than it was among the Nootka for others to take sides. If a man of one clan was killed by a man of another, the aggrieved clan as a body demanded the death of a man of rank equal to that of the deceased. The man selected to be the victim accepted his sentence calmly and died bravely. Under these circumstances the incidence of murder was relatively high.

*K. Oberg (see Bibliography).

All of the Northwest Coast Indians engaged in warfare, but we shall confine ourselves to wars among the Nootka tribes and confederations. These bloody struggles had, of course, an internally integrative function, and they also tore some persons between two loyalties, particularly if their wives were from the enemy side. In contrast to the relative quiet of internal social life, their wars were notably cruel.

One reason for intertribal fighting was to exterminate the owners of territories and fishing grounds, and to seize these properties. The pressures in such cases might be due to population increase, before the arrival of the white men, and to an unequal distribution of resources. For example, the Ahousat people had no salmon streams, while the Clayoquot had them on Lake Kennedy, which empties into the Tofino Inlet, running parallel to the coast, and belonged to the Clayoquot tribe. On the other hand, the Clayoquot had no interseason herring grounds or halibut banks to provide food between salmon runs. As trade was not so much in staple foods as in inedible goods, the Ahousat and the Clayoquot went to war for food.

Another reason for intertribal wars was to avenge an insult to a chief by outsiders. In one example a hostile party caught a chief on a beach, killed him, stuck his body on a pole, slashed his abdomen so that his intestines spilled out on the sand, cut off his genitalia, and tied them over his mouth through a hole in his nasal septum. In another, a chief had died. His retainers wrapped his body in two prime sea-otter skins and placed it up in a tree where passersby could see it and pay their respects. An outsider passing that way climbed the tree and stole the sea-otter skins.

Still a third cause of war was to provide the spirit of a newly deceased chief, or that of his son if one had died, with other spirits to accompany the former on its journey to the afterworld. Sometimes the aggrieved mourners killed a slave on the beach for this purpose, or they might war on another tribe to swell the ranks of their chief's spiritual companions. This practice is, of course, not unique. The Sumerians, early Chinese, Scythians, Natchez Indians, and the Maya all did it, but none of those mentioned were hunters and gatherers. That the Nootkans also followed this practice shows what strides on the road to civilization they had made.

When there seemed to be a reason for one tribe to attack another, a meeting was held and many speeches made. The top chief of the village was supposed to make the decision, but he could be swayed

K*

by lesser chiefs, particularly those called war chiefs, who were known as good leaders in raids and combats. Once the chiefs had made the decision they met in secret to avoid leaks, particularly by women born in the enemy territory.

The chiefs collected intelligence reports from recent visitors to the region to be attacked, and sometimes sent out secret agents to visit relatives among the intended victims. The head chief particularly wanted to know who was currently doing what where, who slept in which house and in which part of it.

The top chief, or a special war chief selected for the purpose, recruited his men, sometimes as many as three or four hundred, trying to muster a larger force than the one to be attacked. He divided his men into squads by houses, had them practice beachhead landings, and briefed them in secret. The war chief's badge of office was a whalebone club with one or both edges sharpened, or a one-piece stone club with a pointed end, used for crushing skulls. The chiefs had special names for these clubs, like "Orphan Maker," comparable to Excalibur for an Arthurian sword. The chiefs also wore body-armor, either of elkhide or of twined hardwood twigs. The other men were armed with pikes of yew with fire-hardened tips, hunting bows, and slings.

As their purpose was to exterminate the enemy, their usual strategy was to conduct a night raid by surprise. There were no naval battles between war canoes, and the raiders seldom attacked by daylight unless their plans had failed, through lack of coordination or because the enemy had been alerted and had held them off until morning. If the enemy expected a raid, they might have had time to post sentries, and to set deadfalls on approaching paths. In one instance which took place early in the 1870s shortly before the end of warfare, the defenders fortified themselves with a double palisade of split cedar logs and loopholes. (By that time they had steel axes.)

The raiders preferred to attack at the time of a ceremony when all of the men would be in their houses. Each squad would be assigned its particular house and each man the name and seating or sleeping position of his assigned victim. One way was to pretend to come in peace and join the ceremony. Then at a signal from the war chief his men would stab their victims. But if they did this they would not be able to wear their war paint.

Usually they painted their faces black, with the war chiefs using charred wolf or mountain-lion bone instead of charcoal. Each man tied his hair into a topknot, and thrust through it double-ended skewers of bone to keep his enemy from seizing it. When they wore that telltale accoutrement they would burst in at the height of the ceremony, or after their intended victims had fallen asleep, and the attackers would post sentries at the doors of the houses to prevent escape.

Timing was essential for the success of the raid. After the war canoes had been beached at some distance from the usual landing place, preferably around a point, guards would be left to protect the canoes, and the squads would proceed by separate paths. If the night was very dark, they might have to hold hands to keep together. The different squads communicated by wolf howls or imitations of the calls of night birds, and each house would have to be attacked simultaneously.

Inside the houses the attackers killed everyone they could, beheading some of them, while women and children tried to crawl out the rear apertures. Meanwhile a number of young men and boys who had come along on their own looted and took slaves. If successful, the attackers burned the houses and went to the main landing place—to which the guards had meanwhile brought the canoes—loaded them, and tried to destroy any canoes they couldn't take.

The war party returned home singing, and displaying the heads they had taken on poles. Then they exhibited the heads on the beach for four days, after which they hid them in the woods. Any women and children they captured became slaves. If they caught a chief alive, they might bring him back to torture him publicly, telling him to perform demeaning acts if he wished to be spared. If he did so, they mocked him and killed him anyway, but if he withstood the pain and insults with the fortitude and dignity expected of his rank, he at least died with honor. Later on, if there was enough loot to warrant it, the chief of the victors could distribute it in potlatches.

If all of the enemy had been either killed or enslaved, or if a few survivors had fled to live elsewhere, the raiders took over the fishing rights and crests of the losers. These rights were not considered as firm nor the crests as honorable as those inherited or acquired by marriage, even after they had been kept for generations, but still the victors kept them until and unless they themselves were defeated.

One long, drawn-out war that had consisted of repeat engagements without clear victory was concluded with a peacemaking ceremony. The chief of the village that proposed it spent two years building a big house, and then invited his enemies, members of two other villages, and they came. They all danced and feasted for four days, and finally one of the younger chiefs of the inviting group danced with a blanket full of eagle down, which he scattered as he danced. The principal chief of the former enemies then said that this act was a good sign, that the eagle down had covered all of the evil deeds that warriors used to do. All the chiefs agreed, the host chief held a potlatch, and the guest went home. The Nootkans fought no wars after that.

12.

Specialization, Wealth,
and Trade

The economic life of hunters and gatherers

In a rough way, the economic life of hunters and gatherers may be split into two categories, forming two ends of a continuous scale. At one end is that of peoples like the Tasmanians, Yaghans, and Kalahari Bushmen, who move about on annual rounds and cannot accumulate much wealth because they have little chance to store it. At the other extreme is that of the Indians of California and the Northwest Coast who are relatively sedentary. Food is abundant. They can amass and store property, and some men can become richer than others. There is no sharp cutoff line between these two extremes, but still the differences are clear.

People who have more food than they need can afford to feed specialists, who provide them with quality goods suited for trade. They are rarely full-time specialists, like our machine toolmakers and diamond cutters, but they are no longer jacks-of-all-trades. In other words, they are approaching the outskirts of the industrial society that we live in, with a foretaste of its complexities and headaches.

In combination, specialization and trade constitute one of the elements in the fabric of society among those that can afford it, making possible the emergence of classes and giving rise to a new kind of leader, the trader or trading chief, the prototype of the commercial tycoon. Trading chiefs are most needed in symbiotic societies, to deal with the white man, Hindu, Japanese, or Malay, but they may also be found among hunting peoples that trade with one another. In any case wealth breeds more wealth, and rich people tend to marry each other. Rank has a way of overriding age grading, accompanied by pomp and display.

In commerical, as contrasted with purely household activities, there are three principal, consecutive steps. They are procuring raw materials, processing them, and exchanging, or selling, the finished product. As this product is normally to be carried about, stored for some time, and traded, it must be something that is relatively compact and will not easily spoil or break. The raw material may be something to be found in but a few places, or, if it is abundant in many places, it must be something that requires the expert skills of specialists to process.

We have previously described examples of hunting peoples moving about to obtain raw materials: the Tasmanians' visit to ochre mines and mollusc beds, the Alakaluf's boat trips to Isla Desolación for pyrites, and the Arctic Eskimos' journeys to soapstone quarries to make kettles and lamps, as well as the offshore probings of Nootka chiefs and their retainers to obtain dentalia shells.

By and large it is not easy to find examples of full-time economic specialization among hunting and gathering peoples, or much part-time specialization either. In the age-old division of labor between the sexes, the man's job is hunting and fighting. He will make his own implements, his boats, or his sleds, but setting up simple houses, making simple containers and garments, is women's work, and women have little time for specialization what with cooking and the care of children. Two conditions foster masculine specialization; a surplus of food adequate to free specialists from the daily food quest, and a need for their services or product among others able to pay for it.

These conditions are not found everywhere, and most of our examples come from the Pacific coastal regions of North America. No doubt they once obtained in western Europe, some of the Middle Eastern countries, and other bountifully endowed regions in which the hunting and gathering way of life yielded to agriculture and pastoralism. But this was so long ago that we are reduced to making deductions, from archaeological sites, that some implements are so intricate and uniform that it took specialists of sorts to make them. We are on firmer ground when we note that some implements, materials, and ornaments were traded far from their sources, but that is as far as this line of inquiry will take us with any degree of certainty.

On the Pacific coast, skilled, specialized workmanship survived well into the last century, and eyewitness accounts of the details are available. For example, one branch of the Maidu in Central California divided specialties between patrilineages. One of them flaked arrowheads, and another built salmon dams. If unrelated persons showed special abilities at one of these crafts, they would be adopted into the appropriate lineages. As a village could contain persons of different lineages, this division of labor on a basis of kinship, real or fictitious, lent an economic element to the social fabric.

The greatest specialization in most of California was in basket making; the greatest in the Northwest Coast was in blanket weaving. Luckily many of our museums have extensive exhibits of these baskets and blankets which the reader is urged to go and see.

Basket making in California

In the southern part of California baskets were made by coiling, using a bundle of grass as the basic coil and binding it with strips of sumac bark or rushes. In the north, however, the Indians made their baskets by twining conifer roots around hazel rods that served as warps, and wrapping the twining elements with strips of colored bark to produce decorative patterns.

In central California these two basic techniques overlapped, and basket making took on a professional cast. Showpieces were coiled; storage and utility vessels were twined. They had single-bundle and three-bundle coiling, diagonal and latticed twining, and wickerwork. The Pomo were the best basket makers in the state, and they were the only people to make twined baskets with definite patterns. The Yokuts made shouldered baskets with feathers attached to the shoulders and neck, and the Modoc overlaid their basket wefts with quills for decoration. Each tribe thus had its own style of basket making, which could be easily identified.

The Maidu turned out many more of these decorated baskets than they seemed to need because most of them were burned on pyres at funeral ceremonies held some years after an important person's death. These mortuary baskets were not utilitarian but symbolic. In making them none but the simplest implements were needed, and no force other than the strength of the human fingers, and no teamwork. All that was needed was the skill of specialists who could be fed by others.

These specialists, called Suku, were not women, but homosexual, transvestite males,* who lived like women and spent their time making these fine feather-decorated objects needed for ceremonies. They themselves were not admitted to the rites because they were not counted as men. Homosexuals are rare in hunting societies, and seldom mentioned in the literature.

*The Maidu also had female transvestites whose function will be stated on page 348.

Northwest Coast specialties: Chilkat and Salish blanket weaving

Among the Northwest Coast Indians most men of any account were specialists to some extent. For example, among the Nootka, specialization included canoe making, woodcarving, stone maul making, sealing, and trapping bears, deer, and elk. These skills were taught boys by their fathers, and an important element in the apprenticeship was learning the secret ritual of each craft that was deemed vital for success. Aside from political leadership, chiefs specialized in whaling. The role of shaman, which depended on a special kind of personality, was not hereditary.

Some specialties also involved women, particularly in weaving. In Chapter 2 we noted that, living in a wet but mild climate, the Northwest Coast Indians got along without fitted garments except when traveling in the mountains. In good weather the men went naked, but they wore shredded cedar-bark raincoats reaching to the elbow when needed, and in cold weather they wore robes or "blankets" under the capes.

Not only is weaving rare among hunting and gathering peoples, but some of these robes are outstanding examples of the textile art. Specialization in weaving them was local rather than individual and the women did the weaving, but not all of the preparation for it. Two of these weaving techniques were outstanding, that of the Chilkat division of the Tlingit, and several of the Salish living along the Strait of Juan de Fuca and on the shores of Georgia Bay, including the eastern side of Vancouver Island, which they shared with the Nootka.

The Chilkat weaving was of Tsimshian origin. Once a Tsimshian chief married a Chilkat woman who learned it. After she had died some of her female relatives got hold of a piece of her handiwork. It was not a robe, but a dance apron, such as the Tsimshians made, but back home the relatives of the deceased carefully unraveled it to see how it was made, and transferred the technique to robe weaving. This new industry flourished, and the Chilkat sold the robes to the other Tlingits who exhibited them at feasts and were buried in them.

Nearly all of the materials had to be imported, and both men and women participated in the process, but in different ways. The warps of the robes were made with a core of shredded cedar-bark twine, and the cedar bark had to be brought from the south. These cores were wrapped with yarn spun from the wool of mountain goats, which the men hunted in the mountains for the women. The wefts were of the same woolen yarn, and no cedar bark showed in the finished fabric.

The dyes were of four colors, blue, black, yellow, and white, and it may be noted that blue is a rare color in the art of any hunting people, because substances from which it can be made are rare in nature. The Chilkat women made it by soaking imported copper in urine. Two of the other three colors were made by soaking vegetable materials in urine also—hemlock bark for black, and lichens from the mountains for yellow. White was the natural color of the wool when thoroughly washed.

The men set up the looms, which were of the one-bar, suspended variety. The men also made pattern boards and painted them with the designs to be woven into the blankets, and made measuring sticks for the women to use in copying the designs off the boards.

Each woman spun her yarn by hand and dyed it, sometimes taking several months in preparation for weaving a single blanket. Then she tied the ends of the warps in line on the cross bar, and twined them together at the top with a special weave. From there on down she wove the body of the robe in a series of vertical panels, instead of carrying the wefts straight across. In that way she could separately reproduce the intricate designs of the panel board. Having twined the top ends of the warps to the bar, she then measured the warps so as to provide for a curved lower border, and tied the ends of the warps in bundles, covering each bundle with animal gut to keep them from getting dirty. The warps for each panel were thus tied together in a single bundle.

The weaving procedure was a combination of twining and twilling. She twined two strands of weft around two adjacent warps, moving over one weft-breadth alternately as she proceeded down the panel, thus producing the twilling. When the panels were finished she joined their edges together with a three-element, false embroidery technique, one that did not leave the joints conspicuous because she used the same method to make borders for the design elements within each panel. She then bordered the sides and bottom of the robe by another technique, braiding.

This whole operation of manufacturing Chilkat robes thus required the coordinated efforts of both men and women, the use of imported materials, and the export of the product. These men and women were not full-time specialists like the Maidu feathered basket makers, but local, part-time specialists, like the old New England farmers who made shoes in their small shops behind their houses in the winter time, or like a tribe of Moroccan mountaineers who used to make gunstocks for trade because they had suitable wood and too little land to feed their families. I know of no other instance of this combination of activities among nonagricultural, nonpastoral peoples.

The Salish robe weavers employed several techniques, not all of which have been adequately reported, and an even greater variety of materials than the Chilkat weavers. They spun their yarn with wooden spindles weighted with heavy wooden or bone spindle whorls to maintain tension. They used not only mountain-goat wool but also the tightly curled hair that they sheared periodically from dogs of a poodlelike breed that they kept for the purpose. To my knowledge the only other animal that was sheared by hunting peoples was *Homo sapiens*. Some of the Australian aborigines cropped their women's scalps to make cordage, but did no weaving.

To these two kinds of wool the Salish weavers added various vegetable fibers, but made little use of cedar bark, and they cleaned their wool by beating it with fine clay, a process analogous to fulling whole pieces of cloth by European weavers. They also spun warps out of eiderdown, to be woven on suspended one-bar looms, though not on their best-known kind of loom, a two-bar variety, for eiderdown would not take stretching.

The Salish two-bar loom was not unique, because in the Plateau country some of the tribes wove robes out of strips of rabbit skin on rectangular frames, but the way the Salish women used looms was more elaborate. Between the two upright bars the weaver first tied a stout cord, stretched tightly. She then took a ball of yarn that she had spun to serve as warp for her fabric. This piece of yarn was long enough to make a continuous, uncut warp. She tied one end of this yarn to the cord, next to one of the uprights. Then she drew it down under the lower bar, up the back side of the frame, over the upper bar, and down to the cord again, and so on until she had mounted the entire warp for her fabric from one side to the other.

She then wove in the weft, hitching the warp around to keep the place where she was weaving in front of her, until she had produced a tubular fabric. Now that the weaving was over, she needed only to cut and draw the string, and the two ends of the fabric parted company, leaving her a rectangular blanket. With this basic technique she could work much more rapidly than could the Chilkat weaver. She could turn out many more blankets in a given time, while remaining free to vary the pattern of the weave, to introduce colored pieces of weft, and thus to create her own designs. Salish robes woven by this and other methods were highly prized and widely traded, being carried down the coast as far as the mouth of the Columbia River.

The elaboration of basket making and weaving techniques in the Pacific coastal regions of North America raises the question as to whether or not they were local inventions. They need not have been, because there were agricultural tribes along the Colorado River. The Pueblo Indians lived not far away, and fancy basket making and weaving techniques could have been inspired by those of agricultural peoples reaching all the way southward to Bolivia.

The answer to this question, which we may never hear, is less important than the fact that these ornate baskets and robes filled needs in the cultures of the coastal peoples. These needs were not so much economic as social. The most elaborate baskets were made simply to be burned, and the most ornate blankets were used far less for warmth than for display. Yet their manufacture kept many fingers busy, turned some men into women, and fostered trade.

Simple trade: the Andamanese and Australians

As far as hunting and gathering peoples are concerned, there are two kinds of trade. The first is an exchange of goods or products between two or more groups of hunters and gatherers. The second one is symbiotic trade, as found among the Mbuti Pygmies and their Negro neighbors; the Birhors and their village marketmen; and the Canadian Indian fur trappers and the Hudson Bay Company. The first is the one we are talking about here; the second takes us halfway out of our field.

One of the simplest trading mechanisms noted by anthropologists is that of the Great Andamanese. In the preceding chapter we told how annual interband meetings were arranged, how they were conducted, and what happened if they led to fights. According to A. R. Brown, the purpose of these meetings was not trade at all but simply to cement relations between bands, by giving each other identical or similar presents. In other words, I give you a bow and you give me a bow, and this makes us friends.

This statement was only a part truth, for, according to earlier accounts recorded when the meetings were still taking place, under the cover of these economically unnecessary exchanges several useful items passed hands that both partners to the swapping needed. One was small slabs of sandstone or other gritstone from the interior, to be used as files or sandpaper in woodworking, and the other was potfuls of pomade, a blend of turtle or dugong fat and ochre, obviously from the coast.

In the preceding chapter we told of the early colonists in Victoria, Australia, encountering aboriginal "kings." On a slope of the present Mount William near Lancefield, the colonists found an aborigine named Billi-billeri working in a native stone quarry. He was digging out stones and breaking them into pieces, and then rudely shaping some of these fragments so that they could later be pecked and ground into axe heads.

Billi-billeri was the headman of a clan that owned the quarry and its surrounding countryside, and he would sell his stones to people from other tribes after the price had been arranged in advance by messengers. Then the purchasers would come to the quarry and camp nearby. They would give him the opossum-skin robes and other objects promised, and take away their axe blanks. If Billi-billeri was not there when the strangers arrived, his sister's husband, who was headman of another clan, would be summoned to come and take his place.

Whoever it was that collected the goods exchanged for the stones, the proceeds were pooled and shared between a number of kinsmen, all heads of different clans, who had inherited their rights to their shares. The offices of these men were hereditary. Because a headman had more wives than other men, there was usually a number of other sons to choose from in case the oldest lacked the necessary qualifications. In any event, what we have just described was a political system based on inherited rights to wealth.

If we move northward to Cape York Peninsula in Queensland, we will find an account of multiple, long-distance trading arrangements described by Lauriston Sharp in 1952, almost a century and a half later than the Billi-billeri episode. Sharp's subjects were the Yir Yoront people, who traded spears for stone axes. Their country was flat, geologically recent, and alluvial, and thus had no suitable stone. They had to get it from quarries, four hundred miles to the south.

They got the stones through long lines of trading partners to the south, and exchanged them for spears, particularly war spears with barbed stingray spines as points; these barbs break off in human flesh and leave nasty wounds. The Yir Yoront made some of these spears, but they got others from people farther north, who also needed stone axe heads.

For a dozen such spears a Yir Yoront man would get one axe head, but 150 miles farther south, at about the middle of the line, the price was: one spear, one axe head. Near the quarries one spear would bring several axe heads. There was no special trading class, because most of the Yir Yoront men took part in this exchange. The trade affected the local social structure principally because these axes, highly prized as they were, belonged to the men. The women, who needed axes for cutting firewood and other purposes, had to borrow them from their husbands, and bring them back as soon as they were through using them. The boys had to do the same. By owning axes the mature men exercised their authority along lines of sex and age. The trade also ensured amicable relations between the groups with which the trading partners had contact up and down the line.

Not long before Sharp's visit to the Yir Yoront some well-meaning missionaries established themselves nearby. One of their first kind deeds was to hand out steel axes to everyone, men, women, and children. The Yir Yoront world almost came to an end. The men lost their authority over their wives, a generation gap appeared, and their trading partnerships collapsed.

Wealth and trade among the Alaskan Eskimo: The Nunivak Islanders

Returning to the New World, let us first see how wealth and trade helped to create a stable social and political framework in two Alaskan Eskimo societies that we have already referred to in previous chapters, those of the hunters of bearded seals on Nunivak Island and of the whalers of Tigara at Point Hope.

Nunivak Island, some sixty miles long and about forty miles wide, lies in seawater open the year round at about 60° north latitude, and within about twenty miles of the Alaskan coast, which is easily reached from the island by umiaks both rowed and sailed. In 1940 the islanders lived in seven villages, all coastal. The smaller villages had only one men's house each, the larger ones two or three. (In the Nunivak dialect a men's house is called *kazigi*, a name commonly used in anthropological literature.)

Some of the Nunivak men were called chiefs, although they held no formal or overt political office. These men had been given a more or less comparable title by public acclaim, as a reward for having given away large quantities of goods in a combination contest and ceremony held by the members of two villages. These gifts were mostly skins, furs, skins full of oil, and other animal products, rather than manufactured goods like clothing and weapons, of which each family made their own. The families kept their supplies in separate storehouses; a rich family might have as many as three. There were also a few poor families that found trouble feeding themselves. They would earn their food by working for rich families, by collecting driftwood for fires, helping build kayaks, and cleaning and sewing furs.

Now a rich man was in many cases the son of a rich father, but not in every case, because to stay rich he also had to be a good hunter and trader. The Nunivak hunters killed seals and walrus, but no whales. The highest prestige came from killing bearded seals out of kayaks in the spring hunts. Bearded seals are large and hard to hold when struck. When the Tigara men hunt them, they harpoon them on ice floes, and when the seal reaches open water it takes two men to hold the line.

Bearded seal skins were needed for boat covers, boot soles, and rawhide lines. The skins of one-year-old bearded seals were particularly valuable in trading with the mainland Eskimo. On the island itself, there was little intervillage trading because all islanders, except for the villagers living at the west end, got the same products from the sea. On steep cliffs near the village were large rookeries of murres, puffins, and small auks. The villagers traded the skins of these birds in units of six skins each, known as a "knot." (Six, incidentally, was also the sacred number and trading unit of the Ainu.)

Also, one islander could get something on credit from another on a promise to pay his debt with something else during the following season. For example, a man who wanted to take a purifying sweatbath before a ceremony and didn't have enough firewood to heat the bath could borrow the wood on such terms. If a man welched on his debt, his only punishment was a loss of esteem, but that was enough to make him pay if he could.

Off-island trade was conducted with other Eskimo only. Before about 1880 the Nunivak men traded only with the Hooper Bay and Nelson Island people, both living on the coast, and the two groups named traded in turn with Eskimo of the interior who rarely if ever came to the coast. The Nunivak traders obtained jadeite for use as tools from a single site in the Jade Mountains near the Kobuk River, and vivianite for making blue paint from a deposit on Nelson Island, both by trade.

Except for these two mineral substances, the Hooper Bay and Nelson Island Eskimo had much the same goods to offer as the Nunivak Islanders did, and thus the former, acting as middlemen, exacted a profit from the transaction until about 1880.

The Nunivak people had a surplus of marine products, such as sealskins, skinfuls of oil, "knots" of birdskins, and the like, but they had no squirrel or wolverine fur, which was needed for their clothing. In July and early August each year, an umiak owner would assemble three or four male relatives or close friends for a voyage. Each man took along his own food and trade goods, and bartered independently; but all worked together in navigating the umiak, and would stand by each other in case of trouble. The umiak owner charged them nothing, for they earned their way.

The Tigaran traders

Tigara, we may recall, consisted of a single village on a spit of land at the end of Point Hope. By about 1900 it had but two men's clubhouses, although it had had seven as late as 1870. These men's houses are mentioned here because they had much to do with the distribution of wealth both at Tigara and on Nunivak Island. During the summer the Tigaran people dispersed, leaving only a few old people in the village.

The spring hunt for bowhead whales was over. Some families went caribou hunting on the mainland; others left to net balugas (small white whales); and still others went trading. It is to be noted that the Tigaran trading unit was the family, not a random boat load of men as with the Nunivak traders, although a Tigaran trading family needed a boat to carry their goods. They loaded it with skinfuls of seal and whale oil, baleen, walrus tusks, and other marine products, and their dogs towed it along shore. If they had no dogs the members of the family towed the umiak themselves.

Some of the families went southeast to a trading center at Hotham Inlet in Kotzebue Sound, others to another center to the northeast at the mouth of the Utorgag River. At Hotham Inlet they met boatloads of other Eskimo from the interior who had brought caribou skins, dried fish, jadeite from the Jade Mountains on the Kobuk River, mammoth ivory, pyrites, and clothing and implements, some made by the inland Eskimo themselves, and others by Athabascan Indians. Not only the Tigarans, but also other coastal Eskimo flocked to this rich market. Eskimo from the head of Norton Sound crossed the Seward Peninsula overland, a trek of a good one hundred miles, and boatloads arrived from Shishmaref and Cape Prince of Wales on the Seward Peninsula, from the Diomede Islands in Bering Strait, from King Island farther south, and from East Cape, Siberia.

In 1649 Russian Cossacks established a trading post at Anadyrsk in northeastern Siberia, about four hundred miles west-southwest of East Cape as the crow flies, and it was not long before European trade goods reached Alaska. Hotham Inlet became the distribution center for these goods. The Bering Strait Eskimo were the middlemen. Furs and ivory moved westward, in exchange for glass beads, iron, tobacco, tea, and Siberian tanned reindeer skins.

At the northern trading center at the mouth of the Utorgag River, the Tigarans originally simply exchanged seal skins, to be cut into lines, and seal oil with the Inland Eskimo in return for caribou skins for clothing. But after the Hudson Bay Company had established its posts on the Mackenzie River during the nineteenth century, the Tigarans and other coastal Eskimo began to obtain English trade goods from the south as well as Russian ones from the east, twenty years or so before direct trade began with the Yankee whalers from Nantucket and New Bedford.

Before the Yankee whalers arrived and decimated the bowheads, the Tigaran trading families, who had done no hunting all summer, could subsist on cached sea-mammal meat from the spring hunts until the bowheads made their return trip to ice-free water. But when the bowheads failed to appear in the fall, these trading families were in trouble. They had to go to the rivers to fish through the ice with gill nets for salmon, salmon-trout, and whitefish, unless they gave up their long-range summer expeditions and traded with the Yankee mariners at home.

What the Nunivak and Tigaran traders did with their wealth

Now that we know how the Nunivak and Tigara Eskimo obtained wealth, the questions remain: What did they do with it, and how did its possession and distribution affect the social structure of these two groups, neither of which was organized by unilateral kinship into clans or tribes, and neither of which had true chiefs?

In the first place, among both groups wealth was not hereditary. However, the capacity to amass it was hereditary to a certain extent, and a man who had the energy, skill, and leadership to obtain wealth was the kind of man likely to be shown respect in any case. In the second place, the wealthy men distributed it to the other people in their village, or, in Nunivak where there was more than one village, among the inhabitants of neighboring villages as well. In both cases membership in and rivalry between men's houses formed part of the system of distribution.

One of the principal ways that this was done in Nunivak was through the mechanism of a so-called messenger-feast. A man who wished to be the principal host at such a feast showed his intention by making a stake of wood and painting it red. He casually displayed this in his men's house so that the boys seated there would see it, and one boy would volunteer to deliver it to the men of the men's house who were thus invited. He also gave the boy a set of smaller sticks, one for each person invited to attend.

Meanwhile the members of the principal host's men's house collected goods to be given in exchange to the guests from the other men's houses. These presents included coils of rawhide line, bundles of walrus intestines, folded skins of bearded and spotted seals, various furs, and some manufactured goods, such as spears and even kayaks. Each of the principal host's housemates contributed what he could, and some gave more than others did. There was no conspicuous rivalry, for each man simply gave what he was able.

At the appointed time the guests arrived, with much ceremony, the hosts going out to meet them and usher them in, until they got to the men's house. The gifts had been hung up on another stake outside the house, and the guests took them down and hung up others in return, which the hosts took. When the men of each side divided up what they had received, the oldest man was given first choice, and so on down the line, by age. The women watched this distribution with considerable excitement.

Then they feasted together at the host group's expense, and went inside where the hosts staged a show. There the heads of the different lineages pushed wooden floats, called "trays," back and forth toward the guests, each "tray" being a model showing in miniature carvings the deeds of the ancestor of that lineage. One end of the "tray" was suspended from the roof, the man or men pushing it holding the other end. Some took two men to push because they were heavy. After this performance the guests gave their hosts more gifts, and departed.

In Tigara the captains of the whaling boats fed the members of their crews and their families during the period before the ice broke and the whales came, so that they would be able to spend time preparing gear and not have to go hunting. Each captain hired a skilled woodworker to make the wooden pot that the captain's wife carried about in order to give the whale a symbolic drink of fresh water. The captain's wife also hired an old women to sew the special mittens she had to wear while carrying the pot, as described in Chapter 5.

During the spring feast that followed the whaling a ceremony was held to initiate new captains. Part of this rite was the famous Eskimo blanket tossing. They set up a walrus skin supported on four corners by tripods of wood, and all around the edge of the skin were hand grips. People grasping these grips could stretch the skin to make the person being tossed rise in the air, and the trick was to leap up, sometimes as high as fifteen feet, and land upright.

First they tossed a boat-owner who had killed the first whale of his life that season. He jumped up onto the skin carrying bundles of baleen, boot soles, skins, and other valuables, and while being tossed he threw the goods out into the crowd, sometimes calling out the names of the persons for whom they were intended, and sometimes letting people scramble for them, especially old people. Then other captains who wished to could follow, but usually only those that had killed no more than three or four whales so far in their careers. After that anyone could jump. In one case it was a woman whose son had recently killed his first seal, and the gifts she threw out had been assembled by her female relatives.

In the fall the members of the rival men's houses competed in games, followed by feasts, and in those and all other feasts held in the men's houses, the poor and otherwise unfortunate persons of the community were fed by the rich men of the house in which the feast was held. When, in the games, one house lost to the other, the losers would bring meat and inedible gifts such as sinews and bootsoles to the other, all would eat the meat, and the other gifts would be divided among the older men of the host's house. By these means people 'were kept busy; the poor, particularly the old men too old for active hunting, were fed and given useful goods; healthy rivalry was sustained; and the rich were relieved of envy. Under this system quarreling within the community was kept at a minimum.

Trading on the Northwest Coast

In the times before European contact the Northwest Coast Indians traded not only in woven robes, but also in copper and many other materials, as we have seen from the lists of materials from which the robes were made. The Nootka, for example, killed sharks and rendered their oil, needed by the tribes farther north, and they also exported dentalia shells and canoes, and imported slaves. The Chinook traders had control of the Columbia River from the falls at The Dalles to the Strait of Juan de Fuca. At the foot of the falls, which was the head of navigation to the sea, they had a lively trading station where they exchanged goods with the Indians living beyond the portage, and they exacted tolls from others coming through the strait.

In 1778 Capt. James Cook found the Northwest Coast Indians using some iron, presumably from Russian sources, from Japanese and other shipwrecks, or both. Captain Cook traded iron tools for sea-otter skins which he knew would fetch fancy prices in China. In the nineteenth century, owing to rivalry between British companies, Boston skippers took over this lucrative commerce, taking metal goods, including firearms, to the Northwest Coast, furs from there to Canton, and tea back to Boston.

As seaborne trade with white men increased, so did the wealth of the Indians. On the other hand, newly introduced diseases reduced their numbers. The result: There were now more positions in the ladder of social rank than there were bodies to fill them, and a scramble for power ensued via the potlatching ceremonies, which reached their peak among the Fort Rupert Kwakiutl, as described in detail by the late Franz Boas. Like totem poles, the efflorescence of potlatching was an artifact of contact with the white man, and potlatching was a substitute for fighting, which the Canadian government had forbidden.

13.

*Gods, Spirits, Myths,
and Tales*

Why hunters need gods

The hunter sees the world around him through the screen of his own culture. He has a spirit that leaves him in dreams and that will quit his body permanently at death. That spirit has to go somewhere and he must create a myth to explain what happens to it. If he has a spirit, so must animals and sometimes trees. In the territory in which he hunts there may be other spirits living in rocks, pools, and hills. Anything dangerous like a rapid in a river or falls, a stormy headland, a deep cave, will have a spirit or spirits in it to make trouble if unappeased.

There are also the sun, moon, stars, and prevailing winds to explain. They must have spirits too. Is the sun a man or a woman? In the tropics where the sun scorches the earth in open country at high noon, the sun may be thought of as an insatiable woman, and the moon a man whom she tires out periodically. In the dim light of the Arctic the sun may be a benevolent man. What is a rainbow but a bridge to the sky? What is thunder but the wrath of a god that controls weather?

Why do the salmon run up the streams in vast numbers some years and not others? Because there is a man in a house under the sea that controls them, depending on how his salmon have been treated. We have seen this concept among the Ainu, who conduct elaborate rites to make sure of their success at salmon fishing. The Northwest Coast Indians believed that the salmon themselves were people who lived in the house under the sea and donned salmon-flesh garments to sacrifice themselves. If their bones were put back in the water they would be reborn every year, but they would not return if they had been offended. Hence the rites concerned with handling the first salmon to be caught in a season, and the prayers to the salmon spirits, became so long and so involved that a special person, actually a priest, had to conduct them. Priests are common enough among food-producing peoples, but among hunters they are exceedingly rare.

Gods exist because people need them. If you believe that you will sicken and die if you violate a tabu that will anger a god, you are likely to think twice before you do it. And if a horrid spirit is going to grab you if you venture into a treacherous cave, you will not enter it unless you absolutely need to. The belief in gods and spirits symbolizes areas of anxiety, and the myths and rites concerned with them promote proper behavior. Proper behavior keeps people from creating antisocial disturbances.

The creator and the ancestors: two different systems

Long ago there was a time when gods walked the earth, or came down to it from the sky; when the earth was created; when the sun, moon, and stars took their place in the sky; when heroes shaped the valleys and headlands; and when animals talked. Some hunters believe that there was once a single creator, who after having finished his work retired and withdrew from close contact with men. He may have returned now and then to intervene when things were going wrong in order to straighten out earthly affairs, and perhaps he will some day come again.

Other hunters pay little attention to the creator, if they mention him at all. They attribute the origin of things to their ancestors, the earth-shaping heroes. If we run through the list of hunters about whose cultures we have the needed information, we will find that the two poles of belief correspond to two different kinds of social and political organization, the simple and the compound. People who have a minimum of social differentiation tend to share their beliefs. People who are divided in one way or another tend to emphasize their differences through separate sets of symbols.

And peoples are interested, some more than others, in how they came into being, and in how they are linked to the lands in which they live; usually both. By and large the believers in a single, lofty, and remote creator live in single territorial groups. Many of them trace their descent bilaterally and have little concern with ancient ancestors. Others may be organized unilaterally, but still live as the others do.

At the opposite pole stand two kinds of people. Some are organized into unilateral clans and extensions of clans, whose members may be scattered in mixed bands or mixed villages. The members of each such clan may have special duties to perform in common ceremonies. Others are people who lay great store by wealth and rank, however they may trace their descent. They care less about an overall creator than about the fabulous deeds of their particular ancestors, toward whom their mythology and their rites are directed.

Believers in a single creator include the Bushmen, Pygmies, Great Andamanese, Semang, Philippine Negritos, some of the Southeast Australian aborigines, probably the Tasmanians, the Yaghans, Onas, Central and Eastern Eskimo, the northern Algonkians and most of the northern Athabascans.

The ancestor worshipers include the Australian aborigines of the northern and central parts of the continent where complex unilateral social systems prevail, and the Northwest Coast Indians, whose wealth and rank are dominant influences, regardless of the way of tracing descent. There also exist mixed or transitional camps, like that of the Ainu. In Ainu theology the creator concept is still strong, but to it is added a plethora of departmental gods controlling fresh water, salt water, the salmon, and various species of land animals, particularly the bear. Men of the six patrilineages also perform minor, secret rites now and then, directed toward their totemic ancestors; but their principal rites have to do with the gods and spirits they hold in common. Unlike the situation on the Northwest Coast, their lineages are not sharply ranked and individual wealth is of little importance.*

The nature of myths

The cosmic deeds of creators, culture bearers, and ancestors have been recorded for generations in the minds of men as exciting and awe-inspiring myths, as least as real as the Book of Genesis is to a fundamentalist Christian. Secular events may be the subject matter of tales, but these too may involve the supernatural. The dividing line is thin, if it exists. Both myths and tales have moral implications. In

*If professional anthropologists see some resemblance between my views expressed above and the conclusions of the *Kulturkreislehre* school of Mödling – Vienna, they may be assured that any similar results may have been arrived at by different methods. One purpose of the Viennese school is to test their idea that monotheism is the original belief of man by studying the religions of the world's most primitive surviving peoples. My purpose was to see if there might be some relationship between the ways in which different hunting peoples are organized socially and politically and the organization of their spiritual worlds, which reflect their own preoccupations.

both, the evil consequences of incest, defilement with menstrual blood, neglect of orphans, and many other antisocial acts are vividly portrayed.

Unlike rituals, which have to be letter-perfect to be effective, myths and tales may improve in the telling because a gifted narrator watches his audience's reaction and finds out which episodes and details evoke the keenest interest; he can build up the successful ones and cut the dull ones. He also knows where to break off and where to begin the next performance, starting the next day with an audience still agog. For these reasons the chronological sequence of episodes may be interrrupted for flashbacks.

Anachronisms are run-of-the-mill in the myths of peoples with no accurate record of sequences of events. Tasmanians told George A. Robinson that the moon came from England, and the Micmac of Nova Scotia say that their trickster-hero Gluskabe once bent the sides of a church bell together so that it couldn't wake them up on Sunday mornings.

Tasmanian myths: primordial astronomy

Let us start our sample of myths with those of the Tasmanians, the most primitive hunters known to us in a material sense, in that they used one-piece stone implements without handles, one-piece wooden spears, had no fabricated containers for carrying water, and no knowledge of fire making. They apparently lived in simple, exogamous, territorial bands with chiefs, and once a year the members of several bands came together to hunt by beating in a circle. The collection of bands that joined each other at these seasonal events spoke a common language and constituted what, in the Australian sense, would be called a tribe. Yet their views of the cosmos were rich in imagery. Our information on this subject comes mostly from information given George A. Robinson by Woorrady, whose technique of wooing we have described in Chapter 10, and who raped and killed his brother's widow, as recounted in Chapter 11.

The stars were important to the Tasmanians because the positions of the stars told them when it was time to burn over the forest, to walk to the coast for shellfish, and to swim to offshore islands to collect the sooty petrel, then nesting. Like many peoples of antiquity

L

they saw configurations of stars and planets resembling men, women, and anatomical parts of men and animals. A black spot in the sky, which was probably the so-called Coal Sack in the Southern Cross, was identified as a stingray which native men were spearing, just as they themselves speared this dangerous fish to keep it from attacking women diving for molluscs.

They also named individual stars and planets and knew their positions at different seasons. When three special stars stood in a vertical line, they predicted fine weather. These stars were apparently Alpha and Beta of the Southern Cross and a third so faint that it is barely visible, if at all, to the white man's naked eye. When a meteorite fell at night they shrieked and hid their heads, for such an event, being unpredictable, was disturbing.

Their origin myths also drew heavily on their knowledge of the stars. Canopus, a bright star in the southern sky, was called Droemerdeener by the Bruny Islanders, who believed that he came out of the sea and fought a rival star called Moihernee, who cannot be identified because it is no longer there. After the battle Moihernee fell down into Louisa Bay where he lived until he turned into a great stone, still to be seen at the time this myth was recited. After his fall Moihernee's wife followed him to earth, and she lives in the sea. Later his children fell down too and entered his wife's womb. They had many children.

Later on the moon, who was a woman, came from the northwest. First she sojourned in the Oyster Bay country where the kangaroo and the abalone asked her to stay. But once when she was roasting an abalone the sun came along and swept her away. Tumbled into the fire by his tempestuous advances, she was burned on one side and rolled into the sea, but after this athletic courtship she rose into the sky where she joined her new husband, the sun. Their children are rainbows. "If you look at the moon," said Woorrady, "you will see the black spots where she was burned."

But neither the sun nor the moon were creators. It was Moihernee who cut the earth and shaped the rivers and islands, and who also created Parlevar, the first man. Moihernee pulled Parlevar out of the earth while leaving certain other creatures underground. Robinson called these earth-spirits "devils."

Parlevar had a tail like a kangaroo and no knee joints, so that he had to sleep standing up. At this point Moihernee's rival Droemerdeener came to Parlevar's rescue; he cut off Parlevar's tail, rubbed fat in the wound, and cured it. Then he gave Parlevar knee joints so that he could sit down, and Parlevar said, "This is very good indeed."

Although Parlevar still had no hole in his penis, Moihernee took care of that too. He either came in the form of Laller, the piss-ant, or sent Laller, who bored the hole, and Parlevar was ready to function.

Moihernee also created the boomer — the great gray kangaroo — by pulling it, like Parlevar, out of the ground. Once in the open the boomer hopped away as far as the seashore, where he sat down and created the lagoons.

On the other hand, it was Droemerdeener who created the kangaroo rat, the wombat, and the echidna, all burrowing animals. Each of these three separately and in turn approached some people who were sleeping and threw stones at them. When each one did so the sleepers partly awakened, and then dozed off again. The animals kept on repeating this performance and made such nuisances of themselves that the men finally woke up and caught them and thrust them into holes in the ground, where they now live. In order to keep them from being a bother, the people were obliged to eat these animals, and have been eating them ever since. The abalone in former times used to speak, but it doesn't anymore. Before diving for abalones, the women stood on rocks along shore, singing and performing an "obscene" dance, the details of which Robinson was too modest to record. Whether this rite was to lure the abalones into loosening their grips on the rocks, we do not know.

The origin of fire according to the Tasmanians

The myth concerning the origin of fire varied regionally. The chief of the Oyster Bay Tribe said that two stars in the Milky Way made fire by rubbing their hands together, and that it was not Moihernee but these same two stars that created Parlevar, who walked down the Milky Way to Tasmania. These two stars were probably Procyon and Gamma in the constellation of Gemini. Natives of the Big River Tribe in the Hampshire Hills said that Parlevar first got fire when lightning ignited trees, which makes excellent sense. A native of Macquarie Harbor, Western Tribe, who had never seen a white man before, said that the first fire was obtained when a white man coughed it out of his throat, and at this the more sophisticated natives in Robinson's entourage laughed, but there is no reason to believe that this statement was intended as a joke. He might have heard of white men smoking, or equated the newly arrived whites, whose skins were ghost-colored, with mythological beings.

The fire that ignited trees was sent by an evil spirit, Rageorapper, who lived in the bush in the form of a large, powerful black man. He brought sickness and death to anyone who violated certain tabus, like touching wood from a lightning-blasted tree or old, imperfectly cremated bones. But most other tabus had nothing to do with Rageorapper for they brought on wind and rain, the antithesis of fire.

Evil spirits associated with dangerous places: Tasmania

Rageorapper, called by different names in different tribes, was a free-moving spirit, more or less identified with the wind and darkness. Certain other spirits were *genii loci*, associated with special features of the landscape, particularly in dangerous places. Once Robinson attempted to explore a seaside cave, but the natives who started to go in with him turned back after a few yards and rushed out in terror, shouting: "The devil is coming!" according to his translation. Inside the cave they had heard the sound of rushing water, possibly the tide.

In the Hampshire Hills in the northwestern part of the Big River tribal territory there is deep snow in winter. There many natives had died of the cold, and it was believed that many spirits who lived there killed strange natives from other tribes. On the uninhabited islands off the northern coast lived other evil spirits. These were the islands to which natives swam to collect nesting sea birds and their eggs, and often drowned on the way.

On the whole, evil spirits were associated with phenomena that disturbed the natives, such as thunder and lightning, death, and illness. They greatly outnumbered the good spirits, of which only one was recorded. He lived near Swansport in the northeastern tribal area, where it was possible to collect vast numbers of swans' eggs in season without danger.

Chiefs and other important men like Woorrady, a great fighter and teller of tales, had captive human spirits inside their bodies, to call on when needed. The chief of the Oyster Bay Tribe had one in his chest that served him like radar, and when he invoked it, his chest muscles twitched. He used it to locate other bands of natives, and it warned him when white men were approaching. Sometimes it left his body at night and walked ahead of him with a torch invisible to others, to light his way.

Other persons, in many cases women, had familiars lodged in mortuary relics, in the form of cremated ashes sewn into small packages of kangaroo skin, with the hair side facing in, and tied to their bodies. Women often took them off and talked to them, and sometimes beat them with sticks so that spirits inside would make them pregnant. One young man of the western tribe who was talking to his amulet said that it had told him that it was thirsty, so he took a drink of water and held it against his stomach.

These amulets were also used in curing, but not always with complete success. Once when some women were diving for shellfish their husbands were waiting on the beach. To amuse themselves they began throwing pieces of kelp at each other. One heavy piece struck a man on the testicles, and he writhed in pain. An old woman took off her amulet and held it against the affected parts, with no effect. Then another woman warmed the palms of her hands over a fire and rubbed his testicles gently with them, until he declared that they felt better.

Australia: Mirawong the songman and the origin of the Pleiades

In Arnhem Land in northern Australia there are special bards known as songmen, comparable to those of the Akoa Pygmies of Gabon. One songman named Mirawong said that he had acquired his gifts as a boy when he was once lost in the forest for four days. Exhausted from wandering about; he sat under a tall tree. He heard a loud crack and saw the trunk open. A little man came out and led Mirawong inside the tree and down a passage to a subterranean land where lived a whole tribe of little men. He stayed with them for four years and they taught him everything he needed to know. Then they put him back under the tree, where his own people found him. They told him that he had been lost for four days.

Once he told Bill Harney, a lifelong associate and friend of the aborigines, a story about the origin of Orion and the Pleiades, in three installments, as follows: Part 1: How a young hunter named Manbuk catches a water girl named Milijun and marries her. Part 2: Flashback—how Milijun and her younger sisters had become seven water girls. Part 3: How the water girls turned first into dingoes and then into the Pleiades, and Manbuk became Orion, the controller of dingoes.

Part 1: In a country wooded with paperbark trees stood a waterfall whose flow was intermittent because of the action of seven water girls. They were sisters, transformed from ordinary maidens by a spell, because they had been involved in the breach of an incest tabu. When the sisters formed a line across the stream above the fall, they held back the water, making it trickle, and when they parted to stand on either side they released the water, which then rushed noisily over the fall.

Now these water girls were covered with slime like catfish, had long hair, and sharp nails. They were very beautiful and sang an irresistible love song. If a man heard it he was compelled to come to them, and they seized him and held him until he was dead. Men whose bodies were found in streams or billabongs had been their victims.

Once a young hunter named Manbuk saw these girls, and they dived to swim toward him, but in order to look at him the first one thrust her head out of the water too soon, and he caught her by her hair. Picking her up in his arms he carried her quickly across ground burned over for hunting, and the other six couldn't follow because of the antagonism between fire and water.

But the captive water girl was frightened, speechless, and in every way useless to Manbuk. So he built a fire and threw green bamboo on it to make it smoke, and held her over it. Off slithered her slime, and then leeches fell out of her pores into the fire. Now she was a normal, beautiful girl with "boy-milk titties," and she told him in his own language that her name was Milijun.

Manbuk and Milijun walked about in the forest and found food in abundance everywhere. Bees and waterfowl swarmed and flocked about Milijun's head, and the dry stalks of yam-plants crackled as they went by, to let them know where the tubers could be dug. In camp, after they had returned to Manbuk's people, Milijun was noted for her kindness to aged and ailing persons. One night, as they lay under a tree, Milijun told Manbuk the story of her life, to be continued in the next narration.

Part 2 (flashback): Milijun's father was named Dunia. He lived on the bank of a tidal creek, and was a hunter, fowler, fisherman, and builder of dugout canoes. (Here follows a long explanation of Dunia's way of choosing and blazing soft-wooded trees, his technique of hewing them into dugouts, and how he traded them.) Dunia's wife was Ninual, a woman of the Fish-Dreaming (Fish totem). They had seven daughters, of whom Milijun was the first-born. When Milijun and the second daughter came to puberty, Dunia tried to seduce them while they were helping him carry fish from his landing place to their camp.

Ninual found this out, but she didn't let on. So she built a hut in the top of a tall baobab tree and took her seven daughters up there with her. When Dunia returned next from fishing, he called to his daughters to come down to the bank to carry fish as usual, but all he got was a faint answer from Ninual in the treetop. Knowing that she knew of his attempts at incest, he gashed his back with the spines of a catfish that he was carrying, but as Ninual continued to invite him to come and join them, and dropped a vine for him to grasp and to be hauled up with, he thought that she had forgiven him, and took hold.

He was pulled high up into the sky, and as he passed the treetop Ninual reached out and cut the vine with her stone axe. Dunia fell, turning over three times, and Ninual cried: "Men that try to seduce their daughters die."

Dunia fell into a lagoon and disappeared. A huge crocodile crawled out, saying in Dunia's voice: "No, I won't die. I will be born over and over again. I will grow fat at each full moon by eating the shades of those who disobey the tribal rules of life."

When the moon grew full Ninual and her daughters could see Dunia's face on its surface, and once when a rainbow circled the moon the mother and her daughters came down from their hut in the tree. After every full moon from then on Dunia's shade fell down and was eaten by the crocodile over and over again, and then he would return to the moon and eat the shades of many babies whose mothers had broken a tabu.

In Dunia's tribe lived an old woman of the Brown-bittern Dreaming, who was immortal. She had stolen the secret of immortality from an elder who had won it in a battle with the spirit of death, and he had lost it when the Brown-bittern woman had wheedled it out of him with her irresistible love song.

It was the Brown-bittern woman's job to capture the spirits of children whose mothers had neglected to sweep up their footprints before nightfall, and to send these infant shades to Dunia to eat. Still lusting after his daughters, and not wanting anyone else to have them, Dunia got the Brown-bittern woman to change his daughters into water girls, and as such they remained until Manbuk found Milijun and made her his wife.

Part 3 (the rains begin): Although Milijun behaved like a normal wife during the dry season, when the rains began she became fidgety. One night when Manbuk and Milijun were sleeping under a big baobab tree, and Manbuk was off guard, he had a dream that left him immobilized. He heard a rumble of thunder, and then soft voices bidding Milijun to grasp a vine that dangled down. She clutched it and began to rise. Finally Manbuk was able to move, and he leapt up, but too late to reach her. He watched her rise. Then, in a great clap of thunder and torrent of rain, she fell back into the lagoon and became a water girl all over again. It was the magic of the Brown-bittern woman that had done this.

Manbuk sat beside the lagoon, looking at his wife, and heard a stick break behind him. Turning, he saw an old man. It was Nartu, headman of the

Sun-Dreaming. Nartu told Manbuk that he lived in a cave and that it was he who sent the Sun-woman out each day to give light and heat. "Are you in trouble, boy? How can I help you?" asked Nartu.

Manbuk told Nartu his tale.

Said Nartu: "Go sun-down way [west] and after many days (he held up five fingers) you will come to my cave, which has a dry patch of ground in front and a burnt hill beside it. Don't approach it by night because the Sun-woman sleeps there and she will burn you with her breath. Go at noon and throw a burning stick into the hole beside my fireplace, and then run away."

Having followed Nartu's directions Manbuk entered the cave, saw many rock-paintings on its walls, found Nartu's fireplace, and the hole where the Sun-woman went each night. He threw in his fire-stick, heard a great rumbling, felt a hot blast of wind, and fled. His skin crackled, and as the Sun-woman in the sky blew a hot wind over the land, everything began to dry up. Manbuk quickly made a water container of bark, filled it with the last of the water about, and ran through a country in which the trees and birds were already dead.

At this point Mirawong paused in his tale to tell Harney that Manbuk had been too angry, had made trouble with the Sun-woman over his girl friend.

Manbuk arrived at the pool of the seven sisters in time to see it dry up. He found the water girls covered with fishy slime. He advanced toward them, and felt raindrops and heard thunder.

Said Mirawong: "Fire and sun heat water girl; rain and water make her lively."

Now the water girls leapt out of the pool and ran, with Manbuk after them, into a "leg" of rain. As Manbuk ran he chanted his emu song that gave his legs speed in the hunt, and the fleeing girls howled like dingoes in the mating season. Manbuk almost reached them when they came to the falling stream and swam upward, in the form of dingoes, into the sky, and he after them. Thus the girls became the Pleiades, a pack of dingoes, and Manbuk Orion, always chasing them.

In the cold weather time, when dingoes whelp, the black fellas watch Orion rise, and go out to catch the puppies and eat them. They are fat, and good tucker.

In narrating this myth, Mirawong also referred to a powerful spirit in the Coal Sack, a spot in the Southern Cross of interest to the Tasmanians as well as the Australians. The spirit mentioned by Mirawong sends down thunder, rain, and storms, and he also punishes young wives who desert their older husbands to run away with young lovers. At such a girl the spirit hurls a fireball. It sinks underground, rises again, and skims just over her head, as a warning. If she elopes again it will strike her dead.

294

Mirawong mentioned this punishment to Harney while a young man noted for philandering sauntered by, and Mirawong raised his voice just enough to make sure that the young man heard him. At the same time Mirawong winked at Harney. He then referred in passing to a second group of transformed maidens who also sang irresistible love songs, but lived in red anthills which, like waterfalls, are good things to avoid. Before Mirawong left he confided to Harney that he had once bought a song sung by the water girls for purposes of seduction, but when sung, it didn't work. The man who had sold it to him had changed the words.

This cosmogenic myth has many facets. It explains how Orion and the Pleiades got to the sky, and what they have been doing up there ever since, in a manner so close to the Greek version that one is led to expect some ancient connection, particularly as a similar account is given in a Chenchu myth from India. It also tells us where the irascible sunwoman goes to spend the night, and how the moon-man is made to wax and wane.

The myth is loaded with moral implications. He who even tries to commit incest will receive supernatural punishment. A man should not let a clever woman wheedle secrets out of him, even if she sings a magic love song to him. A man should never do anything to endanger the ecology of the land just to please a pretty woman. Infants, the aged, and the infirm should be cared for.

Listeners are also given detailed instructions about how to hunt, to fish, to mark trees for future use as canoes, to make the canoes, and to trade. The myth of Manbuk and the Seven Water Girls is thus a concentrated combination of drama, moral admonitions, and technological instructions. In the form given above it has been condensed, and it is but one of the many myths and tales which constitute the painless curriculum to which the youth of Arnhem Land is exposed.

The Andamanese origin myth:
Puluga the Storm Goddess

Nearly a century ago, some of the Andamanese told E. H. Man their creation myth. Although they believed in a number of spirits, by far the most important was a goddess, Puluga, who symbolizes the southwest monsoon that brings violent wind and rains from April to October. She created the earth and its people, and was responsible for almost everything else that happened to the Andamanese from the very beginning. Puluga owned all the wild yams and cicada grubs that the people ate, and all the beeswax that they used in hafting, calking, and cordage. Women who dug yams had to replace the tops to fool Puluga; no one might kill the cicadas that chirp at dawn—the favorite time for surprise attacks; the beeswax, a precious commodity, must never be burned while it was being heated to soften it for use. Such impious acts made Puluga very angry and she punished the people by sending them bad weather.

First Puluga created the earth. It rests atop a huge palm tree growing out of a great jungle under the earth, and this jungle is dimly lighted and inhabited by the spirits of most of the dead. These spirits hunt land animals for there is no sea down there, and the spirits of babies and small children live under a wild fig tree and eat its fruit. The spirits of evil persons, mostly murderers, go to a very cold world in the eastern sky. This world is connected to the world by a bridge which is sometimes visible in the form of a rainbow.

Next Puluga created a man named Tomo. He was black like the living Andamanese but tall and bearded. They are short and beardless. She set Tomo down in a place called Wotaemi near Andaman Strait, between the middle and south islands of Great Andaman, and Wotaemi was the only place on earth that had jungle. She showed Tomo the fruit trees in the jungle from which he could get food, but warned him not to eat the fruit of some of them during the rains. She also gave him fire. [In one version (there are several) she taught Tomo to lay sticks of two different kinds of wood in alternate layers and then she got the Sun to sit on the pile until it began to burn.]

Now that he had fire Puluga taught Tomo how to cook pigs. In those days the pigs were helpless, having neither ears nor noses, and had to be fed. Then Puluga went away, either to her present home in the sky or to her former one on Saddle Peak, the highest mountain in the archipelago.

The first woman was named Chana Elewadi. Some say that Puluga created her after having given Tomo food and fire, and that Tomo saw her swimming near Wotaemi, and she came ashore to live with him and bore him two sons and two daughters. Others say that she came ashore already pregnant on Kyd Island in Shoal Bay off the west side of South Andaman, but in either case the present Andamanese are descended from her.

Before long the pigs had become so numerous that it was a nuisance to feed them, so Chana Elewadi bored holes in their heads and snouts so that they could find their own food. Then the jungle stretched outward from Wotaemi to make room for the pigs. Either Puluga spread out the trees, or Tomo shot arrows with flies tied to them and the flies became trees, but now in either case it was hard to catch the pigs so Puluga came down again and taught the men to make bows and arrows and to hunt. On another visit Puluga taught Chana Elewadi to make baskets and nets and to use red ochre and white clay.

Puluga told Tomo and Chana Elewadi not to work after sunset during the rainy season because if they did it would annoy her cicada grubs, and if the grubs heard an adze chopping wood it would give them headaches, and this would disturb Puluga. She also taught them the parent language of all the Andamanese languages and dialects. [E. H. Man's informants stated that the original language was still spoken near Wotaemi where some of the men were still tall and bearded.]

One day Tomo harpooned a large fish, and the fish lashed the land with its tail so hard that it cut open all the creeks. Tomo lived to be very old, and his descendants multiplied greatly. Puluga then sent them out in pairs all over the islands, with fire and other equipment, to people the land, and these pairs begat the tribes and originated their dialects. Finally Tomo drowned and became a whale, the enemy of turtles, and Chana Elewadi also drowned, turning into a small crab.

Then Tomo's grandson Kolwot succeeded him as the leader, and he was the first man to harpoon turtles. After Kolwot's death the people disregarded Puluga's tabus and she grew angry and sent a flood. Some say that the waters covered the world, but others said that Puluga's old home, Saddle Peak, was left dry. The rising waters drowned everyone except two men and two women who happened to be out in a canoe, and when the waters subsided they landed at Wotaemi; but except from themselves all life had perished from the earth and all fires were out.

Now Puluga re-created the animals, but still there was no fire, so a kingfisher flew up in the sky to Puluga, who was sitting by her fire, and snatched a burning log in his beak and tried to steal it away. But the log was so heavy that he dropped it on Puluga, who became very angry; she picked it up and threw it at the kingfisher but missed him, and it fell to earth at Wotaemi, still burning.

The children of the two couples multiplied and again populated the earth, but they began talking about Puluga and the flood she had sent and decided to kill her. Now she came down to earth for the fourth and last time and said: "Go ahead and shoot me; my body is made of wood." She said that they had disobeyed her orders, digging up her yams, burning her wax, and doing other forbidden things. Then she warned them not to break her tabus anymore and not to plot against her, and she disappeared and has not returned since, and the people have obeyed her.

Some time in the future Puluga, having been quiet so long, will bring about a great earthquake and the earth will turn upside down so that all the people then living will fall into the underworld and the spirits of their ancestors will come back to the surface, where they will live forever without sickness, ageing, death, or marriage, and will be young forever.

This myth is remarkable in several ways. It indicates anxiety about the southwest monsoon, which makes it dangerous for the Andamanese to go out in boats; brings fire-quenching rain; and makes them cold and uncomfortable. Yet the goddess that sends all this trouble each year was also their creator and culture-bearer. They know that their ancestors were not beardless dwarfs as they are, but tall, bearded black people, like the Tasmanians. They describe the original pigs as being helpless and having to be fed; i.e., as domestic animals. And so they probably were, for the Andamans had no native terrestrial mammals.* Carbon 14 dates show that neither pigs, pottery, nor tobacco pipes were present in the Great Andamanese middens before about A.D. 1500, when the Malay pirates and traders began raiding the Andamans and taking some of the Andamanese off into slavery.

A part of the myth not mentioned above states that during the flood the species of palm used by their ancestors in making large, outriggerless canoes perished. The outrigger canoe, certainly not a local invention, was probably introduced at some time before or after A.D. 1500, and harpooning sea turtles probably began no earlier, because the success of the harpoon depends on iron obtained from wrecked European ships. There is not much iron in Arab dhows or Malay praus, which are pegged or sewn. This myth has much to commend it as oral history, not much less truthful than our tale of George Washington and the cherry tree.

The five-fold Yaghan mythology: a complete system

Thanks to the industry of the late Father Martin Gusinde, S.V.D., who visited and studied the Yaghans at four different times during the first quarter of this century, we have a wealth of information about their religious beliefs and myths, which are rich and elaborate, despite Charles Darwin's statement that they had no religion.

There are five separate elements in Yaghan beliefs and myths, only two of which are in any way connected. One of them concerns the high god Watauinewa. He is formless, invisible, and has no special home other than the sky. He is called The One Up There, or Father, or sometimes The Murderer. He controls the weather. He also laid down all the rules of behavior that the Yaghans have to follow, and in case of a serious breach, he brings death to the offender or to a

*Except in a sense for the palm-civet (*Paradoxorus tytleri*), a native of Southeast Asia and the Indo-Malayan islands. It is a parasite that lives in thatched roofs, and could easily have been introduced into the Andaman Islands by Malay sailors.

close relative, particularly to a baby. People do not like to mention his name because it may remind others of deaths in their families. People pray to Watauinewa before going out to hunt on the sea in a canoe, asking for good weather, and they thank him when they return. During funerals they may call him a Murderer, but they take it back later. For over fifty years the English missionaries were unaware of the Yaghans' belief in Watauinewa because, as one of them told Gusinde, "No one ever asked us."

The second element concerns the first settlers. There is no myth to explain the creation of the land; it was always there. The first settlers came from the north, from Ona country. Among them was the Old Sun Man, who once came so close to the earth that he scorched it, and that is why there are no trees on the mountain peaks. The women, who at that time ruled the men, tried to strangle him but he escaped and rose into the sky where he disappeared.

He was replaced by his son Lem, the Young Sun Man, who was very handsome and a great hunter. The rainbow is Lem's brother and the Moon Woman the rainbow's wife. Both brothers are very good-looking, and the rainbow paints his body beautifully. He got his back bent in a struggle with some people who attacked him. They were the relatives of some men that he had lured into the water and then killed with stones from his sling. The reason that he killed them was that, in order to play a trick on people, the rainbow man, who was also a shaman, once lay down and pretended to be dead. While he was lying still, these other men copulated in his presence with his wife and sisters.

Element number three concerns a reversal in the role of the sexes and the transformation of people into animals.

In the old days the women ruled the men, who had to do the housework and sit in the stern of the canoe. The women were able to keep the men in subjection because they had a big hut that they would not let the men into. There they put on conical masks reaching to their shoulders, impersonated spirits, and frightened the men.

Lem had to hunt to feed them and the supposed spirits inside the hut. One day coming back from hunting he saw two girls washing paint off themselves at the edge of a pool. He crept up secretly and overheard their conversation. They were talking about how they fooled the men with their goings-on in the big hut. Lem jumped at the girls and they turned into ducks. Lem then told the men what he had discovered. So they sent the smallest and fastest-running man into the women's big hut, and he tipped over all their masks, and when he ran out he turned into a swamp bird.

Then the next-smallest and fastest man ran in, and so on, until only the men who could not run fast were left. As each man ran through the big hut the women shot arrows or cast spears into their rumps, and these shafts became tails and the men thus turned into different species of animals. Then the other men came in and fought the women, all but two of whom became animals. The hut caught fire, so Lem poured buckets of water on it, which created a great wave and washed some of the animals out to sea, where they became the marine animals.

Then Lem, the rainbow, and the Moon Woman rose into the sky, and very few real people were left, and they were mostly children. The men now knew the women's secrets, and from then on the men kept them from the women. From that time on the men assumed their masculine roles, and began to mount their wives to copulate. Before then the women had mounted the men.

Apart from the story of Lem's wave, there was also a standard flood myth in which all but five peaks were inundated and only a few people and animals survived. In one version the Moon Woman, who was as cross as she was beautiful, caused the flood. In another it was brought on by the spectacled ibis, apparently with Watauinewa's permission. The Moon Woman created a great snowstorm and the snow turned to ice. When the ice eventually melted the sea rose to a line on the sides of the peaks that the Yaghans point out as the high water mark. Apparently this flood came at about the same time as the reversal of the sexes, but this is not definite.

The fifth element is an origin myth concerning two brothers, the elder and the younger Yoaloch, and their older sister. They had other younger sisters, but the latter did nothing of importance. Whether or not the Yoaloch brothers and sisters belonged with the first settlers' group is uncertain. The two brothers gave names to all the places, animals, plants, and objects, and the three of them invented everything. Their older sister originated flint-flaking to make heads for spears and arrows. The younger Yoaloch originated menstruation. Once he was copulating with a beautiful woman. She was the last of the many wives that another man had sent to the brothers, who shared her favors. The woman said to him: "Oh! Your penis is much bigger than your brother's!"

She did not think that the older brother had heard her say this, but he did, and remained quiet. Then the younger Yoaloch's penis swelled enormously and drew blood. The woman thus menstruated, and women have been doing it ever since. When the Yoaloch trio had finished inventing everything and were growing old, they and their younger sisters rose into the sky and became stars.

A lofty weather god who punishes breaches of tabus; the flood; tales of people becoming animals and vice versa; the presence of culture heroes who name and invent everything are all fairly common mythological motifs, and the story of the reversal of the sexes is not unique. On the whole (and I believe that Father Gusinde felt the same way), these Fuegian myths have something of an old-world flavor, and may well be very ancient.

Nenebuc the transformer, a comic hero of the Ojibwa

Frank G. Speck, the authority on the Indians of Maine, also recorded a cycle about a mythological creature named Nenebuc, as told by the Ojibwas living on Bear Island in Lake Temigimi, Ontario.* The cycle is typical of many of the myths of the Northern Algonkian peoples. Nenebuc was what is called a transformer in North American Indian lore, and something of a comic.

Once a young girl had her first menses. She was taken over a hill to live alone and to fast for twelve days, so that she could have a dream. She dreamed of the sun. Her father said: "You must never look at the sun." One day, by accident, she did, and this made her pregnant. So she went to live with the sun. But before she left she said to her father: "You will see your grandchildren soon; just put your wooden dish upside down near the fire, leave it there four days and four nights, and look under it every morning."

The old man did as he had been told. On the first morning he saw Nenebuc, son of the sun, sitting under there, and for four more mornings he looked and saw Nenebuc's four brothers, one by one, each under the dish. Then the old man picked up the dish. One of the brothers had horns. The grandfather sent that one west, and he sent the other three north, east, and south, but Nenebuc he kept at home.

Nenebuc asked his grandfather: "Why haven't I a mother?" But he received evasive answers. Nenebuc scraped a whetstone on a rock and asked it: "Have I a mother?" And the whetstone said: "Yes, you have," and told him the story. Nenebuc grew up fast and he asked his grandfather why he didn't send him out like his four brothers, but his grandfather said: "Because I need you here."

Then Nenebuc had many adventures. One summer he caught no fish because the west wind blew too hard. Nenebuc decided to kill his brother in the west but his grandfather said: "No, don't kill him, just make him blow more gently."

Nenebuc then went west to find his brother. He didn't kill him but he broke off one horn. The West brother told the other three not to blow at all,

*Canada, Dept. of Mines, Geological Survey, Memoir 71.

and the lake grew foul and there were still no fish. So Nenebuc told his four brothers to blow once in a while but not too often, and so they did. Everything was fine at that time, and Nenebuc's grandfather and grandmother died.

Now Nenebuc grew up alone, but he could take care of himself because his grandfather had taught him everything he needed to know, and he started traveling. On the first day he walked across three mountains and killed a goose on each one. Then, when he came to a lake, he was tired. He built a fire, heated some sand, and put the geese in it with their legs sticking up. He wanted to sleep but he was afraid that if he did someone would steal his geese, so he told his rectum to keep watch over them.

He fell asleep, and three or four times his rectum woke him up, saying: "Someone is coming." But his rectum was only trying to fool him. Nenebuc beat his rectum with a club and again fell asleep. When he woke up he found the three pairs of legs sticking out of the sand but the bodies gone, and he asked his rectum why it hadn't warned him; in punishment Nenebuc built up the fire and burned his rectum.

As he walked along his backside began to hurt and he felt a little sick, and he got turned around and followed his own tracks. He thought they were someone else's and he saw what he thought were pieces of dried meat along the track and he ate them, but a titmouse said: "Nenebuc is eating his own scabs." Then he was really sick. As he walked along he encountered a brood of partridge chicks and asked them where their mother was. "Our mother is away," they said. Then he asked them their names and they said: "Jump out and frighten people," so he defecated on them. Before then partridges had been white, but since then they have been brown.

Now Nenebuc finally reached the edge of a cliff, and he lay down close to it to rest. Meanwhile the young partridges' father came home and asked how they had become brown. They told him, and the old partridge followed Nenebuc and pushed him off the cliff. On the way down his scabs scraped off and fell near him. When he saw them he said: "Now the Ojibwa can make soup out of these," for they had turned into rock tripe, an edible fungus eaten during famines.

Nenebuc had many other adventures and quasicomical misadventures during which he was, usually unintentionally, responsible for features of the landscape, the appearance and habits of different species of animals, and finally, the flood. This cosmic episode began when he saw a large snake near a lake, and it turned into a high, rocky ridge in a portage south of Smoothwater Lake. Reaching a sandy shore of that lake he saw some giant lynxes too far away for him to shoot them. Then he made a small wigwam out of bark from a rotten birch stump, got inside, poked a peephole through it, and watched. Curious about the appearance of this new object on the shore, the lynxes sent another large snake to coil itself around it and tip it over, but without success, because Nenebuc held it firmly from inside. Then the lynxes approached and Nenebuc shot one, a female, the wife of the chief of the lynxes, and he wounded her. She then went away, the arrow sticking out of her side, to a hole in a bluff overlooking the lake, on the other side of the lake from the cliff Nenebuc had slid down, scraping off his scabs. Inside this hole was a cave where the lynxes lived.

Next morning Nenebuc saw someone shaking a rattle and singing, in front of the hole that the wounded lynx had entered. It was a shamaness trying to heal the lynx. Nenebuc killed this woman with a club and she turned into a huge toad. He skinned her, put on her skin, went up to the hole singing and rattling, and the lynx's cubs said: "The medicine woman is coming to heal our mother." The cave had a door. They opened it and let Nenebuc in. They fed him. Then he pretended to draw the arrow out but really pushed it farther in, and the lynx died. The cubs then recognized Nenebuc, whose testicles were hanging out of a hole in the toad's skin.

He ran outside, and a great stream of water flowed out after him, and the lake rose. But before the earth was completely flooded he managed to cut some logs and to make a raft. He saw all the different kinds of animals swimming after him, and invited them aboard. After a while he made a rope of roots, tied it to the beaver, and sent him down to bring up some mud, but the beaver failed. Then he sent down the muskrat, who breathed air trapped in its fur, and got some mud, but drowned on the way up. Nenebuc said: "I will dry this mud and after a while you will have the earth again."

Then, knowing that the earth was round like a ball, but not knowing how large it was, he sent the crow to fly around it to find out for him, but he warned the crow not to stop on the way to eat. The crow disobeyed him and ate some dead fish, but when he got back to the raft his feathers, which had been white, turned black. Next Nenebuc sent out the gull, who was also white. He ate just one mouthful of fish, and thus got black patches on his wings. Finally Nenebuc sent out the owl, who ate a hearty meal of fish and never came back, and his plumage remained the same color as before. The place where the owl ate the fish is now called Owl Bay, on the western shore of the lake.

The mud was now dry. The earth resumed its present shape, with hills and forests and rivers and lakes and some swampy regions, and Nenebuc let the animals leave the raft. He himself went to the west, and is still there, lying on his back, singing and pounding on wigwam poles. There he will stay until three years before the end of the world. Then he will rise up again to travel all over the world to visit his animals and the Ojibwa, and he will not die until the world comes to an end.

This transformer cycle is longer than the portions recorded here. From a global point of view, two special elements seem noteworthy. Nenebuc is made to appear rather foolish at times, and the cosmic events that he lets loose are the results of mistakes or chance; he is both comical and serious.

The myths contain a scatological element which may, in part, reflect the critical problem of disposing of fecal matter for people who cannot go outside to relieve their bowels in deep snow in sub-zero weather. This is a tension-creating problem, a putative source of social disturbance, and hence a subject of joking, far more so than the sexual problems expressed in the myths of peoples living in milder climates.

The Nunivak Eskimos' account of the origin of the sun and moon

Still the incest motif can also occur in the North, as among the Eskimo of Nunivak Island, in the tale of the origin of the sun and moon recorded by Ruth Lantis. Once a man was married to a woman who bore no children, so the husband adopted an orphaned nephew and brought him up as his own son, calling him by that name.

Twice, when the men were sleeping in the men's house, the man's wife's lamp went out, and she felt someone cold beside her. She got up, and the visitor left, unidentified. Finally she told her husband and he stayed awake in the men's house to see who might go out. It was his nephew. The nephew went to visit his stepmother again, and his stepfather, who was in the entranceway, saw him. The boy tried to take off his stepmother's boots and parka. She picked up her lamp and ran out. He chased her around the house, carrying his own lamp. She rose into the sky and he followed her. She became the sun and he the moon, and the young man is forever chasing her.

Once he caught her and pushed her, and she fell down and landed on the other side of the bay from the village of Mekoryuk on Nunivak Island. At that place the earth is scorched, and nothing will grow there. The people were afraid that everything would burn up, and so the shaman put on a performance and sent the sun back again.

These tales could go on almost indefinitely, but enough have been told here to show that people in general, in these instances hunters, are interested in the origins of the world about them, and express their anxieties about critical areas of human behavior in myths and tales. The other category of myths, those recounting the deeds of the ancestors of clans, lineages, and the like in segmented societies, have not been covered here because many of them are acted out in elaborate ceremonies, and some of them will be told where they belong, with the ceremonies themselves, in Chapter 15.

14.

*Rites of Passage at Birth,
Puberty, and Death*

Introduction to chapters fourteen and fifteen

In the last chapter we surveyed what, to me at least, is a rather charming system of social controls, directed to people who participate in a common culture, through the vehicle of dramatic myths and tales. These vivid accounts serve to explain the totality of the hunters' universe in a way satisfying to them at their level of scientific knowledge. They also instruct hunters in procedures of behavior that will create the least possible number of disturbances in social relations, and thus not jeopardize their food supply by taking people's attention off their work.

But myths and tales are not enough, in many cultures, to allay the private disturbances that befall individuals through the biological events inherent in the human life cycle — the recognition of a woman's pregnancy, the birth of her child, its period of growth, its coming to puberty, possible illnesses, and certain death. Myths and tales are admonitory, but rites, with which we are now concerned, are therapeutic. They not only smooth the transition of the individual concerned from one state of being to the next, but they also help those most intimately associated with that person to make the necessary adjustments in their own lives. Birth adds a baby; puberty subtracts a child and adds a man or a woman. Death leaves in its wake widows, widowers, and orphans. Something has to be done about these traumatic gains and losses in personnel, and even in our confused modern society, something usually is.

From the moment when a woman knows that she is pregnant to the day that her child is born, and usually thereafter until the child has been weaned, the normal relationship between a man and his wife is interrupted. The baby occupies a disproportionate amount of its mother's attention, and the relationships between the older children in the family, if there are older children, may be temporarily thrown out of gear. At puberty the sex hormones circulating in a young person's bloodstream tend to make a boy rebellious; and the onset of menstruation involves blood, a dangerous substance. In either case, steps must be taken to keep pubescent youth in line.

When a woman has passed menopause her position in the community may be enhanced because she has been released from the proscriptions attendant on periodic letting of blood. Similarly an older but not mentally senile man may, by his own combination of accumulated knowledge, judgment, and personality, have risen to a position of respect and authority. Death brings a shock, the force of which depends to a certain extent on how old the deceased was, and his or her prominence in the community.

Illness does not befall everyone, because some persons suffer sudden and often violent death. But illness may strike anyone at any age, and it may require the services of a diagnostician to determine its cause and a healer to attempt a cure. These functions may sometimes be filled by one and the same person, a shaman, or there may be no shaman at all, as we shall see in Chapter 16.

The disturbance that marriage might create may be overshadowed by its close temporal coincidence with puberty; on the other hand, it may cause no disturbance at all, the basis for the union having already been gradually laid. Marriage is really a social phenomenon involving two preexisting families as well as the bride and groom. It is not in itself a biological event but simply the implementation of two of them, the puberty of the parties concerned. If the bride is a little girl, that implementation may be delayed for several years. The amount of attention that a marriage draws is also balanced by the amounts of attention received by other events in a given society. In our society we tend to make a great fuss over weddings, particularly first ones, but in some societies there are no weddings at all.

In 1909 A. L. Van Gennep invented the term "rites of passage" to specify the rituals that peoples of all cultures, including hunters, perform to ease the transition from one state, biological, social, or both, to another. These rites are not really performed to relax the nervous systems of the individuals concerned. A baby does not know that it is being born. When a man dies, he is dead. A boy who starts to feel his oats when his genitalia begin to function for something besides passing water may not mind this change at all, but he may be throroughly afraid of the privations and ordeals that lie ahead of him, including, in some cases mutilation. The people who are disturbed by these biological events as such are the parents, close kin, widows, and other habitual associates of the person directly affected.

Van Gennep correctly divided each rite of passage into three consecutive parts: separation, transition, and incorporation. In birth, it is principally the mother who may be separated, transformed, and reincorporated. In death it is the bereaved, particularly widows. Only in puberty rites, in illnesses followed by recovery, and sometimes in marriage, do all three steps apply to the protagonist.

Ceremonies of another kind are performed by all hunting peoples whose cultures are well documented. These are the "rites of intensification," so named in 1942 by Eliot D. Chapple and myself. Their functions are to allay the disturbances of a group as a whole caused by some outside event, such as a critical drought, a violent rainstorm that makes the rivers flood, an eclipse, the annual changes in the seasons, or simply to drive away the rain to make hunting possible. Seasonal changes bring with them associated changes in the activities of the people concerned, and consequently in their relations with each other.

When food becomes scarce, a large band may split up into units of a few families each, and the latter may reunite when the grass is green and food is once more abundant enough to feed everyone together for weeks or months at a time. When a large number of people come together after having been separated for half a year or longer, this is the time for fun and games, in the form of rites of intensification. Rites of intensification keep people busy and give them a program of events that maintain order. They may gather their food during the summer and store it for winter use, and in the winter a schedule of contests and dramatic performances keeps them interested and occupied. Contests and performances are most characteristic of peoples whose societies are complex enough to let them present competing teams of clans, moieties, or other complementary units. They culminate in the great annual ceremonies to be described in Chapter 15.

At such seasons people do not deliberately say to each other: "Now that we have plenty of food we can all come together. Let us make fun and hold rituals so that we can keep out of trouble." They hold these rites automatically because they have done so for longer than they can remember. Man is a gregarious animal and loves company. Unless he is a frustrated individual or one with an unusual personality, his greatest pleasure is in doing things together, and his greatest reward the recognition of his peers.

Sometimes puberty rites coincide with rites of intensification because that is a good time to initiate a lot of boys at once. This happens with boys more than with girls because the onset of puberty in boys is gradual and it is possible to wait until enough boys are ready. With girls the first menstruation is a well-marked, dramatic event, and girls are therefore more likely to be initiated one at a time. Also, men's work involves teamwork, and the boys form bonds during such rites that will be useful to them later, whereas when women work together it is for companionship more than for efficiency.

In cases where both kinds of rites are performed during a single ritual cycle, the essential difference between them still remains — to wit, that rites of passage are centered around what happens to an individual because of biological changes, and rites of intensification around what happens to the group as a whole owing to outside forces. But these differences are lost in the action, which combines the two.

Birth

If we begin our account of the rites of passage with birth, we must remember that it is preceded by pregnancy. Once a woman knows that she is pregnant, the rites concerned with birth may begin. In many societies this is a signal for her to cease intercourse with her husband, who must either remain continent or seek his satisfaction elsewhere. In this case he is lucky if he has another wife, unless both are pregnant at once. He may also be obliged by custom to continue to avoid sexual relations with his wife as long as she is nursing her baby. This may cause him considerable hardship unless he finds some other outlet for his libido. Among the Mbuti Pygmies, for example, the husband may be expected to have affairs with unmarried girls.

The Mbuti

The Mbuti, who get through life with a maximum of conversation but a minimum of ritual, are seemingly quite casual about childbirth, but their informality does not hamper efficiency. When the critical moment arrives the mother may be away from camp on a hunt, or merely walking from one place to another. Because women rarely go out alone, she will be delivered where she is with the help of another woman. If she happens to be in camp and the birth is at all delayed, other women lead her into the forest, where births should rightly take place. Her companions seat her close to a tree that has vines hanging from it, so that she can pull on a vine.

While the father is not present at the delivery, he participates in it in one sense; one of the women attending the mother uses one of the father's arrow blades to cut the umbilical cord. In earlier times they used to cut it with a knife that he had made from a sliver of wood or with the cutting edge of a leaf. The blade and the cord (after it drops off) are kept together until the child is old enough to wrap them up in leaves and to carry the package to the bank of a stream, where he buries it in a shallow hole, whence the next flood will wash it away.

Colin Turnbull was told that if the birth takes longer than usual the father removes his clothing, usually only a breechclout, to expose his genitalia. His wife's sister then washes the father's body and massages it. She then returns to the place where the birth is in progress, and when the child has been delivered she comes back to the father, who has to give her a present before he can cover himself again. Everyday thereafter for some time, the father and his wife's brother, if the latter is present, wash the baby with juices from vines that they cut in the forest, and they also tie around one of the baby's wrists, or around its waist, a piece of vine in which a small piece of wood has been incorporated. That piece of wood is supposed to give the baby the strength of the forest, of which it was a part. Until the baby has begun to crawl, neither the father nor the mother may eat meat, not even the flesh of animals that the father himself may have killed.

The Mbuti are supposed to refrain from sexual intercourse between husband and wife for some time after she has borne a baby, but they do not always observe this rule, as the following example illustrates. Once Colin Turnbull witnessed a fracas in a Mbuti camp. A man who also had two older wives nevertheless insisted on having relations with his third, youngest, and prettiest one within a month after she had borne a boy. At the same time he neglected his other two wives, the oldest of whom stamped about the camp one night keeping everyone awake with loud imprecations, upbraiding several people and blaming the young mother in particular. The latter's brother took her side and said it was not her fault. Finally one of the older and most respected men arose, stirred up the central fire, and made a speech saying that the noise would displease the forest, and if the couple kept on having relations the baby would sicken and die.

A month later the baby did grow sick, and some of the people in the camp accused wife number two, who was childless, of having brought about this illness by sorcery. The statement was not made right out, but by implication. The accused woman started to run into the forest and dashed her head against a tree, fell down, and pretended to be unconscious. When she recovered she took refuge in another man's camp a short distance away, but the next day her husband brought her back. Then she made incisions on the baby's skin, and it began to recover. The husband t⸃ ⸃n resumed relations with both his older wives as well as continuing them with the third, and the crisis was over.

The Andamanese

The practices of the Mbuti are fairly complicated, but simpler than those of some other peoples. The Andamanese, for example, who have a very simple kinship system and among whom age grading is the principal cohesive social factor, perform the sexual act with little privacy, owing to the flimsy construction of their huts around the dance floor, and to the dangers, real and imagined, of the dense jungle.

While they seem to have known the relationship between intercourse and conception, they considered intercourse less important than outside agencies. They said that the souls of babies resided in wild fig trees where green pigeons perch, and that the pigeons sent the babies' souls into their mothers' wombs. But if the pigeons failed them and a woman did not become pregnant as soon as expected, she could take steps of her own. She might cook and eat a kind of small frog, or she could go to the shore at low tide and crouch over certain round, water-smoothed rocks on the reef, and the soul of a baby might enter her body from one of these rocks. Or if her husband particularly wanted a child, he might wear a baby sling, normally used by women, while sitting in the camp.

When pregnancy arrived, both the woman and her husband avoided a number of foods, including dugong, yams, and honey. They could eat baby pigs and small turtles, but no adult pigs or large turtles. Some of the older women of the camp acted as midwives, delivering the baby, cutting the umbilical cord with a cane knife, and burying the placenta in the forest. Then they washed the baby, scraped its body with a Cyrena clam shell, and, after a few days, daubed it all over with common clay. If the child died and the mother later gave birth to another, the latter was believed to be a reincarnation of the first one and was given the same name.

The babies were breast-fed until the age of three or four, and if the mother's breasts dried up before then, it did not matter because the babies were passed from hand to hand within the camp, were petted by everyone, and suckled from all women in milk.

The Yaghans

The Yaghans were much vaguer than the Andamanese about where the unborn child gets its soul, but when a woman was pregnant they placed the flowers of the plant *Embothreum coccineum* over her genitalia, after which she held her thighs tightly together. The idea was to make her child as beautiful as those flowers.

During the last two or three months before delivery both parents observe food tabus. The wife may not eat hot meat or hot mussels. Her husband may not eat the heads or hindparts of birds or fish, only the middle portions. Shortly before confinement, neither husband nor wife may eat cormorants. For a few days before and after confinement the mother is not allowed to break or to crush bird bones to get the marrow, nor may she eat sea urchins, which have shells more or less resembling a baby's skull. Her husband may eat them, but only if someone else has cracked the shells. All these tabus are to avoid the chance of bearing a deformed child.

When the moment draws near, other women flock around to give the mother advice, and the husband and other males leave the hut to the women. But if the hut is occupied by several families, the women build a special delivery hut outside. The Yaghans never allow a woman's first child to be born in a canoe, but keep her on shore before it is due. Subsequent children sometimes are born in canoes, with the husband's help if needed. Such a child is given a special name, "Born-away-from-land," plus the name of the nearest place on the shore.

Either one or two women may take part in the delivery, preferably two. The first is an older woman of experience, the second is a woman of the mother's age or younger who may not even be married yet, and whose job it is to catch the baby in her hands when it emerges. The second woman is a friend of the mother, chosen in advance, one who will take care of the baby if needed and who will adopt it if the child's close kin don't. This is a one-episode relationship because, for subsequent births, each child has a different adoptive mother, as Gusinde has called her. Presumably the mother herself stands in this relationship to other women, or the system wouldn't work.

After the delivery the adoptive mother cuts the umbilical cord about five inches from the navel, after having squeezed out the blood into the placenta. If she has a fire handy she burns the placenta, but if not she buries it. If the delivery is difficult and the father is afraid that he may lose his wife the next time, he takes the placenta and feeds it to a dog. Gusinde was told of one case where this was done and the woman had no more children for many years.

After the delivery the mother may eat nothing for an entire day. Her husband may not cut wood in the forest or kill large animals. He may not break bird bones to get the marrow, nor crush sea-urchin shells. Before and after delivery the mother is supposed to eat *Mytilus* mussels to make her milk come. She can eat only certain kinds of fish and only one kind of duck. These tabus seem to have been based less on the attributes of the species in question than on the parts of the coast and sea from which they are obtained. All along the shore live mythological creatures, some of which are extremely malevolent, and different kinds of fish and fowl are concentrated in some of these dangerous spots; the harm might be transmitted to the child through the flesh eaten by the mother. But if there happens to be little other food to eat, the mother cannot be allowed to go hungry. A shaman is now called in. He holds the forbidden food in his hands and blows on it. His breath blows the evil influences away, and the mother can now eat.

Once she has become able to stand up, even on the day of delivery, the mother, the adoptive mother, and the baby—carried by the latter—walk down to the sea. The mother bathes, no matter how cold the water may be, and dries herself with a ball of moss, and the adoptive mother bathes and dries the baby. The mother keeps up this daily bathing for some time, and one mother was said to have bathed four times on the day she had given birth to her child.

Both parents continue to observe the food tabus they had kept during pregnancy, and they do so until the baby's umbilical cord falls off, generally two or three months after birth. A few kinds of fish may not be eaten by either for as long as three years, unless hardship is evident and the shaman blows away the evil, as stated before. For six weeks, or sometimes longer, the parents have no sexual intercourse.

It may be added that the umbilical cord does not just fall off; its separation may be helped a little by an act of the mother. She ties the free end of the cord to the baby's ankle with a string of some kind, so that it will not get lost. When it finally comes loose she wraps the cord in a necklace which she wears until the child is about four, or old enough to catch a nuthatch. Once the child has secured the bird, he ties his own umbilical cord around its neck and lets it loose.

The Ainu

Among the Ainu a pregnant woman was encouraged to rest from her work as much as possible, and when her time came she gave birth to her child in her own house, lying on her side, and attended by her mother, maternal aunts, and sometimes by other women of her secret girdle group. If it was the mother's first child, the delivery might take place in her own mother's house to make sure that enough girdle mates would be there to help her. In either case, all men had to stay outside at that time. If the delivery was difficult, shaved sticks known as *inaus* were set up on the hearth as offerings to the Fire Goddess, and after the child had emerged, one of the attending women thrust her fingers down the mother's throat to make her vomit, so that the resulting muscular constriction would force the placenta out.

For some unexplained reason one of the women then cut a small piece of fat out of the baby's thigh just below the groin, and dressed the incision with the mycelium of certain fungi that grow in the bark of dead elm, oak, and ash trees. The mycelium is a very soft network of cobwebby fibers. It seems most likely that this dressing, which may only incidentally have helped prevent infection, was the real reason for the operation, one intended to imbue infants of both sexes with the spiritual power of those sacred trees.

The trees on which these fungi grow do not include the willow, the most sacred of all trees to the Ainu, but the willow was soon brought into the birth ceremony by the baby's resident grandfather. Before or soon after the birth had taken place he went to a riverbank and cut a green stick of willow and made an *inau* of it. This is a winged *inau* with a mass of shavings tied on it, and its butt end was set in a bundle of reeds representing a pillow. The old gentleman was allowed to enter, whereupon he recited a prayer: "We therefore call upon thee, O willow *inau*, to watch over this child while he is growing up. Guard him and give him strength, together with long life." The grandfather then set the willow *inau* beside the child and departed.

When the Ainu were being created their backbones were made of supple, springy willow, and the backbone was regarded as the seat of life, of that part of the soul that went to the spirit world after death. If a man were killed in battle his backbone would have to be cut in two to liberate his soul. The divine guardian of the willow tree was tutelary for no single lineage, male or female, but watched over the welfare of all Ainu of both sexes.

It may be added that both parents observed dietary restrictions concerned with pregnancy and childbirth, but what they did with the placenta and umbilical cord we do not know. I have searched the literature with this in mind, and haven't found a clue.

The Nootka

During pregnancy, a Nootka mother could eat almost anything except wild rhubarb, which was believed to make the child choke, and she could not eat leftover food kept in a box; it would delay delivery. Thus she was usually the first person to eat her share of a freshly cooked meal, and the first to drink from a bucket of fresh water.

She must not pause while passing through a doorway; this too might cause delay. She could neither weave blankets nor plait baskets, lest such activities snarl the umbilical cord. Neither she nor her husband could look at a dead person or a sea otter, or see an animal dying. The couple could have no intercourse during her pregnancy. When parturition came, her own mother or other female kin took her out to a brush hut built for the purpose, where her mother performed the delivery and severed the cord with a mussel shell. Before and after the delivery her mother gave her some special herbs to eat, steeped in oil. The formula of this herbal tonic was a family secret.

For four days after the delivery the mother stayed in her hut beside a fire, sitting with her legs stretched out, and being fed cod broth by her female attendants. The father spent these days sitting in the big house where he normally lived, eating dried fish. On the fourth day the placenta was disposed of. An elderly female relative took charge. The placenta was wrapped in shredded cedar bark to form a tidy package, but that was not all. If the parents wanted the child to be a good singer, the old woman in charge sang over it; if they wanted a boy child to be a skilled carpenter, they put a chisel and adze in the package. Drucker relates that in recent times a deck of cards was put in the package with a placenta to make the child a successful gambler. The old woman then buried the package in a dry, sheltered place if the baby was a girl; if it was a boy, she buried the package in a swamp to make him able to endure cold.

During these four days following the delivery, the women placed and kept the baby in a temporary cradle consisting of a mat suspended on either side between a pair of poles, with a crossbar to hold up the neck, bark mats for bedding, and a head-pressing device of cedar bark running over the forehead plus bark pads on either side of the head. As the bones of the braincase are malleable at this early age, the Nootka were able to deform their babies' heads in such a way as to elongate them and to increase the slope of the forehead. The Makah of the Olympic Peninsula of Washington State, one branch of the Nootka, did the opposite; they flattened the head from behind and widened it. The Nootka deformed the heads of all babies, including those of slaves.

After four days in the temporary cradle the baby was moved to a one-piece wooden one, hollowed like a canoe, with a projecting headpiece and a footpiece flush with the sides. The baby was bound into this cradle, which was carried vertically. A girl baby's cradle had three holes bored in the footboard for urine to leak through, but a boy baby's cradle did not; he was left with his penis exposed.

The Nootkan treatment of twins

One of the many remarkable things about the Nootka was their attitude toward twins. Most of the subjects of our inquiry do not want twins. They do not want the mother to have to suckle two children at once. There may be a question of birth order, resemblance to other animals that have multiple births, and other reasons for this point of view. One seldom sees twins among hunters, and inquiries about the subject usually bring negative answers for the simple reason that one twin is usually either killed or allowed to die through neglect. Even the Mbuti do this.

But not so the Nootka. To them the birth of twins is a supernatural event, because twins are linked to the salmon spirits, comparable to the owner of the salmon among the Ainu. The twins have power over salmon, and their father partakes of that power, for he is believed to be able to call the dog-salmon upstream. For four whole years, no one is allowed to see the twins except their parents. On the fourth day after the double birth, the parents and the twins are moved to a small plank hut, covered up so that they can't be seen, and when they are moved by boat they are also covered.

In the plank hut, the father drums on a box, the mother shakes a rattle, and other people bring them their food. During the ensuing four years they move about several times, living in isolated spots on restricted diets, and the twins with them. The father takes long walks in the mountains hoping to have some kind of a spiritual experience, and, considering the circumstances, he usually succeeds in this quest. Every night he and his wife sing songs intended to bring in salmon, herring, and whales. After the four years of solitude the family returns to its village, and the food restrictions they have undergone are lifted piecemeal until finally they can eat a normal diet. The twins usually become shamans, and no wonder.

The meaning of birth rites

These five examples were selected because they show a considerable range of variation on a common theme, and because they come from well-documented sources that can be turned to again for other rites of passage. All of them show in varying degree, and for different lengths of time, the elements of separation, transition, and incorporation following the initial event, which is the mother's pregnancy. Dietary restrictions may be regarded as part of the element of separation, and their gradual removal is part of the process of incorporation. The imposition of these food tabus is rationalized as an attempt to keep the father and mother from eating anything dangerous when they are spiritually vulnerable. Functionally they serve two purposes; to implement and to dramatize the element of separation, and to emphasize the importance of the father's role in the production of the baby and in its future care, as well as the more obvious importance of the mother.

Whether or not the people concerned understand the biological facts about conception is not very important. The Andamanese have green pigeons bring babies' souls out of flowering trees; the Ainu believe that pregnancy does not come from one act of coitus alone—the parents must copulate frequently and industriously in order to get a baby. It is becoming increasingly clear that most of the Australian aborigines may not have connected specific acts of coitus with conception until after Indonesian trepang fishermen had begun to visit the northern coast of the continent a few centuries ago. This knowledge or a lack of it has nothing to do with the performance of rites of passage attending childbirth. The important facts are that a child is born, and it has a father and a mother. It will take a good many years before the child can do his share of work in providing food, and meanwhile his parents have much to do.

Whenever a child is born, something has to be done about the placenta right away, and the umbilical cord later on. These are mysterious things, concerned with that vital and magical substance, blood; and as the placenta and cord were once part of the child they remain so in a spiritual sense. Any harm that comes to them may befall the child, or perhaps his successor. The Mbuti rites emphasize their regard for the forest, the Andamanese associate theirs with flowering trees from which they obtain useful fibers, and the Ainu bring in their sacred trees as a part of the ritual content. The Nootka rites emphasize their technical skills and division of labor. In short, the details of any rite of passage, including those of birth, reflect the special preoccupations and emphases of the culture concerned.

Puberty rites

Between birth and puberty, other changes in the lives of children, barring illness and death, are gradual, both physically and in terms of their activities. As these changes create little disturbance among the individuals concerned and among those with whom they live, they seldom require any notable compensatory rites.

Among people who live in relatively compact communities in which there is little privacy, when a girl first menstruates, the flow of blood makes her conspicuous in a ritually dangerous way. Thus her immediate isolation usually has physical as well as social motivation. Among boys the process is less sudden and less visible. Thus it is easier to initiate boys in groups of roughly the same age than it is to initiate girls together, but there are exceptions. Group initiation of boys foreshadows their cooperation in hunting and other masculine activities, strengthening the needed bonds.

The amount of time and attention devoted to puberty rites varies less from society to society in the case of girls than with boys, for two possible reasons. The girls may be expected to keep on menstruating periodically until menopause, while with boys puberty is an event that occurs but once in a lifetime, and his subsequent emissions of semen are not periodic, but voluntary. A girl may not have intercourse while menstruating. Also, men's activities vary much more among different hunting peoples than women's. For example, men who are going to spend most of their time digging roots need less ritual indoctrination at puberty than skilled hunters do. In some societies other problems create more anxiety than a boy's coming to puberty. The Ainu are so worried about the possibility that the annual runs of salmon may fail that they devote an inordinate amount of ritual to allaying their anxiety, and they have no boys' puberty ceremonies at all. Nor do the Kadar, who do not hunt.

The double initiation of the G/wi Bushmen

Like myths, puberty ceremonies are long and full of details. It is impossible to compress them beyond a certain level and still make them comprehensible. Our number of examples will therefore be

M

limited. We shall begin with those of the G/wi Bushmen of Botswana, previously mentioned in regard to incest tabus in Chapter 9, and visualize the situation of a young man who has married a prepubescent girl. For several years he has waited for her breasts to swell and her nipples to assume the tantalizing form of a pair of orange kumquats. Finally the floodgate opens, and she goes to tell her mother.

Her mother is on hand because at this stage of married life the couple is living in the same camp as the bride's parents, and her father may be expected to be there too. The mother and some of her women-friends of about the same age build an unthatched hut of branches, a little way off from the main circle of huts, and lead the girl to it. Inside she is supposed to sit without moving and with her legs straight out, and to remain silent, for four days. She is also supposed to fast, but the other women covertly bring her enough food to keep her going.

Meanwhile her husband has left his connubial hut and gone to sleep with the bachelors under the tree in the middle of the camp. On his way out of his hut he takes his bow, arrows, and spear with him, taking care that his wife does not touch them on her way to the seclusion hut, for should she do so they would be ruined for hunting, and something frightful would befall him, like being eaten by a lion or bitten by a poisonous snake.

On the fifth day of this ordeal, the married women assemble around the girl's hut, and also bring her husband to her. No other males are allowed. Then the girl comes out of the hut, fully clothed. One of the older women sits on the ground, holding between her feet a turnip-shaped, juicy bulb of the plant *Raphionacme burkei*, and slices and shreds it with a split stick. This juicy pulp will be used later in the ceremony.

Now one of the women shaves the couple's heads with an iron blade, in an identical his-and-her pattern, one that the couple themselves choose. It may be an Iroquois-like roach, a series of concentric circles, or a V, with the branches starting above the ears and converging in a peak above the forehead. But if the shaving is done during the summer heat, the couple may prefer to have only the back and sides of the head shaved for an inch or so, in order to leave the mop above as a protection against the heat of the sun, with the peppercorn tufts of hair characteristic of Bushmen teased out and matted with oil and ashes derived from the seeds of another plant, *Ximenia caffra*.

Now the previously sliced and shredded pulp of the first plant is brought out, and with it the attending women wash down the bodies of both participants, starting at their heads and working downwards, reaching under their garments when needed. In this way they give them each a complete bath, taking care that none of the shreds used on the girl touch her husband's body lest he be defiled by menstrual blood. During this bath the girl is told that when she menstruates in the future she must move about as little as possible and must not throw away her soiled pads of grass, which she uses as a tampon, but put them up in a tree.

Once washed, the pair is tattooed. The woman who shaved them now cuts incisions in both of them, just deep enough to draw blood. She cuts them in identical places, from the face down to the hands and feet, and on the back, the most painful place. Her procedure is to make a few cuts on one of them, then to make cuts on the same part of the body on the other one, so that both, in a sense, are cut simultaneously. After each pair of cuttings she mixes the blood of each with that of the other, to join their blood, and while this is going on they are told that they are thus united and the mingling will keep them from harm. The older women also give them advice, such as that they must not talk about each other with their companions of their own sex, and that they must not commit adultery. The cutting is followed by adding pigment to the cuts. In the same impartial fashion, the ashes of burnt medicinal and magical roots are rubbed into the cuts, which will eventually heal into blue, raised scars.

Now one of the women takes one of the girl's arms, raises her to her feet, and leads her into the camp, where the other young women are waiting. Her guide presses an edible plant—which one depends on the season—against the girl's forehead, and says: "This is food." She then dramatically points to the horizon all around in a circle, and says: "This is our world and yours. You will always find food here."

At this point the young women seize the girl and run her around in a circle outside the huts of the camp, and then lead her back into her marital hut. This rapid circumambulation is supposed to symbolize a rainstorm, and the noise that the girls make while running is supposed to represent their pleasure at getting wet. This part of the ceremony is intended to empower the girl to attract rain, which also means food and drinking water.

The husband, who has been standing about quietly and looking embarrassed, joins his wife in their hut, and then the next part of the rite begins. Some of the older women enter the hut and paint the couple in identical patterns with red ochre and fat. Then they lead out the girl and hand her over to her father. Meanwhile the rest of the men have sauntered out from wherever they had been staying, trying to look nonchalant, and join their women and children.

At this point the girl is supposed to be blind. Her father has prepared a loose ball of grass. He holds it in front of his daughter's eyes, snaps it in two, and says: "See your people. This is so-and-so." In this way he introduces everyone to his daughter as if they had never met, and he recounts a biographical sketch of each one. This recitation, of course, gives him a great chance to play one-upmanship on his peers, particularly in terms of the order in which he introduces them, the first being the most favored. Being near the head of the list is supposed to bring good luck at hunting and collecting food. Once everyone has been thus introduced to the girl the others scatter to bring in their ornaments; necklaces of pierced discs of ostrich-egg shell, metal gewgaws obtained in trade, and the like, and they drape them on the girl and on her husband, who has by now emerged from his hut. The couple may wear these during the rest of the day, except for a few that they may keep for several days longer.

At the girl's second, and sometimes at her third, menstruation this ceremony will be repeated. After that the husband cuts a pair of small sticks, carves and burns designs on them, ties them at either end of a thong, and presents this rig to his wife, who wears it around her neck as a sign that she is now a real woman.

Circumcision, menstruation, and wooing among the Mbuti

Once every three years or so the Mbuti boys of a camp, aged between about nine and eleven, are put through a puberty ceremony in their hosts' village along with their Negro peers, and this rite includes circumcision. The Pygmy boys submit to this ordeal simply because it confirms the relationships between the two peoples and allows the Pygmies free access to the village, where they can be feasted from time to time and can obtain trade goods. The Negroes consider that it establishes bonds between age-mates of the two peoples useful in subsequent trading, and also that it brings the forest people into line with their own customs. In this sense the Pygmies may be compared to the "rice Christians" converted by missionaries in other parts of the world. The Mbuti have no male puberty rites of their own except in the sense that they participate in the girls' ceremony, which is known as the *elima*.

The Negro villagers regard menstrual blood with horror, and keep their girls in deep seclusion during menstruation, but the Mbuti have no such notion; to them a girl's first menses is a time of rejoicing and an approach to womanhood. When a girl first "sees the blood" she stays in her parents' hut, or in a special extension built onto it, and when two girls begin to menstruate at the same time they may join up. If one begins a little before the other the first one will wait for the second to join her. In such a case their *elima* hut may not be an extension of that of the parents of either girl, but of the hut of some other couple willing to put up with the noise that is bound to follow. This structure is known as the *elima* house.

Each girl selects a companion of her own age grade to be her helper. The helpers are subject to the same restrictions as the menstruating girls except that they can go in and out more freely. After the helpers have been selected, the girls invite others of their age grade to join the group. An elderly man, in one observed instance a bachelor, served as the "father" of the *elima*, and an elderly woman as its mother. In the case cited the "mother" was a widow. The "father's" role is to quiet the girls down as they grow too noisy, the "mother's" to serve as a chaperone of sorts and to be responsible for the girls' instruction in singing and in what to do when they become mothers themselves. The whole rite lasts about two months. A few more women are also teachers, some married, some simply elder members of the novitiates' age group.

The girls are taught two kinds of songs, the songs that grown women sing, and special *elima* songs. The latter are distinguished from other songs by having special melodies, while the words may be simply repetitions of anything that comes into the girls' minds, or meaningless phrases. As the *elima* songs are sung only on these occasions, they are in that sense sacred. The songs are sung at first in the hut, but later on the girls are taken out into the forest to sing them. While the girls are in the forest they break branches by the paths to warn the boys not to come near them, and if the boys approach, the girls beat them with sticks.

During the *elima* the girls undergo food restrictions. They may not be allowed to eat meat, particularly if the game begins to be depleted

323

owing to the length of the ceremony, and a girl who has not eaten a certain food since childhood because it once made her sick may try it again to see if she can tolerate it in her new condition.

While the girls are in the hut, unmarried boys throng around outside and the girls sally out now and then to chase them and beat them with sticks. Any boy who has been struck is allowed to come into the hut later in the afternoon of the same day. Then the girls beat him again, after which he is allowed to lie down with the girl who had beaten him outside the hut. He must not, of course, be a boy closely enough related to the girl for intercourse to be forbidden. The "mother" makes sure that the girl he lies down with is unrelated to him. The girl whom he chooses (or who chooses him) may change her mind, and not let him copulate with her, in which case he leaves, but if she lets him do so, he is not supposed to hold her in his arms during the act. Colin Turnbull was told by some of the elders that this style of intercourse prevents pregnancy; others said that the girls use special herbal concoctions to prevent it; but, however it is done, the girls apparently do not become pregnant at this time. Boys from neighboring camps may come to visit, be beaten, and be let in, and the girls may leave the hut to go to neighboring camps and whip some of the boys there, in which case the boys are supposed to return the visit.

About two weeks before the end of the *elima* rite the pace changes, and wooing becomes serious and more selective. In the late afternoon, the mothers of the girls inside the hut assemble in front of it with their collecting baskets, sticks, and stones. Now the boys take the initiative and any one of them who wants to enter the hut must get through the line of women outside. The women beat the boys, and if they look with ill favor on one, they may seize him and throw him into a nearby stream. Suitors may fight back by shooting fruit rinds or pebbles at the women with their bowstrings, and a sharp slap with a banana skin can be painful.

In any case, a boy will not get in unless the women want him to, and once he has entered the hut it is the girl's choice whether she will sleep with him or not. If she does, he has to stay there until the end of the ceremony, and the two are considered to be betrothed. During this time the girls paint their bodies and each other's with white clay, in intricate and fanciful designs. One girl observed by Turnbull was particularly proud of her large breasts. She had painted concentric rings on them. Another had stars painted on her buttocks. The girls then come out late in the day to sing and dance, and the boys watch them. Flirtatious behavior is discouraged by the older women.

The ceremonial period ends when the girls go together to the stream to bathe. When they come back they rub their bodies with oil and sing and dance in the camp without further supervision, and go to sleep in their own huts. For a few more days they go about together in the daytime, and then return to normal activities.

After this a boy who considers himself betrothed to a girl, because he has slept with her in the *elima* hut during the latter part of the ceremony, asks her parents' permission to have her come to live with him. If they agree, he must first kill one of the larger species of antelopes and give it to her parents. Until she becomes pregnant the union may be dissolved by either party, but afterward they usually stay together. Whether they live with her band or his depends on a number of factors, including the number of persons in each band.

Not all marriages are begun in the *elima* hut. A boy who has not slept with a girl there may still propose to her parents, and then the whole camp will make the decision, not only concerning the marriage but as to which band the couple shall join. If refused, the couple may go to join a third band, but if they do, the band that accepts them is obliged to give a girl in marriage to the new girl's former band. This latter arrangement may be regarded as an extension of the principle of the exchange of sisters found in many other societies.

In effect, the girls' puberty rites of the Mbuti follow the usual sequence of separation, transition, and incorporation, but like the rites of the G/wi Bushmen they also include the boys. The difference between the two is that among the Mbuti the boys are involved in the rite before marriage, and among the G/wi after it. The beatings that the boys receive from the girls and from the latter's mothers may also be considered as a boys' initiation, for the boys have no separate puberty rite of their own and do not consider their initiation along with the Negro boys in the village to count.

The Andamanese gradually lift three food tabus

Among the Great Andamanese, a girl's puberty is anticipated by a gradual scarification of her body over a period of years. Older women cut linear patterns in her skin, but they are hard to see when healed, for nothing is rubbed in to raise them. When she first menstruates older women decorate her with pandanus leaves—the kind with which women roof their huts—and for twenty-four hours she must sit in a specially constructed hut, with her arms crossed, and during that time she is not allowed to lie down, speak, or sleep. Except for a bath in the sea each morning, she remains in this hut for three days. She is given food, but cannot touch it with her hands; she has to pick it up and put it in her mouth with a skewer.

In the southern tribes of Great Andaman the boys are not scarified, but in the northern tribes coarse, raised scars are cut on their backs at puberty. In both cases the pubescent boys now have to leave their parents' hut and live in a special hut at one end of the dance floor, and the girls have to live in a hut or huts of their own. Both the boys and the girls must sleep in these huts until marriage, but otherwise their movements are not restricted, although their diets are.

Over a period of several years the young people have to refrain from eating three important foods. On the coast these are: turtle and certain fish; honey; and pork. In the interior where turtles are not available a kind of fish shot in creeks is the first of these foods. Each boy and each girl has to undergo a series of three ceremonies allowing him or her to resume eating turtle, honey, and pork, in that order. After the pork ceremony the initiate is allowed to marry. On Great Andaman, because there might be from eight to a dozen young people living in the puberty houses at a time, and each one had to go through all three of the rites separately, staging puberty rites was the principal—and almost continuous—ritual activity of the Great Andamanese.

The turtle-eating ceremony held for one boy took four days. In it he was decorated with, or held in his hands, leaves and wooden objects of three botanical species, *Hibiscus*, *Myristica*, and *Pothos*. All have to do with catching turtles or shooting fish. *Hibiscus* is the source of the strong fibers twisted into ropes for turtle nets and harpoon cords. *Myristica*, a nutmeg tree, was probably bow wood, but we are not sure. *Pothos* is the creeper from the bark of whose roots the Andamanese obtain the bright yellow fiber that they twist into the cordage used in hafting the heads of harpoons and fish arrows. These three substances thus symbolize not the sea creatures caught, but the weapons employed and, by further substitution, the actions of men using them, and finally, the importance of such men themselves. Forbidding the boys to eat turtle until after this rite dramatically separates the boys from the men, as do the other two tabus.

On the first day, one of the older men, or an important visitor, takes charge as master of ceremonies. The rite begins with the boy seated facing the sea, a fire in front of his feet. His arms are folded, his legs stretched out, and his big toes interlocked. He is sitting on hibiscus leaves, has a pad of them behind his buttocks as a miniature back rest, and clutches another bundle of them under his arms. The master of ceremonies now approaches the boy with a dish of cooked turtle fat and meat. He rubs some of the fat over the boy's lips and then over his whole body, while the boy's female relatives, seated nearby, weep loudly.

The master of ceremonies then rubs red ochre all over the boy except for his head hair, then places a piece of turtle fat in the boy's mouth. The boy chews and swallows it. His female relatives again weep loudly. Now the man massages the boy vigorously, rubbing the food symbolically down into his stomach, then working on his arms and legs and making his knuckles and toe-joints crack. Then he spatters a mixture of ordinary clay and water all over the boy's body. All the while the boy has remained seated as at the beginning, and in silence. After this he is allowed to eat turtle meat with a skewer, out of a dish placed beside him. He can use one arm only to do this, and he may move his legs and feet now and then to relieve cramps, but otherwise he must continue to remain seated and silent for forty-eight hours, during which time he may eat only turtle and drink only water.

On the morning of the third day someone otherwise unidentified approaches him with a belt and a necklace made of *Pothos* creeper, and places them around his waist and neck. Now he is allowed to sleep. Later on he goes down to the sea to bathe, and after his return his female relatives repaint him with red ochre and white clay, and he may go back to his hut. Early in the fourth morning an older man takes up a position by the sounding board in the dance floor, and the whole camp assembles. The boy comes out of his hut, and five or six men surround him. The boy and each of the men hold a bunch of *Hibiscus* or *Myristica* twigs in each hand.

Now the leader who had appeared first sings a song on the subject of turtle hunting, beating time with one foot on the sounding board. The women also sing, and they clap their hands on their thighs in rhythm. Once the song is over, the boy clasps his hands behind his neck with his twigs trailing down his back. He leans forward so that his body is horizontal, bends his knees, and then begins an extremely athletic and exhausting turtle dance, imitating

M*

that reptile's movements in swimming. The old man at the sounding board is beating time at a recorded rate of 144 beats a minute, and at each beat the boy has to hop up into the air and down again, and at about every eighth leap he swishes down with his hands and their twigs in imitation of the movements of the turtle's front flippers.

This performance may be repeated a few times, until the boy is too weak to continue. Then he retires to his hut, where he may now speak to his fellow inmates, and after a cooling-off period of a week or two he may resume his ordinary activities, plus eating turtle, but he still has the honey rite and the pork rite ahead of him.

Like turtle catching, honey collecting and pig shooting are dangerous activities. It is the fully initiated men who feed the camp on turtle flesh, honey, and pork, and by making the young people avoid these foods, lifting the tabus seriatim, their elders properly impress them with the importance of their own social position. Thus the age grading which forms the basis of Andamanese society is indelibly imprinted on youthful minds.

Puberty rites of other hunters

The preceding examples are mixed puberty rites involving both sexes, timed to coincide most closely with the girls' menarchy. They are not performed at any special time of year. In most of the other hunting societies girls are initiated singly, while the boys' rites are conducted collectively, in most cases during great seasonal ceremonies when food is abundant.

In northwestern California, among tribes participating in the Northwest Coast culture, female puberty is the concept underlying their greatest rituals. These are annual ceremonies called "world renewal rites," performed to cleanse the world of pollution by menstrual blood. Collective puberty rites for boys may also form parts of more inclusive rites of intensification, as among many of the Australian tribes. Among the Alaskan Eskimo the completion of a young man's initiation also comes during annual rites, after he has killed a succession of animals of increasing size and difficulty, making him at that point eligible for marriage.

Among many of the North American Indians a boy may be sent out in the wilderness to fast, keep vigils, and otherwise put himself in a nervous state suitable for seeing a vision, just as Mohammed was visited by the Angel Gabriel in a cave. The Indian novice may either see or dream of some protecting animal or spirit, and thus he obtains his "power." After this he may be allowed to participate in sexual activities. This is a way of obtaining a personal, totemic guardian, just as his ancestors did in myths. That in some North American Indian societies girls may also see or dream of guardians has been briefly indicated in the first part of the myth of Nenebuc the Transformer cited in Chapter 13.

Death and mortuary rites

Most mortuary rites follow immediately upon a person's death, even before the disposal of the body. They are performed by the individuals most directly disturbed by the loss, although these may include the entire community. The magnitude and intensity of this rite, and the numbers of persons involved, are functions of the degrees of disturbance to all concerned. When a baby dies the rites are minimal because the child's personality has not yet become well enough established to affect many persons outside the immediate family. The death of a man in his prime, a good hunter or fighter or powerful chief, will affect the whole community, and his rites will be correspondingly elaborate. Among some hunting peoples the rites may be held annually to mourn those that have died during the year.

Infanticide and geronticide

Female infanticide as a means of reducing the population in times of extreme want ordinarily evokes no rites, and the baby may even be eaten, as in arid parts of Australia. Nor are rites performed when one of a pair of twins is done away with, or in the case of geronticide through necessity. Among the Caribou Indians of the Barren Lands west of Hudson Bay, sometimes, in winter, the caribou herds fail to appear, and there is a choice between some persons being sacrificed and the starvation of the whole community. The schedule of priorities for survival is as follows. The hunter must be fed because if he is too weak to hunt no one will eat. Next comes his wife, because she can still bear children, and then small children. Male babies have priority over their sisters because they will become hunters if anyone at all is left. Most expendable are the old people, particularly the old women, who outnumber the old men owing to the loss of active hunters through accidents.

When the time comes, no one kills an old woman. Her relatives regret her loss. She commits suicide by simply walking out of the igloo naked, and disappears in the snow. When there are no old people left, girl babies will be killed. This is a heartrending business, because everyone loves children.

In Tasmania, bands of hunters had to keep moving on their annual rounds in order to take advantage of regional differences in the seasonal variations in the food supply. Old people too feeble to walk and too crippled to be carried long distances, or too sick to be moved, were simply left behind in a sheltered place, such as a hollow tree or under an outcrop of rock, with a supply of water kept in a bubble of giant kelp. In his diary Robinson noted that he once came across an old man who had thus been abandoned, and who had crawled around for several days, subsisting on berries. Those who were hopelessly ill were left with a bundle of leaves of the purgative plant *Mesembryanthemum equilaterale*. If the medication worked and they recovered, such persons could follow the tracks of their companions and might rejoin them.

In the rites of passage usually following death, the successive elements of separation, transition, and incorporation may be traced in two sequences, that which concerns the deceased person, and the one affecting those survivors most deeply affected by their loss. In the first instance, death itself initiates the separation, the disposal of the body the transition, and the eventual return of the spirit of the deceased to the company of other spirits in the afterworld constitutes the incorporation. Among people who have territorial clans, the spirit may join those of its ancestors in some totemic spot, from which the spirits of babies may be released upon conception.

As for the survivors, at least in the case of the death of an ordinary man, those most deeply affected are usually widows. After the initial shock, alleviated in part by the attention they get during the funeral, they try to fill the vacuum of their loneliness by turning their attention to others. This can make them both a nuisance and a source of jealousy. The restrictions that they undergo during mourning may help them get used to a less active pattern of living than before, and it also keeps them from disturbing others in the meanwhile.

Separation comes when widows are made to live in a separate part of the camp, rock shelter, or house; transition when they are forbidden to speak to others and may be addressed only by sign language, or through a special intermediary. Incorporation arrives when the widow has become adjusted to her new way of life, or remarries, sometimes as the first wife of a young man, sometimes as the second or other multiple wife of her late husband's brother. In any case, by the time her mourning is over, her husband's soul may have rejoined those of his ancestors, and it is unlikely to bother the people with whom she is now allowed to associate more freely.

The disposal of the body

Returning to the disposal of the body, hunters regard this as a means of isolating the dead person's spirit, but it may be isolated for either of two reasons, to get rid of it entirely or to limit its activities so that it may be used. The concept stated above greatly widens the range of disposal techniques. The easiest way is simply to abandon the body at the place of death, and to avoid returning to that spot until the disturbance is over, usually after several years, when the dead person's spirit has had time to go away. The Mbuti Pygmies used to abandon it before they were taught by the Negro villagers to bury their dead. The Veddas of Ceylon, who lived in rock shelters during the rainy season, did the same. They had so many shelters available that they could afford to leave some of them unoccupied until the remains had disappeared. In tropical rain forests insects and animals make short work of bodies, and if they are buried or covered with earth, the lateritic soil is so acid that bones may disintegrate in less than a year. In 1965 I excavated a cave in a diamond-mining concession in Sierra Leone and found no bones at all, although the soil was full of stone implements and chips. A schoolteacher stationed there told me that she had once buried a dead dog to get its skeleton for use in her zoology class, and when she dug it up a year later even the bones had rotted away.

In other climates people who camp in the same places at least once a year could hardly follow this practice, nor could those who live in permanent or semipermanent villages. Where there are plenty of caves and rock crannies, or hollow trees, these apertures are natural depositories, and frequently used. Where firewood is abundant, cremation is a quick and dramatic solution, particularly if the ground is frozen in winter and burial at that time is out of the question. Another easy method is to secure the body high up in a tree.

But however hunting and gathering peoples dispose of bodies, they usually do so individually in separate places, for graveyards are an artifact of sedentary life. The Maidu of California had special burning grounds, and the Nootka deposited some of their dead on mortuary islets, towing the bodies out to them in unmanned canoes. The Eskimo of Nunivak Island buried their dead in shallow graves, some on top of the other, under slabs of rock in cemeteries located about a quarter of a mile away from their villages. In these burial places skulls and long bones could be seen lying about where they had been disinterred to make room for new bodies. These Eskimo have no fear of corpses or old bones, once the proper rituals have been performed, and, in fact, they formerly made use of parts of bodies as amulets to help them in hunting.

Rites following the death of an Akoa Pygmy

As to whole rites, these may be illustrated by a few examples, beginning with that following the death of an Akoa Pygmy and that of his chief. If the deceased, an ordinary man, has died during the night, the funeral ceremony will begin early the next morning, but if he has died during the daytime his body will be kept overnight to allow a full day for the rites. As the body must not be allowed to grow cold, it is kept in its hut beside a fire, wrapped in fig bark, under the widow's care. His kinsmen place him in a seated position with his arms crossed over his chest and his eyes kept open "to see the spirits." If he has died far enough away from the camp so that rigor mortis has set in, it is a bad omen needing a special sacrifice to appease the ancestral spirits.

In anticipation of the death, the widow and other close female relatives have laid in supplies of white clay to paint themselves with. Now they do so, rumpling their hair and gashing their cheeks until the blood flows. In the rites that follow, men and women are treated equally, with certain exceptions to be noted.

While the women are lamenting, the deceased's eldest son sings the death song, while an uncle responds.

Solo: The animal runs, passes by, dies. It is the great cold.
Response: The great cold of night. It is black.
Solo: The bird flies, passes by, dies. It is the great cold.
Response: The great cold of night. It is black.
Solo: The fish swims, passes by, dies. It is the great cold.
Response: The great cold of night. It is black.
Solo: The man eats, sleeps, dies. It is the great cold.
Response: The great cold of night. It is black.
Solo: The sky brightens, the eyes are put out (like fires). The stars shine.
Response: The cold is below, the light is above.
Solo: The man has passed by, the darkness is gone, the captive is free.
Response: Khmvum, Khmvum, we call to you. [Khmvum is the name of the Creator, the high god in the sky.]

Early the next morning the adult men begin to dance, mimicking the deeds of the deceased. Meanwhile women wash the body and shave it entirely, saving all the hairs to be deposited with it. While so doing, they wail. Some of the men build a special hut for the body in the form of a snail, with a spiral entrance, probably so that the spirits, who can travel only in a straight line, will be unable to enter, and then they move the body into it.

On the following morning the men take out the body and carry it in a crude litter, completely covered with bark, into the forest, and deposit it in a cave, a rock crevice, or a hollow tree, lying it on its side, with its hair beside it. The men return without looking behind them, and wash their hands and feet. Only then can anyone eat.

For four days they mourn, the women being painted white. The men go into the forest to cut bushes of a certain kind, which, when burned, give off an intense, acrid smoke. With this fire they burn the deceased's funeral hut and all of his personal belongings. For four days they keep this fire burning. The men sit around drinking honey wine, while the women do their ordinary work.

Then the men collect the ashes on pieces of bark and throw them into a stream or marsh. They return to the camp and set out hunting. Until they get back they do not allow the first animal killed to bleed freely, and then they sprinkle its blood on the hut in which the person had died.

The death of Ato, an Akoa chief

When a chief died, in this instance Ato, a friend of Father Trilles, the rites were different. During his last illness Ato's people took good care of him, for he suffered from both rheumatism and neuralgia. They gave him hot infusions to drink, cut his skin with a sharp mussel shell, and cupped him, sucking the blood through tubes made of the horns of small antelopes. Then they laid him in the sun on the bank of a stream, covered with hot sand. After this they placed him on a bed of wet leaves on a framework of poles, and built a fire under it, to steam him. Then they immersed him in the river to cool him off. Meanwhile they fed him his favorite foods. When the end came, they laid his body on a strip of bark, and his old wife held his head on her knees and wiped his brow.

The men carried the chief's body out into the forest to dispose of it in the usual way, but in the camp no one mourned. Instead the women collected their belongings and packed them in baskets of plaited hibiscus fiber, for, when the men should return, everyone would have to abandon camp and seek a new site. The women also looked over the old people, to see which ones would be able to walk and which ones needed to be carried on younger people's backs. When the men came back they all set out, under the leadership of one of the chief's sons, and in some cases the band might split at this time. (If a younger son led away his own contingent to set up a camp of his own, he would change his totem from the one inherited from his father, which the first brother kept.)

Several months after such a funeral some of the men would revisit the place where they had left the chief's body. If they found it decayed or eaten by animals, they would leave it undisturbed. But if it were intact and dried, further steps would have to be taken to thwart the chief's ghost. Then they would carry the body back to the old campsite and thence to a place by the stream where the women used to get drinking water and to bathe. Then they would deflect the stream; dig a hole in the deepest part of the bed; put the body in it, tightly bound and standing upright, with a bow, arrows, and spear; weight it down; and let the water flow back. There it would remain in the cold, which Pygmies fear, and its spirit could not wander to harm them.

The Penobscot Indians

In contrast, the Penobscot Indians of Maine practiced a very simple sequence of mortuary procedures. Like the Nunivak Eskimo, they had special cemeteries near their home villages, and if anyone died elsewhere they took pains to bring the body home for burial. As a rule the cemeteries were in sandy soil, which is easy to dig, and if possible, on bluffs or hills overlooking the river.

When a person died, he or she was dressed in his or her best clothing, complete with ornaments, and wrapped in birchbark. Useful objects were placed with the body; in the case of a man a bow and arrows, and sometimes a stone gouge. In modern times the bow and arrows were replaced by a gun.

Before taking the body to the cemetery, relatives and friends would gather at the house of the deceased to mourn. Several old men stood near the body and chanted a short prayer to the dead person's soul, and others joined in. At the actual interment, they sang it again.

If the deceased left a widow or widower, this person soon received a visit from a group of old women, some of whom were relatives of the dead person. The object of this visit was to place the mourning, so to speak, on the surviving spouse. This meant that the latter should wear black clothing (what they wore before they had European clothing we are not sure), avoid sexual intercourse, drink no liquor, and do nothing frivolous or lighthearted that might give offense to the deceased.

These old women kept their eyes open and their ears cocked, and if the mourner broke any of the rules that they had laid down they would soon know of it. Then they would reappear to lift the mourning prematurely, which would disgrace the offender in the eyes of the entire community. But if the surviving spouse behaved as he or she was supposed to do, then the old women would come back after a half year or year or so, at their own discretion, to lift the mourning properly. They would dance a round dance and sing a special song, after which the widow or widower was free to resume normal behavior, and to remarry.

In this uncomplicated procedure we see a double division of labor in which elderly people are uniquely in charge. The old men are concerned with the body and the old women with the survivor. Laying on the mourning, watching out for breaches of conduct, and removing the mourning are simple acts of separation, transition, and incorporation.

The Tasmanians

More elaborate and emotionally less restrained were the funeral rites of the Tasmanians, especially perhaps in the disastrous winter of 1832, when George Augustus Robinson witnessed the disposal of many bodies. Mortuary rites were not uniform over the entire island, although cremation was the most usual technique. When a warrior was killed outside his own country, his enemies would expose his body in a tree, so that its liberated spirit would go home to make its people ill.

Members of one "nation" that lived near the site of Hobart Town used to slice each limb lengthwise to the bone, cut the throat, and stretch the mouth wide open, on each body. Then they would wrap the remains in bark, bury them, and heap stones over the grave. After the flesh had decomposed they would exhume the bones, except for the vertebrae, to wear as amulets. The other tribes considered these people cowards, and when they came into their country to collect eggs, they raided them to steal their women.

On July 30 and 31, 1832, Robinson witnessed a sequence of two cremations which he described in detail in his diary. It was chilly weather and strong gales were blowing in from the southeast. A woman who had been ailing for some time died at 2:00 P.M. on July 30. All of her companions went to get dry wood, and began to pile it in her hut, but Robinson stopped them because, had they burned her in it, all the other huts which were grouped near it would have burned down too.

So they selected an open spot some two hundred yards from the camp and piled the logs in a square, each tier at right angles to the one below it, until the pyre was three feet high. Then they filled the interstices with dry grass and fern, and set pieces of brushwood on end all around it, to a height of about ten feet, leaving an opening for the body. One of the men carried the body in on his back and placed it in the opening, with dry brush under each arm. They closed the gap, and tied around the pyre a grass cord which they had made on the spot.

Other sick persons remained by the pyre in hastily constructed huts, in the hope that the dead woman's spirit would heal them, but the others returned to the camp. The dead woman had left a baby, which other women took turns suckling, and the widower, who was also ill, showed great solicitude for the baby. Everyone wept while making the pyre.

On the next morning the entire group reassembled with torches. Everyone set fire to the pyre at once. Soon it was blazing brightly. Everyone lay on the ground, lamenting and singing a special song. Now and then some of them arose to put more fuel on the fire. When the woman's body was visible, one of the men broke her skull with a pole, and her brains spilled out, unburned. Other men poked the body with poles, until it had been dismembered and was soon reduced to ashes. Then the men who were able to do so went out to hunt, and the sick people who were gathered around rubbed themselves with the ashes.

Meanwhile one of the sick persons, an old man, failed perceptibly, and was writhing with pain. Others carried him to the ashes of the dead woman's pyre and rolled him in them. At his own request they then began to collect wood for his own cremation while he was still alive, and one man, whom Robinson called "the undertaker," took the lead in these preparations. At 3:00 P.M. on July 31 the old man died. Most of the men were out hunting, but those that were left built a new pyre over the ashes of the woman's, and put his body in it in the same fashion.

When the men who had been out hunting returned, they witnessed the second cremation and all lamented loudly, for the deceased was renowned as a bard and a man of great wisdom. After his pyre and body had been reduced to ashes like the first one, some of the participants, who were members of other bands that Robinson had collected for purposes of deportation, gathered up handfuls of ashes to sew into bits of kangaroo skin to use as amulets, as mentioned previously on page 291.

15.

Rites of Intensification and Seasonal Ceremonies

One obvious conclusion that has emerged from our study of cultures of hunting peoples is that hunters are gregarious. When the day's work is done, they like to be together. Some of them who have an abundance or even a surplus of food now and then find ways of coming together in considerable numbers, at suitable times and places, even for weeks and sometimes months at a time.

On such occasions they amuse themselves. They dance, they act out rituals, and they stage dramas and play games. But that is not all that some of them do. Having a whole age-grade collection of pubescent boys, the older men may initiate them together, at once. If there is any time left over, the men may also hold a postgraduate set of ceremonies, either for the preceding class alone, or for the initiated men as a whole. Sometimes they hold no initiation at all, but simply partake of a great, peripatetic round of sacrifices and feasts, a giant winter party, as was the case with the Ainu.

The Ainu bear sacrifice

Sacrificing captive bears was the winter sport and main annual ceremony of the Ainu.* When the snow was deep, members of different settlements visited each other in turn, to sacrifice and to eat yearling bears that they had captured in mid-March when the cubs were just old enough to walk. If the men of one settlement had caught more than one cub (for many are twins), and others had been unsuccessful, then the cubs would be distributed so that each settlement in a given area would have at least one. These bears were fat and tender, even if some had been kept over for a second year.

The bear ceremony seems to have been a means of renewing and strengthening relationships between communities sharing a naturally unified section of a single river valley, communities which in

*Although the Japanese forbade this rite in the eighteenth century, the ban was not completely enforced until as late as the 1930s after one had been filmed. (See B. Z. Seligman, Appendix 2 in N. G. Munro, *Ainu Creed and Cult*. New York, Columbia University Press, 1963.)

340

pre-Japanese times had been allied in war under a paramount chief. When warfare ceased, the rite still served to enable hunters of those communities to cross each other's territories in search of bears — which hibernated on high slopes — without being accused of trespass. This arrangement would also be useful for trading expeditions.

Well ahead of time the chief elders of the participating settlements met in the house of one of them, perhaps the counterpart of the former paramount chief. There they arranged for the route to be followed by the participants, as each community sacrificed, and entertained its guests, in turn. The settlement in which the conference had been held had the right to sacrifice first, and the sequence of routes to be followed had to be coordinated. The round of sacrifices took more than a month, and when they were over it was nearly time to set out to catch a new lot of cubs for the following year.

The choice of the bear as the sacrificial animal, and the fact that the bear lineage was a prominent one, gave the bear men no special privileges. Men of all lineages took part. But in earlier times, well into the nineteenth century, the Ainu also kept and sacrificed other totemic animals and birds, but only within their own settlements. The meaning of this apparent historic sequence is not clear, nor need it be for present purposes.

In the springtime the Ainu kept the bear cubs in their houses, where women in milk nursed them. Sometimes a cub was passed from one woman to another, or several took turns. During weaning women would chew food and feed the cubs from mouth to mouth. When the weather had grown warmer and the cubs had been weaned, they were put in wooden cages in the yard, set on posts four or five feet above the ground. There the women still fed them, fondled them, and watched their reactions, because the bears had to be kept happy.

If a cub growled at a woman it was a bad sign. It meant either that she was menstruating or was not wearing her secret girdle. If she pleaded innocent to either or both accusations, a *tusu* (female medium) might be called to inspect her.

The overindulged pets were kept and fattened in their cages for one year, and sometimes for two. From the economic point of view, fattening bears for slaughter was an expensive luxury because one bear could eat more food than several persons and the bear meat provided by the sacrifice was only enough to give each person a few mouthfuls. Also the women had to collect for the bear the kinds of wild foods it normally ate — roots, berries, chestnuts, and the like.

From the social point of view, rearing cubs gave the "parent" householders status, and provided a subject of conversation, as well as a year-round diversion. But the emotional crisis of seeing an adopted member of the family killed, and then eating the flesh of a half-tame creature that they had nursed, may have helped give some of the women nervous breakdowns, and it may also have helped the men believe the fanciful explanation of the whole cycle which they had been taught.

Their rationalization was as follows. Like other animals, when living in its own country the bear assumes human form, and lives in a house like those of the Ainu, but when seen by an Ainu that "house" looks deceptively like a den. The Owner of the Bears, the Bear *Kamui*, is a huge bear living in a large house atop a mountain or between several peaks, at the head of the local river valley. The Owner of the Bears never leaves his own country, but his deputies live in other parts of Bearland. In March these deputies assume human form. Then a special fire spirit, under the command of Kamui Fuchi, the Fire Goddess, orders them to go visit the Ainu who, in this fantasy, have nothing to do with hunting bears or capturing or killing clubs.

When a deputy bear spirit arrives at an Ainu's house it enters it through the sacred east window and presents the host with gifts, the bearskin and bear meat, which it has brought with it from the mountains. In return the host gives the spirit the hospitality it is due as an honored guest. After the bear spirit has accepted the special shaved stick, or *inau*, made for it, it goes back in human form to the mountains to report to its chief, where the latter accepts the gift. If the deputy gives a favorable report and the gift is satisfactory, then the Owner of the Bears will send out more deputies the following year.

What really used to happen at a bear sacrifice has little resemblance to that tale. No matter who caught and reared the cub, the sacrifice took place in the headman's yard. Well ahead of time the women began getting food ready, particularly dumplings or soft millet cakes. They made these in three sizes: large ones for the bear spirit, middle-sized ones for guests to eat, and small ones to be scattered outside so that children could scramble for them.

The day before the main ceremony guests from nearby settlements began to arrive at the local headman's house, bringing more food. On the day itself the headman or another *ekashi* (elder) prayed at the hearth to Kamui Fuchi (the Fire Goddess), and offered her libations. Then other household deities and spirits were taken care of, and the participants filed out into the yard. The *ekashis* were all dressed in their finest robes and wore fillets of curled shavings. They carried swords which they would brandish at appropriate moments to keep evil spirits at bay.

Some of the men set up a post in the ground, anchoring it firmly, decorated it with fir boughs, and tied *inaus* to its top. Other men then took the bear out of its cage, pulling it through a hole in the floor. They slipped a noose about its neck and tied ropes to its limbs. They tugged and dragged it about the yard, goading and baiting it to make it angry. Still others shot blunt, unpoisoned arrows at it, like bande-rilleros harassing a bull; they brushed it with fir branches, while singing traditional songs.

Then they tied the bear to its post, and a man chosen at the last moment — to keep his identity from the evil spirits — quickly shot it with a poisoned arrow tipped with a bamboo head, trying to hit it in such a place that as little blood would be let as possible. If the blood reddened the snow, no harm was done, as long as none of it touched the bare ground. The bear died, and its spirit began to leave its body.

An *ekashi* prayed to the departing spirit, and bowmen shot magic monkshood arrows over a place where children had previously set up spits of dumplings, like marshmallows on sticks. At this point men carrying two logs approached the bear's body and pretended to strangle it (as indeed was done in still earlier times), acting with clumsy buffoonery. The onlookers laughed. If the bear was a female, they decorated it with a mock necklace and earrings of straw.

The men skinned the body, and caught its blood in cups. All males present drank the blood. The presiding *ekashi* prayed to Nusa Koro Kamui, the Creator, to request his presence at this moment in the ceremony, the time when the bear's flesh and head were handed through the east window into the house. Then the men made offer-ings to their totemic ancestors and the women to their ancestresses, using *inaus* whittled for them by the men. Children scrambled for millet cakes and played tug-of-war.

Inside the headman's house the bear's head had been set up in front of the east window, and by the time the celebrants had returned from the yard, the meat had been cooked. The feast began. Food was placed in front of the bear's head, including some of its own flesh. Everyone present was given some of this sacred meat — some more, others less, according to rank.

After the meal everyone drank and danced, and the party ended with some of the men lying drunk on the floor. How it used to end before the Ainu got liquor, we do not know. After a two days' rest, the celebrants walked to the next settlement and began over again. In a few weeks the younger men would be setting out to seek new cubs for the next year's round.

The Eskimo bladder feast

On the Pacific coast of North America we revisit a stretch of almost three thousand miles in which Alaskan Eskimo, Northwest Coast Indians, and Californian Indians held elaborate winter ceremonies of different kinds which are not easy to summarize. Among the Alaskan Eskimo, the principal motif was the Bladder Feast. It was based on the idea that during the winter rites they could lure the spirits of the sea animals they had killed during the previous year back into their own bladders, which had been saved. Then, during the Bladder Feast, they would return the spirits inside the bladders to the sea — through holes cut in the ice, if necessary. Thus they could hope to ensure the continued abundance of these species on which they principally depended for their food.

During these winter rites, feasts were also given to celebrate the successes of a young hunter in killing his first mammal of several given species, ending with a bearded seal, or sometimes a polar bear. In this way the young hunter progressively entered a state of full manhood, and finally made himself eligible for marriage.

Theatrical productions and potlatches on the Northwest Coast

On the Northwest Coast, dramas were enacted to re-create the mythical events in which the ancestors of the heads of clans or lineages had first encountered the totemic animals or spirits that had given them their power or principal rights, and the use of their crests. These crests were painted on house boards, boxes, and mortuary poles and woven into some of their robes. By means of magic quartz crystals invisibly propelled through the air in pantomime, chiefs of winter villages and of confederations were invited by other chiefs to feasts at which the seating arrangements were as rigidly controlled by rank as at a modern state banquet. Long speeches were delivered, and gifts presented to the guests in order of rank, with the first getting the most.

Some of these parties were potlatches, of which everyone presumably has heard. Whatever the stated reason for holding a potlatch, (and there were many events which could be so celebrated) their principal function was a competitive exchange of gifts. The host would give his guests presents of blankets, sheets of Alaskan copper beaten into standard forms, canoes, and sometimes slaves. The principal recipient would then be expected to stage a repeat performance in which he outdid the first one, but eventually everyone would come out more or less even. The competitors accumulated some of these gifts from their followers of lesser rank, and borrowed others at interest, depending on the circumstances, and redistributed what they had received to the original contributors.

Elaborate, even feverish potlatching, with a competitive destruction of property, including canoes and slaves, reached its peak during the latter two thirds of the nineteenth century after European contact — when imported diseases had decimated the population — and after the Canadian government had put an end to warfare. Then there were more than enough rights and crests to go around; some of the men could earn money in white men's sealing schooners; and the Hudson Bay Company's blankets were available as a convenient medium of exchange.

Such potlatching rose to its zenith among the nobility of the Kwakiutl Tribe, then settled around Fort Rupert in British Columbia. It was described in a detailed and oft-quoted monograph by Franz Boas, but it was atypical, and an artifact of white contact.

The Nootka "shaman's dance," an annual puberty ceremony

Among the Nootka Indians of Vancouver Island the principal winter ceremony was the so-called Shaman's Dance, but it was basically an initiation for boys and had nothing special to do with shamans. It always came at the same time of year, although not every year, but only when there were enough male novices available to warrant it. For this reason the novices varied considerably in age. One pregnant woman went through part of it in order to initiate her unborn child, hypothetically a boy. Thus it was not a simple puberty rite in the strict sense.*

A chief sponsored the ceremony, and other men acted as speakers, captors, drummers, and, for one part of the rite, torturers. Teams of men and women put on separate dances, in three age grades. In the dances they imitated various animals and plants. The old women might imitate something as inactive as a sea anemone, while younger, more vigorous people might play the roles of deer or birds. There were also individual dances or skits, some of them both comic and obscene, like the fumbling sexual attempts of an impotent old man.

During these dances no one was supposed to pronounce the Nootkan word for wolf without paying a penalty. Now and then a middle-aged woman would do so accidentally-on-purpose, so that her clothing would be torn off, leaving her naked. The reason for this word-tabu was that the captors of the novices were supposed to represent the spirits of wolves.

The captors were commoners who had inherited the right to play this part. They went about on all fours, with wolf skins tied on their backs with some of the skin protruding over their heads, and had bull-roarers for tails. They also carried cedar-wood whistles operating on the principle of the double vibrating reed, or shawm, as in the chanter of a bagpipe, and emitting an equally loud and piercing sound.

During the first four days of the ceremony guests assembled in the house where it was held, and they engaged in much noisy rough-housing, practical joking, and smashing of boxes and other objects. The reason for this was that meanwhile the "wolves" were capturing the novices, tearing off their clothes, and sneaking them in through the rear door to the back of the house, where they were made to sit silently behind a curtain, and the uproar that they heard would impress them.

Theoretically, however, the "wolves" had not brought the novices

*The details of the ceremony were long and complicated and varied from village to village and from time to time. There were long schedules and short ones, and some of the boys went through more of it than others did. Philip Drucker's account of it fills 57 pages, and only a brief summary of its major points can be included here. (Philip Drucker, 1951, pp. 386-443).

into the house at all, but had whisked them out to a special place in the woods to instruct them, give them magic crystals to invite guests with, teach them their songs, and decorate them in various ways, particularly with tufts of shredded cedar bark. Actually they lowered the curtain at one point, and some of the boys danced forward to receive rights due them by inheritance, and for them that was the end of their isolation. The "wolves" did take the other boys out into the woods later, whether or not it was to the sacred place where real spirit wolves had once carried the ancestral chiefs who had originated the ceremony. Each village had its own sacred spot.

At one point in the schedule, the speaker asked some men to call the wolves, and one man was sent to sit on the roof to listen for them. Other men sat facing planks which they beat with sticks as if they were drums, making a prodigious noise, and the man on the roof would call down through the smokehole: "Louder, louder, the wolves can't hear you." Finally when the noise had reached its maximum the man would say: "The mountains are trembling now," and the wolf calls could be heard in the distance. Actually the concept of the mountains trembling was not fantasy on the part of the Nootka, for Vancouver Island is earthquake country, and I myself have been through a severe one there.

Now that the "wolves" had been called and had replied, the next step was to bring in the novices, who were supposed to appear out of the woods somewhere up the channel, and men, women, and children set out in boats and on "rafts," being pairs of boats lashed together with planks. When they reached the right place, the "wolves" would make furtive appearances, ducking back into the dense growth. They would appear with one novice, always the one of highest rank, then take him back again, and so on until all had been shown, in anywhere from four to eight appearances. They then came out, and the people on the water landed and put up a mock fight; a chief might drop on the shore and pretend to be dead, overpowered by the strong magic of the "wolves."

Back in the house the dances continued, the novices doing their share, acting as the youngest age grade, and often representing birds. At another special point during these dances some men who had the right to do so seized young men who had the hereditary privilege of becoming war chiefs. Each captor bit his victim in several places on his body where he had pinched up folds of skin. The biting was to deaden the pain of what followed, for then the captor ran a harpoon head through the fold of skin, leaving the harpoon line trailing. After considerable bleeding these harpoon heads were removed by slicing the skin, leaving permanent scars.

At the end of the ceremony each novice's father or grandfather formally introduced him to the assembled group, announcing his new name. In the case of novices whose fathers were of insufficient rank to allow them to do this, the chief who had sponsored the ceremony would introduce them instead. Although rank was shown in this and many other ways during the ceremony, the seating in the house was not by rank; it could hardly have been so because there was too much dancing and milling around.

The Maidu "secret society," another annual boys' puberty rite

So rich were the Indians' stores of acorns, seeds, and other surpluses of food in Central California that they too could devote most of the winter to a succession of rites. Between October and May, the Maidu of the Sacramento Valley performed at least sixteen separate, unique dance ceremonies, some of which were attended by guests from other villages. One of them was the meeting of the so-called Secret Society, which was nothing more than the usual boys' initiation rite more or less coinciding with puberty, and performed when the chief shaman, having decided that there were enough candidates, set the time. Besides him, there were numerous other specialists: the village chief who was chief instructor; his assistant, who taught the boys dancing; various prompters; a singing leader; a clown who mocked serious actors and gave the boys orders which meant that they should do the opposite. A female transvestite was in charge of the boys' sex education. She demonstrated this by copulating with each boy in turn. The whole rite may have taken as long as two months.

We have previously mentioned that the tribes of southern California around the Los Angeles region were organized into moieties, but they also had dance clubs, which were really voluntary associations, because membership in them did not depend on kinship or band affiliation. These bands acted out rites of their own for the edification of others, just as the members of cult totems used to do in Central Australia, as in the oft-cited witchetty grub ceremony, where the members dramatically insured the continued abundance of that insect from year to year.

The Waiwilak ceremonies of Australia

In northeastern Arnhem Land in northern Australia, members of different clans of their two moieties, Dua and Yiritja, act out another set of ceremonies based on an origin myth. This country is flooded between mid-January and May. When the floods recede, the rivers shrink and the land is green. For the next four months all kinds of wild foods are plentiful, and large numbers of people can assemble at sacred ritual grounds from distances as great as eighty miles away. The succession of rites that they perform may consume the entire season.

The origin myth runs as follows.

Two sisters of the dream-time once lived in the Waiwilak country far to the south, where they had incestuous relations with kinsmen. (There seems to have been no one else available.) The elder sister had borne a boy-child and the younger one was pregnant. They were Dua people. They left home and started walking northward through various parts of the Dua territory toward the Arafura Sea, the older sister carrying her baby in a bark-sling on her back. On the road the younger sister gave birth to another male child.

As they went they collected many kinds of vegetable foods and killed many kinds of animals. With these burdens they rested when they came to a great rock called the Python's Back, at the foot of which lies a water hole. Deep down in it lives a giant copper-snake, Yurlunggur, the Great Father. He is the python-totem of the Dua moiety.

The elder sister made fire and the two of them started cooking all the vegetable and animal foods they had collected, but all the plants and animals ran out of the fire, the yams running on legs like men. All of them jumped into the pool and disappeared. They were the totem species of the present-day clans.

Now the elder sister went out to gather bark for her little nephew's bed, and in her search she walked over a shallow part of the python's pool. She was menstruating, and her blood dripped into the water, sinking to where Yurlunggur lay. He was elder brother (classificatory) to the two women. He hissed. Clouds appeared. Rain fell. Water rose in the pool.

The sisters sang the ritual songs and danced the sacred dances to prevent the flood from rising and the python from swallowing them. But during the night all of the snakes, lizards, snails, caterpillars, and other creeping things assembled, for they had heard the call of their father Yurlunggur. The sisters now sang all of the sacred songs that are used today in their ceremonial cycle, starting with the least sacred, known to women, moving on to the more sacred ones known only to men, and ending with the most secret of all, the song of Yurlunggur and the menstrual blood.

When Yurlunggur heard it he crawled out of his hole and into the camping ground. There the two sisters and their children had fallen into a deep sleep, drugged by the serpent's spell. He licked them all over. He bit their noses and made them bleed. Then he swallowed them, the elder sister first, then the younger, and finally the two boys.

Then he stood up, fully erect, on the end of his tail. His head reached high into the sky and the floodwaters rose with him. The other pythons, totems of different sections or clans of Dua, stood up too. Yurlunggur asked them all what languages they spoke, and they told him. All were different. Then Yurlunggur said: "We can't help having so many languages, but anyhow we can all hold our ceremonies together."

While still standing on their tails, the snakes asked each other what they had last eaten, and each one of them named some totemic species. Yurlunggur was asked last, and being ashamed, he refused to answer, but finally the others coaxed it out of him and he told them. At that moment the dry, southeast monsoon began to blow and Yurlunggur fell down, and his fall created the dancing ground at that part of the present ceremonial grounds where the very sacred Djunggan rites have since been held.

As he lay there he spewed out his four victims onto a green ant bed. They were dead. He crawled back into his water hole, keeping his head out to watch. A didgeridoo trumpet (made of a hollow treetrunk or limb) appeared on the edge of his water hole and walked about all by itself. It blew its droning tones over the four bodies. Green ants crawled out of their bed and bit the two women and their infant sons, and they all jumped up.

Yurlunggur crawled once more out of his hole and hit the heads of his four victims with his singing sticks, so that they bled. Then he swallowed them a second time, and again another snake asked him what he had eaten, and he replied: "Bandicoot."

Said the other snake: "You lie."

So Yurlunggur said: "Two Dua women and two Yiritja boys." (This was the first mention of the Yiritja moiety, needed to exchange marital partners with the Dua moiety.)

Once more Yurlunggur fell down, and in falling he created the part of the dancing grounds where the less sacred Ulmark and Kunapipi ceremonies are held. Then he slithered back into his hole and swam through underground waterways to the Waiwilak country, where he crawled out again into the open and spat out the two sisters. They turned into stone, and may still be seen. But he kept the boys and swam back to his own country, where he let them go, and they were the ancestors of the Yiritja people.

While this cosmic drama was taking place in the north, two Waiwilak dream-time men heard the snake's voice from afar, and the thunder and the heavy rain. Knowing that something was wrong they began to follow the two women's tracks and finally came to the place where Yurlunggur had bashed their heads, and they found their blood. They collected it in two bark baskets, and made a didgeridoo trumpet out of the roofpole of the two sisters' hut, and they fell asleep. During the night, when they were dreaming, the spirits of the sisters came to them and taught them all of the sacred songs and all of the rituals, and then departed. In the morning the men awoke and sang and danced all of the songs and rites in the whole cycle, just as they have been performed ever since, and the women have not known the secrets since that time.

In the minds of the aborigines, the Waiwilak myth is as real as the Book of Genesis is to a fundamentalist Christian. The details of the myths and of the rites reenacting them are one and indivisible, while the feat of memorizing the song cycles and the ritual dances and other acts is more impressive than that of a Muslim memorizing the entire Quran, and nearly as great as learning the *Iliad* by heart.

The exact number of rites and their details vary regionally, and even the names and rites of the mythical persons represented differ in various accounts. In all of them cult membership is determined by moiety affiliation, rather than by having been born in a certain locality, as in central and western Australia. In the Murngin region of northwestern Arnhem Land, W. Lloyd Warner observed six rites, of which three are performed by everyone: the Djunggan, the primary circumcision rite; the Kunapipi, a fertility rite which ends with wife exchange and mass copulation; and the Ulmark, a sort of finishing school for the older initiates. We shall describe the high points of the Djunggan and Kunapipi, but omit the Ulmark, which is so long that it may last through two whole dry seasons, and essentially repeats what is in the others.

The Djunggan circumcision rite

The Djunggan rite came first each year and sometimes lasted as long as two months. It had two principal functions: to circumcise the younger boys of several clans, and to pass the older boys of a preceding class a step further toward full manhood.

Its principal symbol is a trumpet representing Yurlunggur, and the first step in the ceremony is for some old men to find a small tree whose trunk has been eaten hollow by termites. Having found it they trim it and test it for its tone and resonance in a hut in a clearing

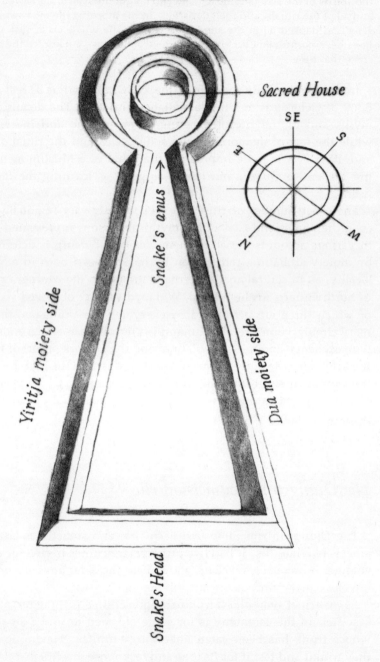

Schematic of
The Snake's Dance Ground

Sacred House

SE

E

S

N

W

Snake's anus

Yiritja moiety side

Dua moiety side

Snake's Head

31. The sacred ceremonial ground used in the Djunggan circumcision rite of the Murngin People, Arnhem Land, Northern Territory, Australia. (After W. L. Warner, 1937)

in the men's camp. By the sounds of this testing the people within earshot know that the Djunggan time is approaching, and men make arrangements to circumcise boys of the proper kinship status, ideally a future son-in-law of the boy's circumciser.

When the boys hear the trumpet blow, their fathers tell them: "The Great Father snake smells your foreskin and is calling for it." Frightened, the boys cling to the women, and the women pretend to fight the men to keep the snake from swallowing their boys.

Now pairs of boys set out on a journey with an older man who is their real or classificatory father's sister's son or a sister's husband, to visit other clans and relatives, and to invite them to the ceremony. The boys may stay out more than a month. Having previously gone about naked and unadorned, the boy is now decorated with white feathers on his body, white paint and armbands on his arms, ochre and fat on his face, a hair belt, and a pubic tassel. His hosts on his route give him presents, and return with him.

Meanwhile the men left behind prepare the camp. Among other things, they set up a tipilike frame of poles lashed together at the apex. They tie leaves to the top and strew other leaves on the ground below and nearby. The poles are named for the Dua, the leaves on top, for the Yiritja. After the circumcision the leaves underneath and to one side, having caught the blood from the boys' penises, will be burned.

The ceremonial grounds are divided into five separate areas, or "camps." On the periphery is the general camp, open to everyone. Next is the men's ground, from which women and children are excluded; within that the "old" men's camp, and its totem house; a fourth and nearby area is the totem "well," in which the totemic emblem, being the sacred trumpet, is kept during part of the ceremony; and finally, the snake's dance ground. These camps have *dal* (power) in various degrees. This power is contagious and dangerous. It is most concentrated in the old men's camp and in the sacred emblem. It is weakest in the general camp.

The snake's dance ground is rather impressive from the engineering standpoint, considering the tools—simple digging sticks—available for its construction.

The lines represent walls of earth ten feet high, covered with leaves. The triangle is about fifty feet long, the snake's head twenty-five feet, while the circular wall enclosing the sacred house is fifteen feet in diameter. The triangle represents Yurlunggur's body with the sisters and their offspring inside it. The sacred house is a windbreak about four feet high—high enough, with its wall, to protect its occupants from view. In it sacred dancers representing monitor lizards paint themselves and hide until the time comes for them to crawl out and do their dance.

After the sacred snake's dance ground has been prepared, or simply refurbished after its last ceremonial use, the men set up the conical pole structures with their leaves in the general camp. The boys have now returned from their journeys. After sunset the women dance around the poles singing, with their knees bent. The men rush out and surround the poles to protect them from the women. Meanwhile the boys have been kept in seclusion. Some of the men go to fetch them and carry them on their shoulders to the snake's dancing ground, and make the boys lie down. The men build a fire nearby and sing a cycle of sixteen songs explaining their totemic animals, birds, and other totems, and perform animal-mimetic dances.

The leader of the whole Djunggan ceremony, who is a Dua man of the Liaalaomir clan which owns the sacred python pool, now calls out the names of the totems of his clan and of other Dua clans with the same totems. An old man then walks to the edge of the enclosure, facing the old men's camp, and calls out the totemic names of the various parts of the country of the Liaalaomir clan, where the swallowing took place.

Then the leader calls for Yurlunggur's tongue. All of the boys who are to be circumcised have their heads covered with women's mats. Four or five men, who have unobtrusively slipped out of the enclosure, blow the trumpet from afar. Then the trumpet appears. Three or four men carry it, and one blows it. He blows it over each boy's head, the men carry it back to the old men's camp, and the mats are taken off the boys' heads. During this episode the older boys see the trumpet for the first time.

The next performance comes when men of the Dua and Yiritja moieties take turns dancing alongside the triangle, imitating the wallaby—a Dua totem—and the gray kangaroo—a Yiritja totem. After this they dance in turn inside the triangle, coming out of the snake's anus on either side next to the enclosure of the sacred house. Sometimes, instead of the wallaby and gray kangaroo, the men dance the rock kangaroo and hawk, to symbolize the practice of burning over the grass for hunting during the latter parts of the dry season, in order to kill rock kangaroos, which are Dua totem animals. The hawk, a Yiritja totem bird, circles in the air during the burning, on the lookout for snakes disturbed by the fire. Meanwhile, in the general camp, an old woman seizes men's spears and chases the younger women to discipline them.

Bloodletting is the next step. Before it, the old men paint the trumpet, which is Yurlunggur, with ochre, which is blood. We must remember that the python is more than just a water symbol or a male sex symbol; it is the most dangerous animal in Australia, comparable to the tiger and the bear in the forests of Asia.

On the day before the circumcision the older men give blood to be used as an adhesive in putting on their costumes. The first time a man gives blood the trumpet is blown over him. This is done because a man who gives blood for the first time is in a dangerous position. Actually some men faint after giving blood, and may even remain in a coma for two or three hours. The trumpet-bearers hold its mouth against the donor's body while the blood flows from his arm, and meanwhile the other men sing three songs, "Human Blood," "The Snake's Totem," and "The Snake's Hiss." After each song the men take turns calling out the names of each one's mother's mother's brother, boasting: "He has a big penis!" "He catches a lot of fish!" and other signal attributes. Each man can call out as many names of persons in that relationship as many times as he wishes. Then they sing five more songs: "The Ground Shaking," "The Snake's Tongue," "Dua Lightning," "Black Rain Cloud," and "Rain Cloud over the Sky."

The men who have given blood now enter a special relationship with all the other men who paint with their pooled blood for dancing. They are, in effect, blood brothers, and can expect hospitality from one another when they camp together or visit.

The blood first given by a man is considered to be the blood from the head of the older Waiwilak sister. The trumpet, when held against the man's body, is the snake swallowing that sister. The songs sung during each such episode of first bloodletting repeat the whole biting and swallowing episode. When the men take the boys away from the women, these men are the snake and the flood is taking them.

On the circumcision day itself, a point of climax is reached. The men paint their bodies with the blood, two men painting each other with brushes made of chewed green sticks. Then the older men paint the boys who are to be circumcised on the dance floor. Dances follow: The Dua men represent Dua totem animals, and the Yiritja men are Yiritja totem animals. The men rush into the area known as the snake's body for each dance and pretend to fight each other.

355

Then the monitor lizard men, who have been making each other up secretly in the sacred house, emerge one by one into the adjoining part of the triangle known as the snake's anus, and the trumpet is blown over each of them in turn. These men represent the snake's children.

On the final day of the Djunggan, the men assembled at the snake's dancing ground paint the stone heads of their spears with blood left over from body-painting, pick up the boys to be circumcised, and carry them on their shoulders, as women carry babies, to the general camp, all of the men in single file. The blood on the speartips represents Yurlunggur, and if the women ask about it the men say that they have killed the snake so that it will go underground, but the men themselves believe that the snake did not really die.

In their camp, meanwhile, the women paint themselves rather crudely with pipe clay and ochre, and dance around the leaves and grass in front of the pole structure where the boys are to be circumcised. After a brief period of general confusion the assembled company divides into two halves, each honking like wild geese, while the leader of the Djunggan cries out the common (not sacred) names of the totems for geese and the places where they are to be found, such as holes left in the mud where the geese have been feeding. Now the men surround the boys, and the women weep.

For each boy, two men lie down on their backs. Each boy is given a shell of water to drink to keep his mouth moist during his ordeal. This will be his last drink until the following day. Then a basket is put in his mouth for him to bite on to help him bear the pain. Some of the women closely related to each boy about to be circumcised whip themselves with twigs to transfer some of his pain to their own bodies. If a boy weeps audibly, the men try to mask his cries by calling out in a loud trill supposed to be a snake's voice. The women dance around the men while the boys are operated on simultaneously. The boy's foreskin is placed in a bark basket filled with water, and given to his father, who is supposed to give it back to his son after the latter has grown up. As soon as the cutting is over, the leader of the rites plucks a feather from the decorated body of each grown man, as a signal that the ceremony is over.

Meanwhile one man picks up each boy and carries him back to the men's camp. Each man who carried one of them then washes his own hands and the boy's wound. The man then warms his hands over a fire-stick and transfers the warmth to the boy's penis, just

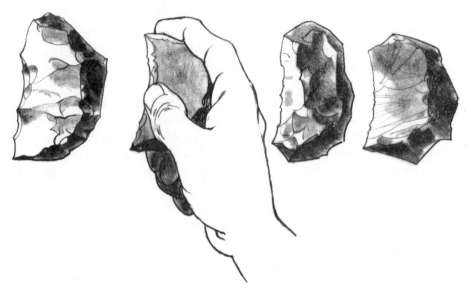

32. Australian circumcision knives

as in Tasmania an old woman warmed the injured testicles of a man hit by a piece of kelp on the beach, as we have seen.

Up to this point the boy has been allowed to eat anything he pleases, but now he is forbidden the flesh of large animals until the end of the next rainy season. On the following day the men build a fire on the part of the men's camp facing the general camp, heat some stones, and place two logs on either side of the fire, and another pair of logs crosswise atop them. This rig is a seat for the boys. Then the men throw lily leaves or bunch-grass soaked in water on the stones, and steam rises. The boys are seated over the stones, and the steam is supposed to enter their rectums, go through their bodies, and come out their mouths. This steaming is intended to make the boy strong, to keep him from being greedy, and to insure him plenty of food later on.

Now the older men warm their hands over the fire, place one hand over a boy's mouth, and rub the boy's navel with the other. While so doing they give the boys instructions as to their conduct as men, such as never to use obscene speech or to go after other men's wives, to obey their fathers and respect their elders, and never to reveal to women and children the secrets they have been taught.

The leader now begins to sing over again the round of totemic songs sung earlier in the Djunggan, beating time with his singing sticks. The men remove the boys from their perch over the stones and seat them on the ground. A man now brings in a bark tray covered with small bites of each kind of food available in the camp and pellets representing other foods then unobtainable.

The food-man now gives a boy a piece of each food in turn, asking him: "What is the name of that food?" Another man seated next the boy whispers the food's sacred name, and the boy repeats it aloud, then swallows it. As he names each food correctly, all the other men cry out: "Yai! Yai!" The men tell the boys that if they reveal these sacred names to the women and children they will be killed, which means, of course, by sorcery if not by violence. The men remove the boys' pubic tassels and replace them with new and different ones, to symbolize their change of status. After this has been done the boys are watched over by older men who keep them away from women and children until their wounds have healed.

After the novices have been dealt with, attention turns to the older boys of the next grade, who have been allowed to see the awesome trumpet for the first time. They are put on a vegetable diet and told not to speak, for a period set by the leader of the rites—usually no more than a week. After this they are taken to the snake's dancing ground and painted with the totemic designs of their clans while the leader, and the men painting the young men, sing the totemic names of the clans, and of the animals and water holes found in the territories of each.

When this is over, relatives of each boy give presents of food, weapons, and other artifacts to the leader of the rites, who shares some of the gifts, particularly the food, with the rest of the older men. Finally, the custodians of the sacred trumpet bury it secretly in mud by the dark of night. The next time the ceremony is held, they dig it up again, and if it is in good condition they use it over again after repainting it; if not, they make a new one.

In this lengthy succession of rites only partly and sketchily recounted here, all of the movements of the Waiwilak myth are sung and acted out, with the climax coming at the bloodletting by the fully initiated men. This individual and collective sacrifice symbolizes the biting and swallowing of the sisters and their sons as a consequence of sacrilege. It also symbolizes death and rebirth. The circumcision itself is not part of the myth, only the statement that the sisters were unable to circumcise their sons as they had intended. The instructions to the young men fall wholly outside the cycle, being a common element in initiations in general.

This recitation of the rules of adult conduct, resembling in a sense the Ten Commandments, in this case follows shock treatment when the adolescent mind is particularly impressionable. It resembles in a way the imprinting observed by students of animal behavior, and even more the instruction by ordeal undergone by recruits in modern guerrilla schools. By these ancient and practical techniques of pedagogy, much may be learned in a necessarily short time, while the camaraderie of the older men who do the teaching is renewed and strengthened. In the latter case the critical event is creating blood brotherhood by mingling the blood from each other's arms.

The Kunapipi

While the other rites of the Waiwilak cycle follow more or less the same routine as the Djunggan, one of them, the Kunapipi, introduces a new element. It is Kunapipi herself, a mother goddess who represents fertility. She is always pregnant, and has a clitoris so long that it drags on the ground. She is said to have first appeared out of the sea at the mouth of the Roper River in eastern Arnhem Land, and to have made her way inland by a zigzag course over a well-known route. According to one version she deposited her children as she passed, and these children became the ancestors of the present population. After the rains each year, she was also held responsible for sending out the spirits of the animals and plants, after being impregnated by the Rainbow Snake, more or less identified with Yurlunggur.

Ronald Berndt estimates that the Kunapipi rite originated after the arrival of Indonesians on the coast, and that in recent times it spread rapidly as a reaction to the effects of white contact, as did the Ghost Dance of the American Plains Indians, the Peyote Cult of the same general region, and the Cargo Cults of Melanesia. Like the other cults cited, it was an ephemeral manifestation, for after the estab-

N*

lishment of missions in Arnhem Land it began to decline owing to the churchmen's disapproval of licentious rites.*

Like the Djunggan, the Kunapipi may also take two months, and in some regions it may begin before the rains have ended. Its overt purpose is to initiate boys into its mysteries, but without mutilation, and the participants decorate themselves with down, feathers, and other materials stuck on with blood. Some wear elaborate head-dresses representing pythons and other creatures. Instead of a snake's dancing ground, the holiest enclosure, also surrounded by earthen walls, represents Kunapipi's womb, and in it are held the most sacred dances. During most of the ceremony the boys being initiated are kept in seclusion under the care of elderly guardians.

The various episodes of the Waiwilak myth are danced with appropriate songs, some borrowed from the Djunggan, and with the usual swallowing and regurgitation. The voice of the python is represented, not by a trumpet, but by bull-roarers. During tense moments clowns appear, in some episodes represented by dancers made up as bush-warblers, silly-behaving birds. The clowns imitate that bird's cry in high, piping voices, in ridiculous contrast to the deep, vibrant tones of the men's singing.

Apart from the womblike earthen enclosure, a hut is set up with forked end-posts and a roof-pole, and covered with bark. This represents the Waiwilak sisters' house. The women also fabricate two tall but lightweight and flimsy dummies, consisting of poles padded with paper bark, lashed with string, and painted. Atop each is a leafy crown simulating palm fronds or pandanus leaves. While profanely these towering mock-ups represent the trees named, in a more sacred sense they represent two pythons, male and female rainbow snakes, actually alive inside the posts.

During the later rounds of dances, men representing male and female animals of various species, the males wearing bark penises, mimic the act of copulation. Notable among them is the opossum, considered to be a somewhat humorous and very libidinous fellow.

Under a full moon, on the last night of the Kunapipi rite, comes its climax, the ritual copulation of the human participants, said to represent the incestuous acts of the Waiwilak sisters which produced their children. This orgiastic ritual has been preceded during several days by suggestive horseplay and sexual joking to raise the libido

*R. Berndt, *Kunapipi* (1951). W. L. Warner (1952) has also described these rites as performed in the Murngin country in considerable detail.

of some of the participants to a fever pitch. Some couples who could not wait have already been practicing in the bushes.

The usual arrangement is for two men in the appropriate kinship relationship to agree to exchange wives. Because there is often a shortage of women, one woman may receive several men. In the dancing which precedes the copulation, some of the women, over-stimulated, hold open the lips of their vaginas and simulate copulation with sticks.

After the dancing the couples pair off, and their usual coital position is for the man to sit on the ground, leaning slightly backwards, with the woman's legs around his lower abdomen; they grasp each other's shoulders at arms length, and thus permit a maximum penetration. In some cases the couple's bodies are separated by paper bark to prevent the woman's sweat from pouring onto the man's body. In any case, after intercourse the male partner wipes the sweat off his own body onto that of his female companion's husband, to keep the former from "getting sick."

Unmarried girls are not allowed to participate in these activities, and the boys being initiated are kept in their camp under close supervision. The next morning the boys are paraded out, suitably painted, and the women assemble with their bodies painted with red ochre. The boys are now secreted in the brush shelter, symbolizing the Waiwilak sisters' house as well as Kunapipi's womb. While the boys are hidden inside, actors perform rites on the roof, lifting up the mock snakes over it, apparently to "swallow" the boys. Finally the initiates emerge, cleansed and reborn.

The Great Hut rites of the Yaghans

Comparable to the Djunggan and the Ulmark were two successive initiations held by the Yaghans. They were called the Great Hut rite and the Men's House rite. If possible they were held in winter, but if too little food was available at that season they were held at some other time when it was more abundant, particularly after a whale had been stranded. When news of such a windfall spread, people would gather from considerable distances, and if they could muster enough candidates to warrant the effort, they might decide to hold an initiation ceremony, which might last from a week to several months, depending on how long the food lasted and how rapidly the candidates learned their lessons. The school might also end when people were getting restive and bored.

We have noted earlier that the Yaghans had no chiefs, no councils of elders, nor clans or other extended kin groups. There was no division of labor other than that between the sexes in a technological or political sense, yet the Great Hut and Men's House rituals were organized in a surprisingly complex way, with eight categories of officials other than the candidates themselves. These were a leader or master of ceremonies, an overseer who had the final authority, a teacher, a number of guards including a chief guard, two sponsors for each candidate, and nurses or baby-sitters who took care of the young children and kept them away from the Great Hut in which the initiations were held until the time that they too would have become eligible.

Members of both sexes were admitted to the Great Hut rite. The girls were allowed to take it only after menarchy, but boys were accepted when their elders judged them to have reached a sufficient level of mental maturity to be able to absorb what was to be taught them, and enough discipline to endure the accompanying ordeals. The age of the male candidates thus varied from about fourteen to twenty-seven. A boy had to go through two successive Great Hut ceremonies before he was allowed to marry; it is not stated whether the girls needed one round or two. At any rate, before the arrival of the missionaries and other whites, Great Hut ceremonies were held often enough so that a competent candidate of either sex could get through young enough to avoid a serious delay in getting married.

The contents of the rites were kept secret from all who had not gone through them, and the very existence of the ceremonies was unknown to the whites, including the missionaries, until 1921, when Nelly Lawrence, the Yaghan wife of a missionary's son, inadvertently pronounced the Yaghan word for Great Hut in the presence of the anthropologist Gusinde. After he had found out, with much difficulty, about the ceremony, he persuaded the surviving Yaghans to stage it, and went through it as a candidate twice. When later he had returned from Austria, his sponsor and mentor in the rite upbraided him soundly for not having gotten married afterward. He died in November 1969, still celibate.

The Great Hut was a long, oval structure built on the same domed principle as the round ones used for habitations, and strong enough to hold one or more guards sitting on the roof, to withstand both the buffeting of the winds and the shaking given the walls by the performers in order to drive inquisitive spirits away. At the end facing the camp was a relatively wide entrance, and at the end facing the forest was a narrower one through which the candidates could slip in and out unobserved by the people in the camp. Each entrance was covered with hanging skins.

The hut in which Gusinde was initiated was about thirty feet long and ten feet wide. The huts had been longer in the old days, sometimes holding fifty to eighty persons. In either case its roof was high enough for people to dance upright along the midline, which served also as the fireplace, bordered with logs. Inside, sticks painted black, white, and red were tied along the walls, and other such sticks dangled from the roof. Their designs were simple bars, circles, and dots, said to be without special meaning.

About forty feet away on the camp side the participants also built an ordinary-looking hut for cooking, to feed all those inside the Great Hut. Four or five initiated women would be cooks. They would take turns preparing the food so that each of them would miss only parts of the performance each day.

The chief guard personified a predatory sea bird, *Leucophaeus scoresbii*, that is often seen with blood on its beak, and he therefore displayed a streak of red paint running from his nose to his chin. He also wore a special headband of white albatross feathers. He or one of his assistants sat on top of the hut to drive away children or strangers with the fierce cry of the bird he was impersonating, and also to keep an eye on novices who might be permitted to leave the Great Hut to relieve themselves, or to gather firewood.

Inside were the leader, an active and nimble man who directed the various parts of the rite; and an older man, the so-called overseer, who quietly directed the leader, telling him when he made mistakes. Inside the Great Hut the seating arrangements were as follows: one sponsor, his or her novice, the second sponsor, a trio of sponsor-novice-sponsor, and so on around both sides of the hearth.

Early in the first day the leader and the overseer entered, first to meditate, and in so doing to prepare for their routines. Then came the other fully initiated persons, including the teacher and the sponsors. Each male novice had either two male sponsors or one of either sex, and the female novices had two female sponsors each. Incidentally, the sponsor-novice relationship held throughout life. The sponsors still gave advice, and their novices took care of them when old. In at least one case a boy's sponsor was his uncle.

Each of these persons wore a forehead decoration made of a piece of albatross or goose skin with feathers on, held in place by a headband, and each carried a dance-wand, about eighteen inches long, pointed at one end, painted white with red lines and dots, and with a ring of down glued near the pointed end.

Shortly after everyone but the novices had been seated, the principal male sponsor of each boy quietly absented himself to decorate himself in a special fashion, for he soon had a special role to play. Later, at a signal from the leader, the guards removed a long strap of hide from one wall of the Great Hut. Holding this strap stretched out, they ran out in single file to the hut where the first novice was hiding, seized him, tied him up, and carried or led him to the Great Hut. The guards then shoved him through the front entrance on his hands and knees, and when he was just inside a man clapped a piece of skin over his head, effectively blindfolding him. At that moment everyone inside began to howl and to beat the ground.

Once the candidate had been seated, still blindfolded, his chief sponsor appeared, painted and otherwise disguised as an evil spirit, Yetaite, who lives underground. Yetaite keeps a sharp eye on people's conduct, and if they don't behave he jumps out of the ground to punish them. The ritual Yetaite had powdered ochre in his rumpled hair, red paint on his face with white lines radiating from his mouth, white paint all over his body, and a feather ornament hanging between his shoulders. With him came an assistant wearing a wreath of twigs on his head, the upper part of his face black, the lower part red.

When Yetaite appeared, others poked up the embers to illuminate the chamber. Yetaite seemed to leap out of the flames, and at the same time someone else removed the novice's blindfold.

Yetaite seized the boy, shook him and pressed him against the ground, while the others present screamed and pounded the earthen floor. After about ten minutes, when the boy was in a cold sweat, the leader of the ceremony cupped his hands over his mouth and shouted: "Hoo-Hoo!" meaning that Yetaite is dead. The Yetaite-impersonator next crouched in front of his victim, and another man sitting next to the boy said: "Look closely, that is So-and-So (quite often the boy's uncle)." That man would be the boy's special sponsor for the rest of the ceremony. The sponsor-novice relationship was one of a greater intimacy than that between the boy and his father, and would remain so for life.

The rest of the candidates were brought into the Great Hut in turn and the performance was repeated, except that the girls were not made to undergo the Yetaite ordeal, but as they saw it done to the boys, they were frightened enough.

After these rigorous introductions the routine began. Except when excused for natural needs, sent out to collect firewood, or led out to be given special instruction in the woods or on the beach, during the rest of the ceremony each candidate had to sit up, cross-legged, in the small space assigned him, motionless and silent. Though rain might drip on his back, no one would plug the hole in the roof. Someone might place a grub or insect on his back, but the novice could not remove it. If a funny story was told, he might not laugh without receiving a reprimand. In punishment for any such breach of conduct or other disobedience, his sponsor and the leader sent him down to the draughty end of the Great Hut, near the smaller entrance, to sit by the door without food for a day or two.

For the first four to six days each candidate was given only one mussel to eat, in the afternoon, and a drink of water, sucked through a bird-bone tube from a snail shell. His sponsor saw to it that he slept only between midnight and about five in the morning. If he fell asleep at any other time someone would poke him saying: "Sometime you will have to sleep upright in a crowded canoe. It is better that you learn to do it here."

During the evening, the novices were led to the beach to bathe. Three times during the ceremonial period they were also taken there to be tattooed, each time in a horizontal line around the chest, except for the skin over the spine. First the lines were drawn with ochre, then the incisions were made with mussel shells, and the ochre was rubbed in. The ensuing marks looked like blue lines under the skin.

Three times a week the novices were given lectures, lasting about an hour each, by the teacher. He was a man of impeccable conduct who sat silently for hours in advance, preparing his speech in his mind. The discourses covered the totality of the Yaghans' rules of adult behavior between the sexes and between members of different age groups. For example, the girls were told that if their husbands began to pursue other women, they should pretend not to notice it for the first few times, and then a husband will probably tire of his affair, and come back.

When the candidates were sent to the forest to collect firewood, they were told not to loiter or eat mushrooms or other snacks on the way, for the spirits living in old treetrunks might see them and report. Actually the guards kept them under secret observation. During the latter part of the ceremonial period the candidates were also led to the beach by some of their sponsors for practical instruction and testing. The boys were taught how various species of animals behave and shown how to harpoon them, with baskets as targets. The girls were taught how to make baskets and to collect shellfish. If a candidate failed to perform satisfactorily, the instruction would be prolonged accordingly.

While all these events were transpiring, the other people in the house sang. Each person sang alone, repeating a single word over and over with variations in pitch, and without melody or harmony. The purpose of this singing was not group entertainment, but to put each singer into a private state of spiritual exaltation. In the late afternoon everyone sang more loudly. They stood up, one by one, holding their dance-wands between the fingers of both hands, and glided with shuffling steps from one end of the Great Hut to the other along the hearth, in which the fire was by now almost out. The candidates were allowed to stand up and dance, accompanied by their sponsors.

The session was over when one man danced down the hearthline and back again, holding his dance-wand horizontally, begging food from those seated, redistributing it to others, and finally eating a little of it himself. He was sending away the spirits that had come to the ceremony. Everyone made a gesture of pulling something toward his or her body, thus putting his or her spirit back inside if it had temporarily wandered out. Then everyone stuck his dance-wand in the ground, hung up his headband, and went to sleep.

The ritual period ended when the people in charge thought that the candidates had learned as much as they could; when someone died; when they ran out of food; or when the participants were getting restless or bored. Then the leader announced the finale. A curtain of sea-lion skins was hung up in the rear of the Great Hut, and the candidates were seated behind it. The people left behind in the camp appeared as audience, and all were painted. A middle-aged man went behind the curtain and led the candidates, now graduates, out. They danced up and down the hearth several times, and then each one's chief sponsor took his or her hand and invited him or her to sit down. This was the incorporation part of the ceremony, the end.

The Yaghan men's house ceremony

The next rite is the *kina,* or Men's House Ceremony, through which all young men who had passed through the Great Hut rite twice were initiated into full manhood. Its candidates might vary considerably in age because some of them would have failed the Great Hut test at least once, before they finally passed.

Its context was the myth of the Great Upheaval and Flood, in which the men stole the women's secrets and thus gained power over them. It might immediately follow a Great Hut rite or a mourning ceremony, or it might come independently, according to the circumstances and the wishes of the men to get together.

The men built a conical log house, decorated it, and chose a leader, who, according to Gusinde, always happened to be a shaman, although it was never specified that he should be. They also let in two older and trustworthy women, needed as actors.

As in the Great Hut rite, novices were brought in blindfolded, then attacked by not one but two spirit impersonators, in this case wearing conical masks reaching to their shoulders and containing eyeholes. When his blindfold was removed the candidate was ordered to unmask the actors by grabbing at their heads. He did so, saw who they really were, and was warned never to reveal the secrets of the Men's House on pain of death.

At one point there was a terrifying ruckus in the Men's House which was easily heard from the camp. The two older women, believed to be captives, had meanwhile pricked the insides of their noses with sharp sticks to make them bleed. They rushed out and cried to the onlookers that they had escaped the evil spirits' murderous attacks, but that all of the men had been killed. Later the men emerged, covered with their own blood let in a similar fashion and wiped on each other. They danced in front of the assembled women and children to show that they had come back to life, and that the evil spirits were dead.

There followed much singing and dancing in the Men's House and the recital of the cycle of the Yoaloch brothers and their sister, which was never rendered in its entirety elsewhere, and of which fragments were given only in the Great Hut. This cycle contains elaborately detailed instructions for all kinds of behavior.

Finally the men, including novices, painted and masked themselves to represent numerous spirits, including those of birds and animals, and appeared from the beach or forest. They danced on the open ground between the Men's House and the camp, moving sidewise, and this went on until food was scarce, the actors and audience grew bored, or both.

Conclusion

The periodic rites exemplified here resemble, in principle if not in detail, those of many other peoples, from hunters to industrial nations. They include Christmas, New Year's Day, and Memorial Day in the United States; and Guy Fawkes Day in Great Britain. On a broader, more international scale they have a counterpart in the Olympic Games.

The overall function of these ceremonies and celebrations is to bring together people who do not see each other from day to day, at times when they can lay aside their work for a day, a weekend, or for longer periods. They are just as basic a part of human nature as speech, the dance, and the visual arts, all of which media of communication are highlighted in the rites themselves.

16.

Shamans and Healing

In the preceding chapters we have written enough about shamans to make them so familiar a part of the hunting scene that they need little introduction here. Stated briefly, a shaman's job is to allay anxieties produced by mysterious causes. These causes are usually believed to be the malicious handiwork of evil spirits, angry gods, or other hostile forces beyond the reach of ordinary men. To thwart them and thus to restore the affected person or persons to health and peace of mind, a specialist needs to be called in. This specialist is someone who has learned how to communicate with spirits and to deal with them on their own terms. He is believed to be telepathic, clairvoyant, and able to move material objects by what modern parapsychologists call telekinesis. The feats of some shamans witnessed by a number of fieldworkers and other western observers have impressed them deeply. Whatever else he may be, the shaman is a gifted artist.

Healing is only part of his business. Some healing is done without the help of shamans, just as we attend to simple illnesses without doctors. The Tasmanians, for example, could relieve a stomach-ache by chewing and swallowing a simple vegetable purge, the leaves of the fig-marigold (*Mesembryanthemum equilaterale*). The Mbuti Pygmies relieved constipation by giving the affected persons enemas of vegetable potions administered through hollow lianas. The Akoa Pygmies of Gabon used for medicinal purposes at least twenty-nine plants botanically identified by Father Trilles. A comparative study of ethnopharmacology among hunters would be both revealing and exhausting, but it is not needed here because it seems that such practices are universal and none of them, apparently, requires the ministrations of shamans.

The same may be said of overt wounds. There was nothing mysterious about the cuts on the chest that Mulka Bill received in a double duel at Mungeranie (pages 257–258) or the surgery by which native Tasmanians amputated an arm shattered by gunshot, the amputee being King Billy, one of the last Tasmanian survivors. (This should not be surprising, for one of the Neanderthal skeletons unearthed in Shanidar Cave, Iraq, had had a withered arm amputated, and the pollens of blood-stanching flowering plants were found in the soil around his bones.)

In inland regions of northern North America, a diet deficient in fat may result in dizziness, weakness, and eventually delusions leading to attempts at cannibalism. Farley Mowat, when he first visited the Caribou Indians west of Hudson Bay, began to feel this when he tried to set out in a canoe. A half-breed gave him a can of melted lard to drink and he was cured. Among the Northern Algonkians, who believe in a mythical cannibalistic monster called Windigo, some persons acquire a Windigo complex. They see real people around them turn into edible animals and try to kill and eat them. Before such a person actually goes berserk, he can sometimes be cured by feeding him large quantities of melted fat.*

Another curative technique, intended for general disability, is for a person to sit in a sweat-house, which works on the principle of the Finnish sauna. In its simplest form this is no more than a frame of poles in which a person sits immersed in steam from water poured over hot stones. Not only does this treatment have therapeutic properties, but it also helps a person in search of supernatural power. It is in common use among many North American Indians and also reaches across northern Asia, where it probably originated.

Among many hunting peoples, some ailments cannot be cured in so simple a fashion as those just mentioned. A mysterious illness, such as a person's gradual loss of energy and appearing to waste away, often seems to be the result of sorcery. The patient's soul may have been taken away, or some ill-wisher may have projected an invisible missile into the patient's body. In order to effect a cure, the soul must be captured and put back, or the disease object retrieved. Both these techniques require the services of a well-trained expert — a shaman, also variously known as a medicine man or doctor.

A shaman has two jobs to do in trying to effect a cure: diagnosis and treatment. He must first find out who or what supernatural being was responsible, and then what steps to take. Some shamans also have other work to do, like controlling weather, and predicting where and when food is to be found. In these roles they are involved in rites of intensification, because weather and food concern the entire community which the shamans serve.

For various reasons, some peoples have no shamans, as in the case

*Vivian J. Rohrl, "A Nutritional Factor in Windigo Psychosis." *American Anthropologist*, February 1970, pp. 97–101.

of the Mbuti Pygmies. Others, like the Tasmanians, combined the noncurative parts of the shaman's work with that of the chief. Among the Birhors the chief, acting as a priest, is in charge of rites to ensure success in the hunt. Some have shamans serving only as healers, while the diagnosis is left to others, or vice versa. Still others have a division of labor between shamans, some healers, and other weather-controllers.

The Ainu: diagnosing and curing

The Ainu have no male shamans. In each settlement the headman, who is also the chief elder, serves as priest in the salmon ritual and other rites, and he must also have memorized the elaborate body of Ainu myths and prayers and know how to perform many rites, including those of healing. In one sense he is also a diagnostician because he practices divination by means of the animal skulls that he keeps in an ornate box in a sacred corner of his house.

If he wishes to predict the outcome of any enterprise, or to determine the guilt or innocence of a person accused of breaking a tabu, he will take the lower jaw of a fox out of his box and place it, teeth up, on top of his head. After appropriate prayers he lets the jaw slide off his forehead onto the mat on which he is sitting. If it comes to rest teeth up, the answer is yes; if down, no.

He can also use this method to check the efficacy of each one of his collection of skulls, to see if they are warding off evil as they are supposed to do, and he will discard those for which he receives a negative answer. This skull-screening is important to him personally in the event that he himself should fall ill. When that happens he places the skulls that have passed the test on a tray near his head, in the belief that they will send away the evil spirit that is afflicting him.

While he may thus take steps for arranging for his own cure, he cannot do it for others who may seek his help. Instead he calls on the services of a *tusu*, or female medium, a diagnostician who has herself been cured of a nervous disease called *imi*, one that particularly affects women. It seems to be a byproduct of the Ainus' chronic anxiety about following correct ritual procedure during the entire annual calendar, and of the hardships entailed. Psychoneuroses were particularly common among women, who lacked the overt, exhibitionistic outlets of the men. Women had to move to new communities at marriage, rarely left home, and worried about the safety of their husbands and sons who went out hunting and might be killed by mistake by a poisoned arrow from a set bow. Nor did they wish to be left as permanently unmarried widows to linger on as cantankerous crones.

The symptoms of *imi* were hysterical neuralgia, eye trouble, chronic headaches, arthritis, and functional paralysis, sometimes accompanied by nightmares and compulsive actions, such as saying or doing the opposite of what was expected or intended. Once she had been cured, such a women would undergo a sudden outpouring of emotion comparable to conversion, but would still behave peculiarly. Women cured of this disease sought each other's company, and other members of the community poked fun at them.

When the evil spirit that had possessed her had been driven out of her body, a good spirit would then hover near her to give her information when she entered a state of trance to perform as a medium, or *tusu*. This spirit might be the goddess of snakes, or that of a friendly fox, caterpillar, or hornet.

When a person fell ill, other members of the family called in the chief elder and a *tusu*. The chief elder put the *tusu* into a trance by incantations and then the *tusu*'s protective spirit, through her mouth, named the spirit responsible for the patient's illness. Then it was the chief elder's job to expel the spirit. He did this by whittling appropriate *inaus* (shaved sticks) dedicated to friendly spirits, and by prayer. In one case, when it was found that the patient was possessed by the spirit of a hornet, the chief elder made an imitation hornet's nest out of wood shavings and waved it clockwise six times around the patient's head.

But if the patient was another women suffering from *imi*, the culprit usually detected was Pauchi Kamui, the powerful, specialized spirit of insanity and hysterical dancing. Then an elaborate performance had to be staged, involving other persons in a sequence of symbolic procedures divided, like a play, into three acts.

The first one took place in the patient's house and its surrounding yard. The elder began by whittling an *inau* for the Fire Goddess, Kamui Fuchi, who had to be invoked first as an intermediary to the other gods and spirits. Having set this up at the hearth, he prayed to her to inform her of his patient's condition. With the help of two female assistants he then led the patient out of doors, where he invoked the spirits of the yard itself, those of the privy, the Sky God, the God of Vegetation, the God of Hunting, and the Owner of the River, at their special stations on the spirit fence, to which were attached many *inaus* and a number of animal skulls.

Then the elder, the patient, and the two female attendants, followed by onlookers, walked down to the river, where they set the stage for Act II. There the elder set up *inaus* for a dozen gods and spirits in ritually prescribed positions, some along the bank for the water deities and others on a spirit fence farther inland for the High Gods. At the lower end of this fence he hung a sword to represent the Fire Goddess, who could not leave the house.

After this the participants built six Houses of Evil, being arches made of reeds, four feet high. At the top of each they tied some stems and leaves of *Polygonum sachalensis*, a plant related to burdock, from the hollow stems of which they also made the model boats in which they floated the visiting salmon spirits back to the sea after the salmon ceremonies. The purpose of these festoons was to send Kamui Pauchi's evil away when the arches were burned.

On either side of each arch they laid a bundle of reeds and herbs possessing magical qualities, and two other bundles were also set beside the *inaus* of the six water spirits on the bank. The two bundles laid beside the spirit fence of the High Gods were different, being made of a species of evergreen bamboo. All of these bundles were switches or scourges, to be used for whipping the evil spirit out of the patient.

Once the stage had been set, the performance moved rapidly First the elder prayed to all the gods and spirits invoked. Then the first arch, the one farthest from the river, was set afire and the patient was made to stoop and pass under it, and as she emerged each of the female attendants beat her six times with their switches, while saying *sotto voce* to the deities: "Pay attention! Pay attention!" This routine was repeated at the five other arches in turn until the patient had reached the bank where the six *inaus* had been stationed.

She was made to walk from one to the other, accompanied by the two women, who picked up their switches at each stage, dipped them in the river, beat her with them, and threw them into the water to float downstream. Finally they reached the *inau* of the female spirit of the undercurrent, and there each of the two attendants picked up two round pebbles, one in each hand, and struck them together to let Kamui Pauchi know that they were ready for him. Then each woman stroked the patient down her sides and front with the pebbles, and one of the women had to repeat this act with the two other pebbles. Then they threw all six of them into the river.

After this the three women walked up to the spirit fence of the High Gods, where the elder stood. Picking Kamui Fuchi's sword off it, he brandished it in the air, slashing and cutting and exhaling "Fuo! Fuo!" in a hoarse whisper, while the female attendants muttered "Fusa! Fusa!" Both phrases meant, as before, "Pay Attention!"

Next the elder held the sword straight up at arm's length and the attendants beat the patient six times each with the bamboo stalks, removed her outer garment, and laid it on the ground. In the old days, when the Ainu were still able to afford it, they threw the robe into the river and let it float away, and .. the patient were only hysterical and not entirely insane, they threw her in too, and pulled her out again. Then the three women returned to the bank, washed their faces, and poured water on their heads. The attendant women reclothed the patient, and led her back to her own yard, followed by the onlookers.

Act III then began. In the patient's yard, the elder prayed to the gods whose *inaus* hung on the spirit fence, the attendants switched the patient again with bamboo, and they again removed her outer garment, which in this case had not been thrown in the river, or her attendants removed it for her. The attendants shook it and hung it out in the open air. Then they led her into her house where they switched her for the last time. The elder burned the *inau* he had carved for Kamui Fuchi at the beginning of the rite, which had now ended.

After all this attention, excitement, exercise, beating, rubbing, singing, playing the leading role, and perhaps having been doused, the patient had every reason to feel better, at least temporarily, if she could feel at all. If Pauchi Kamui's evil were to creep back into her body, she could go through the ordeal again, or she might become a *tusu*. In that role she could inform the elder via spirit communication about what was wrong with other sick people, particularly women afflicted with her own ailment.

It was a great show, an elaborate rite of passage including separation, transition, and incorporation, along with the symbolic antagonism of fire and water, two elements that in this case worked together to drive the evil out of the patient's body and wash it away. The division of labor between the elder and the female medium made it unnecessary for him to go into a trance, an act that would ill befit a dignified man who was both a chief and a priest, and he did not have to make a spectacle of himself by performing sleight of hand or sucking disease objects out of his patient's body. But by having gone through a period of illness herself, and having thus acquired the power of communication with spirits in a state of trance, and by being separated from the rest of the community by her odd behavior, the *tusu* really was one kind of shaman, a diagnostician.

The powerful shamans of the Yaghans

For our second example we return to the Yaghans, whose rites of passage in the Big Hut and Men's House were described in the last chapter. They also held a third, or graduate, school, for those of the Men's House alumni who wished to go on into the shaman's profession. In view of its rewards in prestige, the temptation to do so was great, and many who had ambitions in this direction tried it. Some became minor operators, but relatively few were able to withstand the ordeals of the training schedule and to win out in the contests of personalities that produced shamans of more than local renown.

A really powerful shaman achieved a reputation like that of the one of whom the following story was told. Once there was a long spell of stormy weather; food was scarce, and people asked their shaman for help. He dreamed, and told them that they should go west along the southern shore of the channel on which they were camped, to such and such a place, and wait. In his dream, he said, he saw two female whales who were sisters. Each had a little whale in her belly, almost ready to be born. But a false killer whale (*Pseudorca crassidens*) approached them and threatened them, and they pleaded with him: "Don't kill us, or you will take four lives." But he attacked them anyway, and they were stranded on the flood tide. The people went to the place designated and waited, and sure enough the two pregnant whales were washed ashore, just as he had said. It was Nelly Lawrence, the Yaghan wife of a missionary's son, who told Gusinde that tale, and she added: "There are no shamans like that left nowadays."

There are several ways in which a putative shaman may acquire his guardian spirit, or spirit helper. A man walking in a forest alone may be approached by one of the numerous spirits that live in old tree-trunks, and the latter offers to be the man's guardian. Or he may encounter the spirit of a sea animal on the shore. Or in a dream he may see a giant whale, comparable to the giant elephant of the Akoa Pygmies. This is the most powerful spirit that a shaman could have as his familiar. A man who dreams of the giant whale has received an imperative call that he cannot resist.

The Yaghans' shamans' school

A man with a strong call, from a whale or whatever, may be in a state of semitrance for a few days, fasting and avoiding his fellows. Other people notice his condition and talk about it, and an established shaman may invite him to join himself and others in a session of a shamans' school. When they get enough candidates they will assemble in a secluded place where there is likely to be enough food to feed several families for some time. There they build a conical log house like that of the Men's House ceremony, and the session may last several months. During this time the candidates and their teachers sleep and eat in the house, and must remain chaste for the duration of the course, even if a few frightened women should be admitted as semicandidates who may never expect to become first-class shamans.

The leader is the most prominent among the shamans on the staff, and a few middle-aged men who are not shamans serve as helpers, to provide food and firewood and to prevent disturbance. In the evenings male visitors may be allowed in to observe quietly the candidates' progress.

Everyone in the house is completely naked, and every shaman and male candidate paints himself all over with pieces of lime or dried white clay, shredded off with his teeth and mixed with saliva. When this coat has dried they scratch lines through the paint on each other's bodies. Female candidates, helpers, and visitors paint the upper parts of their bodies white, with red lines running from the corners of their mouths to their ear lobes. This is, apparently, a second-class uniform.

Everyone has his own, assigned seat. The candidates sit with their legs out straight. Each candidate keeps his head from touching the wall behind him with a pad of soft, spongy, rotten wood taken from one of the trees in which guardian spirits live, and if he lays his head on the ground this spiritual insulator must serve as a pillow.

At about four in the afternoon the routine starts with singing, and this keeps up until about two or three in the morning when Sirius and Procyon, the stars into which the Yoaloch brothers were transformed, reach their highest point in the sky. At dawn the candidates awake and are fed, all of the food, such as it is, being cooked in the house. A candidate starts with three mussels a day, plus a mussel-shell of water drunk through a bone tube. Later his ration is cut to two mussels, and finally to one. If mussels are in short supply a fish tail may be substituted for each bivalve. After this meager breakfast, his only meal, each candidate remains silent until noon. On some days they are then sent out after firewood, or, under the supervision of women, to collect mussels which they cannot then eat.

Like many other hunting peoples, the Yaghans believe that a shaman's body is differently constituted from those of other persons, and that the transformation begins here at this school. Each novice takes a ball of fine shavings scraped from wild barberry wood, mixes it with dry white paint, and rubs it on his cheeks, a half hour or so at a time, at frequent intervals throughout the day. This rubbing is supposed to remove his cheek skin and to grow three new layers which are progressively more sensitive, until the last layer of ultra-sensitive skin spreads over his whole body, growing invisibly larger, so that he can feel things about him that his visible body cannot touch, some as much as one hundred yards away. The shamans attentively watch this progress, which they apparently can see. The novice that gets a whole new skin first is considered their most promising candidate.

While these skins are growing and expanding, the shamans frequently hold their cupped hands over the fire and pour its warmth over a novice's head, and they also put warmth into the latter's mouth with one hand. These two movements are said to remove a wall of fog from in front of the novice's eyes so that he can see his guardian spirits and sing to them. The songs they sing are those taught them by their guardian spirits at the time they first appeared to them. Every once in a while one of the shamans puts himself into a trance by singing softly and swaying. Then he falls over, and the novices imitate this performance. Or he may begin suddenly to sing louder, which means that the spirit has entered him and is doing the singing, and gradually this animated singing peters out and dies down as the spirit leaves him. In the evening, the shamans may tell each other about the visits they received from their guardian spirits that day.

Sometimes the spirit-visits become contagious. During the singing one shaman may cry out: "My spirit is coming quite close!" He stands up, bending over; he touches each of the other men and asks: "Who are you?" and receives an evasive answer: "Oh, I am just a native of this part of the country." Others leap up and announce the arrival of their spirits, until the house is full of them, and excitement rises. During the session attended by Gusinde a female candidate named Emilia, whose first husband was a great shaman, pushed a spirit into the fire, whereupon the spirit shot a magical disease object with his sling, but Emilia caught it in one hand and rubbed it invisibly into the hand of Santiago, a male candidate, saying: "I now give it to you!" Then Emilia caught another spirit from the ice on Cape Horn and rubbed it into Gusinde's body.

After such a session the spirits leave one by one, until only one person continues singing, and in a weak voice; but someone may start another round, and so on again until it is time to go to sleep.

In this school candidates are taught to communicate with spirits in dreams during trances, but they also learn more active tricks, such as sleight of hand and swallowing and vomiting up disease objects. This latter type of instruction is probably given privately because it is too secret to be revealed to the mixed audience at the sessions described.

The Yaghan shaman in action

A practicing shaman's activities include healing, weather control, hunting magic, and seeing into the future to foretell events, as in the case of the two pregnant whales that were driven ashore. While shamans normally secure their own food like other men, and are in this sense only part-time or overtime specialists, they nevertheless specialize in their magical practices among themselves, some in healing, others in the use of astronomical knowledge, in controlling clouds, rain, snow, ice, and the movements of sea currents, land animals, and water animals.

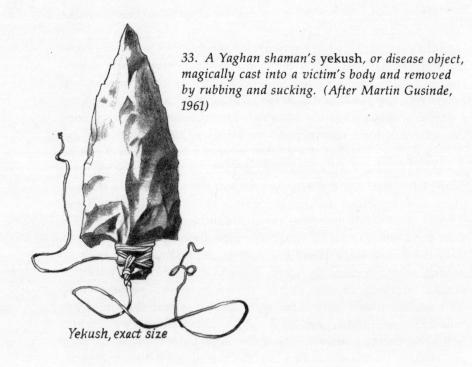

33. *A Yaghan shaman's* **yekush**, *or disease object, magically cast into a victim's body and removed by rubbing and sucking. (After Martin Gusinde, 1961)*

Yekush, exact size

While staging a performance the shaman wears a special costume including a headband of pale gray feathers of the night heron twined together with three strands of tendons, and when off-duty he carries this headdress in a bag. He paints his entire body white and rubs powdered white paint into his hair. Except while healing, which requires rather strenuous physical activity, he usually performs in a so-called dream during which he communicates with spirits and does all sorts of prodigious, supernatural deeds which he announces after he has come out of his trance.

Some of these concern his casting, from a magic sling, a magic arrowhead called a *yekush*. A shaman also has actual stone arrowheads which he keeps in his stomach and can produce by vomiting to convince his audience. So important are they in Yaghan shamanism that the term for shaman is *yekamush*, a derivative of *yekush*. He may shout in a dream, saying: "I have caught a *yekush* thrown by another shaman, in my right hand, and I now put it on the ground in front of me." It is of course invisible, but the audience may believe him whether or not he has moved his hand.

If a person falls ill he may first try a herbal remedy, but to be on the safe side he may also call in a shaman, one whom he trusts. Many ailments, including especially those that affect the nervous system, are believed to have been caused by a hostile person's getting a shaman who is on his side to throw a *yekush* into the victim. The healing shaman paints himself and dons his headband, then puts himself into a partial trance, rubs his patient to find out in what part of the body the *yekush* is located, and then enacts a vivid struggle with the *yekush*, and rubs and sucks until he vomits, and spits out an arrowhead with a string attached to its tang. He exhibits this object in front of his mouth on the palm of his hand, for all present to see, and then he blows it away, and it suddenly vanishes. If the patient should die later, he obviously came to the shaman too late, and if the patient's illness is too advanced the shaman may not produce any arrowhead at all, but simply say that the illness was brought on by the sky god Watauinewa, who is responsible for all deaths.

As for the shaman's powers of prediction, Gusinde witnessed two that came true. On March 22, 1923, a shaman said in his presence: "I see a long canoe approaching with Vigua cormorants in it." Next day a large flight of those birds crossed the channel, something that they rarely do, and in such numbers. And one day at noon Emilia, whom we have already mentioned, said: "The sea is getting white. High waves are rising, with much foam." It was then dead calm. The next day the high sea that she had described rolled in from the east.

When shamans wish to attract the spirits of land and sea animals to them to ensure good hunting, they stretch out both arms, open their hands and clutch the air, then draw their closed hands back to their bodies, open them, then rub them down as far as their knees, whispering "sst!" In this way they capture the creature's spirits and can control their movements.

Sometimes the people gathered on a beach to feast on stranded whale meat keep on eating it after it has spoiled, and many of them become ill all at once. When this happens the shamans bring them together an as audience and perform the concluding rite of the Men's House ceremony, in which attending spirits are dismissed. In this way they make the sick people believe that the spirits that are poisoning them will similarly depart. This is powerful magic, and in putting on this show the shamans exercise vital leadership in a crisis. After European epidemics were introduced, more and more of these performances were needed.

But shamans can also unite communities against each other, as illustrated by the following account. Once there were two brothers both of whom were powerful shamans. They quarreled, and each led his followers to an opposite side of the channel on Ponsonby Bay. The one on the north side had a dream. He got in his canoe and went halfway across the channel, where he met his brother in another canoe, and each of them threw a magic arrowhead into the other's body and returned.

When the north-shore shaman awoke, he told his people this dream and added, "I am now bleeding from the nose and mouth and will die." And so he did, and they lit the customary triple fire as a smoke signal to inform the south-shore people of his death. But as soon as the smoke from their fires rose in the air, they saw three more columns of smoke rising from the south shore. When the two groups got together they discovered that each brother had told the same story when they awoke, and they had died at exactly the same time. They were thus shamans of equal strength.

Australian supershamans: Munkumboles

Our scene now shifts across the stormy southern sea to Australia, and to the fertile Lower Murray River Valley. In this country there are mighty shamans as well as powerful chiefs and wise councillors, and the shamans include healers and weathermakers as well as supershamans who are well versed in the ordinary shaman techniques, but in addition specialize in intertribal relations concerned with peace and war. The name for such a supershaman is *munkumbole*, and he stands at the head of the shamanistic hierarchy. His speciality is clairvoyance, and he is able to see events in both the past and the future.

His role in peace is to meet with other tribal *munkumboles* in a new-moon ceremony, and to work out agenda for the intertribal gathering that would follow, with recommendations based on visions. His role in war is to warn his chief of an impending attack, and to give him precise information on the numbers of raiders to be expected, and the time of their arrival, as well as the outcome.

On the night before the attack, the *munkumbole* sleeps near the chief, with his head on the latter's shield. He sees his chief's men being driven back, rallying, and counterattacking. When he wakes up he sings to the spirit controlling the battle and pleads that his chief be protected from the enemy's weapons. He recounts to the chief what he has seen, and adds that, owing to the latter's great prowess, he saw the chief thrust the spear that brought victory.

Before sunrise the *munkumbole* awakens a herald, who calls to the fighters to get their weapons ready, sees that they have plenty of spears and clubs, and instructs them to leave the camp so that the women and children may be at a safe distance from the battleground. These instructions are given in the *munkumbole's* presence. He then leaves the rest to the chief and departs, for he will take no personal part in the combat, and he may have to join his peers later in peacemaking.

Other and lesser shamans are more active participants in warfare, particularly in vengeance raids against an offending member of another tribe. In the narrative that follows as an illustration of such an activity (one that may have happened in early colonial times, or even before), we must remember that the Lower Murray Valley has been occupied by white men for over a century and that memories of vengeance raids are richly embroidered with magical concepts. We shall make no attempt to separate what really happened, from our point of view, from what was told.

Vengeance with a magic rope

When the kin of a slain man are thirsting for vengeance, one of them, who is not necessarily a shaman, makes a magic rope out of human head hair, or obtains the use of one previously made. These hairs have been cropped from the heads of many persons, living and dead, and twined into a two-strand rope about an inch thick and twelve yards long. Each strand is twisted between its maker's thumb and forefinger and rubbed with ochre and animal fat to make the hairs stick together before the two strands are combined. Once completed the rope is placed in an emu-skin bag with the feathers inside, and it must be allowed to rest there for seven days.

When one of the elders is about to die, a brother or son of the dying man is asked for permission to place the bag under his body so that he may expire on it. Once he is dead, the participants wind the cord

o

about the corpse with one end in its hand, and the other end passing out the door of the hut, where it is held by a man. The body is left with the rope around it until decomposition has reached an advanced stage and the rope has thus absorbed the strength of the deceased's spirit. Now the rope is sensitive to the wishes of whoever is to use it, provided that it be kept warm and dry in its emu-skin bag. On their mission the rope will guide the avenging party through scrub bush and over mountains and rivers, creating a cushion of air just over the ground to speed them on their way.

When the time comes to use this rope, a shaman, who is to be a member of the party, speaks to it, naming the intended victim and telling it what is expected of it. Then twelve kinsmen of the man who is to be avenged carry it to the sacred ceremonial ground and stretch it to its full length. The twelve men stand back from it, chanting a song of vengeance, and dance around it for half a day. The next morning the shaman goes to the ceremonial ground and clears a space free of grass, sticks, and stones, builds a mound the length of a man, and marks on it the outline of the victim's body, with his head to the west, where the spirits of the dead go.

Having finished this effigy the shaman returns to camp to get the other men, and the latter return with the shaman and the rope. The twelve are painted in red ochre and pipe clay. The elders also appear, and sit in a circle around the effigy, but women and children are excluded. Then a stake is driven between the effigy's feet. One end of the rope is tied to it, and the rope is stretched along the midline of the effigy's body straight out to the west, where its other end is tied to a second stake.

The elders now chant a death song, beating the ground with their hands and naming the intended victim. One of the twelve avengers now takes his place at the head of the effigy. He holds the rope loosely in one hand and walks in this position to the end of the rope, over which his hand slides. Then he opens his hands and makes a gesture of throwing some invisible object toward the west, chanting: "You are going, with the sun, into the western sky." The other eleven repeat this performance in turn.

Until sunset the elders continue, at intervals, to beat and chant, and when the sun drops behind the horizon the twelve men stand in a north-south line facing the west, six on each side of the effigy. The shaman now shouts: "Spear the body" and they all jab their spears into the mound. Then they pronounce the victim's name and blow their breaths toward the west. They pretend to weep, walking toward the west, and chanting: "May the victim soon die." Finally they disperse to their huts and the shaman retrieves the rope, and coils it on his bed where he will spend the night.

Seven days later the expedition takes off, traveling by night, and in the instance recounted, mostly along river courses, passing through several tribal territories where different languages are spoken. When they approach an intermediate camp they may make their presence known by beating on a dry gum tree or striking two throwing sticks together. A man who speaks several languages may stand up in back of the firelight to address them in a loud voice, asking who they are and what their mission is. Then the people in the camp will give them permission through fear of the rope, and they indicate this by three blows on a gum tree or three pebbles thrown into the stream. Sometimes the party may be invited to stop and eat. They sit about a hundred yards from the camp, are given food, and carefully burn any scraps to avoid their use in other harmful magic.

When they arrive within a night's march of their destination they camp, and for two or three days send out scouts to locate the enemy camp and to identify their victim. On the evening before their attack they talk with the spirits lodged in the rope, who assure them of their help. Once the victim is asleep the shaman creeps to his hut with the rope, and the others arrive one by one from different directions.

The shaman unwinds the rope, takes a few turns around a throwing stick, and creeps into the victim's hut. With the use of the stick to avoid contact he winds some of the rope around the sleeping man's arms, neck, and body, taking care not to let the victim touch the rope with his hands. While the victim is being tied, all of the participants focus their thoughts on the victim. Then they gently draw on the rope and he follows, still unconscious, and lies down on their knees with his face to the sky. Unsheathing his flint knife, the shaman cuts a slit in the victim's side, below the ribcage, inserts a finger, and pulls out a piece of kidney fat, then presses the sides of the slit back together.

They then lay him on the ground with his head to the west, remove the rope, and leave. Before long the Grandmother Spirit who lives in the Milky Way comes down and revives him. He stands up and yawns once each in the direction of the four cardinal points, with the last yawn pointed west. He returns to his hut and again sleeps. The Grandmother Spirit heals over his wound to conceal the cut, and cleans up all of the blood and other traces of disturbance at the scene of his operation. Then she rises in the air and returns to the Milky Way.

Back in their home camp, the members of the successful mission invite the elders to reconvene on the ceremonial ground to view the victim's kidney fat. They look at it, and one elder gives the shaman a piece of curved bark from a branch of a gum tree, smoked and rubbed with emu fat to polish it. It is to serve as the victim's coffin. The shaman puts the kidney fat in it and takes it away.

Meanwhile the victim feels uncomfortable, and begins to ache, and he gradually comes to suspect that someone has pointed a bone at him or bewitched him in some other way. If the local shaman is unsuccessful at diagnosing and curing his illness, his relatives light a smoke signal to summon in a *munkumbole*, who has a vision telling him who did it, when, and in what way. To prove his point he shows the onlookers a previously unnoticed scratch on the victim's skin. The victim then dies, his soul goes west with the sun, and his fellow tribesmen meet to decide on countervengeance. Then the latter will hold their own rites, and the feud will live on, until the white squatters squat, and few of their descendants have the faintest glimmer of what devious and heroic deeds once went on in their marvelous valley.

And so it goes, the whole world over, and has been going on for ten thousand years, a portentous number. Perhaps someday, as the Andamanese believed, the earth will turn over. Then the dead will live and the living die.

17.

Conclusion: What Can We Learn from Hunters?

The importance of insanity to human survival

What are we to conclude after having read the preceding chapters? A man works for weeks to make a human hair rope six fathoms long and soaks it in corpse juice so that he may use it to mesmerize a victim, whose kidney fat he then cuts out. Does this make sense? Why should the wife of an Eskimo whale-boat owner walk about with a special wooden .bucket several months before the hunt is to take place, in order to give the prospective dying whale a drink of fresh water? Are hunters crazy?

The answer is, of course, that such seemingly irrational acts serve a social purpose. Indeed, *man might be defined as the only·animal that needs to be insane in order to survive.* When he becomes coldly practical, discards his beliefs and rites, begins measuring and counting things accurately, building efficient machinery, inventing weapons of mass destruction, sending men to the moon, and burning up more of the earth's oxygen than its plant life can replace,* he has also begun warming up the wax that will seal his own fate. Who are the crazier, we or the hunters? Their madness is harmless, even useful; ours is lethal.

Material and social adjustments to the environment

But let us start this chapter over again. We need to follow only a few main themes, the first of which is the closeness of fit between hunting and gathering peoples and their environments. Such peoples have had the energy, hardihood, and ingenuity to live and live well in every climatic region of the world not covered by icecaps. They have done so with stone tools and no firearms. In every well-documented instance, cases of hardship may be traced to the interven-

---

*The reader is urged to take careful note of C. LaMont Cole's article, "Are we Running out of Oxygen?" in *Catalyst for Environmental Quality*, Spring 1970. Also reprinted in *Massachusetts Audubon*, September 1970, pp. 29–33.

tion of modern intruders. Starvation came to the Caribou Eskimo only after a few Cree Indians, armed with automatic rifles, had slaughtered a whole migration of caribou in order to cut out their tongues to sell to white canners.

In order to live well, hunters need to know as much about the resources available in their territories as most modern Ph.D.s know about their special subjects, and without books to look them up in. Some hunters are as familiar with the behavior of local animals as are professional ethologists. Others know as much as botanists do about the identification and pharmacological properties of local plants.

Also, without courses in sociology and psychology, or special classes in sex education, they know at least as much about human nature as most of us do: how to get along in small groups; how to deal with the procession of crises in the lives of individuals from conception to death, and with the inherent differences between men and women; and how to relieve the anxieties of all concerned in cases of illness. Sexual abstinence during prolonged lactation, the pruning of twins, a failure to prolong a person's life unnecessarily; these and other measures and abstentions prevent overpopulation more efficiently than does the pill, and also prevent the devastating effect of the crowding syndrome, and the kinds of pollution that we face, including the pollution of men's minds. By keeping a man celibate who cannot kill a large animal, hunters prevent grown men who cannot bring in their shares of meat from passing on their defects, whatever they may be, to future generations.

Relative degrees of cultural complexity among hunting societies

Technical skills vary as much between contemporary hunting societies as they did between archaeological stone tool industries ranging over several hundred thousand years. The simple, unhafted, flake implements of the Tasmanians were less varied and sophisticated than some of the Paleolithic ones a quarter of a million years old. Yet with their simple tools the Tasmanians fashioned efficient one-piece wooden spears and built warm dwellings. In technology the Eskimo stand at the opposite extreme. Some of the most simply equipped hunters had the most elaborate social systems, and the richest mythologies. Wealth and rank arose among hunters who were able to obtain and to store enough food in one season to allow them to spend the following season in rites and games.

Among most hunters every man is a jack-of-all-trades, but where there is more than enough food to go around, talented individuals had the chance to become part-time specialists in crafts as well as in human relations. There is no clear-cut scale on which we can measure the relative complexities of hunting cultures, except to note a special case. With an abundance of salmon the Northwest Coast Indians were socially as complex as some of the agricultural American Indians who planted maize, beans, and squash.

Despite their diversity in emphasis and detail, hunting cultures have much in common. Hunters live and work mostly out of doors. Their senses are acute and, like their bodies, well exercised. Their schedules and routines are seldom monotonous, but often adventurous. Their craftsmanship has to be accurate, for their success is at stake. If badly injured, they must bear pain, and few linger into helpless senility. Among them natural selection is not thwarted, and in their breeding populations they do not build up increasing loads of disabling genes.

A plea for the appreciation of shamans

In the anthropological literature, shamans have often been categorized as natural neurotics who would have been social misfits in a society like our own—the craziest hunters of all. Actually they are exceptionally intelligent and well-disciplined men, as able to hunt as nonshamans are. Their ability to go into a trance is not automatic. Meditation is one way. Dancing and singing monotonously can produce hyperventilation and ecstatic states, as we know from physiological studies of Muslim dervishes, and the same is true of "Holy Rollers." Bushmen and Veddas also go into mass trances.

Being able to swallow and regurgitate objects takes practice and dedication, but it can be done. Once in India I saw a magician bring up several undersized billiard balls from his stomach. Missionaries and other early observers often referred to shamans as impostors, because of their sleight of hand, ventriloquism, and other attention-getting devices. But it is hard to see how these maneuvers are any more fraudulent than some of the symbolic procedures in our own religious ceremonies.

Shamans are also given credit for extrasensory perception, clairvoyance, and telekinesis (which means moving objects by "mental" rather than by "physical" energy). Two close observers of the hunting scene, R. P. Trilles and Martin Gusinde, were not convinced that shamans completely lacked these powers, and new evidence from the Soviet Union indicates that these "psychic" phenomena are being studied there seriously.*

Here a special point may be made. None of these "psychic" activities requires advanced technical equipment; nothing more may be needed than a few quartz crystals or a length of cord to be swallowed. In this sense shamanism may be nearly as old as human speech, and it is only natural to find it more highly developed among the Australians, Fuegians, and Eskimo than it is among ourselves. We have other means of projecting messages through the air invisibly, of predicting the weather and the time when the striped bass will arrive, and of moving things with little physical human effort.

On the relationships between generations in modern and hunting societies

On page 14 of *The Social Contract*, Robert Ardrey has written: "Why the young of our time revolt against the culture that presumably created them is a question for which our anthropologists provide no direct answer." As far as I am aware, and I could easily be wrong, other anthropologists have not stated specifically that the revolt of youth basically stems from a breakdown of communication between generations.

In an overspecialized, overmechanized urban society, our boys and girls have too little direct contact with their parents. Typically, father leaves for his office at 8:30 A.M. and returns at 6:00 P.M. All day he has been interacting heavily with his colleagues — superiors, subordinates, secretary, and perhaps clients or customers, in a ranked hierarchy. He has been jockeying for prestige, as in a potlatch, to see

*Sheila Ostrander and Lynn Schroeder, *Psychic Phenomena behind the Iron Curtain*. New York, Prentice-Hall, 1970.

O*

who can keep the other man waiting on a telephone line. When his busy day has ended, he is tired, and he transmits the hierarchical pattern to his family.

Many boys do not know exactly where father's office is, or what he does there. If father works on classified projects, the boy may never find out, even if he cares. Father returns, drinks a few hasty cocktails, and takes his son's mother out to dinner. As far as the boy is concerned, that is the end of an almost fatherless day. Thus before puberty and during it, the boy is deprived of his father's companionship, of instruction by example, and of a sense of belonging.

When puberty comes the boy feels a great glandular urge to set forth to do something perilous and dashing, to show that he is now a man. He can find no dangerous beasts to slay. He does not need to kill in order to get married. Worst of all, he has no driver's license. But that does not stop him. He drives his family's car, late at night, out onto a lonely stretch of paved road. There he plays chicken with other boys in their families' cars. He drives the vehicle as fast as it will go and suddenly jams on the brakes, to see how much rubber he can scrape off the tires. If he scrapes off more than the other boys do, he is the champion of his unsanctioned, *ad hoc* puberty class, but his achievement does not admit him into adult society. A boy who cannot get his family car may steal one instead, and land up in hospital, jail, or the morgue. When there is no other way for him to show his peers how reckless and dashing he is, drugs may offer the young man a formidable challenge.

His sisters do not see much of their mother, either. Instead of having groceries delivered, mother drives to the supermarket to buy them. Instead of a maid, she has automatic dishwashers, clothes washers, and driers. If she goes out with other women she does not take her daughters with her. Instead of digging yams, grinding seeds, and roasting meat, she heats up frozen foods and television dinners. By the time her daughters come to puberty, mother may have been divorced and remarried, at least once.

Unlike the children of hunters, the boys and girls have no adults to guide them through the puberty ordeals that they need in order to maintain social continuity It is no wonder that they create age-graded micro-societies of their own. The secrecy that once formed a vital part of puberty rites is transferred to their parents, to whom they will not reveal what they have been doing. What with television, paperbacks, and record players, it is also no wonder that much of what they are taught in school bears little relevance to the world they know, and offers less preparation for their vision of the future, because the ecology movement has hit them hard.

Saving our planet from human destruction, and from the destruction of life itself, is only half of our problem. The other half is for us to learn how nature intended human beings to live, and to reestablish continuity with those who may still be alive after the rest of us are dead. If we succeed in the first endeavor, and fail in the second one, *someday, far out in the desert, a few families of hunters may meet, and ask one another: "Where has whitefella gone?"*

*Bibliography of Principal
Works Referred to in the Text*

Baegert, Jacob. *Account of the Aboriginal Indians of the California Peninsula*. Edited and translated by Charles Rau. In Smithsonian Institution, *Annual Report* for 1863, 352–369; for 1864, 378–399; Washington, D.C., 1864, 1865.

LOWER CALIFORNIA

Batchelor, John. *Ainu Life and Lore: Echoes of a Departing Race*. Tokyo: Kwobunkwan (Tokyo Advertiser Press), 1892.

AINU

_____. *The Ainu and Their Folklore*. London: The Religious Tract Society, 1901.

AINU

Bernatzik, H. A. *Die Geisten der gelben Blätter*. Munich: Bruckmann, 1938.

YUMBRI (LAOS)

Berndt, R. M. *Kunapipi*. New York: International Universities Press, 1951.

AUSTRALIA

Berndt, R. M. and C. H. *The World of the First Australians*. Chicago: University of Chicago Press, 1964. (Bibliography contains 409 titles.)

AUSTRALIA

Berndt, R. M. and C. H., eds. *Aboriginal Man in Australia*. Sydney: Angus and Robertson, 1965.

AUSTRALIA

Boas, Franz. *The Social Organization and the Secret Societies of the Kwakiutl Indians*. Report of the U.S. National Museum for 1895. Washington, D.C., 1897.

NORTHWEST COAST

Bridges, E. Lucas. *Uttermost Part of the Earth*. New York: Dutton, 1949.

ONAS

Bird, Junius. "The Alakaluf," Smithsonian Institution, Bureau of American Ethnology, Bull. 143, Vol. 1, 52–79. Washington, D.C., 1946.

ALAKALUF

Brown, A. R. *The Andaman Islanders*. Cambridge: Cambridge University Press, 1922.

ANDAMANESE

Cipriani, Lidio. *The Andaman Islanders*. New York: Praeger, 1966.

ANDAMANESE (ESP. ÖNGE)

Codère, Helen. *Fighting with Property: A Study of Kwakiutl Potlatching and Warfare, 1792–1930*. Seattle: University of Washington Press, 1950–66.

NORTHWEST COAST

Dixon, R. B. The Northern Maidu. Bull. of the American Museum of Natural History, Vol. 17, 1905.

CALIFORNIA

Driver, H. E. *Indians of North America*. Chicago: University of Chicago Press, 1961.

GENERAL

Drucker, Philip. *Indians of the Northwest Coast*. Garden City, N.Y.: Natural History Press, 1963. (Also McGraw-Hill, 1955.)

NORTHWEST COAST

_____. *The Northern and Central Nootkan Tribes*. Washington, D.C.: Smithsonian Institution, Bureau of American Ethnology, Bull. 144, 1951.

NORTHWEST COAST

Gould, R. A. "Chipping Stone in the Outback." *Natural History*, Vol. 77, No. 2, 1968, 42–48.

AUSTRALIA

_____. "Living Archaeology: The Ngaljara of Western Australia." *Southwestern Journal of Archaeology*, Vol. 24, No. 2, 1969, 101–112.

AUSTRALIA

_____. *Yiwara, Foragers of the Australian Desert*. New York: Scribner's, 1969.

AUSTRALIA

Ehrenfels, U. R. *Kadar of Cochin*. Madras: University of Madras, 1952.

KADAR

Empéraire, J. *Les Nomades de la Mer*. Paris: Gallimard, 1955.

ALAKALUF

Fürer-Haimendorf, Christoph von. *The Chenchus: Jungle Folk of the Deccan*. London: Macmillan, 1943.

CHENCHUS

Gusinde, Martin. *The Yamana: The Life and Thoughts of the Water Nomads of Cape Horn*. 5 vols. New Haven: Human Relations Area Files, 1961. (Originally Vol. 2 of *Die Feuerland Indianer*. Anthropos-Bibliotek, Expeditions Ser. 2. Mödling–Vienna, 1937.)

YAGHANS

_____. *Die Feuerland Indianer, Vol. 1: Die Sel'knam* (as above), 1937.

ONA

_____. *Die Twiden: Pygmäen und Pygmoide im tropischen Afrika*. Vienna and Stuttgart: Braumuller, 1956. (Contains a bibliography of 405 titles through 1954.)

PYGMIES

Harney, W. E. *Tales from the Aborigines*. London: Hale, 1959.

AUSTRALIA

Horne, G., and G. Aiston. *Savage Life in Central Australia*. London: Macmillan, 1924.

AUSTRALIA

Howitt, A. W. *Native Tribes of Southeast Australia*. London: Macmillan, 1904.

AUSTRALIA

Kroeber, A. L. *Handbook of the Indians of California*. Smithsonian Institution, Bureau of American Ethnology, Bull. 78. Washington, D.C., 1925.

CALIFORNIA

Lantis, Margaret. *Alaskan Eskimo Ceremonialism*. Seattle: University of Washington Press, 1947, 1966.

ESKIMO

_____. *The Social Culture of the Nunivak Eskimo*. Transactions of the American Philosophical Society, N.S. Vol. 35, Part 3. Philadelphia, 1946.

ESKIMO

Lee, R. B. "What Hunters Do for a Living, or How to Make Out on Scarce Resources." In *Man the Hunter*, 30–48 (see next item).

BUSHMEN

Lee, R. B., and Irven DeVore, eds. *Man the Hunter*. Chicago: Aldine, 1968.

GENERAL

Loeb, E. M. *The Eastern Kuksu Cult*. University of California Publications in American Archaeology and Ethnology, Vol. 33, No. 2. Berkeley, 1933.

CALIFORNIA

Lothrop, S. K. *The Indians of Tierra del Fuego*. Contributions from the American Museum of Natural History, Vol. 10. New York, 1928.

ONA

Lumholtz, Carl. *Among Cannibals*. New York: Scribner's, 1889.

AUSTRALIA

Man, E. H. *On the Aboriginal Inhabitants of the Andaman Islands*. London: Royal Anthrop. Inst. of Great Britain and Ireland, 1885.

ANDAMANESE

397

Marshall, Lorna. "/Kung Bushman Bands." *Africa*, Vol. 30, No. 4, 1960, 325–355.

BUSHMEN

———. "/Kung Bushman Religious Beliefs." *Africa*, Vol. 32, No. 3, 1962, 221–251.

BUSHMEN

———. "Marriage among /Kung Bushmen." *Africa*, Vol. 29, No. 2, 1959, 335–365.

BUSHMEN

———. "The Medicine Dance of the !Kung Bushmen." *Africa*, Vol. 39, No. 4, 1969, 347–380.

BUSHMEN

———. "N/ow," *Africa*, Vol. 27, No. 3, 1957, 232–240.

BUSHMEN

———. "Sharing, Taking, and Giving: Relief of Social Tensions among the /Kung Bushmen." *Africa*, Vol. 31, No. 3, 1961, 231–249.

McKennan, R. A. *The Upper Tanana Indians.* Yale University Publication in Anthropology, No. 55. New Haven: Yale University Press, 1959.

NORTHERN ATHABASCANS

Mowat, Farley. *People of the Deer.* Boston: Atlantic–Little, Brown, 1952.

ESKIMO

Munro, N. G. *Ainu Creed and Cult.* New York: Columbia University Press, 1963.

AINU

Murdock, G. P. *Ethnographic Atlas.* Pittsburgh: University of Pittsburgh Press, 1967.

GENERAL

Oberg, Kalervo. "Crime and Punishment in Tlingit Society." In Tom McFeat, ed., *Indians of the North Pacific Coast,* 209–228. Seattle: Washington Paperbacks, 1967. (Original in *American Anthropologist,* N.S., Vol. 36, No. 2, 1934, 145–156.)

NORTHWEST COAST

Osgood, Cornelius, *Contribution to the Ethnography of the Kutchin.* Yale University Publications in Anthropology, No. 14. New Haven: Yale University Press, 1936.

NORTHERN ATHABASCANS

———. *Ingalik Material Culture.* Ibid., No. 22, 1940.

NORTHERN ATHABASCANS

———. *Ingalik Mental Culture.* Ibid., No. 56, 1959.

NORTHERN ATHABASCANS

———. *Ingalik Social Culture.* Ibid., No. 53, 1958.

NORTHERN ATHABASCANS

Oswalt, W. H. *Alaskan Eskimos.* San Francisco: Chandler, 1967.

ESKIMO

Plomley, N. J. B., ed. *Friendly Mission, the Tasmanian Journals and Papers of George Augustus Robinson, 1829–1834.* Hobart, Tasmania: Tasmanian Historical Research Association, 1966.

TASMANIA

Portman, M. V. *A History of Our Relations with the Andamanese.* 2 Vols. Calcutta: Government of India Printing Office, 1899.

ANDAMANESE

Putnam, P. T. L. "Pygmies of the Ituri Forest." In Coon, C. S., ed., *A Reader in General Anthropology,* 322–342. New York: Holt, 1948.

PYGMIES

Rainey, F. G. *The Whale Hunters of Tigara.* Anthropological Papers of the American Museum of Natural History, Vol. 41, Pt. 2. New York, 1947.

ESKIMO

Rohner, R. P. and E. C. *The Kwakiutl Indians of British Columbia.* New York: Holt, Rinehart, and Winston, 1970.

NORTHWEST COAST

Roy, R. B. S. C. *The Birhors: A Little Known Jungle Tribe of Chota Nagpur*. Ranchi: The G. E. L. Mission Press, 1925.

BIRHORS

Schapera, I. *The Khoisan Peoples of South Africa*. London: Routledge and Kegan Paul, 1930.

BUSHMEN

Schebesta, Paul. *Among Congo Pygmies*. London: Hutchinson, 1933.

PYGMIES

_____. *Die Bambuti Pygmäen vom Ituri*. 3 vols. Brussels: Institut Royal Colonial Belge, 1938 (Vol. 1); 1941, 1948 (Vol. 2); 1950 (Vol. 3).

PYGMIES

_____. *Die Negrito Asiens*. Studia Instituti Anthropos, Mödling — Vienna, Vol. 6, No. 1, 1952; Vol. 12, No. 2, 1954; Vol. 13, No. 2, 1957.

SEMANG

Seligman, C. G. and B. Z. *The Veddas*. Cambridge: The University Press, 1911.

VEDDAS

Service, E. R. *The Hunters*. Englewood Cliffs, N.J.; Prentice Hall, 1966.

GENERAL

_____. *Primitive Social Organization*. New York: Random House, 1962.

GENERAL

Sharp, Lauriston. "Steel Axes for Stone-Age Australians." *Human Organization*, Vol. 11, No. 2, 1952, 17–22.

AUSTRALIA

Silberbauer, G. B. "Marriage and the Girls' Puberty Ceremony of the G/wi Bushmen." *Africa*, Vol. 33, No. 1, 1963, 12–24.

BUSHMEN

Smith, W. R. *Myths and Legends of the Australian Aborigines*. New York: Farrar and Rinehart, (no date).

AUSTRALIA

Speck, F. G. *Myths and Folklore of the Timiskaming Algonquin and Timigami Ojibwa*. Department of Mines, Geological Survey, Memoir 71. Ottawa: Canadian Geological Survey, 1951.

NORTHERN ALGONKIANS

_____. *Penobscot Man*. Philadelphia: University of Pennsylvania Press, 1940.

NORTHERN ALGONKIANS

Spencer, Baldwin, and F. J. Gillen. *The Arunta: A Study of a Stone Age People*. 2 vols. London: Macmillan, 1927.

AUSTRALIA

Takakura, Shinichiro. *The Ainu of Northern Japan: A Study in Conquest and Acculturation*. Translated and annotated by John A. Harrison. Transactions of the American Philosophical Society, N.S., Vol. 50, Pt. 4. Philadelphia, 1960.

AINU

Thomas, E. M. *The Harmless People*. New York: Knopf, 1959.

BUSHMEN

Trilles, R. P. *Les Pygmées de la Forêt Equitoriale*. Paris: Bloud et Gay, 1932. (*Anthropos*, Vol. 3, No. 4.).

PYGMIES

Turnbull, C. M. *The Forest People*. New York: Simon and Schuster, 1961.

PYGMIES

_____. *Wayward Servants*. Garden City, N.Y.: Natural History Press, 1965.

PYGMIES

Warner, W. L. *A Black Civilization*. New York: Harper, 1937.

AUSTRALIA

Watanabe, Hitoshi. *The Ainu: A Study of Ecology and the System of Social Solidarity between Man and Nature in Relation to Group Structure.* Journ. Fac. Sci. Univ. of Tokyo, Sec. 5, Anthropology, Vol. 2, Pt. 6, 1964.

AINU

Witthoft, John, and Frances Eyeman. "Metallurgy of the Tlingit, Dene, and Eskimo." *Expedition*, Vol. 11, No. 3, 1969.

NORTHERN ATHABASCANS,
ESKIMO

Index

healing, 307, 370–386 *passim*; and hunting, 102, 121, 122; Nootka Shaman's Dance, 345–348; school for, 377–379; and twins, 317; Yaghan, 367, 377–382
Shanidar Cave, Iraq, 370
Sharp, Lauriston, 275, 276
Shaw, Thurstan, 23
shellfish, 132–133, 182
shells, 17–18, 22, 172–174
Shillingshaw, J., 253n
Shishmaref, 279
shoes. *See* footgear
Shoshone Indians, 15, 196
shoulder poles, 58
Siberia, 11, 188, 219, 222, 223, 279; clothing, 45; food, 72; tools, 21; travel, 56, 57, 59, 62; whaling, 120
sibling rivalry, 200
sika deer, 91
Sirius, 378
skates, 57
skiffs, three-plank, 64–66
skin boats, 63–64
skin, human, and cold tolerance, 39–40
skins, animal, preparing, 47–49
skis, 56
skull-screening, 372
slate, 21
slavery, 228n, 229–230, 265
sled dogs, 58–59
slings, 96–97
sliver, killing with, 256
slow game, 70
Smith Sound, 98
snakes, 80–81, 351–356, 359, 360; *see also* Yurlunggur
snowshoes, 46, 56
soapstone vessels, 184
songmen, 291
songs: Akoa, 114, 116, 333; Andamanese, 327; Mbuti, 323; Penobscot, 335; Tigaran, 125; Waiwilak, 351, 355, 358; Yaghan, 366–367, 378–379
sorcery, 192, 237, 254–257 *passim*, 262, 311, 371
South Africa, 26, 28, 71, 160
South African Bushmen, 48, 58, 80, 86, 177
South Alaskan language, 222
South America, 3, 10, 11, 46
South Andaman, 241
South Australia, 257
Southeast Asia, 71, 162, 298n
Southern Cross, 288, 294
Spaniards, 29, 58, 62, 96, 97
spears, 74–75, 110, 117–118, 132, 137–139, 148, 275–276
spear-throwers, 75, 77
Speck, Frank G., 62n, 301

Spencer, Robert P., 6n
spinning, 272–273
spirits: belief in, 284–285; of dead people, 245, 331; evil, and dangerous places, 290–291; and hunting rites, 102, 111, 112–114, 119, 381; Shamans' spirit helpers, 122, 376–379
sponsor-novice relationship, 363–365
spring pole traps, 106–107, 108
S-shaped bow, 77, 78
stalking, 83–84
Stanner, W. E. H., 194n
stars, 7, 287–288, 378
steaming, ritual, 357
Stewart, Omer C., 6n
stone: boiling, 185; quarrying, 275, 276; tools, 14–17, 20–21; weapons, 96–97
Strophanthus, 81
Strychnos, 81
Sua people, 98, 101
Sudan, 169
suicide, 262
Suku, 270
Sumerians, 263
sun, beliefs about, 7, 288, 304
supershamans, 382–383
surround, communal, 88
sweat-house, 371
Swansport, Tasmania, 290
"sweetheart" relationship, 260–261
symbiosis, 98, 99, 198, 268, 274
Syrian Desert, 16

Tabus: food, 311–315 *passim*, 318, 323–328; hunting, 100–104 *passim*; incest, 190, 192, 201–203, 206; menstruation, 101, 103, 259; same-name, 210–212; and shamans, 346, 372
Tachu Point, 173
tailored clothes, 44–45, 49
Taimen, 139
Taphrosia purpurea, 140
Tasmania, 16, 43, 71, 77, 89
Tasmanians, 3, 172, 268, 269, 286; boats, 60; body coverings, 39, 42, 43; carrying, 57; and fire, 6–7, 23, 25n; food, 54, 72, 132, 160, 161, 171–172, 181–182; geronticide, 330; hair, 41; illness, 5n, 370; languages, 194; myths, 287–291; shelter, 27, 28; and shamans, 372; social structure, 155, 198, 207, 208, 215, 217, 251–252, 336–337; spears, 74; tools, 389; trapping, 105
tattooing, 321, 365
tea tree, 74
Tehuelche, 29, 31, 96–97
telekinesis, 370, 391
telepathy, 370
Temigimi, Lake, 301

tents, 29, 30–31
termites, for food, 166–167
Texas Coast Indians, 42
Thomas, Elizabeth Marshall, 160, 239n
thongs, 49–50
Thuja plicata, 33
Thule, 18
Thummin, 112
Tiberón Island, 60
Tierra del Fuego, 11, 29, 79, 96, 137, 186–187, 195, 215; *see also* Fuegian Indians; Yaghans; Onas
Tigara, 104, 120–126, 177, 223, 261, 276–282 *passim*
tigers, and the Kadar, 155–158
Tikerarmiut, 104, 120–126, 128, 129; *see also* Tigara
Titicaca, Lake, 60
Tiwi, 74, 155
Tlingit, 20, 188, 225, 226, 262, 271
tobacco, 188
toboggans, 58, 59
Tofino Inlet, 263
toggle traps, 108
tools: flake, 15; for gathering, 154–155; for hafting, 18–20; metal, 10, 18, 228, 282; Ona, 80; Paleolithic, 389; shell, 17–18, 22; stone, 14–17, 20–21, 33–35, 389
tortoise shell, and divination, 112
totems: Ainu, 9, 217–218, 341; Akoa, 334; and marriage classes, 214; Northwest Coast, 9, 228, 344; Penobscot, 231; Waiwilak, 349–350, 353–358 *passim*
tracking, 83, 84–86, 115
trade: Andamanese-Australian, 274–276; of food, 180; Negro-Mbuti, 240–241; Northwest Coast, 173, 282; Nunivak Islanders, 277–278; and social structure, 10; Tigara, 278–279; trading chiefs, 268
trances, 238, 373, 380, 390
transitional systems, 207–208
transvestites, 270, 348
trapping, 104–108, 141–148
travois, 58
tribes, definition of, 194
trees: felling, 23; for shelter, 26–27, 33; honey in, 163–165
Tridacna, 22, 171
Trilles, Father R. P., 81–82, 111, 114, 140, 164, 232–234, 334, 370, 391
Trois Frères, cave of, 87
Trugernanna, 215, 252
trumpet, and Djunggan, 350, 351–358 *passim*
Tsimshian Indians, 225, 226, 228, 271
Tuareg, 228n
tumpline, 57–58
Tungus, 57
Turnbull, Colin, 178, 310, 324

turtle ceremony, 326–328
"Turtle Dove and Her Three Suitors," 232–233
tusu, 341, 372–376 *passim*
twins, 200, 317, 329

Uganda, 241
Ulmark, 350, 351
ulu, 49
umbilical cord, 310, 313–318 *passim*
umiaks, 63–64, 121, 126
unilateral systems, 206–208, 210, 225, 240, 241, 249–251, 285–286
Upper Paleolithic period, 30, 44, 77, 135
Upper Yukon, 84, 89
Urim, 112
Ushuaia, 195, 248
Ute Indians, 196
Utorgag River, 279

Van Gennep, A. L., 307
Van Stone, James W., 126n
Vancouver Island, 126, 173, 271, 345–348
Vavilov, N. I., 160n
Veddas, 27, 163, 166, 198, 207, 331, 390
Vedder, H., 2n
vegetables: food, 72–73, 99, 176, 182, 185–186, 192; for cordage, 50; poison from, 140
vengeance, 248–249, 252, 263, 383–386
Victoria, Australia, 183, 253, 275
Viennese school, 286n

Wabanaki Confederacy, 231
waddy, 74, 252
Waiwilak, 349–361 *passim*
wallaby, 181–182, 354
warfare, 4, 243–244, 250–251, 341, 382–383
Warner, W. Lloyd, 351, 360n
Washington State, 316
Watauinewa, sky god, 298=299, 381
water, 7, 25–26, 59–67, 184
waterproof clothing, 45
weapons, 73–83
weather control, and shamans, 371, 379, 382
weaving, 45, 271–274
weirs, fish, 141–143, 145, 148
Wellington Island, 39, 66
Western Desert, Australia, 25n
Western Ghats, 155
Western Tribe, Tasmania, 289
whales: hunting, 110, 121–130, 180, 223, 279, 281; sharing meat, 177; whaling boats, 64; myths about, 376, 377
wife swapping, 361
Windigo, 371

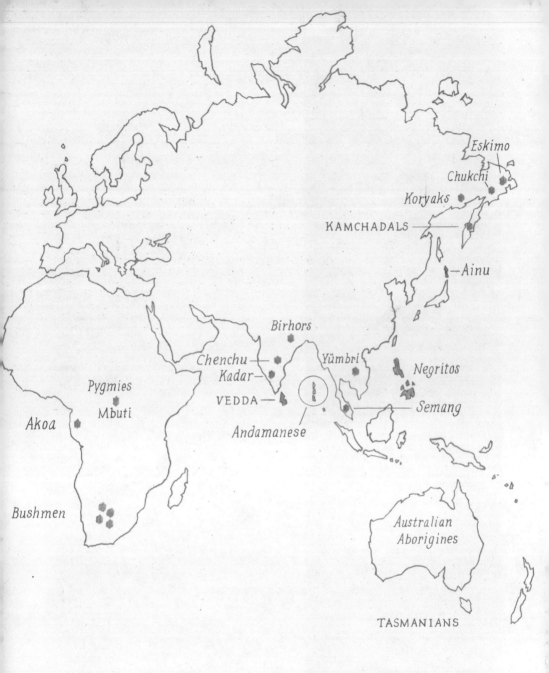

Eskimo

Chukchi

Koryaks

KAMCHADALS

Ainu

Birhors

Chenchu
Kadar

Yümbri

Negritos

VEDDA

Semang

Andamanese

Pygmies

Mbuti

Akoa

Bushmen

Australian
Aborigines

TASMANIANS

CAPITAL LETTERS = Culturally Extinct Peoples